BIBLICAL COMMENTARY ON THE GOSPELS

VOLUME II.

BIBLICAL COMMENTARY

ON

THE GOSPELS,

ADAPTED ESPECIALLY FOR

PREACHERS AND STUDENTS.

BY

HERMANN OLSHAUSEN, D.D.,
PROFESSOR OF THEOLOGY IN THE UNIVERSITY OF ERLANGEN.

TRANSLATED FROM THE GERMAN, WITH ADDITIONAL NOTES,

BY

REV. THOMAS BROWN,
KINNEFF.

VOLUME II.

WIPF & STOCK · Eugene, Oregon

Wipf and Stock Publishers
199 W 8th Ave, Suite 3
Eugene, OR 97401

Biblical Commentary on the Gospels,
Adapted Especially for Preachers and Students, Vol.II
By Olshausen, Hermann and Brown, Thomas
Softcover ISBN-13: 978-1-6667-2165-2
Hardcover ISBN-13: 978-1-6667-2168-3
eBook ISBN-13: 978-1-6667-2169-0
Publication date 5/3/2021
Previously published by T. & T. Clark, 1848

This edition is a scanned facsimile of
the original edition published in 1848.

The page numbers jump from 272 to 277,
however the text flows correctly.

PREFATORY NOTICE.

In the second part of this Volume the Translator has so far departed from the plan of his predecessor as to refrain from translating the Greek terms, except in those cases where it had been done by Olshausen. His object has been to present the work to the English reader as nearly as possible in the same form in which the Author published it to his countrymen.

He is responsible for the contents of the volume only from p. 146.

T. B.

TABLE OF CONTENTS.

PART III.

CONTINUED FROM VOLUME I

	Page.
§ 12. The Calling of St Matthew. Of Fasting, (Matth. ix. 9—17; Mark ii. 13—22; Luke v. 27—39.)	1
§ 13. Healing of the woman with the bloody issue; raising from death the daughter of Jairus,	8
§ 14. Healing of two blind men, and of a dumb man, (Mat. ix. 27-34),	17
§ 15. Sending forth of the Apostles (Matt. ix. 35; x. 42; Mark vi. 7—11; Luke ix. 1—5),	18
§ 16. John the Baptist sends his disciples to Jesus; discourse of Jesus in consequence of this Mission (Matt. xi. 1—30; Luke vii. 18—35; x. 13, 15, 21, 22),	51
§ 17. The Disciples pluck ears of corn (Matt. xii. 1—8; Mark ii. 23—28; Luke vi. 1—5),	79
§ 18. Jesus cures a withered hand (Matth. xii. 9—21; Mark iii. 1—6; Luke vi. 6—12),	85
§ 19. Of the calumnies of the Pharisees; Jesus severely rebuking them (Matth. xii. 22—45; Mark iii. 20—30; Luke xi. 14—26, 29—32),	92
§ 20. The arrival of the Mother and Brothers of Jesus (Matth. xii. 46—50; Mark iii. 31—35; Luke viii. 19—21),	124
§ 21. A woman anoints Jesus (Luke vii. 36; viii. 3),	127
§ 22. The collection of Parables (Matth. xiii. 1—53; Mark iv. 1—20, 30—34; Luke viii. 4—15; xiii. 18—21),	136
§ 23. Jesus in Nazareth (Mark xiii. 53—58; Mark vi. 1—6; Luke iv. 14—30),	165
§ 24. The Baptist's death (Matth. xiv. 1—12; Mark vi. 14—29 Luke iii. 19, 20; ix. 7—9),	177
§ 25. Feeding of the five thousand (Matth. xiv. 13—21; Mark vi. 30—44; Luke ix. 10—17; John vi. 1—15),	181
§ 26. Jesus walks on the sea (Matth. xiv. 22—36; Mark vi. 45, 46; John vi. 16—21),	188
§ 27. Of washing the hands (Matth. xv. 1—20; Mark vii. 1—23),	194
§ 28. The healing of the Canaanitish woman's daughter (Matth. xv. 21—31; Mark vii. 24—31; (32—37; viii. 22—26),	202

	Page
§ 29. Feeding of the four thousand (Matth. xv. 32—39; Mark viii. 1—10),	208
§ 30. Warning against the leaven of the Pharisees (Matth. xvi. 1—12; Mark viii. 11—21),	211
§ 31. Confession of the Disciples; prophecy of Jesus respecting his own death (Matth. xvi. 23—28; Mark viii. 27—9; Luke ix. 18—27),	214
§ 32. The Transfiguration of Jesus (Matth. xvii. 1—13; Mark ix. 2—13; Luke ix. 28—36),	229
§ 33. Healing of the Lunatic (Matth. xvii. 14—23; Mark ix. 14—32; Luke ix. 37—45),	238
§ 34. The coin (Stater) in the fish's mouth (Matth. xvii. 24—27),	245
§ 35. On the character of the children of the kingdom (Matt. xviii. 1—35; Mark ix. 33—50; Luke ix. 46—56),	250

PART IV.

OF CHRIST'S LAST JOURNEY TO JERUSALEM, AND CERTAIN INCIDENTS WHICH TOOK PLACE THERE.

(Luke ix 51, xxi 38, Matth. xix. 1, xxv. 46; Mark x. 1; xiii. 37.)

§ 1. Report of the Journey by Luke (Luke ix. 51—xviii. 14),	282
§ 2. James and John are incensed against the Samaritans (Luke ix. 51—56),	284
§ 3. Of following Jesus (Luke ix. 57—62; Matth. viii. 19—22),	289
§ 4. The sending forth of the seventy disciples, with the address of Jesus to them (Luke x. 1—24; [Matth. xi. 20—27]),	293
§ 5. Parable of the tender-hearted Samaritan (Luke x. 25—37),	301
§ 6. Mary and Martha (Luke x. 38—42),	306

ORDER OF THE SECTIONS OF THE GOSPELS,

ARRANGED AFTER EACH GOSPEL.

MATTHEW

	Page		Page
Chap. ix. 9—17	1	Chap. xiv. 22—36	188
,, ix. 18—26	8	,, xv. 1—20	194
,, ix. 27—34	17	,, xv. 21—31	202
,, ix. 35—42	18	,, xv. 32—39	208
,, xi. 1—30	51	,, xvi. 1—12	211
,, xii. 1—8	79	,, xvi. 23—28	214
,, xii. 9—21	85	,, xvii. 1—13	228
,, xii. 22—45	92	,, xvii. 14—23	238
,, xiii. 46—50	124	,, xvii. 24—27	245
,, xiii. 1—53	136	,, xviii. 1—35	250
,, xiii. 53—58	165	,, vii. 19—22	289
,, xiv. 1—12	177	,, xi. 20—27	293
,, xiv. 13—21	181		

MARK

	Page		Page
Chap. ii. 13—22	1	Chap. vi. 45, 46	188
,, v. 22—43	8	,, vii. 1—23	194
,, vi. 7—11	18	,, vii. 24—37	902
,, ii. 23—28	79	,, viii 22—26	202
,, iii. 1—6	85	,, viii. 1—10	208
,, iii. 20—30	92	,, viii. 11—21	211
,, iii. 31—35	124	,, viii. 27	214
,, iv. 1—20, 30—34	136	,, ix. 1	214
,, vi. 1—6	165	,, ix. 2—13	228
,, vi. 14—29	177	,, ix. 14—32	238
,, vi. 30—44	181	,, ix. 33—50	250

LUKE

	Page		Page
Chap. v. 27—39	1	Chap. iii. 19, 20	177
,, viii. 40—55	8	,, ix. 7—9	177
,, ix. 1—5	18	,, ix. 10—17	181
,, vii. 18—35*	51	,, ix. 18—27	214
,, x. 13—15, 21—22	51	,, ix. 28—36	228
,, vi. 1—5	79	,, ix. 37—45	238
,, vii. 6—12	85	,, ix. 46—56	250
,, vi. 14—26, 29—32	92	,, ix. 51	282
,, viii. 19—21	124	,, xviii. 16	282
,, vii. 36	127	,, ix. 51—56	284
,, viii. 2	127	" ix. 57—62	289
,, viii. 4—15	136	,, x. 1—24	293
,, xiii. 18—21	136	,, x. 25—37	301
,, iv. 14—30	165	,, x. 38—42	306

ORDER OF THE SECTIONS OF THE GOSPELS, IN VOLUME I.

ARRANGED AFTER EACH GOSPEL.

MATTHEW.

	Page		Page
Chap. i. 2	35—73	Chap. viii. 1—4	239—248
„ iii. 1—12	148—161	„ viii. 5—13	248—255
„ iii. 13—17	161—167	„ viii. 14—17	255—260
„ iv. 1—11	167—179	„ viii. 18—27	260—269
„ iv. 12—17	179—182	„ viii. 28—34	269—286
„ iv. 18—22	182—183	„ ix. 1—8	286—292
„ iv. 23—7, 29	183—239		

MARK

	Page		Page
Chap. i. 1	35	Chap. i. 35—39	260—267
„ i. 2—8	143—161	„ i. 40—45	239—248
„ i. 9—11	161—167	„ ii. 1—12	286—292
„ i. 12—13	167—178	„ iv. 35—41	267—269
„ i. 14—15	179—182	„ v. 1—20	269—286
„ i. 16—20	182—183	„ v 21	286—292
„ i. 29—34	183—260		

LUKE.

	Page		Page
Chap. i. 2	73—117	Chap. v. 1—11	260—267
„ iii 1—20	148—161	„ v. 12—16	239—248
„ iii. 21—23	161—167	„ v 17—26	326—335
„ iii 23—28	35—43	„ vii 1—10	248—255
„ iv. 1—13	167—178	„ viii. 11—17	255—258
„ iv. 14, 15	179—182	„ viii. 22—25	268—269
„ iv. 31—41	255—260	„ viii. 26—39	269—286
„ iv. 42—44	260—267		

※* This table was given with the translation of the first volume of Olshausen for the Foreign Theological Library, but was wanting in the translation of the Continental Translation Society. It is now given for the convenience of those possessing that translation, and it will be understood that the paging refers to it.

COMMENTARY

ON

THE GOSPELS.

§ 12. THE CALLING OF ST MATTHEW. OF FASTING.

(St Matth. ix. 9—17, Mark ii. 13—22; Luke v. 27—39.)

ST MATTHEW touches by the way upon the occasion of his being called to the office of an apostle, but without enlarging on his own personality (Subjectivitat[1]); sacred as might be to him the moment that called him to the immediate presence or proximity of our Redeemer, yet he remains with his spiritual eye steadily and immoveably fixed in pure contemplation of the sublime phenomenon which he wishes to represent to his readers. He only mentions his calling on account of the events that were connected with it. Both St Mark and St Luke give to him who was called on this occasion the name of *Levi;* yet, the affinity of the narrative itself, together with the identity of the discourses

---

[1] This keeping in the background of their own persons on the part of the Evangelists, so apparent in the Gospels, is a highly important feature in their distinctive character, it manifests them as chaste historians, that were purely absorbed by their noble and sublime subject. Against the inauthenticity of St Matthew, as little can be inferred from his not here making himself known, as against that of St John, for the same reason. The position of this event appears, no doubt, unchronological, but St Matthew, in the first place, does not pretend to observe any chronological order, and in the second, this calling certainly already presupposes an earlier invitation of St Matthew by Christ.

GOSPEL OF ST MATTHEW IX. 9—13.

that are connected with it, compel us to regard the names, though different, as intended to denote one and the same person. The experiments made to represent them as denoting different persons, have turned out to be very weak.[1]

Ver. 9. Ματθαῖος = מַתִּיָה, "Matthew," Θεόδωρος, "Theodore."— The τελώνιον, "place where toll or custom is taken" = בֵּית הַמֶּכֶס, "house of tribute, custom house," which properly signifies, according to *Buxtorf* (Lex. Talm. p. 1065), an exchange.—The call, ἀκολούθει μοι, "follow me," as well as the δεῦτε ὀπίσω μου (iv. 19 comp. with ver. 22), "follow after me," implies not only the corporeal following to which our Lord here invites him, but the internal spiritual following, which is the real ground for the former. A previous acquaintance with St Matthew is presupposed, for otherwise our Redeemer would not have invited Matthew to leave his official duties; the latter had, no doubt, already taken the necessary steps to relieve himself from those duties.

Ver. 10. St Matthew received joyfully the Saviour, who had called him to a nobler office; he prepared for him a δοχὴ μεγάλη, "a great banquet," = מִשְׁתֶּה, "feast," Gen. xxvi. 30. This word is met with, also, in St Luke xiv. 13. (Concerning τελώνης, "a publican, i e, tax-collector," and ἁμαρτωλός, "a sinner," see on Matth. v. 46.) The Evangelist contrasts our Saviour, who had chosen a publican or tax-gatherer for his apostle, with the Pharisees, who would not even permit that intercourse should take place with these unfortunate beings, devoted to the world, in whose hearts, however, frequently the noblest longing after the truth was excited. Yet do these Pharisees not appear exactly as though they had been wicked and malicious; they must be regarded rather as being incapable of comprehending, in consequence of their confined position, the free action of the love of Christ. Our Lord, therefore, affords them an insight into a much purer life than they were aware of, or could comprehend.

Ver. 12, 13. Jesus describes, in a few words, his sacred office as the Physician of mankind The man exposed to contagion may do well in shunning the diseased person; but the physician

---

[1] St Mark ii. 14, calls Levi τὸν τοῦ Ἀλφαίου, "the son of Alpheus" This Alpheus is in every respect another person than the father of James (Matth. x. 3), for the existence of any relationship between St James and St Matthew, or Levi, is not rendered probable by any circumstance whatever

hastens to him to remove his suffering. As a ἰατρός, "physician," the physician of souls, Jesus represents himself, according to Exod. xv. 26, where Jehovah himself says to the wretched (people of) Israel: כִּי אֲנִי יְהוָה רֹפְאֶךָ, "for I am the Lord that healeth thee." In the passage forming a parallel to this, in which Jesus speaks of his destination (ἔρχεσθαι, "to have come," = to the more usual ἔρχεσθαι εἰς τὸν κόσμον, "to have come into the world," the appearance on earth of one belonging to a higher order of things), δίκαιοι, "righteous men," stands as an exposition by the side of ἰσχυροί, "sound, whole," as ἁμαρτωλοί, "sinners," by the side of κακῶς ἔχοντες, "those that are sick." Without prejudice to the doctrine of the universal sinfulness of mankind, we yet see that the sacred writers frequently draw a line of distinction between men (comp. on Luke xv. 7); sin, as it were, concentrates itself in some individuals. But these are often the very men on whom, in his free grace, the Redeemer first has compassion. The righteous (those that are, according to the law, less liable to punishment) frequently perform the character of the jealous brother on the calling home of the lost son (comp on Luke xv. 11 seq.) The word καλεῖν, "to call," expresses the ministry of our Redeemer with reference to the ἁμαρτωλοί, "sinners;" it signifies the gracious calling of our Lord to partake of his feast of joy (Comp. on this word, and its relation to ἐκλέγειν, "to choose, select," on Matthew xxii 14.) St Luke adds: εἰς μετάνοιαν, "to repentance," which is a spurious interpolation both in St Matthew and St Mark, the μετάνοια, "repentance" (see on M iii. 2) being viewed as the first step towards the kingdom of God. St Matthew adds, moreover, to the idea a reference to Hos. vi. 6. (The word πορεύεσθαι, "to go forth, to proceed," is used as redundant in a sense analogous to הָלַךְ, "to walk, to go forward") The dazzling brightness of the coming sun clearly shines forth in the words of the Old Testament seer, the life manifested in self-denying love appears as outshining all other sacrifices: חֶסֶד חָפַצְתִּי וְלֹא זָבַח, "mercy have I desired, and not sacrifice." Hence, the sacrifices do not seem abrogated in these words; but, on the contrary, consummated in the veritable Sacrifice, of which all the others are but types. The expression חֶסֶד, "grace, favour, mercy," = ἔλεος, "pity, compassion, mercy," signifies love, in so far as it manifests itself, i e. as it is displayed, towards those that are unhappy, and where it affords no enjoyment to the bestower, but only a pure self-sacrifice. Such an explanation of the γράμματα ἱερά, "sacred words," to the γραμματεῖς, "scribes, expounders of the Scriptures (see note 1, p. 327), was for themselves a powerful exhortation to the μετάνοια, "repentance."

Ver. 14. After this, these same Pharisees (according to St Luke), or rather certain disciples of St John who happened to be present (according to St Matthew), or both in common (as St Mark, sinking all distinction between the two, says), bring forward another peculiarity of the circle of the disciples of Jesus—the abandonment of fasting and standing prayer (Luke v. 33), on which things even the Baptist himself, according to his Old Testament point of view, laid great stress.

Ver. 15 The Redeemer immediately goes to the root of these outward and peculiar formalities, as one who always penetrated into the depths of the spirit, i e. who always viewed things in their spiritual bearing, and sets at once before them the difference of the economies of the Old and New Testament. In the first place, says Jesus, the peculiar nature of the kingdom of God does not rest on such external matters—the life thereof will hereafter exhibit itself in the church in a far different analogy with the Old Testament. He concludes by comparing himself to a bridegroom, and his disciples to the friends of the bridegroom, and leaves them to draw from this comparison the inference necessarily required to illustrate the point at issue or before them As marriage is the season for the most indwelling sentiments of joy, so must also be our Lord's appearance in the world; streams of light and of life overflow all hearts, eating and drinking, gay enjoyment, appear as the sensible outward manifestation of the inward joy and happiness of the spirit. Suffering, as exemplified by fasting, could only supervene by the death of the bridegroom; but then, indeed, it would be a suffering the more bitter and the more acute. The remarkable parts of this parable are, *in the first place:* that the disciples are designated υἱοὶ τοῦ νυμφῶνος, "sons of the bridal-chamber" (= παρανύμφιοι, companions of the bridegroom in the bridal-chamber, νυμφών = חֻפָּה,[1] "the veil, or veiled chamber"),

---

[1] חֻפָּא. This is the name which the Jews of old gave to the veil, or covering, which was supported by four posts, beneath or within which the marriage ceremony was always performed It resembles very much the canopy used in the Church of Rome on high festivals, which is generally borne over the individual who is to perform high mass, and who,

they express metaphorically, indeed, together with all believers, the bride herself. (Comp. Ephes. v. 23 sqq.) There is, however, also admissible another legitimate view taken of the disciples, according to which they appear as the first rays of the rising sun of the spiritual world sent forth among mankind; hence they are exhibited as introducing the heavenly bridegroom, as it were, to his earthly bride In the second place, it is obscure how the ὅταν ἀπαρθῇ, " when he shall be taken away," is to be brought into connection with the expression νηστεύσουσιν, " they shall fast,'' by which it is followed. If we assume it to signify the death of the Redeemer on the cross, it then would appear as though its meaning were: that the church would fast during the whole time of his absence and until the period of his return in glory. This idea, however, cannot well be received as truly conformable to our purpose, because the resurrection of our Redeemer at once dispelled again the sorrow for his death, and yet our Saviour could hardly have intended to say that his disciples would only fast the one day during which he remained in the grave. We must look, therefore, for a spiritual conception, or mode of viewing of the question at issue, which, dispelling the difficulties, grasps the eternal bearing which the words of our Lord display. For his words are spirit and life (John vi. 63), and as such, therefore, they must possess for the church in all ages their spiritual signification. What Christ here says is applicable to his disciples of all times, sometimes they do rejoice, and sometimes they fast. It is manifest that the question at issue is not so much respecting the bodily presence of our Redeemer (ἐπιδημία αἰσθητή, " the visible sojourning"), which, for example, was certainly no bridal joy to Judas, as his internal spiritual presence in the souls of men (ἐπιδημία νοητή, " perceptible sojourning"). But this presence of our Redeemer is more glorious and efficacious *after* his resurrection than it was *before* The words of Jesus, understood in this sense, afford as their result the profound idea that an internal vicissitude takes place even in believers, which is a vicissitude of light and darkness (Jam i 17), inasmuch as there reigns within them at one time a nuptial joy, and, at another, grief for the departed bridegroom has the ascendancy, and that,

on such occasions, invariably carries the tabernacle, i e the sacred vessel containing the host. It is not unlike a four-post bedstead, the lower portion of it, of course, being removed, and is in use among the Jews at the present day, to whom it is known under the above name.—T according to these alternations, their outward life also assumes varied hues depending more or less thereon. Yet the joyous disposition is viewed as predominating under the New Testament, whereas it is the grave and serious frame of mind which reigns under the Old Testament.

Ver. 16, 17. But since the remark of the Pharisees and of the disciples of St John contained something which seemed to require a reply (ver. 14), our Lord demonstrates to them in conversation, by means of two parables or similes (St Luke v. 36 uses, on this occasion, the expression παραβολή, "a parable," which may here be applied in the more extended sense of the word: see on this head Matth. xiii.), that the two dispensations do not admit of being confounded together. The new spirit demands the new form, and even though we may meet in the New Testament life with forms which are nearly related to the Old Testament state of things, yet are they different from those phenomena of life which existed purely under the law. Both similes certainly express the same meaning; but they differ in regard to point of view from which they are conceived, and the difference between these two points of view explains the difference which exists between the similes themselves.[1] In the former, that which is new is viewed as something merely

---

[1] *Neander* in his Kl Gelegenheitsschr (smaller occasional works) p 144, explains these similes in such a manner, that he does not admit them to have reference to the Old and the New Testament, but as bearing upon the disciples of John, who here appear as the interrogators, so that Christ laid open or explained to them that which caused their surprise at the difference of their own way of life and that of his disciples. For, this surprise was founded on the circumstance that they, the disciples of John, were as yet moving in the sphere of obsolete or antiquated Judaism, and were not able to conceive or comprehend the spirit of his new doctrine. Hence, it would avail them little even were he to invite them to adopt the new way of life of his disciples. The old garment of the old nature cannot well be mended with a single patch of new cloth, wherever regeneration has not as yet taken place, there the mending in detail will not be durable Although this view contains much that is commendable, yet do I decide in favour of that exposition according to which the contrast existing between the Old and the New Testament forms the main point of both similes, the *whole connection* imperatively demands this The difference of the similes is sufficiently explained by the remarks made concerning the different points of view from which they are taken, which is equally well suited to assist in the solution of other difficulties to be met with in the parables of the Gospel history. (Comp on Luke xviii. 1 sqq.)

incidental, as a means to remedy antiquated evils and necessities, for in this light the Gospel must have appeared to the Pharisees, looking down from their own confined point of view; and in the second simile, on the contrary, that which is new is regarded as that which is essential, that which is old is regarded as the mere form—thus, according to the truth, did they stand in relation to one another. Thus, by the combination of both similes, our merciful Lord, ever ready lovingly to aid and have compassion on human weakness, ministered fully to the wants of the whole human species. The Pharisees themselves could not but see that they were unable to screen the imperfections of their dispensation, i.e. that of the Old Testament, by the superinduction of the Gospel element, which could produce as little beneficial effect as a piece of new cloth would, if put on an old cloak or garment. ($'E\pi i\beta\lambda\eta\mu\alpha$, "a patch," is only used in this place; according to *Suidas*, it is $\tau\grave{o}\ \tau\tilde{\omega}\ \pi\varrho\omega\tau\acute{\epsilon}\varrho\varrho\ \dot{\epsilon}\pi\iota\beta\alpha\lambda\lambda\acute{o}\mu\epsilon\nu\sigma\nu$, "that which is laid upon what was there before." A patch or piece of cloth, in as far as it is viewed as filling up a rent, is called: $\pi\lambda\acute{\eta}\varrho\omega\mu\alpha$, "a filling up" '$P\acute{\alpha}\varkappa o\varsigma$ from $\dot{\varrho}\acute{\eta}\sigma\sigma\omega$, "to rend, to tear," signifies a piece torn off, a rag; $\ddot{\alpha}\gamma\nu\alpha\varphi o\varsigma$, "not yet fulled, or dressed.") St Luke v. 36 views the simile in a different light. He conceives a piece torn off a new garment, and applied to the mending of an old one. This involves a double disadvantage. For, in the first place, damage is done to the new garment, and, in the second; the new piece agrees not with the old garment. This mode of viewing the simile is evidently based on the endeavour to render these two similes more homogeneous in themselves, for, according to the view of St Luke, the New Testament would be the *new* cloak, as compared with, or in contrast to, the Old Testament; but it is for this very reason that we prefer the representation of St Matthew and St Mark; the narrative of St Luke appears somewhat modfiied (The reading: $\dot{\alpha}\pi\grave{o}\ \dot{\iota}\mu\alpha\tau\acute{\iota}o\upsilon\ \varkappa\alpha\iota\text{-}\nu o\upsilon\ \sigma\chi\acute{\iota}\sigma\alpha\varsigma$, "rent from a new garment," as contained in the text of St Luke, is no doubt authentic, it has perhaps been omitted, merely in order to assimilate the narrative of St Luke to the description given by both the other Evangelists) In the second simile is brought forward, in a prominent manner, the relation existing between form and substance, as seen from the New Testament point of view; the substance must produce, by means of its innate creative power, a form analogous to its own character; whenever human self-will forces the spirit into obsolete forms, the immediate result is a rending of the form, and at the same time an unsuccessful and irregular operation of the substance; its innate power reveals itself, no doubt, but only in irregular phenomena, which are, on the whole, anything but salutary. The simile is as simple and comprehensible as it is wonderfully profound and full of fine meaning. As, for instance, the comparison of the life-principle of the Gospel with the most spiritual-physical production leads to various ideas. (The ἀσκοί, *utres*, "bottles sc. of skin;" according to the eastern custom, skins, inwardly smeared or lined with pitch, were used for the preservation of wines; these vessels were convenient for transport on asses and camels.) St Luke adds, moreover, another trait (v. 39) which is highly characteristic, and which is pointed at the Pharisees. The loving Saviour finds an excuse for those hearts that have grown up in the habitual practice of the old statutes and habits, and does not think it unfounded or unreasonable that they should find it difficult to step beyond the magic circle of old spiritual habits, and venture themselves on a new and tempestuous (sprudelndes) element of life. The old, although in itself more austere (as is the Old Testament, when compared with the New), becomes mitigated and rendered pleasing through habit; we cannot reconcile it to the taste at first (εὐθέως, "immediately"). But this very expression, at the same time, gently invites us to enter the new life of the spirit which was brought by our Redeemer to mankind.

§ 13. HEALING OF THE WOMAN WITH THE BLOODY ISSUE. RAISING FROM DEATH THE DAUGHTER OF JAIRUS.

(St Matthew ix. 18—26; St Mark v. 22—43; St Luke viii. 40—55.

After recording these conversations, which took place at the feast given at his own house, St Matthew proceeds to present Jesus before us as a worker of miracles *Storr* (Evang. Gesch. des Joh. p. 303,) is no doubt right in saying, that St Matthew (up to ix. 35,) has brought together all that which occurred in his dwelling, and before his own eyes; hence, with regard to the chronology, we must here unhesitatingly follow St Matthew, inasmuch as the other two Evangelists immediately pass over with vague formulas from the two parables to other narratives. (Comp. St Mark ii. 23; St Luke vi. 1.) But it must appear the more striking, that St Matthew describes the very events which occurred immediately after his calling, in his own immediate presence, in a manner so little graphic, whereas both St Mark and St Luke present the occurrence in so minute and picturesque a form. The features which they add to the narrative before us, are, as usual, it is true, partly unessential, as for example, when they give the name of the Archon, the age of the damsel, the circumstance of the woman suffering from the issue of blood having sought the aid of physicians; yet, other traits there are which enter deeply into the general character of the narrative, as the sending of messengers to inform Jairus that the death of his child had taken place, the notice that Jesus perceived within himself that virtue had gone out of him. Here, then, in a way not to be mistaken, do we find the *fact* itself once more proved that St Matthew, in his narratives, writes without precision, and apparently not as an eye-witness; the only question is, whether the *inferences* drawn from this fact are correct, if we for this reason deny to St Matthew the authorship of his Gospel. A want of clearness and precision in his narration, a limited power of comprehension in matters connected with external circumstances, is all that can be concluded with safety therefrom. But all this may consist very well with the character of an Apostle with whom spirituality, in the sense of mental superiority, (Geistreichheit) is no requisite, but spirituality of thought. Besides, St Matthew did not lay himself out to notice, in a more special manner, the outward form of events, as is the case with St Mark. Besides, in both narratives related in this section, our Redeemer presents himself to our view once more as a heavenly manifestation, such, indeed, as the most inward longing of humanity sighs for, as the ideal perfection of itself With the most holy and most pure will of God, he combines a fulness of divine life-bestowing power, which was poured out in a life-giving stream over the fields of this poor world of man, through which he passed. Raised far above the miseries and necessities of earthly life, he does not withdraw his blessed presence therefrom, but on the contrary, he lovingly descends into the lowest regions of misery, causes death and sin to be swallowed up for ever, and wipes away the tears from off all faces (Isa. xxv. 8).

Such a Redeemer the prophets had prayed for, with a glowing and heartfelt desire, and in the hope which springs from faith, had promised him, at the command of the Spirit,—we see him rule and act in the New Testament, both in his Divine and human character, as an incomparable phenomenon, which attracts towards itself, with an irresistible and enchanting power, all those hearts that are susceptible of noble impressions. He is truly the Saviour of his own body! (the church) Ephes. v. 23.

St Matthew ix. 18, connects that which follows through the passage ταῦτα αὐτοῦ λαλοῦντος αὐτοῖς, literally, "while he was speaking these things to them," in a direct manner with that which preceded it. ("Ἄρχων, "a ruler, chief person," is here = ἄρχων τῆς συναγωγῆς, "a ruler of the synagogue," (Luke viii. 41,) ἀρχισυνάγωγος, (Mark v. 32,) chief or moderator of the synagogue, who directed the convocations, רֹאשׁ הַכְּנֶסֶת.[1] Instead of εἰσελθών, "coming in or to," must be read, no doubt, εἷς ἐλθών, "one coming," since St Matthew frequently uses εἷς, "one," for τις, "a certain one," (viii. 19; xvi. 14; xviii. 28; xix. 16,) according to the analogy of the Hebrew term אֶחָד, "one," which is in the Aram. lang. חַד.—The name Ἰάειρος is = יָאִיר, "Jair," Numb. xxxii. 41, Deut. iii 14). Jairus, according to or in St Matthew, at once declares the damsel already dead, whereas, according to St Mark and St Luke, this announcement is made only at a later period by messengers; but, because St Matthew wished to omit this particular circumstance, he was therefore necessitated, in order to bring forward the occurrence in a complete manner, to represent the child as dying, when her father hastened to Jesus to pray him for aid. There are some persons who on this occasion, or on reading this narrative, imagine experiments to have been made on the dead child; in that case the message of the servants would refer to their insufficiency for

---

[1] Each synagogue, according to Jahn, (Archaeologia Biblica, § 372,) had several elders, who were presided over by a person selected from among themselves, and who was called רֹאשׁ הַכְּנֶסֶת, ἀρχισυνάγωγος, or as the text has it, "ruler or moderator of the synagogue, (house of prayer)" a title which was not seldom applied likewise to all of them. The office or duty of the elders was to convene assemblies, to select as well as to invite all such persons that would have to read in the assembly, and to address it, and to preserve order throughout the proceeding, and in the synagogue itself.—See also Vitringa de Synag. Vet. lib. ii. c. 11 —T

awakening once more the dead body. St Luke viii. 42 observes, by way of digression, that the child was 12 years old, and that it was the only daughter of the Archon. (The expression μονογενής, must be viewed as St Luke vii. 12, i e. as "only born.")

Ver. 19. The disciples went with our Lord, who followed the call of the agonised father, and both St Mark and St Luke depict the scene, showing what a crowd of people followed, and how they thronged Jesus. (St Mark v. 24, συνέθλιβον, "they thronged;" St Luke viii. 42, συνέπνιγον, "they pressed hard upon.") Rudeness, curiosity, and good-will, were mingled together in the motley crowd, Jesus bore with them all.

Ver. 20. And now there pressed forward a woman that was diseased with an issue of blood; she had suffered for 12 years,— had employed physicians and human aid, but all in vain; nay, her disease had even rendered her poor. (The expression δαπανάω, "to spend," of Mark, = προσαναλίσκω, "to spend entirely," of St Luke, signifies to expend, to lavish, but with the accessory notion of lavishing in vain. St Luke viii. 43, βίος, "life, living," *opes facultates*, "riches," Luke xv. 12, 30; xxi. 4) She appears as a picture of one despairing of human aid in the greatest distress. The faith of the woman was great, but still she imagined that she required by all means a bodily touch in order to be cured; she went behind Jesus to touch the hem of his garment. Unlike that strong believer the centurion (Matth. viii. 8), she knew not that the power of Jesus was efficacious even from afar off. A mistaken shame, no doubt, might have prevented the sufferer from discovering her situation to Christ; she trusted to obtain aid, even though she were only to touch his garment. It is evident that she was struck with the idea of a sacred atmosphere, which enveloped the heavenly visitant, into the middle of which she must strive to enter. She conceived the garment as the conductor of the powers. (Comp. Matth. xiv. 26.) The woman's ideas could hardly have been free from material notions concerning the wondrous powers of Jesus; but happily it was not the imaginations of her *head* that were to cure her, but the faith she harboured in her *heart*, and this was ardent, and pleasing to our Lord. (Κράσπεδον = ציצת, "fringe, tassels," Numb. xv. 38; Deut xxii. 12. Comp. on Matth. xxiii. 5.) But only St Mark and St Luke describe more explicitly the effect produced by this touch of the believing woman, and that which was consequent upon it. St Mark v. 29 uses the significant expression: ἐξηράνθη ἡ πηγὴ τοῦ αἵματος, "the fountain of the blood was dried up," to signify a radical cure of the deep-rooted disease; and adds: ἔγνω τῷ σώματι, "she perceived in her body," i.e. she experienced a peculiar *bodily* feeling, which afforded her the conviction of the malady being removed. Μάστιξ, "a scourge," sc. Θεοῦ, "of God," comp. 2 Macc. ix. 11, every disease, rightly understood, is the consequence of sin; hence, the punishment of God, which is intended to lead to a knowledge of these. Comp. the comment. to Matth. ix. 2.) But with this, both narratives combine a description of the conduct of Jesus towards the healed woman, which is altogether peculiar to this narrative St Mark observes, v. 30, that Jesus perceived that a virtue had gone out of him; St Luke, in explanation, adds, that Jesus himself uttered the words: ἔγνων δύναμιν ἐξελθοῦσαν ἀπ' ἐμοῦ, literally, "I perceive that power has gone forth from me." The disciples, in their spiritual non-age, seek for the cause of the question of Jesus in the pressure produced by the people, and wonder at the conduct of Christ; but he, looking round with a searching eye, (περιεβλέπετο, "he looked round," Mark v. 32,) and the woman, feeling herself discovered, comes and confesses, δι' ἣν αἰτίαν ἥψατο αὐτοῦ, "for what cause she touched him," and indeed ἐνώπιον παντὸς τοῦ λαοῦ, "in the presence of all the people," as St Luke, ver 47, adds, not without reason. What strikes us *first* in this description is, that Jesus makes use of the expression δύναμις ἐξελθοῦσα ἀπ' ἐμοῦ, "power has gone forth from me. In consequence of this, the imagination begins to reason, i e. to draw conclusions, that the power has operated by an *involuntary* process, whereby the action would become inconsistent The words in themselves, however, evidently do not imply that the power emanated from Christ involuntarily; but we should as little take offence at the idea of the actual emanation of the power, as when the church teaches that the Spirit proceedeth from the Father and the Son, and that it is poured out into the hearts of the faithful. The fulness of spiritual life, which our Redeemer bore in himself, revealed itself as is the nature of the spirit, in its creative and curative character, and that is what is expressed in the words δύναμις ἐξέρχεται, "power went forth," as the radiance beams forth from the fire when it shines and warms.[1] This veritable mode of expression, on the

---

[1] Hence it is, indeed, that all those passages, as for example St

other hand, forms a powerful contrast to that empty view according to which Jesus is said to have ministered and cured without the pouring forth of power from within him. But the view that the efficacy of Christ took place in this case involuntarily, seems to be favoured, because of the question, Who has touched me? in connection with the passage, I felt a virtue go out of me; if Christ indeed knew not that he had performed a cure, and whom he had cured, the whole transaction appears as magical, and is quite unworthy of the Lord. Every one of his cures must be viewed as an act well known to Christ, and which stands in a perfect connection with the person to be healed, and with his moral condition. Meanwhile, in the reflections which follow, this feature becomes apparent likewise in this case. It was the moral cure, indeed, that had induced our Lord, who had well perceived her bashful faith, and who did not desire to bring upon her shame and confusion, to draw her from her concealment, and to bring her forward to the light. Without addressing her, he compels her of herself to come forward, and to overcome the false shame which had prevented her from coming freely and openly before our Lord, and laying before him her necessitous case. In her secret approach to our Lord, in order to touch his garment, was, no doubt, contained faith; yet therein her mode of proceeding was not pure and single-minded; the fear of man and a false bashfulness were at the bottom of all this, and these had as yet to be overcome. It would have been, nevertheless, too hard upon her to have required from her solicitation *previous* to the cure being effected, and that she should have spoken out openly before the people; hence, our amiable Lord mitigated the hardship by permitting her to do so after the cure had been performed, and thus he assisted her in her course through the narrow pathway. But he could not disburden her entirely from this affair, for it was subservient to her birth into the new life. Thus we attain the moral point of view of this event, and in Christ we shall perceive everything contributing to man's temporal and everlasting welfare, planned and arranged in due order, according to the measure of his boundless love. Only we might ask, whether it was not untruth to inquire,

Matth. xiv 36; Mark iii 10, vi 56; Luke vi 19, in which it is narrated, that many people supplicated our Lord to permit them to touch his cloak, and that they were cured, afford no difficulties, because the cures here appear clearly as the actions of his will τίς ὁ ἀψάμενός μου; literally, "who is he that toucheth me," when he knew of her? But if we only consider that Christ wished to bring her to a confession, and that the concealing of the conviction cannot possibly here be in question, no one can find herein a stumbling-block and offence, as little as if a father were to put the question to the mass of his children, who has done that? well knowing the guilty one, and yet being desirous to obtain his free confession of his guilt.[1]

Ver. 22. After this conquest of the woman obtained over her old nature, it was time to comfort her, and to cause to grow up freely and healthily the faith which at first had revealed itself but timidly. During the process or course of the cure, the δύναμις, " power," of Christ appears as the *causa efficiens*, " efficient cause," and the πίστις, "faith," of the woman, as the *conditio sine qua non*, "the necessary condition;" both in their combined effects achieved the work. Our Lord gave her peace, not only in mere words, but in the essential efficacy of the Spirit.

St Mark and St Luke proceed to record what form circumstances assumed in the course of Christ's progress to the house of Jairus. There came messengers (ἀπὸ τοῦ ἀρχισυναγώγου, "from those of the ruler of the synagogue," sc. δοῦλοι, "servants,") and announced the death of the child, (see above on Matth ix. 18,) beseeching him not to trouble Jesus. The Redeemer comforts the trembling father, who was wavering in his faith, and arrives at last at the house. Both narrators anticipate, i.e. observe here, as if by way of digression, that Christ took with him into the house only certain persons named by them; the careful St Mark mentions it once more in its right place, in ver. 40.

Ver. 23. According to the custom of the Jews, who hastened their funerals in an unusual manner, Jesus found funeral music already there (αὐληταί, "minstrels"), and crying (St Mark has ἀλαλάζειν), wailing (κόπτεσθαι, *pectus plangere*, "to beat the breast," = lugere, "to mourn"), mourners assembled before the dwelling. The Redeemer interrupted their noise with the words: οὐκ ἀπέθανε τὸ κοράσιον, "the damsel is not dead," without

---

[1] According to *Euseb*. Hist. Eccl viii. 10, there was set up in Caesarea Paneas the statue of Christ cast in bronze, representing the woman suffering from the issue of blood in the act of touching his garment. We have no reason to doubt the veracity of this narrative, inasmuch as the fact is in itself anything but improbable

minding their derision. This declaration of Christ is so plain and natural, that persons ought never to have ventured to tamper with it.[1] The miracles of our Lord require no hand to help them forward; their very want of ostentation adds to their grand and stupendous character. The addition ἀλλὰ καθεύδει, "but she is sleeping," does not permit us to view or comprehend the first expression as though it meant "she is not dead, inasmuch as it is my intention to resuscitate her," or "inasmuch as what I intend doing must be regarded as being already accomplished." The contrast: οὐκ ἀπέθανε, ἀλλὰ καθεύδει, "she is not dead but sleepeth," which is repeated verbatim by all the three Evangelists, permits of no prevarication. We have here, consequently, *no raising from death in the true sense of the word*, inasmuch as it is probable that the child was in a state of deep fainting or trance;[2] but even if viewed in this light, is the act

[1] *Strauss* and *De Wette* are of opinion, that the Gospel writers see in this narrative a raising from the dead, this they only do, no doubt, in order to be able the more easily to declare it mythical. I cannot agree with *Schleiermacher*, who sees herein a raising from death, because Christ declares openly, she is not dead Assuming it to be a raising from the dead, the words οὐκ ἀπέθανε, "she is not dead," will then contain an untruth, for even if Christ did raise her, she must have first been dead In John xi 11 we read of Lazarus, κεκοίμηται, "he sleepeth the sleep," which might well be used, considering the ambiguity of the word, but Christ could not have said of him, οὐκ ἀπέθανε, "he is not dead" It is, therefore, only the passage in St Matth xi 5, that affords some semblance, where it is mentioned along with many other miracles of Christ, νεκροὶ ἐγείρονται, "the dead were raised up" That seems to presuppose or imply, that St Matthew had been relating some instances of raising the dead, but, this passage excepted, his Gospel contains no narrative of the kind But a reflection such as this must not be assumed in any way in St Matthew, the passage xi. 5 betrays a very general character, and in it may quite well stand χωλοὶ περιπατοῦσι, "the lame walk," even though no history of the kind has been related, just as all notice of the cures of demoniacs is wanting, although St Matthew had already related such. Finally, we might conclude, from the plural νεκροὶ ἐγείρονται, "the dead are raised up," that St Matthew must have related many raisings from the dead. In passages such as these, the Evangelists added for their readers, from tradition, those portions necessary for their completion. But, even if this occurrence is no raising from death, it still remains a miraculous act For, the miracle is contained in the cure of the child of her deadly disease, which had plunged her into the sleep of death.

[2] Physicians distinguish *syncope* (fainting) from *asphyxia* (suspended animation, apparent death), by the latter they understand the state of suspension of *all* vital functions, i.e that state of the body (during life) in which the pulsation of the heart and arteries cannot be per-

performed by our Lord of less importance? Does he not present himself through such open declarations in the light of the purest moral grandeur? The moment of actual death, which cannot be fathomed by human knowledge, Jesus could seize upon at its individual instant, and hence he declares that it has not yet taken place here; but the circumstance of his knowing it, that he knew it long before he arrived, that he understood how to fix the time and circumstances thereof; herein, indeed, is contained the miracle of this act. What was unknown to all of them (St Luke viii. 53, εἰδότες ὅτι ἀπέθανεν, "knowing that she was dead," because they had tried every means to raise the dead) was known to him, without having seen the child; and he expressed openly what he knew, and produced thereby life and faith. This open declaration contributed in no way whatever to diminish his miracle in the eye of those that were present; but, on the contrary, it was thereby elevated, raised more glorious (St Mark v 42, St Luke viii. 56). Having here likewise in view the moral impression, Jesus collects from among the rude mass (in whom derision is as easily excited as stupid astonishment) a small flock of sensitive souls; to them he permitted the undisturbed enjoyment of beholding the return to life of the damsel in all its touching expression, in order that they might thereby be excited, sacredly and solemnly, to express their thanks to God. But our Lord commanded them to conceal this impression in the deepest recesses of their hearts, in order not to lose again, through their busy talkativeness, the little spark of life but just ignited (Mark v. 43, Luke viii. 56. Concerning this, comp. the Comment. on Matth. viii. 4.) The careful St Mark records, moreover, what happened in the presence of the parents, and of St Peter, St John, and St James. (Respecting the presence of these three apostles only on many occasions, comp. on Matth. x. 2.) Jesus took her by the hand and called, טְלִיתָא קוּמִי (Talitha cumi), "child, or damsel, arise." (The noun substantive is the Syriac form of טָלֶה, which signifies lamb, and which was frequently used when speaking of children.) It were

ceived, in fact, it is a total suspension of the powers of the mind and body. It is this which must here be supposed. The history of Eutychus (Acts of the Apostles xx. 7 sqq) is very similar to it. Of the youth mentioned, St Paul says· ἡ ψυχὴ αὐτοῦ ἐν αὐτῷ ἐστίν, "his life is in him," words which explain the passage occurring in our narrative (Luke viii. 55,) ἐπέστρεψε τὸ πνεῦμα, "the spirit returned."

best here to look upon the calling of Christ to the damsel, his life-bestowing word, as the medium of resuscitation. Of the application of any other means not the slightest mention is made, and there is no reason for supposing that such was the case; it is not absolutely impossible but that they might have been used, inasmuch as Jesus makes use, in other cases, of certain means or remedies (see on Mark vii. 33) But, because all is recorded in a plain straightforward manner, where it did happen, hence it is natural to suppose, that where no such thing is spoken of, even there also it did not take place Christ and his apostles, free from every charlatanism, represent the most wonderful occurrences in the most plain and simple manner, and as our Lord, when feeding thousands with a few loaves, true to his human nature, nevertheless commanded them to collect faithfully and minutely the crumbs which remained, so in like manner also does he who is himself the life, and who shall hereafter awaken all the dead with his voice (John v 25), command that the little child whom he has raised from its trance, and whom he confesses *not* to have been dead, should be supplied with food (St Mark v. 43, Luke viii. 55). He thus permits everything to proceed in a simple human way, and manifests, indeed, thereby a truth of the internal life, which forms, in a peculiar manner, the true foil to his great actions.

§ 14. HEALING OF TWO BLIND MEN, AND OF A DUMB MAN.

(Matthew ix. 27—34.)

St Matthew alone relates that, during the time which Jesus spent in his house, he cured therein two blind men and a dumb man. The words: αὐτῶν δε ἐξερχομένων ἰδού κ. τ. λ. (v. 32), "as they went out, behold," &c, immediately connect the cure of the dumb man with that of the blind men. The nearly similar narrative recorded by St Matth. xii. 22 sqq. must be regarded, therefore, as a different event. The accusation of the Pharisees: ἐν τῷ ἄρχοντι τῶν δαιμονίων ἐκβάλλει τὰ δαιμόνια, literally, "he casts forth the demons through the prince of the demons" (ver. 34), will be inquired into more fully in that place Since these two narratives of the cures here effected offer no difficulties that may not be solved by means of the remarks previously made, hence, the only circumstance deserving of notice is, that the κωφὸς δαιμονιζόμενος, "dumb man possessed with a devil" (ver. 32), must be considered as perfectly distinct from a dumb man, suffering from organic imperfection. The former is dumb in consequence of psychical influences which his body is in subjection to This, no doubt, must have assumed the form of a species of mania; but this mania must not be viewed as an imagination, but as the consequence of real effects produced by the powers of the enemy Their being vanquished by the light-giving power of the Redeemer, restores in the sufferer the just balance of the psychical and physical relations. This mode of viewing the *Scriptures* which ascribes real effects to real causes, but which more especially does not acknowledge the existence of psychical phenomena without their adequate spiritual causes, certainly appears as simple as it is profound.

§ 15 SENDING FORTH OF THE APOSTLES.

(St Matth. ix. 35—x 42; St Mark vi 7—11, St Luke ix. 1—5.)

After having represented Jesus in chaps. viii. and ix. as a worker of miracles, St Matthew gives in chap x. a collection of the Redeemer's laconic sayings similar to that given in the Sermon on the Mount. A transition expressed in general terms, such as we have seen already in St Matthew iv. 23 sqq, here leads him thereto He remarks how Jesus wandered about, how he taught, and how he healed the sick. A confinement of his benefits to Galilee alone is not herein to be traced; on the contrary, the words of St Matthew are so generalised that it is evident that a fixed designation of the localities of the various occurrences never entered into, or formed part of, his design. But then the Evangelist sets forth how the minute perception which our Redeemer obtained in his wanderings into the state of the people excited in him the most heartfelt compassion for the calamitous situation of the people of God—and it was indeed this which formed the motive of his sending forth the disciples. (Concerning σπλαγχνίζεσθαι, "for the bowels to have yearned, i.e. to have felt great compassion," see on Luke i. 78, it signifies or expresses very properly the maternal compassion for her helpless child Instead of the usual ἐκλελυμένοι, "fainting"—ἐκλύεσθαι, "to become faint, exhausted," used when speaking of the failing or exhaustion of powers of any kind, Gal vi. 9; Heb. xii. 3—the more rare mode of expression ἐσκυλμένοι should no doubt, as by Griesbach, be adopted in the text, "worn out by the cares of life, and scattered [ἐῤῥιμμένοι] by wolves, like sheep without a shepherd" Respecting this figure, comp John x. 3 sqq.) The general idea with which this is connected: ὁ μὲν θερισμὸς πολύς κ. τ. λ., "for the harvest truly is plenteous," &c, stands, St Luke x. 2, in a closer, more definite connection on the sending forth of the seventy disciples, whence we refer to our comment on that passage. St Matthew only introduces it here as betokening the fundamental disposition of the soul of Jesus, from which emanated the idea of sending out the twelve apostles, which is given in immediate connection therewith. The idea thus expressed marks likewise the development of the time and of the people for the reception of the divine doctrine, as well as the need of such teachers as were able to remedy their true necessity in an effectual manner.

The body of the twelve apostles, it is evident, is here assumed as already existing, of its formation the Evangelist speaks as little as of the calling of the single members, if we except the fragmentary notice (iv. 18 sqq) Both St Mark and St Luke prove themselves here likewise more accurate in their relations; they combine their catalogues of the apostles with the remark that Christ has expressly chosen and installed them as a body (St Mark iii 14, καὶ ἐποίησε δώδεκα, ἵνα ὦσι μετ' αὐτοῦ, literally "and he ordained twelve that they should be with him." More precise yet is Luke vi. 13, προσεφώνησε τοὺς μαθητὰς αὐτοῦ, καὶ ἐκλεξάμενος ἀπ' αὐτῶν δώδεκα, οὓς καὶ ἀποστόλους[1] ὠνόμασε, literally "he called to [unto him, as the English version has it] his disciples, and of them he chose twelve, whom also he named apostles.") According to the narration of St Luke alone, is the significancy of the installation of the apostles rendered very prominent. He remarks at vi 12, ἐξῆλθεν (ὁ 'Ιησοῦς) εἰς τὸ ὄρος προσεύξασθαι, καὶ ἦν διανυκτερεύων ἐν τῇ προσευχῇ τοῦ Θεοῦ, which signifies: "he went out into the mountain to pray, and was passing the night in prayer to God." Thus then it would appear that our Redeemer pre-

---

[1] The expression ἀπόστολος, "apostle," stands here as the proper official title for the twelve (With regard to the relation of this term with similar expressions, see the Comment on 1 Cor xii 28)

pared himself by nocturnal prayer, and then in the morning installed the twelve apostles. If we consider that the election of this body of men, in whose hearts the first germs of truth were to be deposited, depended upon a careful selection of persons, we shall then be able to form an idea of the importance of that momentous act; it was the moment in which was laid the foundation-stone of the church. The twelve who formed the representatives of the spiritual Israel[1] were to constitute within themselves a complete *unity;* hence they had to perfect one another mutually in their requirements and dispositions, and to bear within themselves the germs of all the various acts and decisions that manifested themselves in the church at a subsequent period in grand phenomena. Only as the discerner of all hearts (John ii. 25) was it possible for our Lord to lay the foundation of such a body of closely united minds, which might exist, and represent the whole spiritual creation, that was as yet to be called into existence. In his own person all was concentrated in one holy unity; but as the ray divides itself into its various colours, so in like manner went forth the *one* light which emanated from Christ into the hearts of the twelve in various modified degrees of brightness. Thus only and through this mediation could not only a few individual men, but all might be equally satisfied with the Gospel food according to their several necessities and dispositions. A striking feature in the election of the twelve is, that *Judas Iscariot*,[2] the betrayer of our Lord, was admitted as a member of this most narrow circle. Faith, however, perceives herein the wondrous leadings of the grace (Gnadenfuhrung) of our Lord. Evil becomes everywhere intertwined and mixed up with the *good*, in order that it may be overcome by the redeeming power of Christ. As the serpent was not wanting in Paradise, nor Ham in the ark of Noah, so it was necessary, in like manner, that there should be a Judas among the twelve, if the circle they formed was to represent an exact type of Israel. Not, as though he had been predestined to evil—the Scripture knows nothing of the *reprobatio impiorum,* "Divine reprobation

---

[1] This is represented figuratively in Rev. xxi. 14. The twelve, as distinct from St Paul, seem to have had likewise a special reference to the bodily Israel (Comp on Matth x. 5, 6, and the Introduction to the Epistles of St Paul)

[2] Concerning what has been said of Judas Iscariot, comp on Matth. xxvi. 24, John xiii 27

of the wicked" (comp on Rom. ix.)—but in order to afford him the opportunity to overcome the evil that dwelt in him by the aid of our Lord. The luckless man, no doubt, because he did not avail himself of his opportunities, became the instrument of the betrayal of our Lord, but his *destination* was by no means such. The God of mercy only ordains everywhere in this temporal system of the world the intermixture of good and evil, in order that the latter may be overcome by the former, or when it does not permit itself to be overcome, in order to consummate or perfect the good by the contrast with the evil; for although Judas did bring our Lord to the cross, yet must he himself, through the very act, assist in laying the foundation of everlasting redemption.

With regard to the *first* sending forth of the twelve, which took place under the eyes of our Lord, this is also narrated by St Mark vi. 7—11 and St Luke ix. 1—6, but without the imparting of the instruction given, so explicitly as is done by St Matthew in chap. x.[1] But it is evident that various elements are again brought together in this discourse of St Matthew (ch. x.) St Luke ch. x. relates the sending forth of the seventy disciples, a subject on which St Matthew observes a silence, and gives on this occasion a discourse addressed to them by Jesus; this, as also Luke xii, wherein Christ administers admonitions separately addressed to his disciples, contains many elements of the instruction given to the apostles, as contained in the tenth chapter of St Matthew It contains nothing, it is true, which would be unsuitable for this occasion, so that we might unhesitatingly assume, in this respect, that the words were so spoken by Jesus, yet it is improbable, for this reason that St Luke gives the same passages in a more suitable combination, whereas the connection existing between the isolated ideas throughout the discourse of St Matthew is frequently only loose or vague. The simplest way would be to assume that St Matthew intended to bring together, in this chapter, those principles of action which Jesus gave to his apostles at various periods of time for their guidance

---

[1] The hypothesis raised by Dr *Paulus*, (in his Comm. vol ii. p 34,) that St Luke and St Mark are narrating a subsequent sending forth of the twelve, has originated from the endeavour to connect the isolated Gospel-narratives into one compact whole, in accordance with the respective periods in which the events took place But this hypothesis is altogether void of internal probability.

in their position with regard to the world in general. This becomes, indeed, the more probable, because many expressions occurring in the instruction (comp particularly on Matth. x 23) reach beyond the then horizon of the disciples who were to be sent forth. The special reference of the instruction to the impending mission of the twelve has become in the hands of the Evangelist altogether of a general character, so that we have received, in this discourse or address of Jesus to his disciples, an universal code of instruction as regards themselves and their *united* apostolical ministry, yea, as regards all missionaries for all future times. How far this may have been the design of St Matthew I leave undecided,[1] but the Spirit that spoke through him has given to his representation this rich and bounteous fulness

Ver. 1. Jesus, sending out the twelve by two and two, in order to afford them mutual support (Mark vi 7), gives them firstly, an authority to legitimate to themselves the power of healing (ἐξουσία, "full power") It is obvious that the communication of such healing powers could only take place through the communication of the Spirit. Hence we find here the first trace of a communication of the Spirit by Jesus to his disciples, which is strengthened in John xx 22, and which is represented as being consummated at the feast of Pentecost. From this results also the relation which their wonderful cures hold to the other ministrations of the apostles. The external ministry of healing was the first and most subordinate, their purely spiritual ministry through the word they could only commence after the feast of Pentecost. In like manner did our Redeemer, in the first place, cure the bodies only, but he afterwards exercised his redeeming power in the cure of souls. The loss which the church sustained, indeed, was therefore not so great, when at a subsequent period the spiritual gift of healing left her; that which is of far more importance remained behind, the word for the redemption of souls Besides, we find, moreover, a remarkable analogous case of such a communication of the Spirit to others in Numb. xi. 16 sqq, wherein it is related how Moses imparted the Spirit that was upon him unto the seventy elders of the people. This mode of viewing the Spirit does not in the

---

[1] On this point comp *my* "Festprogramm uber die Aechtheit des Matth" "Programme of the authenticity of the Gospel of St Matthew." Part ii p 17

slightest degree border on materialism, but is only a representation thereof in its most peculiar nature. As God is love, and as love is itself the self-imparting being, so it is, in like manner, the nature of the Spirit, as being of the divine substance, to communicate itself everlastingly, pouring itself in a life-bestowing and strengthening current into the hearts of men. A Spirit that would not or could not communicate itself would be unspiritual, or an anti-divine Spirit. Now, Christ, as the express image of the invisible Father, pours out everlastingly a full stream of the living Spirit, but communicates thereof to every one according to his necessity and receptive power. Inasmuch as Jesus chose designedly neither distinguished nor learned disciples, but, on the contrary, such as were poor and despised in the eyes of the world (1 Cor. i. 27), hence they required the more a Divine power from above to enable them to fulfil those duties which their office imposed upon them. This power would act through them, pure and undisturbed in its operations, as by pure instruments, and the less their minds had been formed and impressed by human influence, the more were they fitted thereby to become such instruments in the hands of the Spirit.

Ver 2. Here follows the catalogue of the apostles, which we here present for the convenience of the reader, together with the other lists of the same (as given in St Mark iii 13 sqq., St Luke iv. 12 sqq ; Acts of the Apostles i. 13 sqq.), in the form of a comparative table:—

St Matthew.	St Mark.	St Luke.	Acts of the Apostles.
	1. FIRST CLASS.		
1. Σίμων, "Simon."	1. Πέτρος, "Peter"	1. Σίμων.	1 Πέτρος.
2. Ἀνδρέας, "Andrew."	2 Ἰάκωβος	2 Ἀνδρέας.	2. Ἰάκωβος.
3. Ἰάκωβος, "James."	3. Ἰωάννης.	3. Ἰάκωβος	3. Ἰωάννης.
4. Ἰωάννης, "John."	4 Ἀνδρέας	4. Ἰωάννης.	4. Ἀνδρέας.
	2. SECOND CLASS		
5. Φίλιππος, "Philip"	5 Φίλιππος	5. Φίλιππος.	5. Φίλιππος.
6 Βαρθολομαῖος, "Bartholomew."	6 Βαρθολ.	6 Βαρθολ.	6. Θωμᾶς.

St Matthew.	St Mark.	St Luke.	Acts of the Apostles.
7 Θωμᾶς, "Thomas"	7 Ματθαῖος.	7. Ματθαῖος	7. Βαρθολ.
8 Ματθαῖος, "Matthias"	8. Θωμᾶς.	8 Θωμᾶς	8. Ματθαῖος

3. THIRD CLASS.

9 Ἰάκωβος Ἀλφ, "James the son of Alpheus"	9 Ἰάκωβος Ἀ.	9 Ἰάκωβος Ἀ.	9 Ἰάκωβος Ἀ.
10 Λεββαῖος, "Lebbeus" Θαδδαῖος, "Thaddeus"	10 Θαδδαῖος.	10 Σίμων ὁ Ζηλ	10. Σίμων ὁ Ζηλ
11. Σίμων ὁ Καν, "Simon the Canaanite"	11 Σίμων ὁ Κ	11 Ἰούδας Ἰακ	11. Ἰούδας Ἰακ.
12 Ἰούδας Ἰσκ, "Judas Iscariot."	12 Ἰούδας Ἰ	12 Ἰούδας Ἰσκ	

The order observed in these four catalogues, according to three classes,[1] is so similar, that they cannot be supposed to have originated by mere accident, and yet the individual statements somewhat vary, which throws an obstacle in the way of referring them back to a written source or foundation. Hence, it is most natural to suppose, that each of the writers above referred to arranged them, according to their importance, as it had then been acknowledged by the universal consent of the church. Those that were less known and less active were placed the last, and those that were best known the first. Meanwhile, modifications of a trifling nature took place therein, for example, St Matthew and St Luke both place the pairs of brothers together, whereby Andrew is placed before James and John; St Mark and the Acts of the Apostles, on the contrary, place the three chief apostles foremost, St Peter being at the head. Among those that were pretty equal in point of importance, as Philip, Bartholomew, Thomas, and St Matthew, arbitrary transpositions take place But the notion that some of

---

[1] All agree together as to the placing of Peter, Philip, James A, and Judas Iscariot, but they disagree as to the position of those that stand between the above named apostles Yet, the classes themselves remain unchanged

the apostles filled a more important station than others, is forced upon the reader's mind, by the Gospel-history, in a manner not to be repelled. This is especially the case with St Peter, St James, and St John, who appear as the flower of the twelve. On several important occasions, Jesus took them only with him as his most intimate companions. (Besides St Mark v. 37; St Luke viii. 51, comp. likewise St Matth. xvii. 1; [St Mark ix 2; St Luke ix 28;] St Matth. xxvi 37; [St Mark xiv. 33;] also St Peter and St John only, John xxi. 19, 20). The disciples thus surrounded our Lord in wider and still wider expanding circles; nearest to him were the three, then came the other nine, after them the seventy, and finally, the multitude of his other disciples. Undeniable, then, as is the difference which existed between the disciples of Christ, yet does not this imply that there existed any more intimate initiation (esoterische Gnosis) for those standing nearest to him. The secret, or mystery of Christ, at once the highest and the simplest truth, was to be preached from the house tops It is not to be doubted, however, that some penetrated infinitely deeper into this same mystery than the others, and hence, became far more fitted to move in more immediate proximity to our Lord. With regard to the apostles individually, St Peter stands at the head of them all. St Matthew calls him πρῶτος, "the first," which, is, no doubt, not altogether accidental. (For particulars, see on Matth xvi 18) Concerning the cognomen Πέτρος, "Peter," given to Simon, see on John i. 42. *Andrew* stands very much in the background throughout the Gospel-history; *James*, the son of Zebedee, appears only in connection with the two coryphaei of the company of the apostles, St John and St Peter.[1] According to xii 2 of the Acts of the Apostles, he died early the death of a martyr ('Ανδρέας, "Andrew," = אַנְדְרִיָה, "Andrijah," which is derived perhaps from נָדַר, "to vow, to consecrate")—With regard to *Philip*, see on John i 45; he, too, was from Bethsaida *Bartholomew* (בַּר תַלְמַי, "Bartolmai," = son of Ptolemy,) however, seems, according to John i. 46, to be identical with Nathaniel of Cana (John xxi. 2). The Gospel-history observes a silence with regard to the latter,

---

[1] As concerning the cognomen Βοανεργές, "sons of thunder," attributed to John and James by St Mark iii. 17, compare the explanation on Luke ix 54

Philip appears in the act of speaking in John xiv. 9.—Θωμᾶς, הַתְּאוֹם, "Teom," Δίδυμος, "the twin." (Concerning whom comp. the comment. on John xx. 24.)—Ματθαῖος, "Matthew," with the addition, or adjunct, ὁ τελώνης, "the publican;" this points to Matthew as the author of the Gospel, inasmuch as it is wanting in all the other catalogues of the apostles, and inasmuch as an adjunct of this kind is found to no other name.[1] Only the author himself could have added it with propriety; in his mouth it became a memorial of the undeserved mercy that had been shown to him. Concerning the different persons called *James*, comp. on Matth. xiii. 55, and the introduction to the Epistle of St James. I must here briefly remark, that I consider James the son of Alpheus, as being a different person from James the brother (cousin) of our Lord, more especially on account of the passage John vii. 5: οὐδὲ γὰρ οἱ ἀδελφοὶ αὐτοῦ ἐπίστευον εἰς αὐτόν, literally: "for not even his brethren believed on him." For it is only after the ascension of Jesus that we find the ἀδελφοὶ τοῦ κυρίου, "the brethren of the Lord," among the assembled believers (Acts of the Apostles i. 14); it is, therefore, not likely that any one of them should have been among the twelve. The person of *Simon* with the cognomen ὁ Κανανίτης, "the Canaanite," is described in a manner not to be mistaken, by the explanatory cognomen: ὁ ζηλωτής, "the zealot," which St Luke gives of him in his Gospel, as well as in the Acts of the Apostles. Κανανίτης, from קָנָא, "to be zealous." He belonged, no doubt, to the sect of those Jewish zealots of whom mention is made by Josephus (Bell. Jud. iv. 3, 9). His demagogical zeal, which had hitherto taken an external form, was subsequently directed towards the attainment of internal freedom. More difficult, however, is it to identify the person of the Λεββαῖος, "Lebbeus," whom St Matthew calls Θαδδαῖος, "Thaddaeus." In the first place, in so far as concerns the matter of the text of St Matthew, it must be ob-

---

[1] *De Wette* (on this passage) brands this observation as one having no weight, but is any other apostle besides named after his worldly calling? Is St Peter designated the fisherman, or anything of the kind? Besides, in addition to this, the word publican has an opprobrious signification, as may be seen in the phrase, publicans and sinners. Such a cognomen none but St Matthew alone could bestow on himself. Least of all would an author of the Gospel, living at a later period, have made use of it, as such an one could only have an interest thereby to extol St Matthew.

served that the reading is various. The addition ὁ ἐπικληθεὶς Θαδδαῖος, "who is surnamed Thaddaeus," is omitted in many Codices It appears to me, indeed, also, as though it does not properly belong to St Matthew, who makes no use of this form of speech in any other passage, when referring to a name. It is probable that it may have crept into the text from some gloss which, being made on its margin, might have expressed the very probable supposition that the Thaddaeus of St Mark was the same person with the Lebbeus of St Matthew. *Mill* preferred to regard this addition as a reference to the name of St Matthew. He looks upon Λεββαῖος as being analogous with Λευί, and hence, derived the addition from some one, who wished to direct the attention to the circumstance, that both St Mark and St Luke call St Matthew *Levi*. The identity of the names, however, cannot be proved. Λεββαῖος is probably derived from לֵב, "heart," so that it signifies *cordatus*, "brave, courageous." Θαδδαῖος is perhaps synonymous with Θευδᾶς (see *Buxtorf.* Lex. Talm p. 2565, sub verbo תַּד, *mamma*, "the breast or pap," in the Hebrew language שַׁד). But both names are wanting in St Luke (in the Gospel as well as in the Acts), instead of it he has: Ἰούδας Ἰακώβου, "Judas, the son of James," who, on the contrary, is mentioned neither in St Matthew nor in St Mark. That there was a Judas among the twelve (not Iscariot) is clearly pointed out by St John xiv 22, and may easily be the same person with this Lebbeus or Thaddaeus. The ancient church had adopted this view at an early period (*Hieron* ad h. l. calls him τριώνομος, "triple-named") Altogether without foundation is the view adopted by many modern commentators, that the name Ἰακώβου, "of James," ought to have been completed, not by υἱός, "son," as is done in other cases, and usually also in this, but by ἀδελφός, "brother." This Judas, then, would appear to have been the author of the Epistle of Jude, which forms a part of the canon of the New Testament, and a brother of James the son of Alpheus and Simon Zelotes; all, however, are supposed to have been the ἀδελφοὶ τοῦ Κυρίου, "brethren of the Lord," a view which we shall endeavour to refute when we come to treat on St Matth. xiii. 55, and St John vii 5, and in our introduction to the Epistle of St James and St Jude. There exists throughout no real ground for departing from the customary mode of supplying the ellipsis, and on this account we cannot help looking upon this Judas, who is also named Lebbeus or Thaddaeus, as a different person from Judas the brother of our Lord. The passage St John vii. 5, must here serve as a clue to lead us to the truth; from which we learn that the brethren of Jesus believed not on him, and consequently that it was impossible that they, or any one of them, should have been admitted into the band of the apostles. Finally, 'Ιούδας 'Ισκαριώτης, = אִישׁ קְרִיוֹת, "a man of Karioth," (Josh xv. 25)[1] This explanation is given in more than one manuscript on St John vi. 71; xii 4, in the words ἀπὸ Καριώτου, "of Kariotos." Other derivations, as for example, from שֶׁקֶר, "falsehood," are obviously intended to convey a prophetic allusion to his treacherous act; but even this of itself shows the pure character of our Gospels, that they, while they abstain from every kind of laudatory expressions concerning Christ, and his acts, as well as his discourses, avoid, in like manner, every kind of reproachful allusions to Judas. The single remark which they make, referring historically to the name of Judas, is, ὁ παραδοὺς αὐτόν, "who betrayed him."[2] This only excepted, they allow the stupendous facts contained in the history of Jesus to speak for themselves, and this simple, truthful portraiture of them places light and shadow in their most striking contrast at once before us And thus viewing everything in the sense or light of pure objectivity, they disdain every kind of mean or paltry subjective censures.

Ver. 5. To this band of the twelve St Matthew now makes Jesus direct his discourses. It must appear remarkable that this discourse should proceed on the ground of Jewish exclusiveness, inasmuch as the disciples are forbidden to go to the

---

[1] *De Wette*, agreeing with *Lightfoot*, has declared in favour of the derivation of this appellative from the word אַסְקוּרְטְיָא, "a leather apron," or אַסְכָּרָא, "strangling" The parallel passages in St John, however, are entirely opposed to this explanation, the assertion, that אִישׁ קְרִיוֹת, "a man of Karioth," or קְרִיוֹתִי, "the Kariothite," could not have been added as a surname to his proper name stands altogether without proof

[2] The passage containing the words here alluded to, is given in x 4 of the Gospel according to St Matthew, and runs thus. 'Ιούδας 'Ισκαριώτης, ὁ καὶ παραδοὺς αὐτόν, literally, "Judas Iscariot, who also betrayed him"—T

Samaritans and the Gentiles (St Luke x 1, in his discourse to the seventy, as the representatives of the collective Gentile world, of whom alone St Luke gives this relation, seeing that he wrote for the information of Gentiles, does not contain this restriction) Jesus, however, never appears as the disturber of the exclusive privileges vouchsafed by God to the Jewish people (see on Matth xxi. 33); on the contrary, he acknowledges these (Matth. xv 24), and confines his own ministry, on the whole, to Palestine. He indicates, indeed, that is, he points in a significant manner to *that* time when this exclusiveness will be done away with (John x. 16), and ministers in the mean time, altogether incidentally, to the necessities of Gentiles and Samaritans, whenever their faith *constrained* him to do so. (Comp Matth. xv 21 sqq., John iv.) A mere accommodation to the weaknesses of the disciples is herein out of the question; it is the veritable necessity of the circumstances of the time and the immediate destination of the twelve that are to be considered. It was only at a subsequent period that St Paul received the express command to labour for the Gentile world (Acts of the Apostles ix. 15). The Redeemer also, on his final departure from this earth, extended the sphere of action of the twelve likewise over all nations (St Matth. xxviii. 19). But it was necessary first of all to prepare, in the nation of Israel, a hearth to receive the sacred fire, and to keep its glowing heat in a state of concentration even unto the end After the sure establishment of the church in the bosom of the people of God, and after the infidelity of the mass thereof had been fully ascertained, the stream of life was then first shed abroad over the whole Gentile world.

Ver 6 Πρόβατα ἀπολωλότα, "lost sheep," must here be taken in the sense of sheep who have gone astray and been separated from their shepherd (comp St Luke xv. 4), with reference to Jerem. l. 6, צֹאן אֹבְדוֹת הָיָה עַמִּי, "my people has been lost sheep"

Ver. 7. The main substance of the announcement is the kingdom of God, as then present or at hand (comp. Matth. iii. 2; iv. 17), but in the form announced by St John. (See St Mark vi. 12, ἐκήρυσσον, ἵνα μετανοήσωσι, literally "they preached that they should repent.") The directions given to the disciples, together with their destination on occasion of this first sending forth (mission), was quite a different one from that which *followed the pouring out of the Holy Ghost* The apostles themselves as yet took their stand on the point of view (ground) of the Old Testament, and preached repentance, as did the Baptist before them, and baptised with water as he did (John iv. 2); at a subsequent period, however, they preached the forgiveness of sins, the soil having been prepared beforehand by the preaching of repentance.

Ver. 8. With this is connected the promise of miraculous cures, as the first outward and visible sign or manifestation of the future redemption (comp. Matth xi 5). The exhortation δωρεὰν δότε, "give as a gift" (freely ye have received, freely give), was the natural result of the circumstances in which they were placed; the disciples might easily have permitted themselves to be led away to receive presents, and thus imperceptibly not to regard the faith, but the splendour and greatness of the sick persons, and thus to inflict an injury on their own souls; their portion was only that which would supply the necessaries of life (Very important critical authorities omit the passage: νεκροὺς ἐγείρετε, "raise dead men," others place this passage after λεπροὺς καθαρίζετε, "cleanse lepers," which, it is not unlikely, points to a marginal gloss (Randglosse). *Mill* and *J D. Michaelis* therefore consider the former as being an addition of a later period. We might suppose, indeed, that they had been added for the purpose of increasing the glory of the apostles, only no instance of such a miracle is related, and this of itself makes it more probable that the omission resulted from the circumstance of there being recorded no raisings from the dead performed by the apostles. But it does not follow, that, because no instance thereof is given, no case of the kind should have therefore occurred)

Ver 9, 10. This endowment with spiritual riches our Lord combines with the exhortation to go forth in the external garb of poverty. This remark, however, that there was no necessity for outward preparations for the journey, is, in reality, only another view of their riches. By going forth without being possessed of any human means, they but lived upon the rich treasure of their heavenly Father. The correct exposition of the passage is obtained best from a comparison with St Luke xxii. 35—37. There Jesus reminds his disciples, a short time before his sufferings, of that rich and glorious time when he was able to send them forth without any earthly preparations being made for their journey, and remarks that the times now were different (inasmuch as these were the days in which the bridegroom would be taken from them), and that now it was necessary for every one of them to prepare and arm himself as well as he could to the utmost of his powers The general idea, therefore, is to be rendered thus: We live at a time of rich blessings (it is the hour in which the light is in the ascendant, and which forms the contrast to St Luke xxii. 53, $αὕτη\ ἐστιν\ ἡ\ ὥρα$, $καὶ\ ἡ\ ἐξουσία\ τοῦ\ σκότος$, "this is the hour and the power of darkness," to which passage comp the Comment.), when it requires no human preparations, "love will guide you, and love will provide you!" The separate points brought forward must not be anatomised, but must be taken in all the grandeur of freedom, in which they were viewed by the apostles themselves. St Mark vi. 8 permits them to take a $ῥάβδος$, "staff," but the two other prohibit even that;[1] St Matthew prohibits even the $ὑποδήματα$, "sandals," St Mark permits them. It is a paltering with words (Mikrologie) to insist here on a difference between $ὑποδήματα$ and $σανδάλια$. The words: $ἄξιος\ ὁ\ ἐργάτης\ τῆς\ τροφῆς\ αὐτοῦ$, literally "the workman is worthy of his meat," of St Matth. x. 10, affords the best point of view The Redeemer, who had himself no place wherein to lay down his head, places his disciples likewise in the position of a reliance upon pure faith; as the labourers of God,[2] they were to rely upon him therefore that which was necessary for their bodily wants; for the exercise and proof of their faith they went forth without any careful preparations, such as are and must be invariably made by the man that has not faith. It is likely that some of the disciples had indeed some money with them; therein they would have acted by no means against the commandment of our Lord, except that they had taken it with them *from unbelief*. Hence, this commandment, too, must be viewed, in spirit and life, in its relation to the disposition and faith, and bears in itself its eter-

---

[1] *Gratz* in his Commentary on St Matth. vol i p. 519, is of opinion that Jesus only forbade them to take with them a *supply*, not that he prohibited their taking the staff which was in their hands, or the shoes that were actually on their feet Strange! who ever carries with him a supply of walking-sticks on a journey?

[2] The expression $ἐργάτης$, "labourers," points to a figure of speech herein contained, according to which mankind is compared to a vineyard, or to an arable field, wherein spiritual work is to be performed. (Concerning this, see on St Matth xiii 1 sqq)

nal truth, applicable to all the labourers in the kingdom of God at all times and in all places; this word of our Lord, however, must never be viewed without the reference to St Luke xxii. 35 sqq., which is necessary for the complete comprehension thereof.

Ver 11. There follow now more special precepts with regard to their spiritual ministry. The passage ἐξετάσατε τίς ἄξιος, literally "inquire who is worthy," does not refer to honourable or noble persons, but to the poor (Matth. v. 3), longing, needy in spirit (Matth. ix. 12), to them only could the annunciation of a Redeemer be an εὐαγγέλιον, "Gospel, i.e. glad tidings." In this same city they were not to change their residence, but abide in the same place; he exhorts them to peace and quietness during the unquiet course of their journey. (This very idea is expressed in St Luke x. 7, with an additional remark, concerning which see the commentary on the passage referred to.)

Ver. 12 The apostles, as those in whom dwelt the spiritual powers which our Redeemer possessed *without* measure (John iii 34), and which he had apportioned to them *according* to their capabilities of receiving them, are enjoined to communicate their gifts. As the sun sheds abroad his rays both upon the good and the evil, so must they, too, bless the house into which they enter; their blessing, if given to the impure, will *return back* upon them This mode of expression flowed from an essential conception of that which is spiritual, and its effectual working; justly compared to the (rays of) light it pours itself forth, and returns again to its source,[1] blessing and intercession is, according to this view, an exhalation and an inhalation of the Spirit. These are figures of speech, but such as contain a substantial and profound meaning. Led by the Spirit, the apostles enter a house, and say: εἰρήνη τῷ οἴκῳ τούτῳ, "peace to this house" (Luke x. 5), not as a mere empty phrase, as the שָׁלוֹם לָכֶם, "peace unto you" of the Jews, but as the innermost expression of their nature and of their office. The blessing will cling to the place where it meets with welcome, (ἄξιος, "worthy," must be applied again, in the Gospel sense, to all those that are in need, and long for salvation and mercy,) wherever blessing meets with no resting-place, there it returns to those that pro-

---

[1] This mode of viewing is rendered more especially prominent in the representation of χάρις, "grace," and πνεῦμα, "spirit," given by St John Comp. St John vii. 38, 39

nounced it, as to its source of life. Hence, the Spirit here appears as that which itself has life, forming for itself fountains in those from whom it emanates, and to whom it returns, whenever it finds no resting-place wherein to settle, in order to create a new source (John iv 14; vii. 38).

Ver. 14 Wherever the feeling of need, and mark of a longing to appropriate that which is divine, is wanting, the messenger of Christ departs thence; he only comes in order to bring to the sick the message of healing. The ἐκτινάσσειν κονιορτὸν, "shaking off the dust," is a mere symbolical representation of total and utter separation and renunciation (Acts of the Apostles xiii. 51, xviii 6). To express an idea by means of an act is in the Old as well as in the New Testament, as, indeed, throughout the whole of the east, a very common process; this kind of language or speech is to the sensual man more impressive than mere words (comp on Matth xxvii. 24).

Ver 15. Sodom and Gomorrha stand here as the symbols of justice, as the chastiser of alienation from God. But the vastness of the guilt is in proportion to the degree of purity and clearness in which that which is Divine has presented itself to him who has hardened himself against its impressions. Whoever turns away the messengers of Christ, shows himself more callous than the ancient sinners of Sodom, because they express and represent that which is Divine with more purity than Lot and his better contemporaries (as regards the whole idea here hinted at, comp. what is further adduced on St Matth. xi 22, 24)

Ver. 16. After thus portraying the favourable side of the apostolical ministry, its dark side is not withheld from their view in their relative position with regard to the enemies of the kingdom of Christ. The λύκος, "wolf," is as truly the emblem of cunning malice as the πρόβατον, "sheep," is the figure of simple purity, harmless and defenceless, it stands opposed to the wild and ferocious power that knows no restraint. This is a significant picture, unfolding the position of every follower of the Lamb (Rev xiv. 4) among the perverse race of the children of this world. The language of our Lord is confined to very significant animal symbols, in order to exhort to *prudence*, which is a virtue that can be acquired by the faithful only after a hard struggle, he fears the character of the old serpent, and prefers to *suffer* rather than to *deceive* In the περιστερά, "dove," the emblem of the Holy Spirit (Matth iii. 16), is reflected the purity of the soul (ἀκέραιος = unmixed, pure, without guile); in the term ὄφις, "serpent," (Gen. iii. 1) is expressed cunning, prudence. (Φρόνιμος, "prudent, practically wise," φρόνησις, "practical wisdom," derived from φρένες, signifies, in Biblical anthropology, the power of thought, understanding, which manifests itself in reflecting on the circumstances of life, comp. on Luke i. 17.) It is difficult to amalgamate this wisdom of the serpent with the purity of the dove, but it is not impossible, as is testified by the commandment of Jesus. Yet, in the course of the Christian development, let cunning suffer rather than simplicity of heart, if their union cannot as yet be consummated

Ver 17, 18. Here the glance just cast at their impending sufferings, on account of their confession of Jesus, is laid open in a fuller view. Their life, which has moved hitherto in a narrow sphere, will be brought forward into the publicity of the great world, according to the hint of our Lord, and earthly tribulations of all kinds await the preachers of heavenly peace (comp on Matth xxiv. 9); the συνέδρια, "councils," signify the high court of justice in the provincial cities (see on Matth. v. 21, thus also in Mark xiii. 9). The discourse ascends from things of trifling importance to those of greater moment The ἡγεμόνες, "governors," here spoken of (comp. on St Matth. xxvii 11), are the Roman pro-consuls; the βασιλεῖς, "kings," were the tetrarchs (Acts of the Apostles xii. 1; xxvi. 2). Concerning εἰς μαρτύριον, "for a testimony," see on Matth. viii. 4 In the sufferings which the children of God have to experience from the world, on account of the name of Jesus, is developed their true character, that of suffering and self-sacrificing love.

Ver. 19, 20. As a consolation for the prospect of such sufferings, our Lord promises them special help from above. The disciples, inexperienced and unskilled in language, are referred to the Spirit of all wisdom. The μὴ μεριμνήσητε, πῶς ἢ τί λαλήσητε, "take no thought how or what ye shall speak," excludes all human calculation, and refers the disciples to a principle of a higher nature, to the Spirit from on high We find the idea expressed already in Is 1 4, that it is a gift given by God to know how to speak a word in season (comp. Luke xxi. 15). Of course, this does not exclude the application of the natural powers, they are rather to be looked upon as sanctified by this Spirit. Hence, the term μεριμνᾶν, "to consider, take thought," is to be viewed as the anxious collecting of one's own strength, as is seen in the unbelieving, natural man, who is unaware of a higher source both of power and life. But such a relying on the powers from above would become *enthusiasm*, firstly, where the conditions of aid from above are wanting, i.e. repentance and true faith, and in the second place, where internal impurity designs to apply them for wicked purposes. In order to confirm more and more the conviction of such an aid from above, Jesus adds. οὐ γὰρ ὑμεῖς ἐστε οἱ λαλοῦντες, κ. τ. λ., " for it is not ye that are speaking," &c Thus, then, the isolated individuals disappear wholly in the great struggle of light and darkness; the question here is the cause of God; *this* is pleaded by his Spirit dwelling in those instruments which he consecrates for himself. Through this mode of viewing the matter, the individual person gains an invincible power, inasmuch as, having departed from his isolated state, he becomes aware of his nature, as a member of a great invincible community The πνεῦμα πατρός, " the Spirit of the Father," forms next a contrast with the spirit of the disciples themselves, hence the heavenly principle appears as already operating within them, although it has not as yet developed itself in its full power (comp. on John vii. 39)

Ver. 21. Thus far the discourse has contained nothing that was not in accordance with existing circumstances; but the verses which follow seem all at once to take a different view, that is, they seem to refer to circumstances such as are treated of in chap. xxiv. They point to a field or sphere of action of a more vast extent than that which would present itself to the disciples on this their first mission Our Redeemer would speak to them, no doubt, of persecutions even unto death, but only in the last days of his earthly ministry[1] (comp on St Matth. xxiv. 10, 12). Analogous, however, to this were the relations of the disciples throughout the whole of their ministry; and in so far these verses are applicable even here. The Gospel is now represented as overstepping the natural conditions of earthly life. The new element of life, which it has brought into the world, is stopped in its course neither by family ties, nor by the barriers of friendship or relationship; it appropriates to itself everywhere susceptible minds. But in consequence of this, it

---

[1] Very decisive in this respect is the passage of the Gospel of St John xvi 4, to which see the exposition.

calls forth also its contrast in the minds of all those that are callous to its influences, and the Gospel of peace brings the sword into the bosom of families; for, being the word of God, it divides asunder the joints and marrow (Heb. iv. 12). The history of the spreading of Christianity proves the literal truth of these prophetic words of our Redeemer. (Compare the Acta Martyrii Perpetuae et Felicitatis, printed in *my* Monum. hist. eccl, vol i. p. 96 sqq) But inasmuch as phenomena of this kind could not have made their appearance at the time when our Redeemer spoke these words, hence these remarkable words of Christ display a prophetic character.

Ver. 22 The hatred of all men that are taken with the principles of this world is directed more especially towards the name of Jesus Natural virtue the world may find lovely or amiable, for the world perceives it to be a blossom of its own life. But it hates what is especially and specifically Christian, for it feels that in it is its death (Jam. iv. 4). The reference made to the impending persecutions required a hint concerning the necessary earnestness of purpose that would be requisite in this struggle and endurance The σωτηρία, "salvation," here is connected with ὑπομονή, "patience, patient endurance." The words εἰς τέλος, "unto the end," contain a reference more especially to the individuals, not to the tribulation of the whole, for death itself brings at once to every single member of the company of the faithful the end of trouble and the beginning of everlasting safety. Yet does the passage sound (and ver 23 confirms this feeling, that the meaning of these words extends further) as though it belonged to some prophetic discourse concerning his second coming. That the mention thereof, on the first sending forth of the disciples, appears not to be in accordance with the existing circumstances, will be presently more fully developed.

Ver. 23 With a view to the impending persecutions, Jesus once more recommends prudence; he advises them to avoid them as much as possible, in order not to endanger their souls by a wilful entering into, and abiding in, peril. The church has ever acted according to this precept, and it was only *Montanistic rigour* which sought, at a subsequent period, to prohibit the avoidance of persecutions. (The passage: κἂν ἐκ ταύτης κ. τ. λ., "and if from this," &c., is no doubt genuine; its omission in some Codices has originated most likely from the similar terminations of the clauses [homoioteleuton] The reference to the return of Christ and the end (which was already perceptible in ver 22) is brought forward very clearly in the concluding words The Son of Man is to return before the disciples who are to be sent out shall have wandered through all the cities of Israel (τελεῖν, "to finish," scil ὁδόν, "the journey".) What here forms a difficulty is, that it appears not to have been the design of the mission that the disciples should travel through the whole land, the mission took place, for the most part, for the perfecting of the disciples themselves. From the feeling, therefore, that the connection of the passage demanded a reference to something about to happen immediately, emanated the declaration: "you will not require to hasten over all the Jewish towns under the persecutions that you will meet with, I shall be with you again ere that." Yet to this view of the words, which, grammatically speaking, is possible, does not suit, in the first place, the grave ἀμήν, "verily," and in the second, it is not Jesus that comes back to them, but it is they that came back to Jesus (Luke ix. 10). Finally, the phrase ἔρχεται ὁ υἱὸς τοῦ ἀνθρώπου, "the Son of man cometh," has a determinate dogmatical acceptation; it always refers to the παρουσία, "advent, second coming of the Messiah." But of this Jesus cannot well have spoken, if we consider the whole connection of the passage. And nothing is gained, indeed, by referring the coming of our Lord to the resurrection, the outpouring of the Spirit, or indeed to the destruction of Jerusalem, for all these things were as yet too remote from the disciples during the first period of their sojourning with Christ. It is according to the nature of things that the notice of the *second coming* should be conditioned by that of his *departure from them*, but of the latter our Saviour had not as yet spoken. It was only at a later period that he permitted his disciples to obtain an insight into both events, shortly before, and at his transfiguration (St Matth xii 40, xvi. 21, 27; xvii 1 sqq , St Luke ix. 22, 31), on which solemn occasion it was that Divine messengers first revealed to the human comprehension of our Lord himself the Divine resolution in its whole extent, as concerned the redemption of mankind through his sufferings. Hence, if we can say with the greatest probability that the passage is not here given in its original connection, so it is equally true that St Matthew has interwoven it here in the discourse of Jesus in no unsuitable manner. For, the words, which make mention of the second coming of Jesus, extend by anticipation the horizon of the reader beyond the immediate subject in question. They amalgamate the first sending forth of the disciples with that of a subsequent period, and form thus *a general* instruction for preaching disciples This freedom, which the Evangelists, especially St Matthew, have permitted themselves to assume in the treatment of the elements of the Saviour's discourses, specially with a view to the more perfect treatment thereof, must always have something striking in it. (Concerning this comp § 8 of the Introduction) But that which would have destroyed the character of the Gospel, if applied thereto by an uncongenial spirit, only tends to add to its splendour, thus put in practice by the congenial Divine Spirit. The individual decisions of Christ resemble pearls and jewels, which the Evangelists work into, and freely apply to, the most varied and beautiful wholes. (Compare on this passage the comment. on St Matth. xxiv 1 sqq.)

Ver 24 Jesus, in continuation, proceeds to intimate to the disciples their future fate, by comparing them with his own person. This passage is given in St Luke (vi 40) in a different connection, and with the addition: κατηρτισμένος δὲ πᾶς ἔστι ὡς ὁ διδάσκαλος, signifying literally: "but every one made perfect shall be as the (in the text αὐτοῦ, "his") teacher," in which the expression κατηρτισμένος must be viewed as signifying "perfectly educated, accomplished," so that the meaning of the words would be: "the accomplished scholar resembles his master in all things " (Comp concerning these words what has been said on Matth. v. 1, with reference to the connection of the discourse in St Luke [vi 20 sqq]) But thereby the idea becomes involved in difficulties, inasmuch as the remark forces upon the reader's mind the idea that many scholars surpass their teachers. The reference to the proverbial mode of speech, which is contained in these words, is evidently of no value, for another proverb says. πολλοί μαθηταί κρείσσονες διδασκάλων, "many disciples surpass their masters." The first condition of a good proverb (and any other than *good ones* our Lord cannot possibly have made use of) is, that it be the expression of truth. However, this difficulty is removed, if we consider that the scholar who surpasses his teacher at the same time ceases to be, in the spiritual sense of the word, his pupil; as a scholar, he can go no farther than his master; hence, if he goes farther than the one master, he must then have had another, and if no human one, he must have had the Spirit, who has developed that which was dormant within him. These words, which, viewed in this manner, possess in every case their *relative* truth, are admirably fitted, in their *absolute* sense, to the relative position of the disciples with Christ. He, the image of the Father, could be surpassed neither by his disciples, nor by any person whatever at any time, he is Lord and teacher in the absolute sense, and, compared with him, no man existing gets beyond the sphere of his dependence and state of instruction. In this relation, then, it is likewise absolutely true, that whatever happened to the master, must also happen to the disciple

Ver 25 As the point or apex of the inimical disposition is rendered prominent, the circumstance of the world's regarding that which was Divine, in its purest manifestation, as that which was *diabolical*, i.e. as being in connection with the prince of darkness, which implies, at the same time, its contrast, and hence that the world also sees that which is Divine in that which is diabolical, and thus that it will establish a total confusion of the elements of good and evil If such be the case with the sun, what must happen to his rays; if the master is treated thus, what will not be done to his servants, in whom is but reflected the glory of the Lord. (Οἰκιακός, "household servant," comp. ver. 36, *domesticus*, with reference to the οἰκοδεσπότης, "the master of the house." The passage refers back to St Matth. ix 34, ἐν τῷ ἄρχοντι τῶν δαιμονίων ἐκβάλλει τὰ δαιμόνια, literally: "he casts forth the demons through the prince of the demons" [comp xii 24]) This expression is not different from ἐπικαλεῖν Βεελζεβούλ, "to call Beelzebub," for, in order to be able to drive out devils through him, he must be in the subject casting them out. Besides, as regards the name, Βεελζεβούβ = בַּעַל זְבוּב, "Beelzebub," German *Fliegen-Baal*, 2 Kings 1 2, was an Ekronitish deity, so called because a power was ascribed to him of removing troublesome flies. (As Zeus, "Jupiter," had the cognomen or epithet ἀπόμυιος, "the driver away of flies," μυίαγρος, "fly catcher.") In the New Testament, on the contrary, the reading βεελζεβούλ is to be preferred, inasmuch as the Jews changed the name of the idol here referred to out of derision into a contemptuous form. This form of name (derived from בַּעַל, "Lord," and זֶבֶל, "mire"), signifies, namely, the Lord of mire or filth. (Comp *Lightfoot* on St Matth xii 24.) Ingenious is the interpretation given of this name by *Dr Paulus*, according to which the form would be solved into the words בַּעַל זְבוּל, Lord of the dwelling, that is, of the subterranean one; to this would answer the οἰκοδεσπότης, "master of the house," of Christ. But that the prince of darkness is named after a national deity is accounted for, because, according to the decisive Scriptural view [see on 1 Cor. viii. 5], the Gentile life, which is connected with idolatry, appears as the element of darkness.

Ver 26, 27. Christ preserves the state of mind of the disciples in a state between fear and implicit faith; by means of the former he urges them on to earnestness, and by means of the latter he preserves them from faint-heartedness. Very striking is it, that the trust or confidence is based upon the certainty of a future disclosure of all existing mysteries, which is the fundamental idea of all the four members of the discourse comprised in these two verses The unveiling in itself of what is hidden, could, it is true, never be the foundation of confidence, were the secret or mystery something evil, it then would cause fear and consternation; for the bosom, however, which harbours that which is holy, as yet unexposed to view, and not understood by surrounding beings, there is nothing certainly more consolatory than that the time of revelation is approaching, for it is indeed also the time of the victory of the good Ver 27 contains the explanation of the preceding verse; the two members contained in each must be viewed according to the *parallelismus membrorum*, "parallelism of the members." The ἐν τῇ σκοτίᾳ, "in darkness," stands opposed to κεκαλυμμένον, literally, "that which has been covered," and denotes the unintentional darkness or obscurity that rests upon anything, as, for example, in this case the advent of the new life into the hitherto unrecognised land of Galilee; but the passage εἰς τὸ οὖς ἀκούειν, "to hear in the ear," on the contrary, is contrasted with κρυπτόν, "that which is hidden," and denotes here the intentional hiding or secreting of that which is to be communicated, in this case the disclosure of the mysteries of the kingdom of God in the closed or exclusive circle of the disciples. In these words the future free announcement of the Divine decrees, in all their bearings, and the unfolding of all the mysteries of God in the church, through the Spirit, is hinted at Mysteries, or secrets to be kept back, are things unknown to the church. (In the interpretation of the phrase· κηρύσσειν ἐπὶ τῶν δωμάτων, "to preach upon the house-tops," the ancient forms of houses and roofs must be borne in mind.)

Ver. 28. The general precept: μὴ οὖν φοβηθῆτε, "fear not, therefore," of ver. 26, is connected in ver 28, in a clearer and more explicit manner, with the true object of fear, and the false objects thereof are excluded. With a retrospective view to ver 21, Jesus observes, that the enemies of *corporeal* or *physical* life should form no object of fear to the child of God, inasmuch as their power cannot reach the *true* life. In the passage: μὴ δύνασθαι τὴν ψυχὴν ἀποκτεῖναι, literally, "not having power to kill the soul," their merely external power, which is not able to penetrate into the sphere of spiritual life within which the believer moves, is expressly hinted at. This power is however contrasted with another, and that power the Lord *commands* them to fear. The following reasons *would appear* to compel us to understand thereby the prince of darkness.—1st, Had these words a reference to God, the expression φοβεῖσθαι, "to fear," contained in the same verse, would have to be regarded in two different senses,[1]—in the first place, in the sense of *metuere*, "to fear, to be afraid of," and in the second, in that of *revereri*, "to stand in awe, to reverence;" 2d, With this the verses 29, 30, in which God is described as a protector in times of danger and necessity, do not agree; upon this is based the exhortation, μὴ οὖν φοβηθῆτε, literally, "fear ye not therefore," of ver. 31, but this would form a contradiction with the φοβηθῆτε, in the sense referred to above, which is, moreover, so emphatically reiterated in St Luke xii 5; 3d, It appears improper to say of God that he destroys souls, inasmuch as it is he that saves them Decisive, however, against this is the fact, that the devil never appears in Scripture as he who condemns souls to hell; his whole sphere of activity stands under and in subjection to the power of God (James iv 12) And inasmuch as ver. 33 clearly expresses the possibility of apostacy and denial of the Messiah; hence, the passage is best conceived in such a manner as to make it appear that the Redeemer intends to give

---

[1] No weight is to be placed upon the change of φοβεῖσθαι τινά, "to fear such an one," and ἀπό τινός, "because of such an one," even the former combination may signify *metuere*, "to fear," but in the sense of *revereri*, "to reverence," it certainly is not found with ἀπό, "because of, on account of." In the profane use of the language, "to be afraid of," "to reverence," is expressed by φοβεῖσθαι πρός τι

therein a powerful *exhortation* to earnestness of purpose, for the preservation of and confirmation in their calling. The change of the meaning of φοβεῖσθαι cannot, it is true, in that case, be avoided; but then, such like occurrences are frequently met with. But the exhortation, μὴ οὖν φοβηθῆτε, contained in ver. 31, has, according to this mode of conception, a reference to the presupposed fidelity of the disciples. (Concerning γέεννα, comp. on Matth. v. 22.—The contrast formed by ψυχή, "soul," and σῶμα, "body," is by no means contrary to the threefold existence [trichotomie] of human nature, as taught in the Bible; the ψυχή here is the πνευματική, "spiritual life." In another view, πνεῦμα, "spirit," and σάρξ, "flesh," may be perfectly well regarded as integral portions of the human nature.)

Ver. 29. As the contrast to fear, Jesus refers them to the almighty aid of God, for whose kingdom they were contending. He who feeds the sparrow and numbers the hair of the head, would assuredly protect the life of his faithful ones! The term στρουθίον, "sparrow," stands here, as frequently in the Septuagint = צִפּוֹר, "any bird, great or small." An ἀσσάριον, translated "farthing," was the tenth part of a denarius.[1]

Ver. 30. In a special providence is comprised the comforting idea of this doctrine. It combines, as throughout nature, things most sublime with things the most insignificant, into an harmonious whole. Thousands are fed, and the crumbs are collected; the Redeemer rises from his grave, and the linen is left carefully folded together.

Ver. 32 The whole assumes more and more a general keeping, although it may be seen, indeed, from the parallel passage of St Luke xii 2 sqq that the words were originally uttered in a different connection, the discourse comprises or keeps gradually more and more in view, the whole collective body of the disciples of Jesus as engaged in their conflict with the world. Besides, Christ here appears as he, the confession of whom has

---

[1] The ἀσσάριον, above referred to, is a brass coin of about the value of three farthings, and, as we see in the text, is equal to the tenth part of a δραχμή, an Athenian silver coin worth about eightpence three farthings, or *denarius*, which, according to A Boeckh's "Staatshaushaltung der Athener, vol. 1 p. 16," was worth about sevenpence halfpenny value The Latin name of this coin is *As*, its value, about three farthings and one-tenth of a farthing, it is called by the Rabbinical writers, אִיסָר —T.

a decided influence upon everlasting bliss or everlasting woe, whose testimony is available in the sight of God and his angels. The confession before men (as the enemies of that which is good) forms the contrast with the confession of Christ before the heavenly host. Whoever takes upon himself, in this world, the ignominy of appearing as a true worshipper of Christ, that person will also be received as such at the manifestation of Christ in his glory. The contrast, however, in like manner, is placed immediately by the side of it; as the latter terrifies, so does the former allure. Of course, the whole has a reference to believers only, those who have acknowledged our Lord as that which he is, and now either dare openly to confess their belief in him, or are tempted through fear to conceal it; the latter procedure must extinguish the light of faith that was kindled in them, and consequently exclude them from the kingdom of God.

Ver. 34. But inasmuch as the fear of strife and persecution might easily deter them from an open confession, our Lord points out, in a very distinct manner, that the Gospel, according to its nature, must of necessity lead to strife. Not as though strife itself were the *object* thereof, (its real object is that peace in which strife terminates,) but such strife is, nevertheless, a necessary *consequence* of Christ's entrance into the world, or into a human heart. But since absolute holiness is revealed in the person of Christ, while the κόσμος, "world," nevertheless, comprises in itself both good and evil in a mixed state, therefore the spirit of Christ (μάχαιρα, "a sword," Ephes. vi 17,) divides or cuts off the evil (διαμερισμός, "division," Luke xii. 51), and whoever cleaves thereto, is separated or cut off therewith.

Ver 35, 36. The consequence of this dividing power of the Gospel Jesus now sets forth, in the same manner as above, in v 21, 22. The most intimate relationships and connections which are based on corporeal or physical affinities and terrestrial love, are at once divided or cut through by the sword of the Spirit, which altogether annihilates them, if the unholy element be clung to, and ennobles them, if place be everywhere given to the Holy Ghost. That which our Lord lays down here, as required of those who believe in him, namely, a separation from all, even the most intimate earthly ties, on account of the covenant with him, already was declared by Moses of the Levites·
"Who said unto his father and to his mother, I have not seen him; neither did he acknowledge his brethren, nor know his

own children: for they have observed thy word, and kept thy covenant. They shall teach Jacob thy judgments, and Israel thy law." (Deut. xxxiii. 9, 10, comp Gen. xii 1.)

Ver. 37. The love of Christ must be stronger than either paternal or maternal love. (Comp. Luke xiv. 26, wherein is found the yet stronger expression: μισεῖν πατέρα κ. τ. λ. "to hate father, &c." (Very significant is the οὐκ ἔστι μου ἄξιος, "is not worthy of me;" for, Christ himself is the object or aim of the true believer, he longs after him as he is, in the power of his resurrection and his sufferings. (Comp. on Phil. iii. 10) This mode of action of the Gospel, this requisition of the whole man thereby, makes the world to foam and rave with fury, for this reason it creates for itself another Christ, who leaves good and evil to dwell peaceably together in undisturbed quietude. Moreover, had Christ not been the Truth and Life itself (John xiv. 6), it would have been a violation of the most sacred duties, had he demanded the disregard, for his sake, of the dearest ties of relationship. God alone must we obey, rather than father and mother, and, therefore, Christ alone, because in him we behold the Father (John xiv 9). For this reason it is that, by esteeming his person higher than what we hold dearest and holiest, no duty whatever is violated, on the contrary, each duty is purified and ennobled. The commandment: "honour thy father and mother," therefore, is not abrogated thereby, but fulfilled (Matth v. 17), inasmuch as man conceives himself in Christ as the child of the father of all fathership (Ephes. iii. 15).

Ver. 38. With the requirement of a separation from earthly ties, which the faith in the Redeemer, if it be a living one, at all times presupposes, is connected the prospect of a course of life full of sufferings, the end of which is death. What a full consciousness of his glory and blessedness must our Lord have been possessed with, when he did not hesitate to place before them such a picture of the life of his faithful ones!—The σταυρὸν λαμβάνειν, "to take up the cross," spoken of *before* the crucifixion of our Lord, must be explained from the general custom, according to which malefactors had to carry their cross to the place of execution; in the mouth of Christ, and spoken previous to his suffering, these words assume a prophetic character. *Fritzsche* (on this passage) distinguishes between λαμβάνειν, "to take or bear," and αἴρειν τὸν σταυρόν, "to take *up* the cross" (xvi. 24), so that in the latter is expressed the signification of the *willing* taking up. The passage, ἀκολουθεῖν ὀπίσω, "to follow after," evidently implies a *bearing* of the cross, as the adjunct of the *taking* up of the cross, together with its ultimate result, the *death* of the cross. The life of every individual professing Jesus, which is on earth necessarily toilsome, inasmuch as he lives for ever in danger, and, as he sacrifices his own will to the divine will, is compared unto a continual dying on the cross. That which is here taken in its connection, has an immediate reference to life in the first ages of Christianity, under *bodily* dangers and persecutions, retains its truth at all times with reference to the *internal* life-struggle of believers, whence it is that this figurative mode of expression finds its application also throughout the whole Scriptural language (Gal. ii. 20; v. 24; Rom. vi. 6)

Ver. 39. From this one view of Christian sufferings, the persecutions and perils of death therein, the glance extends itself more widely over the subject in general; the regeneration of the new life is conditioned by the death of the old one. That here by ψυχὴν ἀπολέσαι, "to lose life," cannot be meant the mere loss of the bodily life for the sake of Jesus, is manifest, partly because not all the apostles died in consequence of persecution, and yet the remaining alive without guilt or fault cannot possibly have been counted to their disadvantage, and even a death by persecution may be conceived (as indeed not unfrequently occurred), which does not correspond with the requirements herein expressed; for instance, if it occurred as the result of vanity, or fanatical excitement The ψυχὴν ἀπολέσαι, "to lose life," can be therefore only a spiritual sacrifice, through which alone the bodily death becomes a sanctified one. In the expression, ψυχή, "soul, life," the signification of *soul* and *life* are amalgamated with each other (compare on vi. 25); hence, the question on this passage is of a *twofold* soul, of which the *one* becomes lost, the moment the *other* is preserved. If we put life instead thereof, then is it a twofold, or double being, or existence, of a higher and lower kind, of which man has the choice. (The same idea is expressed in the same words, in Matth. xvi. 24, 25; John xii. 25. However, in the place of εὑρίσκειν, "to find," St John gives φιλεῖν, "to love," which is more intelligible; the expression, εὑρίσκειν, here signifies to gain, to attain to.[1])

[1] Comp. Hebr x. 39, at the words. περιποίησις ψυχῆς, "the saving of the soul."

This passage will assume a more definite form by paraphrasing it in the following manner: ὁ εὑρὼν τὴν (σαρκικὴν) ψυχὴν, ἀπολέσει αὐτὴν (sc. πνευματικήν)· καὶ ὁ ἀπολέσας τὴν ψυχὴν (σαρκικήν), εὑρήσει αὐτὴν (πνευματικήν), "he that findeth his (fleshly) life shall lose it (that is the spiritual life); and he that loses his life (the fleshly one) shall find it (the spiritual one)." The innermost personality, the *ego* (self), remains, but in true self-denial it becomes dead to sin, the unbelieving man, on the contrary, cleaves to his natural state of being, and retains it, but the germ of the more exalted life can never in him attain the dominion. The mode of expression here made use of by the Redeemer is explained in the simplest manner, by the assumption that the personality of man (the ψυχή) is conceived as standing between two powers, the influences of which he may receive into himself, and by means of which he may be changed or transformed into their nature. Now, inasmuch as man is already by his nature more especially exposed to the one (the evil) power; hence, the question in the work of renovation is, to forsake the old sinful life, which has grown up together with the *ego*, and to enter instead thereof into the new life of light. This transition, or going over from life to life, is a death; but out of this death springs up a new and more exalted life. Important hereto is the addition, ἕνεκεν ἐμοῦ, "for the sake of me," which stands opposed to all self-devised means of sanctification and perfecting of the spiritual life. A crucifying of the flesh and self-denial undertaken *for one's own sake*, for one's own consumnation, or perfection, are abominations in the sight of our Lord, for they are in that case always the fruits of secret presumption and pride.[1] They must be undertaken, on the contrary, from a love

---

[1] Throughout the religions of farther Asia (*Hinterasien*), especially Buddaism, is interwoven the idea of self-denial, but being, as it is, without Jesus, without that perfect ideal of holiness manifested in the flesh, the practice thereof gives birth to the most frivolous and silly exhibitions. The addition, therefore, of ἕνεκεν ἐμοῦ, "for my sake," is of the greatest importance to the rule of self-denial, and, at the same time, a remarkable testimony to the divine dignity, or Godhead of Jesus; for, it would have been the highest presumption to have required that all things should be disregarded for his sake, had he himself not been something *more* than all things (das Geschaffne, i.e. created nature). In the work of J J Schmidt (uber die altere religiose, politische und literarische Bildungsgeschichte der Volker Mittelasiens, i.e. "on the religious, political, and literary history of civilisation among the ancient nations of Central Asia" Petersburg, 1824), we find characteristic traits

to Jesus, from a sense of obedience to him, from the motions of his Spirit; in that case they create or bear lovely fruits, and effect that sanctification, without which no man can see the Lord (Heb. xii. 14). The via media, or happy medium between idleness on the one hand, and self-seeking activity on the other, is not easily found; the originator of faith must here in like manner be himself the finisher thereof (Heb. xii. 2).

Ver. 40. As a comfort for the difficulties which our Lord has placed before his own people, there follows in conclusion a noble idea, wherein is expressed how infinitely dear to the Lord of the universe are all those who are valiant for the truth.[1] As Christ is the representative of the Father, so does he consider, in like

of such mistaken notions of self-denial, for example, "Shaggiamuni, (the Buddha of the Mongol tribes) as a king's son, encountered once in his walks a tigress with her young, who was nearly dead with hunger. Penetrated with compassion, and there being nothing at hand wherewith to restore her, he withdrew himself under some pretext from his followers, returned to the tigress, and laid himself down before her that she might tear him in pieces But perceiving that she was too much exhausted to attack him, he forthwith made an incision in his skin, and so placed himself before her that she might lap the blood which flowed from the wound, whereby she became gradually strengthened, so that she was able to devour him altogether" What puerilities, when compared with the spectacle afforded by the life of an individual living in a state of true Christian self-denial, and following the precepts of Jesus! Far more noble were the ideas conceived even by noble-minded Muhammadan Mystics of former times, as for example, Dshelal-ladin Rumi, who thus beautifully expresses the necessity for the death of the *old man*, that thereby the *new creature* may be brought to life.—

> Death ends indeed the cares of life,
> Yet, shudders life when death is near,
> And such the fond heart's deadly strife
> When first the loved one does appear
>
> For, where true love is wakened, dies
> The tyrant *self*, that despot dark;
> Rejoice thou, that in death he lies,
> And breathe morn's free air, with the lark.

It must be admitted, however, that there exists a wide difference between the conception of the idea itself and its realisation, or practical execution.

[1] St Luke x 16 exhibits the reverse side of the picture in the words: ὁ ἐμὲ ἀθετῶν κ. τ. λ, "he who despiseth me," &c Ideas in accordance with this are also met with in the Rabbinical writings, for example, si quis recipit viros doctos, idem est ac si reciperet schechinam, i e. manifestationem summi numinis. "If any one receiveth, i e entertaineth, men of learning, it is the same thing as though he were to entertain the *Shekinah*, that is, the manifestation of the supreme Deity" Concerning this passage comp *Schöttgen.*

manner, his disciples as representing him, hence, whosoever, therefore, receives his disciples, receives the Lord of the universe himself (Mark ix. 37). But, the δέχεσθαι, "to receive," as may be more immediately seen from the verses which follow, must be conceived with emphasis in this manner: "Whosoever receives you with a knowledge of what ye are, and because of this your spiritual character, he receives God," and hence receives all the blessings, according to the history of the patriarchs, which are conferred by a visit from the Lord. There is comprehended, therefore, in the term, δέχεσθαι, "to receive," not the mere outward reception (hospitio excipere, "to receive into the house as a guest"), but more especially the opening of the heart, and of the whole life of the inner man, so that we may receive the Lord's disciples, although we ourselves had not wherein to lay our heads.

Ver. 41, 42. But in order to place in its full and true light the greatness of the glory of believers, and to portray the blessedness of those that receive them, our Redeemer concludes with a remarkable parallel. His disciples, the representatives of the new Christian life-giving principle, he compares with the pious men of the Old Testament, προφήταις καὶ δικαίοις, "with prophets and righteous men," and thus infers, that in so much as the former occupy a more exalted station than the latter, by so much the higher and more glorious will be their reward. Firstly, as to that which concerns the gradations of rank, or consequence, the name, μικροί, "little ones," here given to believers, is remarkable. We may regard it as equivalent to the Rabbinical form of speech, according to which קָטוֹן, "little," forms the contrast to רַב, "great," and as the latter signifies a teacher, a master, so the former denotes a scholar, a servant But this does not go the whole length; the expression here is to imply or denote (comp. Matth. xviii 6) something peculiar to the disciples of Jesus. In the first place, this is to point out the state of dependence of the disciples, as is clearly discernible from the context, who appear in this world like helpless children given over as a prey to want and misery, but who are sustained by the help of their heavenly Father that dwelleth on high. But then, in the second place, the expression here refers likewise to the child-like, innocent, and more especially to the lowly-mindedness of those that have been born anew, who, although exalted and honourable in the sight of the Lord, are conscious of their own honourable position, yet without any presumption whatever. (The text, xviii. 6, explains this more fully.) In contrast with this μικρότης, "littleness," of the disciples, is placed the piety of individuals spoken of in the Old Testament, which, although in reality inferior, possessed somewhat more of outward show; its two principal forms are brought forward, viz. προφητεία, "prophecy, the prophetical office," and δικαιοσύνη, "righteousness, justice." In the former is displayed, in a peculiar manner, the fullness of enlightenment by the Spirit of God (which often, however, as for example in the case of Jonah, might be combined with mean personal qualities); in the latter, preciseness in the observances of the law (comp. on Luke i. 6). The δικαιοσύνη, "righteousness," here appears as the higher gradation of religious life under the Old Testament, inasmuch as it presupposes a higher degree of development of the individual character than the προφητεία, "prophecy, or prophetical office" Far above both stands the New Testament life, in which regeneration taking its rise in the heart acts outwardly on the life. These three gradations of προφήτης, "prophet," δίκαιος, "just or righteous man," and μικρός, "little one," are brought forward in connection with those who shall receive them, and to every such person the μισθός, "reward," is promised of him whom he receives. (Concerning the abstract idea of μισθός, "reward," comp the remarks made on Matth. v. 12.) In a legal point of view, the expression is wholly appropriate, and it harmonises also with the evangelical view, in thus far that love, which in this case appears as the principle of action, carries its reward in itself. Hence each person seeks after and receives his reward according to the principle which he harbours in his bosom. But as a condition of the μισθός it is furthermore added, in what manner the reception must take place· εἰς ὄνομα προφήτου, δικαίου, μαθητοῦ, "in the name of a prophet, of a righteous (man), of a disciple" In this εἰς ὄνομα is contained the key to the whole, rather obscure, passage; it corresponds to the Hebrew בְּשֵׁם, "in the name" (to assume a confounding of the prepositions εἰς and ἐν is unnecessary), so that the name expresses the character, the true nature of the individual to be received. According to this, the passage contains a rich meaning; it expresses the moral principle, that every action must be measured according to the disposition from which it emanates, and declares that the disposition is the result of the whole internal mental position of the

E

man. Hence it is not the *isolated act* of receiving which is regarded as the ground of reward, but it is the *position, i e. disposition of the soul* (Seelenstellung) from which it emanates; and in the reception itself the person received is not alone considered, but the degree of knowledge and of clear-sightedness with which the person is received as the individual he or she pretends to be. Hence the sense of these remarkable words is this: Whosoever receives an Old Testament prophet for the very sake of his spiritual character, and who is hence endowed with the susceptibility for this point of view, and the ability to recognise him as such, the same person is rewarded according to his Old Testament position, the very same takes place with regard to the righteous man. But he who receives a disciple of Jesus, and hence affords refreshment to a child of God and a citizen of the kingdom of heaven, even though it were by means of the merest trifle (as a lower counterpart of δέχεσθαι, "to receive"); hence, he who is able to discover in them the resplendent nature of that which is Divine under their insignificant outward appearance, he who can love it, and do good to it under the form of its representatives, shows thereby that he himself is called upon to act from this point of view, and consequently that he will receive the reward which it involves. But this is an everlasting one (οὐ μὴ ἀπολέσῃ τὸν μισθὸν αὐτοῦ, "shall in no wise lose his reward"), in which it is intimated that the Old Testament awards to the righteous men thereof promises of a more earthly character. The idea is exceedingly spiritual, and therefore so frequently misunderstood by the expounders thereof. For therein is evidently contained likewise this idea that the individual occupying a lower point of view can never be received as one occupying a higher position, because he is wanting in the higher life; but the person occupying a higher point of view may be received as one of a lower position. The disciple of Christ must always be regarded as having passed through the law Many a benevolent pious Jew would therefore receive the apostles as prophets and righteous men, because regarding them from his own point of view, he could not perceive in them anything higher, but he who was able to discern in the messengers of Christ that specific new thing which they brought with them, and who therefore was drawn to them from the love which he bore to the thing itself, would receive from them that full rich blessing, the new birth; while, at the same time, those also standing in the other degree if turning towards them with a heart of love, bore off their blessing therefrom. Hence the little ones herein appear as bestowing blessings in every direction, "truly, as dying, and *yet* as those that live; truly, as poor, and *yet* as those making many rich, as having nothing of their own, and *yet* as possessing *all things*," (2 Cor. vi. 9, 10).

§ 16 ST JOHN THE BAPTIST SENDS (HIS DISCIPLES) TO JESUS. DISCOURSE OF JESUS IN CONSEQUENCE OF THIS MISSION.

(Matth. xi. 1—30; Luke vii. 18—35; x 13—15, 21, 22)

Ver. 1. It is true that St Matthew, in concluding the discourse with the words. διατάσσων τοῖς δώδεκα μαθηταῖς, "commanding the twelve disciples," gives it once more plainly to be understood that he considers the foregoing discourse as destined for the disciples who were to be sent out; but he is silent with regard to their journey itself. St Luke ix. 10, on the contrary, relates their return, in like manner, as he does that of the seventy in x. 17. With a vague καὶ ἐγένετο, "and it happened," St Matthew connects another occurrence therewith, namely, the narrative of the inquiry of St John through his disciples In the Gospel of St Luke vii. 18, the same narrative is connected with the history of the raising from death of the youth of Nain, but here, too, is the connection given very slightly with the general formula. καὶ ἀπήγγειλαν Ἰωάννῃ κ. τ. λ., "and they reported to John, &c." Hence, in this case also nothing of an exact nature can be ascertained concerning the chronological order of the events Worthy of remark, however, is the exceedingly minute agreement of the Evangelists in this section, as well in isolated expressions (for example in ver. 23), as more particularly (Matth. xi. 10) in the Old Testament quotation from Mal. iii 1. The Septuagint translates this passage precisely according to the Hebrew text, but the two Evangelists deviate in an uniform manner from both.[1]

We have here in St Matthew, moreover, another discourse, formed, in like manner, out of various elements, inasmuch as St Luke gives the elements here brought together in another de-

---

[1] On this point comp Matth iii 3, Mark i 1

finite connection. The narration of the mission of the two disciples of St John is made use of by St Matthew only as a means of connecting therewith these discourses of Jesus, in which are portrayed the different positions of the people with regard to the person of Jesus. The proud understood Jesus as little as they did St John; the humble recognised that which is Divine under the most varied forms, because they themselves, in fact, were seeking after this only. With this is very aptly connected chapter xii

Ver. 2. With regard, then, to the mission of the disciples of St John, this occurrence leads us to an examination of the internal position of the Baptist. The latter appears here in prison (at Machaerus, according to *Joseph.* Antiq. Jud. xviii 5); it is only in a subsequent chapter (xiv. 3 sqq.) that St Matthew gives us, in a supplementary clause, the necessary information concerning his imprisonment. It is in the prison that the Baptist hears of the ministrations of Jesus, and this induces him to send to him two of his disciples with the message or inquiry: σὺ εἶ ὁ ἐρχόμενος, ἢ ἕτερον προσδοκῶμεν, "art thou he that should come, or do we look for another?" (The expression ὁ ἐρχόμενος, "he who is to come," has a dogmatic signification, it denotes the Messiah, perhaps according to Psalm cxviii. 26, בָּרוּךְ הַבָּא בְּשֵׁם יְהֹוָה, "blessed is he that cometh in the name of the Lord,"[1] and in Heb. x 37 Christ is even called with reference to his advent, i.e. second coming [παρουσία], ὁ ἐρχόμενος, he at whose future coming all things obtain their fulfilment.) The question or inquiry of the Baptist accordingly seems to express an internal uncertainty concerning it, that is to say, whether Jesus is the desired Saviour or not, and such a question must appear singular in the mouth of the Baptist after his strong declarations of faith, and after the experiences he had had concerning the relation in which he stood to Jesus (comp. St Matth. iii., and especially John i. 23). Hence many people have felt disposed to regard this question, in one view, as being calculated for a confirmation of the faith of his disciples, who were beginning to grow weak in faith, and in another view, as containing an incitement to Jesus himself to hasten the carrying out of his plans. To the

---

[1] *Hengstenberg* (Christol. vol in p. 468 sqq) derives the expression, on very plausible grounds, from Mal. iii. 1; but there is no doubt that many passages of the Old Testament acted together to give this expression currency in its more definite dogmatic form

first remark no weight whatever can be given, for the decisive declarations of their master would have completely sufficed to the disciples of St John (John i. 29), as we see in the instance of the apostles, but the other remark contains something that is true. To St John it might appear, indeed, as though Jesus were too cautious in his proceedings, inasmuch as he did not understand his internal ministration to the souls of men. The only difficulty is to suppose that St John, if he had himself stood unshaken, should want to induce our Lord to embrace another manner of action; even the form of the question is of such a nature that it bears a reference rather to the subjective position of the inquirer. If we examine the passage which at present claims our attention in a perfectly unbiassed manner, it would then appear more natural to look for the ground of this inquiry in the mind of St John himself. Internal experience is the best instructor for the comprehension of such occurrences. In the life of every believer are to be found moments of temptation, in which even the most firm conviction will be shaken to its very foundation; nothing is more natural than to conceive such moments or periods of internal darkness and abandonment by the Spirit of God, even in the life of St John. We have too much accustomed ourselves to consider the Biblical character under a certain fixed form, as unchangeable; but it is evident that the internal vicissitude of light and darkness must be presupposed in every isolated individual (our Lord himself excepted, whose nature was a peculiar one, and regarded *per se*, must be so), even where we are not informed thereof, inasmuch as it is this struggle between light and darkness which contributes to the perfection of the life of the saints. Hence, wherever such clear and simple statements call for our attention, as in this case, with regard to St John, there is no ground whatever for doubt. In his gloomy prison at Machaerus, a dark hour, no doubt, surprised the man of God, an hour in which he was struck with the quiet unobtrusive ministry of Christ, and wherein he fell into internal conflict concerning the experiences he had heretofore had. This is clearly pointed out in the words of Jesus: μακάριός ἐστιν ὅς ἐὰν μὴ σκανδαλισθῇ ἐν ἐμοί, which means literally, "happy is he whosoever shall not be offended in me" (ver. 6), words which contain, at the same time, censure and consolation. For truly it would have been a sad thing for the poor captive had he not stood firm in the hour of temptation, had he really taken offence; but, in this case, he was merely tempted to it—and blessed is the man that endureth temptation (Jam. i. 12). But inasmuch as there is no victory for sinful man without a struggle, hence was likewise the Baptist destined to pass through this struggle. But that he endured this struggle, and vanquished, is manifest from the very circumstance of his inquiring of Jesus himself. That he inquired of him *in this manner* shows his state of temptation, but that he, in his state of temptation, inquires of no one but *himself*, manifests his faith in him; especially inasmuch as the free life of the Redeemer, so very different from his own, must have appeared something very astonishing in the sight of this most austere preacher of repentance (comp on Matth. xi. 19). The question of St John is nothing but another: "Lord, I believe, help thou my unbelief," and this prayer was granted by our gracious Lord. Whosoever asks of God, whether he be God, whosoever asks of the Saviour, whether he be the Saviour, is in the right path to overcome every temptation, it is only thus that he can ascertain it with certainty Hence it is that the words of Jesus concerning St John which follow (ver. 7 sqq) form no contradiction to the supposition that he sent the messengers to Jesus in an hour of severe temptation. Even thereby did he prove that he was no reed to be shaken by a breath of wind, but that he was firm as the foundation of the earth in his faith, and that he withstood the effects of every tempest But if there be no tempest, how can firmness prove its strength? It was therefore in the time of his greatness, when the fulness of the Spirit dwelt in him, that God made use of the Baptist for *his* purposes to serve humanity; in the time of his littleness or poverty, and when forsaken, it was then that God perfected him within himself

Ver. 4, 5 Referring to prophetic passages, such as Is xxxv. 5, 6; lxi 1, Jesus replies to the question by facts; the messengers find the Redeemer in the midst of his Messianic labours; they can only report that he is the Redeemer. They saw his ministry bodily; the spiritual types of the corporeal procedure were made palpable to them by his discourse; amidst the cures effected by our Lord resounded the word of everlasting salvation (Concerning πτωχός, "poor," comp. Matth. v. 3) The εὐαγγελίζεσθαι, "to be evangelised, to have the Gospel preached," here signifies to hear the Gospel, to receive the glad tidings. The conception. the poor preach the Gospel, is forbidden by the passage, lxi. 1 of Isaiah, which is here kept in view. This is a magnificent mode of proceeding! the only thing suited to convince them of his Messiahship Concerning the person of St John not one word is mentioned—the only thing given or applied to him as a consolation and exhortation is the μακάριός ἐστιν, "happy, or, blessed is he." But if we ask why our Lord did not enlarge more fully thereon, then it must indeed be answered, that such struggles are to be fought through in the inward man only, the question itself was already to our Lord a signal of approaching victory, therefore he left him entirely to himself, without interfering any further with him. (Concerning σκανδαλίζεσθαι, "to be offended, to be scandalised," see on Matth. xviii. 8.)

Ver. 7. But before the people, who might have misunderstood such a question, Jesus expressed himself more fully, and depicted to them the noble figure of the serious, or grave warrior, in order that they might know, on the one hand, what they possessed in him, and on the other, that they might discern what he was incapable of bestowing on them. Some of the disciples of St John that were present might have given an immediate cause for his so doing. He is silent concerning himself; this he leaves in the most solemn repose, for the whole subject he makes the words, μακάριός ἐστιν, ὃς ἐάν μὴ σκανδαλισθῇ ἐν ἐμοί, literally, "happy is he who shall not be offended in me," suffice. But the manner in which our Lord enlarges, in ver. 7—9, on St John, in the presence of those surrounding him, is of a rather obscure nature. It is difficult to obtain the right meaning of all the various objurgatory questions. The passage, κάλαμος ὑπὸ ἀνέμου σαλευόμενος, "a reed shaken by the wind," may be taken in a figurative sense as speaking of a light-minded individual (as Ephes. iv 14; Heb xiii. 9); or, without any figure, of the reed which grew on the banks of the river Jordan, which afforded sport to the winds In the latter case the sense would be: you must have had indeed an object in view, when ye hastened into the wilderness, it cannot have been your intention merely to look at something of an empty character, something common-place, as for example a pliable reed, or soft garments. The third question must, then, indeed denote the right thing; they wished to see a prophet, and this also was St John the Baptist. The whole train of thought would be meanwhile rather poor,—it would be best to adhere to the one question, "You wanted to see a prophet, is it not so? Well, then, you have seen him, and the greatest one too, only obey him!" But if we turn to the other mode of interpretation, we shall here too meet with a stumbling-block The idea: did ye go forth in order to see a light-minded or vain man is uncommon; for who would go to the wilderness to see such a man; or, who could imagine that St John should be such an one? But if it be said, the unsuitable question itself is intended to express that they certainly thought no such a thing, then the question will be, to what purpose then was this brought forward? The passage contains, at any rate, something of an obscure character, if we do not compare it with ver 16 sqq. This latter passage shows, that Jesus keeps in these questions in view the character of the multitude, and that he portrays therein its contradictions The multitude evidently flowed out into the wilderness in order *to see* a prophet (as though there was something in a prophet to be looked at; they did not desire *to hear*); they might have known very well that a true prophet would manifest or reveal himself to them; but as soon as they perceived his moral earnestness, he no longer pleased them; their impure heart had longed for a prophet after their own mind. This internal contradiction, of hastening to the prophet, and then of wishing that he were not what he is, and that he might be what he cannot be, that is *like unto themselves*, this our Lord, who searches the heart of men with eyes of fire, unfolds to them The $\kappa\acute{\alpha}\lambda\alpha\mu o\varsigma\ \acute{\upsilon}\pi\grave{o}\ \acute{\alpha}\nu\acute{\epsilon}\mu o\upsilon\ \sigma\alpha\lambda\epsilon\upsilon\acute{o}\mu\epsilon\nu o\varsigma$, "a reed shaken by the wind," they are themselves, as is fully demonstrated in ver. 16, 17 "Ye thought to find a pliable pseudo-prophet, one who would give way to all the whims or humours of sin, one that would be in every respect like unto yourselves? Ye thought to find a sensual instructor, one who would flatter your sensualities? Ye thought to behold a prophet like unto that which you depicted him to yourselves, mighty, glorious, but sparing sin? Yes, you have obtained one; but he is another Elijah" After this there follows in the first place a further description of the Baptist, and of the nature of his ministry, to which is joined the parallel of the person of Jesus and of St John, with the observation, that the same character of the multitude which St John did not please, took offence in like manner at him, although his manifestation differed in every respect from that of the Baptist; and for this sole reason, that being sinners, they could nowhere, in any form of godliness, *find* the likeness of themselves, while yet in reality it was only themselves they were everywhere *seeking* The proud judges of the children of light, who are displeased at one time with one thing, and at another time with another thing in them, require, therefore, before all things, to accommodate themselves to humility, the babes (νήπιοι, ver. 25) that appear therein, therefore, seize upon that which is divine in whatever varied forms it may appear, inasmuch as it never and nowhere is the *form* that constitutes with them the question, but it is the *substance* which they always and everywhere look for.

Ver. 9 The portraiture of St John begins with the words, ναὶ καὶ περισσότερον προφήτου, "yea, and more than a prophet." That the Baptist was more than a prophet (that is, that he was above the point of view, or position of prophets in general, in his development), is to be inferred from Malachi iii. 1, wherein a messenger is spoken of that is preparing the way for the Messiah. (Concerning this comp. Matth. iii. 3.) Through this office the Baptist obtained a peculiar position, inasmuch as he occupied the intermediate space between the old and the new covenant; nevertheless, as he still belonged, according to the whole tenor of his life, to the old one, he only formed the link of the chain, by means of which both the circles of religious life are fitted one to another. (Comp what has been said above on Matth. iii 1)

Ver 11 But our Redeemer proceeds yet further in his exaltation of the Baptist, as he places him above the prophets, so also does he place him above all γεννητοὶ γυναικῶν, "those born of women." The ἐγείρεσθαι ἐν = הָקִים בְּ, "to have been raised up or among," has the signification to raise up, to call forth some one from among a great mass of people, for some special purpose, so that the sentence may be completed by ὑπὸ τοῦ Θεοῦ, "from or by God" (John vii. 52).—Γεννητὸς γυναικός = יְלוּד אִשָּׁה, "born of woman," Job xiv. 1, xv. 14 (γεννήματα γυναικῶν), signifies man in general, but with the accessory notion of frailty and impurity. The expression, therefore, has its contrast in the phrase, γεννητὸς ἐκ τοῦ Θεοῦ, "born of God," thus was the first man and Christ, and so are the believers that are begotten of the Spirit through him (John i 13) To this contrast do these concluding words of the verse refer, wherein the μικρότερος ἐν τῇ βασιλείᾳ τῶν οὐρανῶν, literally, " the lesser person (i e. the least) in the kingdom of heaven," is placed above St John. (On the expression, μικρότερος ἐν τῇ β., "the least in the kingdom," must be compared what has been said on Matth. v. 19, where μέγας, "great," and ἐλάχιστος ἐν τῇ β, "the least in the kingdom," form contrasts to one another.) "Man, though occupying the lowest position in the development of that Christian life which has been brought by Jesus into humanity, stands nevertheless higher than John "[1] With regard to this remarkable idea, it must also be observed, that the μείζων εἶναι, "to be greater," which the Redeemer here applies to all those of the kingdom of God, must here be conceived in a Christian sense, so that he who is greater is at the same time more humble, divested of all selfishness and sin, quite in the sense of St Matth. xx 25, 26. Hence, those that are in the kingdom of God occupy in so far a higher position, in proportion as they are endowed with the power of attaining this position of divesting themselves of what is purely their own; this, therefore, is the general character of all the members of the kingdom of God; the difference which exists among themselves only consists, partly in the gradation, i e degree of power for receiving the exalted principle of life, which separates the internal man from sin (hence also from pride) in all the designs and actions of his being, and partly in the more or less rich endowment with those powers on which depends the varied sphere of action of each single individual. It *then* becomes self-evident, that the εἶναι ἐν τῇ β. τ. οὐρ., "to be in the kingdom of heaven," cannot here signify that an individual belongs to the visible church of Christ, inasmuch as the great net of the kingdom of God contains likewise many rotten or worthless fishes (Matth. xiii 47) On the contrary, the meaning of the expression is here evidently limited by the preceding γεννητοὶ γυναικῶν, "born of women," whence we must assume the passage, βασ. τ. οὐρ., "kingdom of heaven," as equivalent to γεννητοὶ ἐκ Θεοῦ, "those born of God" Hence, the β. τ. οὐρ. is here the kingdom of God viewed as an ideal kingdom. This collective body, with all its members, our Redeemer places, in the words of ver. 11, above that whole body to which St John belonged, together with the

---

[1] The comparative μικρότερος needs not to be taken as a superlative, comp Winer's Gr p 221 The reference of the expression to Jesus himself. "I the lesser one in the kingdom of heaven am greater than he," is evidently quite inadmissible It would have been a pseudo or mock-humility had Christ called himself less than St John.

prophets of the Old Testament Hence, the whole passage is to be applied to those only that are truly regenerated, to many members of the external community of the church not even a position equal to that of the representatives of the Old Testament can be accorded. But this passage will always contain, nevertheless, a considerable difficulty, in so far as the question arises as to whether no regeneration took place under the Old Testament? In order to answer this question, we must distinguish between *regeneration in the narrower and wider sense of the word*. In the *narrower sense of the word*, the expression regeneration signifies the communication of a higher life and of a higher degree of knowledge, which can only be effected through the principle of the Holy Ghost, the pouring out of which on mankind was conditioned by the glorification of Christ (John vii 39) Accordingly, in this more confined sense of the word a regeneration is out of the question with the saints of the Old Testament Abraham, Isaac, and Jacob, as all the other holy men of the Old Testament, only beheld the Redeemer as he that was to come, without having experienced the real effects of his power (Heb. xi 13, 1 Pet i. 10—14) Hence, they descended into the sheol, "grave," and only attained to the resurrection through Christ. (Compare on Matth xxvii. 52, 53.) On the contrary, in the *wider sense of the word*, every important consequential change in the inward man may be called a regeneration, and such an one was experienced, no doubt, by Abraham and Jacob, whence they may be justly regarded, but more especially on account of the new name conferred upon them, as the prototypes of the new birth Accordingly, the meaning of the words, οὐκ ἐγήγερται ἐν γεννητοῖς γυναικῶν μείζων Ἰωάννου τοῦ βαπτιστοῦ, literally, "there has not arisen among those born of women one greater than John the Baptist," would yet have to be more exactly determined. It is not probable that Jesus wished to place Abraham, Jacob, and others, as subordinate to the Baptist; these are to be regarded, not only as the corporeal ancestors of the people of God, but in a more especial manner likewise as the fathers of the faithful, and this in a glory of surpassing brightness. For, we must distinguish or admit degrees of development and various grades or positions among the members of the Old Testament, as we do among the members of the church of the New Testament. We see a distinction already made above (Matth. x. 41) between προφῆται, "prophets," and δίκαιοι, "righteous men;" here we may to a certain extent find a third classification indicated, viz. "the regenerated of the Old Testament." In that case the Baptist would be merely represented as a δίκαιος, "righteous man," in the noblest sense, under the law,[1] as a true representative of the law, but to whom the life of faith from above (as it had been already imparted to Abraham and Israel, who occupy their position more as the representatives of the high order of things belonging to the life under the Gospel which was thereafter to be revealed, than that of the life according to the law of Moses) was a kingdom from which he was excluded.

Ver. 12. After having portrayed the person of the Baptist, our Redeemer proceeds to the description of the peculiar characteristics of the time, which leads him on to the objurgatory discourse contained in ver. 16 "Great as is the man, whom God had chosen as his precursor for the kingdom of the Messiah, so is the time in which he acts, in like manner, rich in blessings; hence, the more guilty are those who do not avail themselves thereof." The ἡμέραι Ἰωάννου, "days of John," must be viewed as referring to the period of his public appearance, with the preaching of repentance, as the *terminus a quo,* "the period from which," i e. the commencement; in the words ἕως ἄρτι, "until now," the *terminus ad quem,* "the period to which," i e. the conclusion, is only in so far to be viewed as denoting that the favourable period yet lasted, but which must not be conceived by any means to be concluded at the time then present. The idea of a time blessed with the thriving of all that is good, is peculiarly expressed in the passage: ἡ βασ. τ. οὐρ. βιάζεται, signifying, "the kingdom of heaven suffers violence." A similar expression occurs St Luke xvi. 16: ἡ βασ. τ. Θ. εὐαγγελίζεται καὶ πᾶς εἰς αὐτὴν βιάζεται, literally, "the kingdom of God is proclaimed as glad tidings, (is preached) and every one rushes into

---

[1] *Hengstenberg* in his *Christol.* vol iii. p. 472, has misunderstood this view of mine, as though I denied to the Baptist faith and repentance, what I wish to say is, that he does not represent the former in an eminent degree, hence, St Paul could not have made use of the Baptist as a type of the life of faith, in the manner in which he represents Abraham as such in Rom. iv But no δίκαιος, "just or righteous man," of the Old Testament can be supposed, according to Heb. xi, without πίστις, "faith," only the faith of the Old Testament had not as yet, like that of the New, the inward possession of divine things, but only the hope thereof, as is clearly expressed in the passages quoted Heb xi. 13, 1 Pet i. 10 sqq

it." With this idea perfectly corresponds that which follows in our text: καὶ βίασταί ἁρπάζουσιν αὐτήν, "and violators seize upon it." The words of this verse are no doubt to be taken in such a sense as to express but one side of the manifestation of which our Lord is speaking. At that period, full of mighty agitations, there was expressed by mankind in general, and by the Jews in particular, a passionate longing, and a sincere desire for a change of the existing circumstances, which broke forth with so much the more violence, the more or the longer it was suppressed. In so far as the innermost substance or origin of this desire was truly pure, in so far could the βασ. τ. Θ., "kingdom of God," be regarded as their object; but in so far as there was in it something of an unwholesome nature, and as it appeared intermixed with much that was spurious, it was called a βιάζεσθαι, "a forcing themselves in," and an ἁρπάζειν, "a seizing by force or violence," is ascribed to it. For, even if the expressions were to be viewed as denoting primarily the greatness and extent of zeal and earnestness for divine things, which excited so mightily the minds of men at the time of our Lord, yet, is the refined censure of the manner in which this zeal is expressed, not to be mistaken in the choice of the expressions. Had it been the design of our Redeemer to render prominent the other side of the same manifestation, he then might have said: the heaven is, as it were, opened, streams of the Spirit are poured forth with life-giving power over mankind. But it rather suited his purposes to set forth the actions of mankind. With this is very admirably connected Luke vii. 29, 30, in which passage the passionate longing of the poor after the truth is contrasted with the proud contempt thereof of the Pharisees. (The δικαιόω, "to justify," forms a contrast with ἀθετέω, "to reject or despise," the former signifying to regard as just, to approve, as we find it immediately after in St Matth. xi. 19 [see the comment. on Rom. iii. 21], and the latter to contemn, to despise.)

Ver. 13. The peculiar circumstances of the spiritual world, as they then existed, Jesus explains more distinctly, according to St Matthew, in the observation, that the law and the prophets only extended as far as St John; with him, then, commences, or, more properly, he represents the great turning point of the old and the new world. This idea appears in a different connection in Luke xvi. 16, but with St Matthew it forms so intimate a part of the whole, that we may regard it as being here authentic. For, if the entire economy of the Old Testament concluded or ceased with St John, then it was natural that, with his appearance, a mighty spiritual commotion should pervade mankind, which being, as it were, spiritual labour-pangs, would give birth to an existence of a higher order. But in the manner of expression of this verse, we are struck, in the first place, by the combination of the νόμος, "law," with the prophets, so that it also appears as prophesying. The νόμος = תּוֹרָה, here designates that element from which proceeded the prophets as its representatives, and it is the internal nature and power of the law to prophesy of Christ. Awakening the knowledge of sin, it creates the desire to know the Redeemer, without yet quite satisfying it. In the second place, the question is as to how προεφήτευσαν, "they prophesied," is to be explained. It might be taken as signifying, "the manifestation of prophecy lasts up to (until) St John," himself included. But in the first place, John himself was, properly speaking, no prophet in the sense of the Old Testament, he only *bore witness* of him who was already present, and invited mankind to repentance, and in the second place, the prophesying ministry continued even *after* St John (Acts of the Apostles xi. 28). Hence, it is much better applied to the prophecies themselves: "With St John the prophecies will cease, i e. will be fulfilled, they do not extend beyond him." But this idea seems to be unfounded, inasmuch as many of the prophetic oracles extend to the most remote futurity, until the foundation of the kingdom of God on earth shall have been entirely accomplished. But the words which follow, (ver. 14,) compel us, nevertheless, to decide in favour of this assumption, in them St John is represented as the Elijah, and it is this, indeed, which points to the end of all the prophecies (Mal iv. 5). Hence, it is probable that we must add this text to the many others wherein, as well according to the words of Christ, as likewise those of the apostles, all things are represented as consummated in their time. (Comp. 1 Cor. x. 11.) The exposition, however, of these remarkable decisions, cannot here be given, but will be found on St Matthew xxiv.

Ver. 14. As it were by way of addition, and for confirmation, Christ adds, moreover, that the John here spoken of is the promised Elias. With regard to the idea of the appearance of Elias, to which a reference is made by the passage, ὁ μέλλων ἔρχεσθαι, "which was to come," this passage is based on Mal iv. 5,

הִנֵּה אָנֹכִי שֹׁלֵחַ לָכֶם אֵת אֵלִיָּה הַנָּבִיא, "behold, I will send you Elijah the prophet." The Septuagint has taken altogether a correct view of these words as referring to the Tishbite; as, in like manner has Ecclus. xlviii. 1. For, the grammatical construction requires a reference to a definite historical person, on account of the expression הַנָּבִיא, "*the* prophet." The case would be somewhat different, were the reference to this particular person not to be viewed in its figurative sense through ἐν πνεύματι καὶ δυνάμει 'Ηλίου, "in the spirit and power of Elias," as it is in St Luke i. 17. This would be even more probable, if the New Testament did not impart or furnish more exact information thereon. According to St Matthew xvii. 3, Moses and Elias appeared to the transfigured Redeemer as messengers sent from heaven, through which narrative the figurative interpretation of that promise is rendered improbable. But what here is striking, is the declaration that John is the Elias, since he himself declared, according to John i. 21, that he was not. Yet, though this be not done by the text εἰ θέλετε δέξασθαι, "if ye wish to receive (it)," yet, the whole connection existing between this passage and those elsewhere treating of Elias, implies,[1] that the Redeemer called him so *in a certain relation*, viz because he acted ἐν πνεύματι καὶ δυνάμει 'Ηλίου, "in the spirit and power of Elias," as says the Scripture (Luke i. 17); Elijah, that zealous preacher of repentance, has, as it were, his after type in St John. But the question is, whether it is to be believed that the Old Testament prophecy above referred to has been completely fulfilled in the appearance of St John, or in the mission of Elijah, on occasion of the transfiguration of Christ. One feels inclined to doubt it, when we read that the prophet Malachi adds, (iv 5,) that Elijah would be sent: לִפְנֵי בּוֹא יוֹם יְהוָה הַגָּדוֹל וְהַנּוֹרָא, "before the coming of the great and dreadful day of the Lord." The supposition, therefore, that this pro-

---

[1] The opinion of *Hengstenberg* (in the passage referred to, p 474) that the passage, εἰ θέλετε δέξασθαι, "if ye be willing to receive it," was to indicate that the non-acknowledgment of Elijah, in the person of St John, was based on a faulty spiritual disposition, is probable, indeed, on account of the following: ὁ ἔχων ὦτα κ. τ. λ., "he that hath ears, &c" so that the meaning would be · "if you but wished to comprehend it, he is the Elijah that is to come" This does not affect, nevertheless, the main idea, that is, that the appearance of the Baptist cannot exhaust the prophecy of Malachi.

phecy, although—as implying a reference to a certain person, it be fulfilled—must be regarded as being as yet unfulfilled (comp. on Rev. xi 6) seems not improbable As it is the nature of all the Old Testament prophecies that the object of the prophecy can be represented in a previous manifestation, without its meaning being thereby completely exhausted, so it is in like manner here. The period at which Christ lived was by no means, it is true, the prophesied יוֹם י׳ הַגָּדוֹל, "the great day of the Lord;" but that entire period, up to the destruction of Jerusalem, bore a certain resemblance to the latter days, and had, in like manner, an element (the Baptist St John), which typified the future appearance of Elijah. It is probable that from this chain of ideas proceeded the indefinite εἰ θέλετε δέξασθαι, "if ye wish to receive (it)."

Ver. 15 But in order to direct the whole attention to these manifestations of the time present, Christ adds the solemn, grave words: ὁ ἔχων ὦτα ἀκούειν, ἀκουέτω, literally, "he that hath ears to hear, let him hear." (The term ἀκούειν, = שָׁמַע, "to hearken," intelligere, "to understand, comprehend," hence, ὦτα, "ears," = אָזְנַיִם, "the two ears," which is frequently used when speaking of the faculty of the understanding.[1]) According to Christ's view, therefore, his discourse must have contained something not less worthy of investigation than requiring it, and this fact is the reason of his admonition, which then would form the motive of this address; and that the words have not as yet lost their profound sense, would appear evident from the remarks already made

Ver. 16, 17. That which was indicated in ver. 7 is here carried out in figurative language; our Redeemer censures his capricious contemporaries, by comparing them with humoursome children whom it is impossible to please in any way, that understand neither mildness nor severity. (On γενεά = דוֹר, "generation," those living at any one period, comp. on Matth. xxiv 34. The text of St Matthew has been altered here in various ways; instead of ἀγοραῖς, "in the market-places," ἀγορᾷ, "in the

---

[1] Similar forms are used by the Jewish teachers, as, for example, in the Zohar qui audit audiat, qui intelligit intelligat, "he that heareth let him hear, and he that understandeth let him understand" Besides the Gospels, the formula ὁ ἔχων ὦτα κ. τ. λ is very frequently met with in the Apocalypse, but is wholly wanting in the Gospel of St John

market-place," has been adopted, instead of ἑταίροις, "to their fellows," ἑτέροις, "to others," in place of which St Luke has ἀλλήλοις, "to one another." The usual reading, nevertheless, both for internal and external reasons, still deserves the preference.) The expressions αὐλέω, "to play on a pipe or flute," θρηνέω, "to wail or lament," refer to children's play of a jocose and a graver kind. But the whole figure would be misunderstood, were it to be viewed, as though the children who are speaking represented Jesus and St John, the representatives of mildness and severity, while the other children addressed or spoken to, represented the capricious people; both classes of the children, the speaking ones and those spoken to, on the contrary, are to be considered as the representatives of the capricious contemporaries of Jesus, so that the meaning is, "this generation resembles a host of ill-humoured children, that cannot be pleased in any way, the one part desiring this, the other part that, so that, after all, no degree of useful activity is attained by them."

Ver. 18, 19. This figurative discourse is immediately followed by the literal declaration that John was too severe for them, and Jesus too lax (For the particulars on δαιμόνιον ἔχει, "he hath a demon," comp. Matth. xii. 24.) The difference existing between the dispensations of the Old and New Testament appears here, in a striking manner, in the description of their respective representatives, notwithstanding the misrepresentations which they undergo. In the person of St John, we find the strict observer of the law, who displays in his public appearance a rough moral severity, and who abstains from every intercourse or communion with the sinner; in the Redeemer we see, on the contrary, the impossibility of sinning, coupled with a merciful love, which induces him not to withdraw himself even from the most wretched of sinners, inasmuch as their impurity is unable to defile his heavenly purity, whilst his Divine light is able to break through their darkness and enlighten it. St John is a noble manifestation of humanity, an earthly flower; but Jesus stands forward as the image of that which is heavenly, as the offspring of a more exalted world. Blessed was the man then, blessed is the man now, whosoever he be, that is not offended in him, but who receiveth him even as he is! The words· καὶ ἐδικαιώθη ἡ σοφία ἀπὸ τῶν τέκνων αὐτῆς (St Luke adds, πάντων, "of all"), "but wisdom is justified of her children," form the conclusion of this idea. These, as well as many other words made use of by our Lord, resemble multilateral polished jewels, which send forth their splendour in more than one direction, a peculiarity which is not foreign even to the spiritual or intellectual sentences of the wise men of this world. Considered by themselves, they may be viewed *in various ways as being full of meaning;* but connected with that which precedes and follows them, *one* meaning of course must be most conspicuous. The expression τὰ τέκνα τῆς σοφίας, "the children of wisdom," evidently points to a contrast with that which goes before, wherein the children of folly are described in the very act of their foolish decisions. (Hence the καί, "and," is = ἤ, "and, but," &c., and must be taken in its adversative or disjunctive sense, and δικαιοῦσθαι, "to have been justified," must be taken as above in Luke vii 29, in the sense of being approved just, hence to acknowledge as such, to praise, to laud.) The idea then would be this: "but wisdom (which is found fault with, or reprehended by, foolish men) is justified, defended, and represented by her children as wise," namely by their conduct with regard to her institutions; to which Matth xi. 25 sqq , in which the νήπιοι, "babes," appear as the truly wise men, forms a very suitable sequel. (Neither the aorist nor the signification of δικαιοῦσθαι, "to have been justified," are in favour of the translation: "Wisdom is *reprehended* by her children.") But this idea acquires a peculiar charm when we consider that the Scriptures speak of wisdom not as of an abstract idea, but as of a heavenly personification, nay, speak of Jesus himself as wisdom. (See on Luke xi. 49, comp. with Matth. xxiii. 34, Ecclus. xxiv. 4 sqq , John i. 1.) For the Redeemer here appears as speaking according to his Divine nature, and the ἐδικαιώθη, "has been justified," the aorist, thereby obtains a peculiar significancy. The same manifestation which he censures at the time then present, that is, that foolish men take offence at the ways of wisdom, has presented itself at all times; but the children of wisdom have at all times justified their mother, and will still continue to do so even at this day. Hence the Redeemer here appears as the bestower of all spiritual blessings from the beginning of time, as the generator of all the earthly representatives of wisdom from the commencement of the world, which he now at length personally represents in its entire fulness and glory, concluding thereby the process of its gradual development.

(We must reject all those expositions of the passage which lead to the exclusion of the contrast with that which goes before, such as the one according to which the sense after, καί, "and, or but," is completed by means of λέγουσιν, "they say," so that the proposition: ἐδικαιώθη κ. τ. λ., is put, so to speak, into the mouth of the censorious Jews, according to whose notions the τέκνα σοφίας are mere *pretended* children of wisdom.)

Ver 20. The reproving speech which follows, St Luke x. 13 sqq gives in a more original connection with the mission of the seventy; but St Matthew has interwoven it very appropriately into his context. The whole discourse of the Redeemer was already a reproach against his contemporaries; in the words which follow, the censure is uttered in its sharpest severity against those who had seen his glory displayed in the most open manner. Besides, the whole passage represents the same principle (viewed only in another light) which we have already dwelt upon at x. 41 of the Gospel of St Matthew. As, therefore, the reward is not modified according to the deed itself, but according to the disposition wherein it originates, and the consciousness by which it is accompanied, so is, in like manner, the punishment not measured by the external appearance of the deed, but according to the internal disposition of which it testifies, and the consciousness thereof which it presupposes The guilt of Tyre, of Sidon, of Sodom, here appears lessened, because the position of their inhabitants was altogether a more unenlightened one than that of the Jews at the time of Christ, and because that which was Divine appeared to them in a far less dazzling form But at the time of Christ the feeling of necessity was awakened, and in the person of our Redeemer this necessity was met by the purest manifestation of that which is Divine, which, moreover, condescended to the frailties of human kind by events which, occurring outwardly and visibly, were calculated to produce an effect on them; but men hardened themselves nevertheless against these powerful impressions of the Spirit, and did not repent; hence this mightily increased their guilt. By the greater guilt of the latter, however, the guilt of the former is not in any way diminished; it remains what it was, but compared with more thorough manifestations of sin, its relative position is distinctly recognised.

Ver. 21. Χοραζίν, "Chorazin," which is only mentioned in this place, was a little town in Galilee on the shores of the Lake of Genesareth, near the city of Capernaum. Some expositors are disposed, without any reason, to write this word Χώρα Ζίν, "the region, i. e. the wilderness of Zin." It is evidently cities that are here spoken of (ver 20) In that place was situated the better known city Βηθσαιδά, "Bethsaida," derived from בַּיִת, "house, place," and צֵידָה, "hunting, fishing;" hence the place, or city of fishers The two together appear as the representatives of that favoured region, wherein the foot of the Redeemer had wandered so long, and where his hand had dispensed blessings. *Tyre* and *Sidon* are named, on the contrary, as the rich voluptuous representatives of rude sensual enjoyments, which, as such, had been already denounced on various occasions by the prophets of the old covenant (comp. Is. xxiii). The passage μετανοεῖν ἐν σάκκῳ καὶ σποδῷ, "to repent in sackcloth and ashes," is the well-known Old Testament description of an earnest disposition to repentance, which is manifested in corresponding external forms (1 Kings xxi 27; 2 Kings vi 30; Jon iii. 6, 8)

Ver 22 The words ἡμέρα κρίσεως, "day of judgment," appear, in their most general sense, as the period which is finally to come wherein will take place the separation of all those phenomena of good and evil, which, during the passing course of this world, have appeared in a mixed form (For the exposition, comp on Matth. xxiv) Ἀνεκτός, or ἀνεκτός, "tolerable, endurable," derived from ἀνέχω, "to bear with, endure" (see concerning the same idea Matth x 15). The comparative, as well as the whole passage, taken in its connection, leads to the notion of a difference existing between the degrees of punishment awarded to the wicked, some are, as it were, *in mitissima damnatione*, "in the mildest or least terrible condemnation," as St Augustine says This notion of the relative nature of punishment seems to lead to the supposition that it may be likewise abrogated, which must be admitted unhesitatingly, when speaking of the lower forms of sin, concerning which see on Matth xii. 32.

Ver 23 The same thing applies to Capernaum (see on Matth. iv. 13) in a higher degree This insignificant Galilean country town had become the stationary place of abode of the Messiah, and had thereby gained a higher importance. For, the choice of the town by our Redeemer as his place of abode, must evidently not be considered as having been the result of mere chance, but as intimately and spiritually connected with the call and susceptibility or receptivity of its inhabitants The nucleus of the kingdom of God *might* have, and *should* have developed itself in this place Instead of this, however, only a few joined themselves to our Lord with a feeling of complete decision, whereas the others remained without faith in their unholy way of life. Hence the more dazzling the light was to which they opposed themselves, the longer it shone upon their darkened hearts, the more their guilt was increased. This is expressed in the terms: ἕως ᾅδου καταβιβασθήσῃ, "shalt be brought down to hell," words that are perhaps the result of Old Testament texts, such as Ezek. xxxi. 10, Isa. xiv. 15, lvii. 9, that occurred to the mind of our Redeemer when they were uttered. The expression καταβιβάζεσθαι, "to be brought down," is found in the New Testament in this place only; it is the contrast or reverse of ὑψωθῆναι, "to be exalted, i.e. to a condition of honour, dignity," &c., whence the former expression is to be taken in the sense of being cast or thrown down, *dejici*. A contrast to οὐρανός, "heaven," is formed by the ᾅδης,[1] "the abyss of hades," ᾅδου οἶκος, δῶμα, "the dwelling-place of hades" = שְׁאוֹל, "hell, grave." Such expressions, borrowed from the Greek mythology, which is, indeed, alluded to in 2 Pet. ii. 4, wherein there occurs the expression τάρταρος, the Holy Scripture adopts unhesitatingly as long as they existed in the mouth of the people, and had a true or solid foundation The simple and true fundamental idea of heaven and hades is this, that good and evil, which are already separated internally even on earth, although they here appear externally to stand on an equality with one another, will be ultimately separated likewise externally. Hence, in so far as the ἡμέρα κρίσεως, "the day of judgment," here refers to the act of reducing to their ultimate element or principle what appears here to be mixed up together, the casting down into the hades here signifies the devolution of individual evil into its primeval element. At the great division which is to take place in the universe, each individual life will be attracted to, and governed by the power of that element to which it has granted an admission into itself He who has admitted the Spirit and light of Christ, will be attracted by him into his kingdom of light; he who has permitted the spirit of darkness to rule in

---

[1] Concerning ᾅδης, comp on Luke xvi 28 By *hades* here is understood, according to the general acceptation of the Old Testament, the Gehenna.

his heart, will become the prey of the powers of darkness, according to the guilt of the individual, which can be determined by God only (see Matth vii. 1), because it depends upon the degree of the impression made by the light upon the man, and against which he had hardened himself. It ·is strange that some persons should have considered external prosperity as indicated in this text!! "Thou art a right opulent and prosperous city; but thou wilt decline very much." That which man cherishes in his heart, that finds he even in the word of God; he makes for himself a God, and makes his Redeemer speak that which suits him best, and as he would have it spoken. (Comp. 2 Pet. ii 20) The more guilty Capernaum is contrasted, moreover, with Sodom with the remark: ἔμειναν ἄν μέχρι τῆς σήμερον, "it would have remained until this present day." These words, if they are not to be considered as a mere empty phrase, are remarkable, inasmuch as they show that our Redeemer speaks even of that which is past as of a thing not of absolute necessity. He here acknowledges evidently the freedom of the human will, and the possibility of its having been otherwise, if men had been obedient to the will of God. This so morally important view of history, as altogether based on the free actions of individuals, constitutes the foundation of the whole Scriptural doctrine.

Ver 25. That the words which follow were not spoken in an altogether immediate connection with those which go before, is pointed out by St Matthew himself in the transition, ἐν ἐκείνῳ τῷ καιρῷ, "at that time;" it appears as though this formula implies a space between that which precedes and that which follows. St Luke x 21 sqq. gives, with apparent precision, these words in their appropriate connection. Hence, we have reason to assume, that St Matthew has followed once more his custom of bringing the elements of discourses into a connection peculiar to himself, inasmuch as it was by no means his intention to describe the life of Jesus in chronological order, but only to illustrate his ministry from general points of view. The same Spirit that had spoken through the Lord, guided *him* likewise in the choice of order and arrangement. This is also again perceptible in the position of the verses which follow; they form a more than commonly suitable contrast to the severe denunciation of unbelievers which precedes them; they are a commentary on ver. 19, ἡ σοφία ἐδικαιώθη ἀπὸ τῶν τέκνων αὐτῆς, "wisdom is justified of her children." The whole passage (ver. 25—30), moreover, is remarkable in St Matthew, on account of the sublime flight of ideas displayed therein; it is quite the language of St John. It is evident therefrom, that it is the same Jesus that speaks in St Matthew and St John, only the subjects of his conversations are different; and it is for this reason that each of them represented him in the manner in which their individual subjectivity has permitted them to recognise him. The verses 25—30, henceforth, open an insight into the most internal recesses of the heart of our Redeemer, that was burning with love for his brethren. Aware of his divine majesty and glory, he inclines humbly to the lowly, and endeavours to comfort the forsaken. Hence, it is the true substance of that which is Christian, the condescension of that which is divine towards the feeble and poor, which is here celebrated in inspired language, by the side of which all human greatness, wisdom, and glory, sink into the dust. St Matthew commences: ἀποκριθεὶς εἶπεν ὁ Ἰησοῦς, "Jesus answering said," on the expression, ἀποκρίνεσθαι, "to answer," according to the analogy of the Hebrew, עָנָה, "to answer," see on Luke i. 60. On the other hand, St Luke, x. 21, renders prominent the internal exultation and rejoicing in the spirit of the Lord, ἠγαλλιάσατο τῷ πνεύματι, "he was glad in the spirit." It cannot mean here, τῇ ψυχῇ, "in soul," inasmuch as this would point rather to the human individuality of the Redeemer, as in St Matth. xxvi. 38. The point at issue here is a pure objective joy, which is participated in by the world of spirits, and which is represented in a state of perfection in the internal life of our Lord.) Christ commences with the praise of God on account of his ruling Providence. (Ἐξομολογεῖσθαι = הוֹדָה seq. dativ. to praise, to laud. Rom. xiv. 11, more freq. in the Septuagint.) God is represented under the well-known Old Testament designation of the Lord of the Universe, evidently with an intended contrast to the νήπιοι, "babes"= μικροί, "little ones" (Matth. x. 42), πτωχοὶ τῷ πνεύματι "poor in spirit" (v. 3). For, in the acceptation of νήπιος is implied not only the idea of that which is undeveloped, but also of that which is inexperienced, helpless, as it is here used by way of a contrast with the σοφοί, "wise," and συνετοί, "prudent;" the former of which expressions refers more to that which is divine, whilst the latter bears more upon that which is earthly; the σοφία, "wisdom," is a result of the νοῦς (intellect), but the σύνεσις, "prudence," is that of φρενες (understanding) [1] Hence, it cannot be said, in a direct manner, that the wise and prudent had a *false* wisdom and prudence, they had in their knowledge much that was true, and were indeed more developed or learned than the disciples of our Lord But their wisdom and prudence was at best an *earthly one;* hence, it was subject to many infirmities, and was thus unable to penetrate into the depths of that which is divine; Christ, on the contrary, brought a *heavenly* wisdom, and the first condition for the reception thereof, was poverty, the being void of man's individual wisdom. Hence it was that human wisdom was in itself a hindrance to the reception of the pure light, that sent forth its rays from the opened heavens; and those hearts that were simplest and most despised, that were aware of their poverty and blindness as concerned divine and human things, but which nevertheless burnt with longing after truth, received it soonest and most profoundly. (Comp. 1 Cor. i. 19 sqq) This wonderful dispensation of God, that the Lord of heaven and earth espoused the most wretched and poorest; this is that which is here exultingly celebrated by our Lord. The expression, ταῦτα, "these things," therefore, comprehends in one view all that which was peculiar in the life of Christ, and which has been conferred upon mankind through his ministry This came to all human beings that could comprehend it by ἀποκάλυψις, "revelation." Human σοφία, "wisdom," is a fruit or result of intellectual activity, and spontaneous determination; the heavenly wisdom, on the contrary, is the effect of the divine operation on human receptivity, which is the root of the life of faith But whilst πίστις, "faith," belongs purely to the καρδία, "heart," the σοφία, "wisdom," in its heavenly form, is the blossom of the νοῦς, "mind, intellect." But the ἀποκάλυψις, "revelation," is placed as a contrast to an ἀπόκρυψις, "concealment," an expression which might be considered as being in favour of an absolute doctrine of predestination, comp Matth xiii. 13, 14. There is nothing, nevertheless, which forbids us to view ἀποκρύπτειν merely as signifying "not to reveal," so that the sense would be, "they are left to their earthly wisdom" We here pass over, therefore, for the present, the reference to predestination, which will hereafter frequently occupy our attention.

Ver 26. The Redeemer once more breathes forth his feeling

[1] Comp *my* Opusc theol (Berol 1833), p 159

of thankfulness towards the Father; ναί sc ἐξομολογοῦμαί σοι, literally, "I acknowledge thanks to thee." (On εὐδοκία = רָצוֹן, "will, pleasure," see on Luke ii 14.) In so far as the divine will is the pure emanation of his being, inasmuch as God never *wills* aught else but what he is, herein is comprehended the idea, that this very grace, which conferred true heavenly knowledge on the poor and childlike, is the effect of the pure forbearing love of God, which is revealed in the communication of his own nature. The *love* of God, the pure contrast of *envy*, permits him to descend into the souls of men, more especially into poor and needy souls Of this wondrous love of God, which is unknown to man, and which he cannot comprehend without illumination from on high, inasmuch as man only loves splendour and abundance, but not poverty, the person of Jesus himself is the proof least to be mistaken; in him dwelt the fulness of the Godhead in the bosom or form of humanity, and yet was this divine manifestation the least brilliant and the most humble From the Father, the Lord of heaven and earth, the Saviour makes a transition to himself, the visible representative of this pure love of God, and describes himself as the active dispenser of that which he has celebrated in the Father, he then invites all the poor, all the needy and wretched, to partake of his fulness of God.

Ver. 27. The transition from the Father to the Son may be reconciled through the following idea: "the instrument, by means of which the Father reveals himself as everlasting mercy, is the Son himself" The Saviour proceeds first on the idea of his divine power: πάντα μοι παρεδόθη ὑπὸ τοῦ πατρός, "all things are delivered to me by the Father." The expression, πάντα, "all things," refers back to the above-named κύριος οὐρανοῦ καὶ γῆς, "Lord of heaven and earth," so that the passage forms a parallel to the word of the Lord, ἐδόθη μοι πᾶσα ἐξουσία ἐν οὐρανῷ καὶ ἐπὶ γῆς, literally: "there is given to me all authority in heaven and earth," (Matth. xxviii. 18) wherein Christ, the Son of God, is represented as the ruler of the world, to whom is due, as to the Father, equal honour and worship, and in whom only the Father reveals himself to mankind (John xiv. 9.) But as the βασιλεία, "kingdom," is coeval with the Father, so is it *given* (παρεδόθη), to the Son, inasmuch as he is likewise man, whence the Son will also restore it into the hands of the Father at the end of the kingdom of God, i e when all things shall be subdued unto him (1 Cor xv. 28) Proceeding forward from this fundamental relation, the Redeemer places before them his relative position to the Father in point of the ἐπίγνωσις, "knowledge or recognition," and from thence deduces that all true ἀποκάλυψις, "revelation," to the babes of which he has spoken, passes *through him* only; hence, that all knowledge gained without him, and beyond the sphere of Christ, is mere human knowledge, and, consequently, worthless. Our Lord represents to them, therefore, first of all, the mutual relation existing between the Father and Son: οὐδεὶς ἐπιγινώσκει τὸν υἱὸν εἰ μὴ ὁ πατήρ, οὐδὲ τὸν πατέρα τις ἐπιγινώσκει εἰ μὴ ὁ υἱός, "no man knoweth the Son, but the Father; neither knoweth any man the Father, save the Son." It is remarkable, that the early fathers frequently pervert this passage in their quotations (on this subject see *my* history of the Gospels "Geschichte der Evangelien," p. 295 sqq.). *Irenaeus* even says, in a passage (Adv. Haer iv. 14), that the heretics have caused a perversion designedly, according to which they read, first, οὐδεὶς ἐπιγινώσκει πατέρα εἰ μὴ ὁ υἱός, "no man knoweth the Father but the Son," but this is very improbable, because *Irenaeus* himself very frequently transposes the two members of the verse. The reading is not, according to the manuscripts, a contested one; hence, the only question is, why the position of the members should be the one it is. The ἐπίγνωσις τοῦ υἱοῦ, "knowledge of the Son," is here, no doubt, placed at the head, because it forms the main question. What Jesus wishes to say to his followers is, that man can attain a true knowledge of God through the Son only, for, "no man can come unto the Father except by me" (John vi. 65). Were the position to be received as a purely absolute one, οὐδεὶς τὸν πατέρα ἐπιγινώσκει, εἰ μὴ ὁ υἱός, "no man knoweth the Father, save the Son only," would probably have been placed at the head. But in the contrasting nature and power of the two members is indicated that peculiar mutual operation which exists between the Father and the Son,[1] according to the expressive, σύ, πάτερ, ἐν ἐμοί, κᾀγὼ ἐν σοί, "thou, O Father (art), in me, and I in thee." The Father beholds himself in the Son, as his εἰκών, "image," ἀπαύγασμα τῆς δόξης, "the brightness of his glory" (Heb i 3); the Son sees himself again in the Father, so that the Son is the self-manifestation (*Selbstobjectivirung*) of the Father, which as a divine, and hence ever-

---

[1] On the recognition of the Father by the Son, and of the Son by the Father, comp. the valuable texts John x. 14, 1 John ii. 13, 14.

fasting act, hath begotten the Son as an everlasting being. (For the particular details concerning the relation existing between the Father and the Son, see on John i.) This mutual act of recognition, and of being recognised, by the Father and the Son, the Son, as the λόγος, "word," as the manifestation of the Father who dwelleth unseen within him, communicates to the world of man. (Comp on 1 Cor. xiii. 12; Gal. iv 9) The revelation depends, it is true, upon the *will* of the Son (ᾧ ἐὰν βούληται, "to whomsoever he willeth"), but this will must not be viewed as an *arbitrary one*, but as under the guidance of merciful love, and wisdom. If any one should here say, that the Son having communicated the knowledge of God to any person whatever, as indeed he has ever communicated it to certain individuals, it hence naturally follows, that it is no longer the Son only who recognises the Father, but that it is likewise this or that man, or many men, who, together with the Son, recognise the Father,— we should then answer, that it is Christ, who, in the individual recognising God, recognises the Father by his own spirit (Gal ii. 20), hence, when the whole church shall hereafter recognise God through the spirit of Christ, even then it is the Son only, who, nevertheless, in that infinite mass of individuals, recognises the Father, inasmuch as they are all *one* in Christ (Gal. iii. 28; 1 Cor. xii. 12). Accordingly, it is clear, that the ἐπιγνώσκειν, "knowledge, recognition," does not here signify a mere comprehension by knowledge of divine things (in which human wisdom indeed consists, the knowledge of which concerning God has no power to create the divine life), but it is the life of God in man, and of man in God, which is, it is true, not *without* the knowledge of him, but which contains within itself both his nature and the knowledge thereof The true ἐπίγνωσις τοῦ Θεοῦ, "full knowledge of God," hence, is based upon divine love, i.e. upon the communicableness of his nature to the world of his creatures Only light beholds light, only that which is divine recognises that which is divine

Ver. 28. The verses which follow, for which we are solely indebted to St Matthew, and which, at the same time, seem here to be altogether in their proper place, are a commentary on the words, οἱ πτωχοὶ εὐαγγελίζονται, "the poor have good, or glad tidings," preached to them, contained in ver. 5 He, to whom all things have been delivered by the Father, calls to him the heavy laden—not the rich, the great, and the glorious—that is to say, he bestows himself upon them. Both expressions, κοπιῶντες καὶ πεφορτισμένοι, "those labouring and heavy laden," denote the same position, the active side of which is rendered prominent by the first, and its passive side by the second, i.e. the position of existence under sin and its consequences. The sense of suffering beneath the yoke of sin can only emanate from that which is divine dwelling within man; the ungodly feels at his ease under it. Hence, in so far as the divine life dwelling within men strives after a deliverance from the yoke of sin, they are called κοπιῶντες, "the labouring;" and in so far as they experience its oppression, without being able to free themselves from its shackles, they are called, πεφορτισμένοι, "the heavy laden." The removal or abrogation of this whole position is promised by the Redeemer in the ἀνάπαυσις, "rest." The belief in him brings back the lost harmony that formerly existed between the internal and external life, and with it peace and rest to the soul. (Comp. Jerem. vi. 16. The acceptation of ἀνάπαυσις corresponds with the one of St John: ζωὴν ἔχειν καὶ περισσόν, "to have life and more abundantly" [John x. 10] As soon as the magnet of life has found its pole of attraction, peace and rest are the immediate result. The powerful and ever-enduring ἀνάπαυσις, "rest," is εἰρήνη, "peace")

Ver. 29, 30. But as that which is holy in man is encumbered, or burdened, as with a heavy load, in consequence of the sin within him and around him, so in like manner doth the divine life, with its demands, appear to man as something onerous and oppressive, because the disunion in man is not removed forthwith by his entrance into the element of good; and hence it is that our Redeemer speaks of a ζυγός, "yoke," and φορτίον, "burden," which he himself imposes. But the same appears as χρηστός, "easy," and ἐλαφρόν, "light," when compared with the burthen of sin. From this latter, indeed, man's nobler self suffers in an immediate, i e. a direct manner; hence, it produces the deepest oppression of the soul, and this characteristic it was that distinguished the oppressive yoke of the Pharisaical statutes, as born of sin, and as checking the development of the divine life (see on Matth. xxiii. 4); *the burthen of Christ, on the contrary, is only felt by man so long as he is still encumbered with sin*; but the nobler self feels the spirit and life of Christ as its homogeneous element, and thus the believer can exult and sing praises in the inner man, although he be outwardly perishing daily (2 Cor iv 16). This struggle with sin the believer must *enter upon* according to the bidding of Christ (ἄρατε, "take up," signifying the positive activity on the taking up of the struggle, comp on Matth. x. 38), and *learn* of Christ. Jesus, accordingly, represents himself here, in a manner not to be mistaken, as the ruler and prophet (teacher), who imposes the yoke of his rule, and who offers his own doctrine for acceptance, only he is a clement ruler and teacher, in contra-distinction to the servitude of sin, and of all that has originated therefrom, as for example the Pharisaical statutes, and it is even this mildness, or clemency, which is made use of by the Redeemer, as a motive to invite to the reception of his yoke. Together with this connection of ideas, there seems, moreover, to exist in this passage another one. For the expression ζυγός μου, "my yoke," cannot be explained merely as the "yoke which I (as the ruler) impose on others," but it may likewise be viewed as the "yoke which I myself bear," so that it is equivalent to the cross of Christ. Regarded in this light, the passage: ὅτι πρᾷός εἰμι κ. τ. λ., "because I am meek," &c, obtains a new signification. Those who belong to Christ are to learn, namely, from the meekness with which Jesus bears his cross or yoke, and acquire a like disposition of mind, for thereby every yoke becomes easy, and every suffering may be overcome. If each person takes to himself the burden of sin as a burden common to all men, if he endures the sufferings of time as the consequences of the collective guilt of mankind, he then will stand in the position of self-denying love, *take* the yoke upon himself (and not exactly have it placed on him), and find therein rest and peace for his soul, for disquiet emanates from self-will, which is averse to its due share in the bearing of the burthen of sin. According to this combination of ideas, then, our Redeemer regards himself also as a bearer of the cross and of the yoke, as he was made like unto men, his brethren, in all things; only he bore not the yoke for his own sake, but for our sake With this mode of interpretation alone the expression: ταπεινὸς τῇ καρδίᾳ, "lowly in heart," is consistent. With reference to his subjects, a ruler may be said to be πρᾷος, "meek," but not ταπεινὸς, "lowly;" hence, as little as God is ever said to be ταπεινὸς, "lowly," just as little is the Redeemer so, according to his Divine nature, ταπεινοφροσύνη, "lowliness of mind, humility," is clearly a characteristic of the creature, and Christ calls himself ταπεινὸς, in so far only as he is man, and in so far all that is peculiar to human nature becomes him, as fitly as that which appertains to the Divine nature. Holy writ expresses the act of incarnation of the Son of God by κενόω, "to empty, to nullify," and the humiliation, i.e. the becoming lowly of the Son of God as man by ταπεινόω, "to humble, abase." (For the particulars comp. on Phil. ii. 6—8.) This shows that the Redeemer intended to speak in this place not merely from the position of his Divine nature, but also that he brought into view the human part of his being (two natures which are to be conceived, generally speaking, as having existed in his sacred person in a wonderful, to us incomprehensible, state of combination); HE to whom all was delivered over by the Father, he himself bears with us the yoke, hence he, too, in like manner, takes hold of the heavy burdens of life, and is both master and servant in one and the same person (comp. Matth. xxiii 4, 11), he gives not only commands, but he also assists in the execution thereof, inasmuch as he causes them, by virtue of his spirit, to appear easy (1 John v. 3) But the expression τῇ καρδίᾳ, "in heart," implies that the humility of the Redeemer is to be ascribed to his most inward mental life, in which this humility is only the expression of the decision of his holy will; hence humility appears in him as a thing of free choice, as the emanation of free-will. It thence follows that there is certainly a difference between ταπεινὸς τῇ καρδίᾳ, "lowly of heart," and τ. τῷ πνεύματι = שְׁפַל רוּחַ, "humble in spirit," Proverbs xxix. 23 (comp. Ps. xxx. 18 [Septuag] with πτωχὸς τῷ πνεύματι, "poor in spirit," Matth v 3). The latter expression is a predicate, i.e. a thing peculiar to sinful man, and is only in so far praiseworthy as the recognition of poverty and of wretchedness is the condition of all help from above; but as such this expression cannot be applied to Christ. He was ταπεινὸς τῇ καρδίᾳ, "lowly in heart," but exalted and rich τῷ πνεύματι, "in spirit," inasmuch as the decision of his will and the inclination of his heart did not aspire upwards, but was directed towards that which was lowly. *His* ταπεινοφροσύνη, "lowliness of mind," therefore, is = ἔλεος, "mercy." But the notion of ταπεινοφροσύνη, "lowliness of mind," in both its forms, used when speaking of the perfectly Holy One, and of sinful man, is peculiar to Scriptural language. The Septuagint use it beforehand in the Old Testament as equivalent to אֶבְיוֹן, "needy," עָנִי, "poor," דַּל, "humble," corresponding with the πτωχός, "poor," and ταπεινὸς, "humble, lowly," of the New Testament. In the profane language of antiquity, this expression is extremely seldom used, and then in an honourable sense (as for example by *Plutarch*). The peculiar use of the *word* is bound up with, or depends upon, a peculiar *idea* which belongs to revealed religion. Whilst we meet everywhere in natural man with a struggle after that which is *high*, which is the result of an obscure sense of his *deeply* fallen state, the Scripture teaches more darkly in the Old Testament, more distinctly in the New, that the humbling ourselves into the depth of poverty is the safest way to salvation and to the highest degree of exaltation. Only in the deepest depth of repentance and of bitter self-recognition, which produces a merciful love towards our fellow-men, the soul can receive the Divine power of life, and rise again to its former highest degree of exaltation. In the life of our Redeemer, who from love became like unto sinful man, this way is exemplified, which alone leads to peace.

§ 17. THE DISCIPLES PLUCK EARS OF CORN.

(Matth. xii. 1—8; Mark ii. 23—28; Luke vi. 1—5.)

In the twelfth chapter of St Matthew, which follows, the Evangelist records several individual occurrences, among others also a cure (ver. 9 sqq.), which, nevertheless, held together by a common bond, render likewise prominent the plan of St Matthew to arrange the life of Jesus according to certain rubrics. It is, namely, the polemics of the Pharisees directed against Jesus, that hold together in this section the individual parts, and on account of which the various occurrences seem to have been recorded. It is probable, especially according to the more minute accounts of St John, that the polemical attacks of the Pharisees against Jesus assumed a more decisive form, after he had arrived in Jerusalem for the celebration of the feast (John v. 1 sqq) But inasmuch as St Matthew attends neither to time nor place, since he designs to confine his communications neither to Galilee, nor to any other part of the country,[1] continuing his narrative, on the contrary, without any statement of

---

[1] The opinion frequently expressed by modern critical writers, that St

localities, merely making it his aim, to place before the eye of his Jewish readers the life of Jesus in its various aspects, hence, we must likewise here renounce any exact order of the individual occurrences, and this the rather, inasmuch as any such references drawn from the internal evidence of the narratives themselves, could turn out no otherwise than arbitrarily. (Comp. the early parts of vol ii. of Dr *Paulus'* Comm.) An impartial comparison of both the other Evangelists will lead to the same result. For, even if St Mark immediately connects the narrative of the cure of the withered hand with the plucking of the ears of corn, yet does he differ, in iii 7—9, so-very much from St Matthew, and enters in the course of these verses into so many totally different circumstances, that nothing can be gained therefrom in point of chronological order, even though he returns, iii. 20, once more to events which Matthew relates also in this chapter. But more stirking yet is the manner in which St Luke differs from St Matthew, inasmuch as he enters, in his parallel to St Matthew xii. 22 sqq , into the great record of the last journey of Jesus to the feast (Luke xi 14 sqq), and then returns again, at the end of the chapter, to viii. 19 sqq.

The first narrative, then, that of the plucking of the ears of corn by the disciples, is introduced by St Matthew with the altogether vague expression, ἐν ἐκείνῳ τῷ καιρῷ, "at that time," a formula which admits of wider and narrower limits, and which corresponds to the general καὶ ἐγένετο, "and it came to pass," of St Mark. But St Luke here uses a peculiar expression, ἐν σαββάτῳ δευτεροπρώτῳ, "on the second Sabbath after the first." Something more decisive might probably be adduced for chronology from this formula, were its signification not so completely indeterminate. The word seems to have been formed by St Luke himself, and is to be met with neither in the biblical writings, nor indeed elsewhere. According to the usual opinion (which originates with *Scaliger*), the expression, δευτερόπρωτον σάββατον, is made use of to signify the first Sabbath after the second day of the passover, so that it may be resolved into, σάββατον πρῶτον ἀπὸ δευτέρας ἀπὸ τοῦ πάσχα, "the first Sabbath after the second day from the passover." For, according to the Mosaic institution (Levit. xxiii 11), the first-fruits of sheaves were offered to the Lord on the second

Matthew only wishes to record the sojourn of Christ in Galilee, has been refuted in *my* "Programmen uber die Aechtheit des Mt," Program concerning the authenticity of St Matthew day of the passover (מִמָּחֳרַת הַשַּׁבָּת, "on the morrow after the Sabbath"), and from this day seven Sabbaths were counted to the day of Pentecost Hence, the Sabbath following this second day of the passover is the one called δευτερόπρωτον, "the second after the first" Hence, also, the plucking of the ripening ears by the disciples accords very well with this opinion, nevertheless it is to be considered that the harvest continued until the day of Pentecost, which was in fact, properly speaking, the feast of harvest; the disciples, therefore, might have strayed through the fields also at a later period. Jesus, furthermore, must have left Jerusalem very soon to have wandered in the fields of Galilee, on the very first Sabbath after the feast, which, as is well known, is celebrated during a period of seven days In fine, the explanation itself is certainly ingenious, notwithstanding, and possibly correct but proofs are wanting for the support of it We may imagine that every first Sabbath of two closely connected with one another, and, as it were, belonging to one another, may have been called in this manner, this case however frequently occurred. For, on the three great festivals, the first and the last of the seven days were celebrated, and these might very easily fall out on Sabbaths, so that two days of rest followed one another; in like manner was it with the new moons. The first day of both would thus be called δευτερόπρωτον. In favour of this explanation, although it likewise cannot be proved, would be the omission of the article, which points, in a manner not to be mistaken, to many σάββατα δευτερόπρωτα (Besides, the Hebrew שַׁבָּת or שַׁבָּתוֹן is translated by the Septuagint now as σάββατον, "Sabbath," and then again as σάββατα, "Sabbaths," in like manner do both forms occur in the New Testament)

Ver. 2. The plucking of ears of corn, in so far as it was made use of to appease hunger, was permitted according to the law (Deut. xxiii. 25), only the application of the reaping-hook was forbidden. But the Pharisaical micrology, i.e. captiousness, which had perverted the plain Mosaic commandment of external rest into a painful institution, added the plucking of ears on a Sabbath to the forbidden labours. They divided all affairs into thirty-nine main classes (fathers), among which there were again many subdivisions (daughters).

Ver. 3, 4 Jesus, therefore, endeavours to raise them from their narrow-minded position to a spirit of greater freedom, in such a

G

manner, too, that he places before them, from the law itself, the free application thereof, the result of which is to be a spiritual reception and administration of the law, together with its ordinances. The first example adduced is that of David. The well known narrative of this occurrence, which took place on David's flight before Saul, is found 1 Sam. xxi. 1 sqq. The ἄρτοι προθέσεως = לֶחֶם פָּנִים, "shew-bread," were placed upon small tables in the sanctuary of the ark of the covenant (Exod. xxxv. 13; xxxix. 36). The addition made by St Mark ii. 26, ἐπὶ Ἀβιάθαρ, "in the time of Abiathar," presents a difficulty. For, according to the relation given in the Old Testament, it was not Abiathar but his father Abimelech who was then high-priest; the expression ἐπὶ, however, cannot well be viewed otherwise than signifying: *at the time of*, at the time of performing the office of (comp Luke iii. 2; iv. 27; Acts of the Apostles xi. 28). *Beza* wished to regard this passage as an interpolation; yet there is no ground for this, the manuscripts are, with a few exceptions, in favour of it. It would be most simple and natural to suppose that the Evangelist has confounded the father with the son, which might easily have happened, inasmuch as Abiathar was the more celebrated of the two. If this be not admitted, to which I can nevertheless see as little objection, as to the adoption of various readings, it then would be as well to assume that the father likewise bore the name of Abiathar, although no proof can be given in favour thereof.

Ver 5. St Matthew and St Mark here complete between them the discourse of Jesus. St Matthew, in the next place, gives still another example from the Old Testament, from which it may be seen that the law, as concerning the rest of the Sabbath, is to be taken in a spiritual sense (on this comp. John v. 17, wherein Jesus infers, from the incessant, creative activity of God, likewise an unlimited activity for himself.) According to Numbers xxviii. 9, certain offerings had to be made by the priests in the temple on the Sabbath; this act of offering presupposes active exertion of various kinds, and yet the priests were guiltless as regarded these acts. The σάββατον βεβηλοῦν = חִלֵּל שַׁבָּת, "to profane the Sabbath," Ezek xx. 16, must be viewed, therefore, as signifying: "they would (according to your false notions) desecrate the Sabbath." The ἐν τῷ ἱερῷ, "in the temple," is here evidently made use of to form a contrast with βεβηλοῦσι, "they profane or desecrate," to wit, "in the place where, on account of its holiness, one would least expect it."

Ver. 6. From the temple Jesus proceeds forward to existing circumstances. Of the two readings, μείζων, "one greater," and μεῖζον, "a greater thing," the latter, as the more difficult, is no doubt to be preferred; it has no unimportant authorities in the manuscripts. Μείζων, "a greater person," could only form one peculiar contrast with νόμος, "the law," i e. with the original promulgator of the law, hence with Moses, but the neuter gender draws a parallel between the relations of the priests to the temple in general, and the relations between the disciples and Christ. The sense then is: "the point which is here at issue is something of much greater importance than that which concerns the temple service; and hence, if the law could be there conceived and treated with spiritual freedom, how much more may it be done here." That the relations, it is true, were here much more important, solely arose from the importance of his person, and in so far the μείζων, "a greater person," affords no room for false interpretation; at ver 8 the same idea is expressed with greater precision.

Ver. 7. If this whole deduction from the Old Testament had already brought before the minds of the Pharisees how little they had comprehended the spirit of the sacred book, so does the Redeemer still further continue, according to St Matthew, to place this fact before their eyes in a yet more decisive manner They had wished to reprove the disciples as transgressors of the law, and yet had they themselves transgressed it by this very censure. Their mere external views had prevented them from penetrating into the spirit of the writings of the Old Testament, and hence it was that they were unable to comprehend the meaning of the profound words of Hosea (vi 6). ἔλεον θέλω καὶ οὐ θυσίαν, "I will have mercy and not sacrifice" (comp. Matth. ix. 13.) In these words were already expressed, in the language of the prophet, the spiritual point of view to which the human race was to be transferred through the Gospel, according to which it was not the external action, as such, but the internal disposition, more especially the disposition of self-sacrificing merciful love, which is the thing that is truly well-pleasing to God. But it was this very merciful love that was wanting in the censure of the Pharisees; they did not aim at a true correction of the disciples, they were not urged forward by a pure zeal for the cause of God, on the contrary, it was envy and innate bitterness of heart that prompted them to attack the disciples, and hence they persecuted the Lord in his disciples by their apparent or mock zeal for the Lord. They condemned the innocent (κατεδίκασαν τοὺς ἀναιτίους, "condemn the guiltless"), for the disciples had not plucked the ears of corn out of tedium, and for mere pastime, but from hunger (ver 1), they had abandoned whatever they themselves possessed, and engaged in their labours for spreading the kingdom of God; they were thus deprived of the necessary means of sustaining their lives. Hence they occupied a position similar to that of the servant of God, David, who, together with those belonging to him, hungered, in like manner, in the service of the Lord, they were also like unto the priests that had to work in the temple on the Sabbath, and who thus appeared to transgress the law of the Lord for the Lord's sake, hence they also might have eaten without hesitation of the shew-bread; whatever belonged to God belonged to them. The disciples, therefore, appear here as priests of a higher standing in the spiritual kingdom of God, to whom belonged, in a higher degree, what the law itself had *assigned* to the priests of the old covenant [1]

Ver. 8. The concluding portion of the discourse of our Redeemer refers back to the exalted rank of his person (and consequently likewise of his disciples). In St Mark ii 27 it is preceded by a noble idea: τὸ σάββατον διὰ τὸν ἄνθρωπον ἐγένετο, οὐχ ὁ ἄνθρωπος διὰ τὸ σάββατον, literally: "the Sabbath was made on account of man, not man on account of the Sabbath." Inasmuch as σάββατον, "the Sabbath," here stands synecdochically for the law and all its institutions, these words contain or imply the contrast between the micrological, i.e. contracted, narrow-minded, view of the Pharisees concerning the Old Testament and the free and spiritual one of Christianity. According to the former, the commandments themselves, and the external legal

---

[1] In the parallel passage, Luke vi 4, the Cod D has a remarkable addition, which has probably originated in an apocryphal Gospel: τῇ αὐτῇ ἡμέρᾳ θεασάμενός τινα ἐργαζόμενον τῷ σαββάτῳ, εἶπεν αὐτῷ· ἄνθρωπε, εἰ μὲν οἶδας τί ποιεῖς, μακάριος εἶ, εἰ δὲ μὴ οἶδας, ἐπικατάρατος καὶ παραβάτης εἶ τοῦ νόμου, "on the self-same day, beholding a certain man working on the Sabbath, he said to him· O man, if indeed thou knowest what thou art doing, blessed art thou; but if thou knowest it not, thou art accursed, and a transgressor of the law" (on the sense of this addition, comp the remarks on Rom. xv. 22)

obedience to them, is the end of man's service, and in this sense the law is an oppressive yoke; but according to the Christian view, man, and his exaltation into the image of God, is the great object, the commandments, and his outward obedience to them, are only the *means* that lead to this end. This acceptation permits the law to appear in its true nature and signification as a love-gift of our paternal God, who causes man to move so long only in the leading strings of external ordinances, as until he becomes able to receive the internal law into his heart (Jerem. xxxi. 33). Hence it is impossible that *the expression,* ὁ υἱός τοῦ ἀνθρώπου, "the Son of Man," *should be parallel to the* ἄνθρωπος, "man," of Mark ii. 27, *in the concluding idea, which is common to all the three Evangelists·* κύριος τοῦ σαββάτου ὁ υἱὸς τοῦ ἀνθρώπου, "the Son of Man is Lord of the Sabbath." For although sinful man does not exist on account of the law, but the law, on the contrary, on account of man, still there would be something very inconsistent in saying: that he is the *Lord* of the law, or even of any one of the legal institutions. He only could say this of himself, who was the perfect, the first of men. Hence υἱός τοῦ ἀνθρώπου, "Son of Man," must here be regarded as a contrast to ἄνθρωπος, "man," and that this expression, therefore, implies the Messianic dignity of Jesus. As the Lord of heaven (1 Cor. xv. 47), although walking the earth in human insignificance, the Messiah is above every lawful institution, inasmuch as his will is the law itself; yet does he never appear as abrogating any law, but as consummating it in its spiritual sense (Matth. v. 17). In this manner does the Redeemer consummate the law of the Sabbath of the Old Testament, inasmuch as he recommends an internal dedication of the soul, and rest in God.

§ 18 JESUS CURES A WITHERED HAND

(Matth. xii 9—21; Mark iii. 1—6; Luke vi. 6—12)

Ver. 9. The same subject is yet further developed on another occasion, where Jesus heals a sick person. He makes use of this occurrence in order to afford to the Pharisees, who, notwithstanding all their hostile feeling, had not been given up as yet by our Lord, an insight into the spiritual comprehension of the Old Testament. The transition-formulas however here employed by Matthew are unquestionably very vague. The μεταβὰς ἐκεῖθεν, "having departed thence," is made use of to connect this occurrence immediately with the preceding one; but we see from Luke vi 6 that there was at least a period of eight days between them, and that the event to be narrated happened on another Sabbath. The words: εἰς τὴν συναγωγὴν αὐτῶν ἦλθεν, "he went into their synagogue," prove how completely the marking of the separate localities was overlooked, for nothing has been previously mentioned to show who are meant by the αὐτῶν. (The χεὶρ ξηρά, "withered hand," = ἐξηραμμένη of St Mark, is, as the expression so naturally derived from the appearance teaches us, a hand disabled by paralysis, and deprived of the power of life; a mere luxation is here out of the question.[1]

Ver. 10. The Pharisees, according to St Matthew, endeavoured to entrap Jesus by means of an insidious question; St Mark and St Luke only allude in general terms to their malicious intentions, without letting them speak. (The word παρατηρέω, "to observe or watch narrowly," Luke often uses in the sense of *insidiose observare*, to observe treacherously, xiv. 1; xx. 20.) It has another cognate signification, Gal. iv. 10, *superstitiose observare*, "to observe superstitiously." The notion of anxious observation is common to both.) But Christ perceived their intention or design, not merely from the question (for the latter might indeed have originated likewise in a well-disposed intention), but through his gift of searching the hearts of men, which was wholly different from a mere reflective supposition concerning their intention. (Comp. on John ii. 25. Concerning the expression διαλογισμοί, "reasonings, thoughts" [Luke vi. 8], see on Luke ii. 35; Matth. ix. 4). St Mark and St Luke again treat of the outward impression of this event in a more graphic manner than St Matthew. They inform us how Jesus ordered the sick man to come before him, so that he could be seen by

---

[1] In the apocryphal additions to the authentic gospel of St Matthew, such as St Jerome found them in the Gospel of the Nazarenes, this sick man was declared to be a *caementarius*, "mason" Hieronym Comm. in Matth. p 47 writes that he said; caementarius eram, manibus victum quaeritans, praecor te, Jesu, ut mihi restituas sanitatem, ne turpiter mendicem cibos, "I am a mason, seeking my food by (the labour of) my hands, I beseech thee, O Jesus, that thou restore my health, lest I begin with shame to beg my food." (Comp. *my* Geschichte der Evang. p 78)

all, and how he, directing the looks of those present on the sufferer, endeavoured to rouse up the consciences of those men who had grown callous in their mistaken state of legality. The question, however, which Jesus proposes to the assembled Pharisees (Mark iii. 4; Luke vi. 9) is of a rather singular character. It appears, namely, as though the question at issue should not have been the ἀγαθοποιῆσαι, "to do good," or κακοποιῆσαι, "to do evil," but the ποιῆσαι, "to do," and μὴ ποιῆσαι, "not to do." But it is this misleading contrast from which the Redeemer wishes to withdraw them, and to point out to them that the not-doing may very often be a sin; but then it was clear that man should no more sin on the Sabbath than on any other day, consequently, concludes Christ, it is under peculiar circumstances not only permitted, but also a *duty* to act on the Sabbath-day. The law, then, of Sabbath observance, is thus reduced by our Lord to the more exalted one, which forbids us to commit sin.

Ver. 11. St Matthew further narrates that the Redeemer appealed to the conscience of each single individual, asking whether he would not draw out his sheep on a Sabbath from a pit if it had happened to fall therein. Jesus infers *a minori ad majus*, i.e. comparing small things with greater, how much more is not the faithful shepherd of human souls bound to save, on the Sabbath-day, a little sheep of his human flock which had fallen into the well or pit of perdition! This it is, which is indeed a veritable Sabbath-work, a true service of God! The same idea, in a different connection, is to be found Luke xiv. 5. For βόθυνος, "a pit," St Luke has φρέαρ = בּוֹר, "a well." The Pharisees remained silent (Mark iii. 4), hence they confessed themselves to have been overcome by the truth of the reasoning, (Luke xiv. 5); this susceptibility, coupled with so much stubbornness, awakened very opposite sentiments in the heart of the Redeemer: περιβλεψάμενος αὐτοὺς μετ' ὀργῆς συλλυπούμενος ἐπὶ τῇ πωρώσει τῆς καρδίας αὐτῶν, "having looked round about upon them with anger, being grieved concerning the hardness of their hearts" (Mark iii. 5), a sorrowful and very painful wrath is by no means a contradicting feeling; it is only in sinful man that the over-boiling rage stifles the more gentle sensations of sorrow and sympathising grief; but in the Redeemer, as also in the heart of God, the flame of wrath is identical with that of love, for whilst he hates the sin, he has compassion in his heart for the being that has given place thereto. (The substantive πώρωσις, "hardness, callousness," is only to be found besides in Rom xi 25; Ephes iv. 18 The verb, on the contrary, is met with very frequently. It is derived from πῶρος, *callus*, and signifies, in the first place, hardness of heart, insensibility, more especially to spiritual and moral impressions. In the second place, it is connected with the notion of τύφλωσις, "blindness," because blindness is a corporeal insensibility to the impressions of light.

Ver. 13. After this deeply heart-affecting address, the Redeemer heals the sick man ('Αποκαθίστημι, "to restore," used when speaking of bodily healing = שׁוּב, "to revert, to restore," Exod iv. 7 In like manner, Mark viii. 25. It signifies, properly speaking, *in integrum restituere*, to restore to the former original situation. Often also in the spiritual sense, as for example Matthew xvii. 11.

Ver. 14. The discovery of sin awakens either repentance, or, if man is insensible thereto, bitterness of heart, thus it was with the Pharisees. The host of priests, attacked in the most hidden mystery of their sins, united together for the defence of their kingdom, hence the question at issue was no longer concerning the opposition of solitary individuals, but it was a mighty body, the opposition of which was called forth by the light which emanated from Christ. According to Mark iii 6, the cunning Pharisees endeavoured at once to enter into a coalition with the temporal power; he writes: μετὰ τῶν Ἡρωδιανῶν συμβούλιον ἐποίουν, "they took counsel together with the Herodians." These Ἡρωδιανοί, "Herodians," were the courtiers and adherents of Herod Antipas, the ruler of Galilee (Matth. xxii. 16; Mark xii 13), whom the Pharisees undertook to win over to their interests, because they could effect nothing without the aid of the temporal power[1] Hence their infamous designs became evident also in this; they hardened their hearts against the beneficent influences of the Holy Ghost, ἐπλήσθησαν ἀνοίας, "they were filled with madness," as St Luke vi. 11 says very significantly of them, for every departure from God is foolishness.

Ver. 15 But inasmuch as the hour was not yet come in which our Lord was to be delivered into the hands of his enemies (Matth. xxvi 45), he left them, and withdrew into a state

---

[1] The uncritical *Epiphanius* describes the Herodians as a religious sect (Epiph. haer Ossen p. 44)

of retirement. The narrative of St Matthew xii. 15, 16, exhibits the same kind of general formula, which is so often met with in him (iv. 23 sqq ; ix 35 sqq) According to the parallel passage (Mark iii. 7 sqq), Jesus went to the lake of Genesareth, and among the masses of the people that sought him here also, there were not only persons from Idumea, Tyre, and Sidon, but likewise from Judea and Jerusalem (comp iii. 22, where there are expressly mentioned, γραμματεῖς ἀπὸ Ἱεροσολύμων καταβάντες, "scribes who came down from Jerusalem"), which clearly proves, that Jesus had already exercised his ministry in Judea and Jerusalem Many events recorded by St Matthew and St Mark probably occurred in or near Jerusalem, only the Evangelists neglect to make mention of the localities; of a confinement to Galilee of the scene wherein Jesus ministered before his last journey to the feast, no trace is to be found. According to the further narration of St Mark (iii 9), the pressure of the people, that became irksome to our Lord (θλίβειν, "to crush") was so great, that he had to enter into a vessel in order to instruct them from thence. (In the passage, ἵνα πλοιάριον προσκαρτερῇ αὐτῷ, "that a small vessel should be in waiting on him," the expression, προσκαρτερεῖν, is used in the sense of being at one's disposal, *praesto esse*, "to be ready at hand") But even here also Jesus endeavoured earnestly to (ἐπετίμα, "he charged") procure that his dwelling-place and his dignity should not be made known (ἵνα μὴ φανερὸν αὐτὸν ποιήσωσι, "that they should not make him known," Mark iii. 12, Matthew xii. 16). According to the context, this command of Jesus bears principally on the circumstance, that he wished that every political movement in his favour, on the part of those Jews that were impressed with false notions concerning the Messiah, should be avoided, in order to deprive his adversaries of every, even merely apparent, occasion for accusing him. (Comp. on this subject on Matth. viii. 4)

Ver 17 St Matthew avails himself, moreover, of this quiet retirement of Jesus, which formed so striking a contrast with the tumultuous enterprises of subsequent false Christs, in order to quote a remarkable passage from the Old Testament (Is. xlii. 1—4), wherein this character of the Messiah is brought prominently forward. The Messiah is described therein as being possessed of the same qualities of gentleness of which he had spoken, Matth. xi 28—30 (On the ὅπως πληρωθῇ, "that it might be fulfilled," comp. Matth i. 22.)

Ver. 18. This quotation, also, from the Old Testament, is treated in a peculiar manner St Matthew does not follow either the Septuagint, nor verbatim the Hebrew text; on the contrary, he makes use of the text for his own purpose in an independent translation. The Septuagint has, in the first place, added in the translation its own exposition. it adds to Is. xlii. 1, Ἰακὼβ ὁ παῖς μου, Ἰσραὴλ ὁ ἐκλεκτός μου, "Jacob my servant, Israel my chosen one." The reference of this passage to Israel, that is to say, to the collective total of the truly faithful among the nation, is, in truth, not incorrect, but Matthew could not make use of it for his purpose (at least, not without explanation); hence, he adheres to the words of the original text, בְּחִירִי, "my chosen one," עַבְדִּי, "my servant," which, as a matter of course, had a more immediate reference to Jesus, and the word, הֵן, omitted by the Septuagint, he renders, ἰδοῦ, "behold." The evangelist, however, correctly explains these words as having reference to him, inasmuch as the Redeemer is not merely a member of the collective body of the true worshippers of God in Israel, but because he is their representative; and that the prophet himself, in his prophetic spirit, looked for such an one, is evident from many expressions, especially ver 4 (לְתוֹרָתוֹ אִיִּים יְיַחֵלוּ, "for his law the islands shall wait.") The ᾑρέτισα, "I have chosen" (in Hebr. אֶתְמָךְ, "I will uphold," and according to the Septuagint, προσεδέξατο, "hath accepted, received"), derived from αἱρετίζω, "to choose," which occurs in this place only, deviates from the meaning of the original text, yet could תָּמַךְ, "seize, lay hold on," αἱρέω, "to take hold on, to choose," be well understood in this manner:—The expression, יוֹצִיא, "he shall cause to go forth," the Septuagint renders better by ἐξοίσει, "he shall bring about," than does St Matthew by ἀπαγγελεῖ, "he shall declare, announce" The expression was perhaps chosen on account of the prophetic discourses of Christ concerning the judgments which follow.

Ver. 19. The words of this and the following verses extol the gentle character of this beloved Son of God. The first two expressions St Matthew has transposed, the words of the Hebrew text being, לֹא יִצְעַק וְלֹא יִשָּׂא, "he shall not cry, nor lift up" (the Septuagint has ἀνήσει, "shall take up, lift up," instead of, ἐρίσει, "shall strive." In what follows the בַּחוּץ, "without," (LXX. ἔξω) is rendered freely, ἐν ταῖς πλατείαις, "in the streets," here no doubt in reference to the foregoing ἀναχωρεῖν, "withdrawing, retiring" (εἰς τὴν ἔρημον, "into the desert"), ver. 15.

Ver. 20 As ver. 19 records the quiet, noiseless ministry of Christ (for whatever was of a turbulent character in his ministry did not emanate from him, but from the people, the Lord himself always endeavouring to quell every tumult), which the Jews, who were given to outward show, in no way expected from the Messiah, who, according to their vain notions, would appear with a noisy splendour and tumultuous glory; so in like manner does this verse express his condescending affability, ministering to the necessities of the suffering and feeble. The expressions, κάλαμος συντετριμμένος, "a bruised reed," and λίνος τυφόμενος, "smoking flax," are natural figures of speech for a broken, perishing life, it is represented as the business of the Messiah, again to excite and to strengthen it The last words of Is. xlii. 3, לֶאֱמֶת יוֹצִיא מִשְׁפָּט, "he shall cause judgment to go forth unto truth" (which the Septuagint renders, εἰς ἀλήθειαν ἐξοίσει κρίσιν, "he shall carry out judgments unto truth"), St Matthew has rendered, with a deviation, ἕως ἂν ἐκβάλῃ τὴν κρίσιν εἰς νῖκος, "till he send forth judgment unto victory," which latter expression would refer to לָנֶצַח, "to victory, mastery, destruction" (comp 2 Sam. ii. 26). One might suppose, that the Evangelist had another reading before him, or, that the εἰς νῖκος, "unto victory," is an exposition of εἰς ἀλήθειαν, "unto truth,"[1] for the carrying out of the κρίσις, "judgment," to the ἀλήθεια, "truth," is indeed the victory.

Ver. 21. The first words of Is. xlii. 4, which St Matthew considered less suitable for his purpose, he has omitted; but the concluding words, לְתוֹרָתוֹ אִיִּים יְיַחֵלוּ, "the isles shall wait for his law," he renders, τῷ ὀνόματι ἔθνη ἐλπιοῦσι, "in his name shall the Gentiles trust," which agrees verbatim with the Septuagint. Here is to be observed the exact harmony with the Septuagint against the Hebrew text in the former deviation; it can hardly be explained otherwise than by a various reading, for the very term, לְתוֹרָתוֹ, "to his law," must have appeared to St Matthew

---

[1] Others, as for example *Gesenius* (on this passage), translate אֱמֶת by *mildness*, a signification which *Umbreit* justly does not acknowledge or admit, in the treatise thereon, which will be presently quoted.

as very suitable to his purpose With regard to the exposition of this passage, as having reference to the Messiah, *Umbreit* has once more defended it, in these latter times, in his beautiful treatise on the Servant of God. (*S Heidelberg* "Studien und Kritiken," vol. 1 part ii) This intelligent expositor has seized very correctly the idea of the suffering and victorious innocence and the moral power in the Servant of God, who is no other but the Lord and King Jehovah; only, he appears to overlook the identity of the Servant of God in the various passages. The difficulty of combining his various (apparently contradictory) predicates, i e. qualities or titles, with one subject, disappears with the supposition of the idea of the representation of a multiplicity by an unity. The various explanations of this difficult passage concerning the Servant of God (from Is xl.—lxvi), according to which is understood therein the entire nation, or the righteous, or the prophets, form no direct contradiction to the biblical-messianical ones, for in the idea of the Messiah all this is indeed contained. The Messiah represents the ideal of the true Israel, while the righteous men and prophets represent the true Israel as it actually existed.

§ 19. OF THE CALUMNIES OF THE PHARISEES JESUS SEVERELY REBUKING THEM

(St Matth. xii. 22—45; Mark iii. 20—30; Luke xi 14—26, 29—32.)

A more intimate connection of the narrative which follows with the preceding one is in St Matthew out of the question, inasmuch as in accordance with the formula having a general reference to that which precedes (ver. 15, 16), a mere τότε, "then," carries forward the discourse. In Luke xi. 14 sqq. we find ourselves transposed into a perfectly different territory, and Mark iii. 20 leads us back again to the mission of the twelve, where a vague καὶ συνέρχεται πάλιν ὄχλος, " and there came together again a multitude," is immediately connected with the narrative of their return. The addition however of οἱ γραμματεῖς, οἱ ἀπὸ Ἱεροσολύμων καταβάντες, "the scribes which came down from Jerusalem," of ver. 22, renders it probable, that a festival in Jerusalem had preceded it. But, on the one hand, it is uncertain *what* festival here is to be understood; and, on the other, it may be imagined, that the journey of these scribes had no connection whatever with a festival, that could be assumed only in case it had been remarked, that these doctors were Galileans. But inasmuch as this is not said, we may conceive that they were emissaries, sent by the principal men of Jerusalem, and these might arrive at any time in Galilee. At any rate, we shall do well in not wishing to decide upon that which is left undecided. St Mark (iii. 21), moreover, puts forth a remarkable notice, which will occupy our attention presently (on Matth xii 46), he, however, proceeds at once to relate the impudent accusation made by the Pharisees against our Lord, without referring to the cause which called it forth. Thus, St Matthew represents the opposition of the Pharisees in its gradual development, until it attains its climax in the accusation of a connection between Christ and the kingdom of the evil one, and of his being mad.

Ver 22 According to the record of St Matthew, the cure of a demoniac, who was both blind and dumb, was the cause of these impudent accusations of the Pharisees. (St Luke xi. 14 only mentions his dumbness, but without denying that he was at the same time blind.) The sick individual must have suffered from a very peculiar disease, for it is only in this manner that we shall be able to explain the remarkable surprise of the multitude (Matth xii. 23, ἐξίσταντο πάντες οἱ ὄχλοι, "all the people were amazed," the verb, like the substantive, ἔκστασις, " ecstacy, astonishment," is often made use of in the language of the New Testament when speaking of violent fear or astonishment; Mark ii. 12, v. 42, Luke v. 26, Acts of the Ap. iii 10), and their inference from the cure (Concerning υἱὸς τοῦ Δαβίδ, " the Son of David," comp on Luke i. 35) Besides, it is quite clear, that the sick person is not called, δαιμονιζόμενος, "one possessed with a devil," *because* he was dumb or blind, or because he was both at one and the same time; on the contrary, these phenomena in him were accompanied by other physical and psychical affections, which leads to the supposition of spiritual influences (comp the remarks made on Matth ix. 27 sqq.).

Ver 24. The more dazzling an appearance the performance of Christ assumed—the purer and more perfect the healing of a highly unfortunate being, who seemed to be cut off from every participation of life, appeared, which thus excited astonishment and sympathy in the simple masses of the people—the more fearfully was the wrath of the priestly host, which perceived well, that the ministry of Jesus would destroy their domination, stirred up. They breathed blasphemy into the heart of the simple-minded, stating, that the power by which they were thus moved was not the result of that which was holy, but of that which was unholy. Inasmuch, therefore, as mighty effects lead to the conclusion of powerful causes, they accused him of an intercourse with Beelzebub. (Comp. on Matth. x. 25.) The accusation noticed above (Matth. xi. 18, δαιμόνιον ἔχει, "he hath a devil") was less severe The δαιμόνιον ἔχειν, "the having a devil," it is true, is by no means equivalent to μαίνεσθαι, "the being mad," as St John x. 20 clearly proves, where both are combined by means of καί, "and," consequently they cannot be identical, unless the author wished to have uttered a gross tautology. The expression, μαίνεσθαι, "the being mad," may be conceived, it is true, as the *consequence* of the δ. ἔχειν, "the having a devil," and being, if not a necessary, at least a very common result of the δ. ἔχειν, it may in this case be understood as having actually existed. But in itself, δαιμόνιον ἔχειν, "to have a devil," signifies only to be ruled over, to be guided by an evil spirit = ἔχεσθαι ὑπὸ δαιμονίου, "to be possessed with a devil." Hence the difference existing between this expression and the one made use of in xii. 24 consists in there being *here* asserted a direct influence of the ἄρχων τῶν δαιμονίων, "prince of the devils," whereas *there* merely that of any evil being in general; and therefore, that the performance of miracles through the powers of darkness presupposes a peculiar wickedness of disposition, whereas in the δαιμόνιον ἔχειν, "the having a devil," there is rather supposed an unconscious state of dependence upon the evil spirit.

Ver. 25, 26. Jesus perceived their internal wickedness (St Luke vi. 8), and the evil thoughts of their hearts (on διαλογισμοί, "reasonings," διανόημα, "thoughts," ἐνθυμήσεις, "desires, lusts, imaginations," see on Luke ii. 35, Matth. ix. 4); he at first endeavoured to instruct them by means of reasoning, and a representation of the circumstances. (According to St Mark iii. 23, ἐν παραβολαῖς, "in parables," comp on this head on Matt xiii. 3. The parabolical character of this discourse is particularly obvious in St Mark iii. 27) This endeavour of the merciful Redeemer, who knew what was in their hearts, is full of consolation; it permits us to suppose, that he discovered in their hearts likewise the germs of something better, to the vivification of which he might direct his attention in the course of his instruction. Had these luckless beings, who called light darkness, and who converted that which was holy itself into an unholy thing, not been blinded by their passion, they then would have committed the sin against the Holy Ghost (Matth. xii. 32), and thus have been deprived of all hope of forgiveness. But, in the latter case, it would be likewise inconceivable, that the Redeemer should have spoken words fitted to effect their deliverance to such as could not be redeemed from their errors! For Jesus endeavours, in the first place, to display before them the contradictory character of their accusation. He compares a kingdom, a city, a family, in short, any social union whatever, with the kingdom of Satan, and concludes by saying, that inasmuch as nothing of the kind can maintain its existence without a certain order and cleaving together of the members, so in like manner neither can the kingdom of darkness. ($\mu\epsilon\rho i\zeta\epsilon\sigma\theta\alpha\iota$, $\delta\iota\alpha\mu\epsilon\rho i\zeta\epsilon\sigma\theta\alpha\iota$, "to be divided, disunited," denotes an internally divided existence, mutual strife, it is the contrast to $\dot\epsilon\nu o\tilde u\sigma\theta\alpha\iota$, "to be united." In like manner, $\dot\epsilon\rho\eta\mu o\upsilon\sigma\theta\alpha\iota$, "to be laid waste, made desolate," $o\dot u\chi$ $\ddot\iota\sigma\tau\alpha\sigma\theta\alpha\iota$, "not to stand firm," is to be cut off from existence and subsistence $=$ $\tau\acute\epsilon\lambda o\varsigma$ $\ddot\epsilon\chi\epsilon\iota\nu$, "to have an end," Mark iii. 26.) The whole argument, moreover, appears to possess something of an obscure character; it would seem, namely, that the character of the kingdom of darkness consists in the very fact that peace and unity are wanting therein, and that strife rules there instead, hence, how can a conclusion be drawn from the nature of the kingdom of darkness *against* strife? We might feel inclined to reply to the remark of Christ concerning the accusation of his adversaries, "that inasmuch as the evil principle is engaged in strife with itself, this it serves as a proof that it can have no lasting existence." But, this difficulty will be removed, when we reflect, that our Lord does not say, no kingdom (or city, or household) in which there exists a division (that is, among the members constituting the union) can stand; for in that case we would have to say, that there is no kingdom, city, or household that can stand, inasmuch as there exists none in which there is no strife or division at all, he rather expresses himself thus wisely: no kingdom, or any similar social union, can have existence, if, as such, it be divided against itself. Hence, if strife be not silenced in a kingdom as soon as ever it enters into contest with another kingdom, then must it be regarded as dissolved; but if it only remain in this *state of opposition,* retaining its living unity, the internal division among its individual members does not abrogate its existence. Hence, that there is a division in the kingdom of darkness, Jesus does by no means deny; on the contrary, it is its nature; but he at the same time maintains that it forms a complete union, as opposed to the kingdom of good. And it is for this reason that it is also said. $εἰ ὁ σατανᾶς τὸν σατανᾶν ἐκβάλλει,$ "if Satan cast out Satan." This passage cannot be used in order to prove that $σατανᾶς,$ "Satan," stands for bad angels in general (comp. above on Matth viii. 28), on the contrary, it signifies (as the article shows) the $ἄρχων τῶν δαιμονίων,$ "the prince of the devils." This one, as the representative of the whole, cannot be *against himself,* otherwise he could not (and, together with him, his kingdom, which is himself) maintain such an opposition against that which is good. However, that here "is, moreover, assumed a kingdom of evil spirits, cannot possibly be doubted when viewed exegetically," even according to the opinion of *Dr Paulus* (see volume ii. p. 89 of his commentary), and hence it will be necessary to have recourse to artificial means, in order to remove this troublesome doctrine from the Holy Scriptures.

Ver. 27, 28 After this display of the absurdity contained in the idea that Beelzebub would attack his own kingdom, Jesus passes on to another objection. Jews also cast out demons ($οἱ υἱοὶ ὑμῶν,$ ' your sons"[1]), the Pharisees and Scribes are considered as the fathers of the faith, hence of the faithful Jews, wherewith then ($ἐν τίνι,$ "by whom, in whose [name]) do they cast them out? This discourse is based on the principle or assumption: no effect without a cause; now, inasmuch as the Pharisees acknowledged the cures of Jewish exorcisers, they were necessarily bound to assume a cause for them. An evil power they could not assume, partly from what has been previously said, and partly because the general popular notions would not admit thereof, hence there was no alternative but to assume that this was done by means of a *good* power. From these minor demonstrations of beneficent power, which appear seldom and isolated in a prominent manner, the Lord excludes the mass of cures of the incurables to whom HE had afforded relief, and in-

[1] *Chrysostom* understands by this expression the apostles, he, no doubt, thought we should not ascribe to the Jews the gift of exorcising demons.

fers therefrom that the kingdom of God is at hand The βασι-
λεία τ 9, "kingdom of God," must here be conceived, in an indefinite general sense, as that order of things in which that which is Divine manifests itself as victorious in this temporal system of the world. This was very justly connected with the appearance of the Messiah, and in so far the expression signifies, indeed, the Messianic period. (For ἐν πνεύματι, "with the Spirit," St Luke has, xi. 20, ἐν δακτύλῳ Θεοῦ, "with the finger of God," according to the Hebrew אֶצְבַּע, "finger," comp. Exod. viii. 19, הִיא אֶצְבַּע אֱלֹהִים, "this is the finger of God." It is = יָד, χείρ, "hand," a figure significative of power, only with the accessory notion of a finer manifestation of the divine power, and one more difficult to be perceived) That the Jewish notions of evil spirits, and of their expulsion, were mixed up with much superstition, there can be no doubt. *Josephus* (Bell. Jud. vii. 6 3) relates, that there grew a root in the neighbourhood of Machaerus, by means of which evil spirits were driven out, whom he considers as πονηρῶν ἀνθρώπων πνεύματα, "the spirits of evil men." The same writer relates, in his Antiquitates (viii. 21. 5), an instance of exorcising by means of such roots, with the aid of the incantation-formulas of Solomon. In like manner is an evil spirit exorcised (Tob. viii. 2) by means of the liver of a fish. Yet such an admixture of superstition does not prove that there is no truth at the bottom of the thing itself, with which that which is in itself false may be joined. We may imagine that many Jewish exorcists (see Acts of the Apostles xix. 14) performed acts by faith in help from above, which had a resemblance to the cures of Jesus; the same, however, must be regarded as feebler and isolated exercises of spiritual powers.

Ver. 29. How essentially Jesus comprehends the struggle between good and evil is evident from the third parable,[1] wherein he infers, from the nature of the contrast, that such phenomena, as manifested themselves in his ministry, could only be conceived as the result of an absolute preponderance of power. The kingdom of darkness, as a social union, here forms the opposition to the kingdom of good, both kingdoms being viewed in

---

[1] The parable is based on the passage of Is. xlix 24, 25, where the Hebrew גִּבּוֹר, "mighty man," corresponds to the ἰσχυρός, "strong man." The description of St Luke quite agrees with the prophetic language, according to the version of the Septuagint.

their personal representatives But *real* as the manner may be in which the opposition is conceived, yet does it appear by no means as an *absolute* one, inasmuch as in the good there always resides the power of conquest. St Luke carries out the figure more carefully. The evil spirit is viewed as an armed man who guards his castle (αὐλή stands for palace, as in Matth. xxvi. 3, a great pile surrounded with fore-courts and halls). Only an ἰσχυρότερος, "stronger man," can overcome him, can deprive him of his armour (πανοπλία), and divide the booty. (Σκῦλα, "spoil, plunder," St Matthew and St Mark have σκεύη = כֵּלִים, "vessels, furniture," which frequently signifies arms, in which sense it may form a parallel with πανοπλία. As the contrast to σκῦλα, which are contra-distinguished from equipment or armature, it might be conceived as furniture and possessions in general) This parable indicates, in its application to the special circumstances that here form the question, that the redemption of individuals fettered by the chains of darkness is only possible through the preponderating power of light. But the great practical truth which is taught or promulgated in this parable is this, that the evil *in abstracto* is not a mere μὴ ὄν, "non-existent," not mere deficiency in the being filled with the knowledge of God, but something real, although, it is true, not a thing substantial or absolute, like the good. The reality of evil is contained in the *disturbed relation* of the powers to one another. This disharmony, however, is a real existence in the universe; acting powerfully, it emanates from one point, and can therefore be subdued only through a power of a more mighty character, acting harmoniously. The harmony proceeds likewise from a centre-point, from the Redeemer; his redeeming efficacy is the harmonious principle of life which overcomes the disharmony

Ver. 30. After these discourses of Jesus, which are directed to the comprehension or understanding, his language assumes another colouring; it takes a more decisive turn in the direction of earnest exhortation He remonstrates with the Pharisees and Scribes—who, as the representatives of the theocracy, had they faithfully done their duty, should have been *for* the Redeemer and his cause—that in their position mere indecision concerning him was a decision *against* him (Both the parallel members of the verse contain the same idea The contrast of συνάγειν, "to gather together," and σκορπίζειν, "to scatter abroad," is borrowed, no doubt, from the figure of collecting treasures of any kind.)

Hence, notwithstanding the earnestness expressed in this discourse, the idea breathes forth, nevertheless, a stream of mildness; the Redeemer does not regard them as absolute enemies, but he views them as yet as undecided friends, expressing, however, distinctly at the same time that indecision is their perdition. Were we to say that this expression refers perhaps to other Pharisees who had not uttered that impudent accusation, it must be observed that this is by no means intimated in the speech, Christ's former manner of speaking to his calumniators evidently admits here also this more lenient interpretation. But this normal rule forms an evident contrast to the similar one: ὅς οὐκ ἔστι καθ᾽ ὑμῶν, ὑπὲρ ὑμῶν ἐστι, literally "he who is not against you, is for you" (Luke ix. 50; Mark ix. 40). The expression, however, refers to persons having no absolute call to labour for the kingdom of God, in whom, therefore, the want of decision against the truth is at once as certainly a favourable sign of their well-intentioned disposition as the absence of a decision in his favour on the part of the Pharisees formed a sign of their impure disposition. A reference of this normal rule to the kingdom of darkness (so that μετ᾽ ἐμοῦ, "with me," and κατ᾽ ἐμοῦ, "against me," would have to be explained as referring merely to the subject, forenamed in the context, the first person being only used proverbially so as to yield this meaning, "the common remark, 'he who is not with me,' &c., may justly be applied to the devil,") is here entirely out of the question.

Ver. 31, 32. With this idea is moreover connected a description of the terrible guilt into which all those plunge themselves who war against Jesus (κατ᾽ ἐμοῦ, "against me"). But in order to put this guilt in its true light, our Lord compares it with other very culpable actions, especially with blasphemies. This difficult passage requires a careful consideration, on account of its dogmatical meaning[1] In the first place, with regard to the various views or opinions given to us by the Evangelists, St Luke xii. 10 contains a similar idea, but in a more abbreviated form. It stands there in a completely different connection from the one in which it here stands, and in a

---

[1] On the *sin against the Holy Ghost*, comp the instructive treatises by *Grashoff* (Stud 1833, part 4.), *Gurlitt* (Stud. 1834. pt. 3) and *Tholuck* (Stud 1836, pt 2) Yet, from a fear of being led too far, I have in the following sheets but seldom taken notice of the points therein treated of.

far less suitable one. The comparison of his account with that of the others does not contribute to advance our understanding of the passage. St Mark contains the words in the same connection, but more briefly and less decidedly. In St Matthew alone the idea appears in a state of complete development, and we find it here proved once more that he understands how to make up, by carefulness in the communication of the discourses, for the want of attention to external matter. Hence, if we follow St Matthew, the result of the general idea will be: that all sins can be forgiven, with the exception of one, which St Matthew calls. εἰπεῖν λόγον κατὰ τοῦ πνεύματος ἁγίου, βλασφημία τοῦ πνεύματος, literally "to speak a word against the Holy Ghost, the blasphemy of the Spirit;" St Mark, on the contrary, calls it βλασφημεῖν εἰς τὸ πνεῦμα τὸ ἅγιον, "to blaspheme against the Holy Ghost." In order to illustrate the idea, a further addition is made, that βλασφημίαι, "blasphemies" (according to St Mark), and words against the Son of Man (εἰπεῖν λόγον κατὰ τοῦ υἱοῦ τοῦ ἀνθρώπου, literally "to speak a word against the Son of Man," according to St Matthew) would be forgiven, *except* the sin against the Holy Ghost only. We cannot say, therefore, that ver. 31 and 32 express quite the same thing, for even if ver. 31 contains a preliminary remark that the sin against the Holy Ghost cannot be forgiven, yet does ver. 32 express strongly the important new idea that even the sin against the Son *can* be forgiven, but that *one* not; to which is added, moreover, the new emphatic remark: οὔτε ἐν τούτῳ τῷ αἰῶνι, οὔτε ἐν τῷ μέλλοντι, literally "neither in this world, nor in the future one." This single idea forms, nevertheless, a difficult subject for explanation, because it stands partly isolated, inasmuch as no passage of the New Testament treats any further of this sin nominatim, and partly because it is in itself obscure, and stands in connection with other difficult doctrines, as, for example, the doctrine of the Holy Ghost. Difficulties such as these cannot be removed by means of grammatical and philological researches; every one solves them according to their agreement with his own fundamental views. A correct explanation of such a passage necessarily presupposes the position which an individual occupies with regard to the knowledge of Christ; taken separately therefrom, the passage *must* be misunderstood. According to the comparison of Heb. vi 4 sqq, x. 26 sqq, 1 John v. 16, all such views must be discarded, *in the first place*, as have a tendency to reduce the sin against the Holy Ghost to local and temporal circumstances,[1] so that it may not have been committed in any sense either before or afterwards. *In the second place*, every explanation is to be discarded, which is void of a due regard to the moral earnestness contained in the words, inasmuch as it affixes to the words: "that sin committed towards the Holy Ghost cannot be forgiven" (notwithstanding the addition, neither in this world, nor in the one to come), the meaning, that it can be forgiven, only *with more difficulty* than other sins. But *finally*, the true knowledge of Christ must discard likewise every explanation of this remarkable passage, which comprehends, by the sin against the Holy Ghost, an *act* altogether independent of the moral position of the individual sinning, for it must ever be regarded as the result of a previous sinful development of life. As the two first modes of viewing it destroy the profound meaning of the word of God, and connect the most important moral circumstances with localities or vague phrases; so does the latter mode of viewing lead to errors which overburthen conscience, inasmuch as an unhappy being may easily be plunged into sin in an unguarded moment of his life, which is sometimes described as the sin against the Holy Ghost Certainly as regards the Biblical exposition thereof, even the already quoted passages (Heb vi. 4 sqq.; x. 26 sqq ; 1 John v. 16) lead to the possibility of a fearful increase of sin, in which man is as little disposed to believe, as in the development of good, as it is taught in the doctrine of Christian justice or righteousness ($\delta\iota\kappa\alpha\iota o\sigma\acute{\upsilon}\nu\eta$ $\tau o\~{\upsilon}$ $\Theta\epsilon o\~{\upsilon}$, "the righteousness of God.") For even if the expression: $\beta\lambda\alpha\sigma\varphi\eta\mu\epsilon\~{\iota}\nu$ $\epsilon\iota\varsigma$ $\tau\grave{o}$ $\pi\nu\epsilon\~{\upsilon}\mu\alpha$ $\tau\grave{o}$ $\ddot{\alpha}\gamma\iota o\nu$, "the blaspheming against the Holy Ghost," is wanting in those passages, and even if, in fact, the point at issue is something else, viz the loss of the more exalted life in Christ already received, whereas the question at issue seems to be the refusal of the one to be received,[2] yet is the comparison of such parallel passages

[1] Who does not recall here to his mind the strange definition given by *Reinhard* (Dogm p 321) of the sin against the Holy Ghost, concerning which this writer says delictum quorundam Judaeorum (!) qui summa pertinacia ducti, miracula Jesu, quorum evidentiam negare non poterant, a diabolo proficisci criminabantur "a sin of certain Jews (!) who incited by the most determined opposition, when they could not deny the evidence of the miracles of Jesus, denounced them as proceeding from the devil" This exposition is the more inapplicable, inasmuch as the gospel-history does not say that the Pharisees who held the language (Matth xii 24) had *committed* the sin towards the Holy Ghost, they only appear as likely to do it, and it is against this that Jesus warns them

[2] Lucke says on 1 John v. 16, (p 233) that the sin against the Holy

not *unimportant*, namely, as we recognise therefrom the powerful conception of the words οὐκ ἀφεθήσεται, "it shall not be forgiven." As a parallel in another view the remarkable passage from Matt. x. 41, 42, presents itself to our notice. For, as there was expressed in this passage of St Matthew, already explained above, the gradation of good and the reward to be expected thereby, so is here taught, in like manner, the parallel gradation of evil, and its concomitant perdition. Only, the degrees are here not so clearly defined as in the passage x 41, 42, but it is evident from an accurate examination that here too are to be distinguished *three* degrees of sin, as there of righteousness. That the βλασφημία τοῦ πνεύματος, "blaspheming of the Spirit," or the εἰπεῖν, "speaking," (sc. λόγον, "a word," κατὰ τοῦ πνεύματος τοῦ ἁγίου, "against the Holy Ghost," is the deepest degree of guilt, is generally acknowledged, but how the εἰπεῖν λόγον κατὰ τοῦ υἱοῦ τοῦ ἀνθρώπου, "speaking a word against the Son of man," is to be distinguished therefrom, is altogether doubtful. Some have been disposed to regard the ὁ υἱὸς τοῦ ἀνθρώπου, "the Son of man"= ἄνθρωπος, "man," as we find it in Mark iii 28: πάντα ἀφεθήσεται τὰ, ἁμαρτήματα τοῖς υἱοῖς τῶν ἀνθρώπων, "all sins shall be forgiven to the sons of men." (According to the Hebrew בְּנֵי אָדָם, "sons of man.") But, this mode of interpretation is altogether inadmissible, for this simple reason, that the singular, ὁ υἱὸς τοῦ ἀνθρώπου, "the Son of man" with the article, is never used as a general designation of man; on the contrary, it is the name of the Messiah, and stands parallel with the πνεῦμα ἅγιον, "Holy Ghost." The sin against the Son of man accordingly becomes apparent as something peculiar through the formula: καὶ ὅς ἂν, "and whosoever" (ἐάν is a less authorised reading) εἴπῃ λόγον, "speaketh a word." After having observed in the second part of ver. 31, that: the βλασφημία τοῦ πνεύματος, "blasphemy of the Spirit," will not be forgiven, the sin against the Son of man is mentioned in especial with

Ghost is a species of the ἁμαρτία πρὸς θάνατον, "sin unto death," spoken of by St John in the passage referred to I am rather inclined to place it on a level therewith, than to consider it as subordinate thereto, for we might even say that the sin designated by St John is the sin against the Holy Ghost The difference between the two expressions appears to consist merely in this, that the name *sin against the Holy Ghost*, places the object before us, and that the sin is referred thereto. The name *sin unto death*, on the contrary, places in the foreground the consequences of the sin, as regards the subject committing the sin (Compare Lehnerdt's treatise on the text 1 John v 16. Konigsberg 1832) the remark, that *it* also will be forgiven.—More obscurely indicated the *third* class certainly is, inasmuch as the Father is not expressly mentioned together with the Spirit and the Son; but in the words: πᾶσα ἁμαρτία καὶ βλασφημία ἀφεθήσεται τοῖς ἀνθρώποις, literally: " all sin and blasphemy shall be forgiven to men" (Matt. xii. 31, comp. Mark iii. 28,) is necessarily contained the reference to the Father. For, every sin, especially every blasphemy, has in its remote sense a reference to God [1] A blasphemy can by no means be uttered either in reference to angel or man. Here accordingly appear three degrees of sinfulness, firstly, sin against God the Father, secondly, against the Son, and thirdly and lastly, against the Holy Ghost. For the two former degrees there exists the *possibility* of forgiveness, (on the supposition of repentance and faith,) for the latter only it is excluded Hence, this gradation affords the safest guide to a just interpretation of the text. For, as it has already been observed above on Matth. x. 41, 42, that the merit of an action is determined both according to the importance of the object on which it is conferred, (so that it is not a matter of indifference in a political point of view, whether I confer a benefit on a peasant or on a king, on a prophet or on a righteous man,) and also according to the point of moral development occupied by the individual performing the action; thus also is it exactly with regard to the augmentation of the sin. The internal position or nature of the subject or individual acting, and the relation in which the action stands to the object thereof, determine the degree of guilt. The Redeemer had here to do with persons who recognised as their calling the occupation with divine things, and who had attained to a certain degree of internal, i. e. moral development; the higher this was conceived to be, the more perilous became their position, if

---

[1] It is only apparently that some passages form a contradiction thereto, passages, in which, as in vi 11, of the Acts of the Apostles, βλάσφημα ῥήματα λαλεῖν, " to speak blasphemous words," is applied as referring to man, for, in that passage, Moses is looked upon as a divine ambassador, hence, the will of God is blasphemed in his person, whence it is added in words to explain this· εἰς Μωυσῆν καὶ τὸν Θεόν, " against Moses and God " In Rom xiv 16, τὸ ἀγαθὸν, " that which is good," is placed only for that which is Divine, just as in 2 Peter ii. 2, where ὁδὸς τῆς ἀληθείας, " the way of truth," stands for the ordinance of God Of course, what applies to Moses, applies likewise to the apostles (Comp. Rom iii 8, 1 Cor iv 13, x 30) This with reference to the remarks of *Grashoff*, as above cited, pages 955, sqq

they, notwithstanding, gave themselves up to sin. A child is incapable of committing a blasphemy, because it has no knowledge of God; hence, it only talks at random, or utters *words void of sense*, because its internal nature is incapable of comprehending that which the words refer to. But, the Pharisees, who bore within themselves the knowledge of Divine things, and who, notwithstanding, hardened themselves against his exhortations, required this warning; that men can grow so completely callous towards the impressions of what is Divine, that no reconciliation is for them any longer possible; such a word, uttered with the force of love, might yet rouse their heart from the state of carnal security in which they were staggering along on the brink of the abyss. But the Saviour of the world wishes nevertheless to deprive no one of the consolation of forgiveness, he adjudges it to all ἁμαρτία, " sin," and βλασφημία, " blasphemy," pre-supposing, as a matter of course, true repentance and right faith. The ἁμαρτίαι, " sins," as distinguished from βλασφημίαι, "blasphemies," are sins, the immediate object of which is man, or any other creature; βλασφημίαι, " blasphemies," on the contrary, denote sins that have a reference to God himself In order to be able to commit these, a knowledge of God is therefore pre-supposed, and then a degree of sinfulness which goes beyond, or oversteps the light of this knowledge.[1] Such an internal situation is nevertheless represented as one, which still affords a hope for redemption, the predominance of grace is able to stir up in the inner man the concealed susceptibility for that which is good. But, if the higher revelations of the Divine nature of Christ also be firmly rejected; if the moral development be increased to the degree of capability to receive the Holy Ghost, and if man from impurity close his heart to the light thereof, forgiveness and redemption then become impossible, inasmuch as the *internal susceptibility* of being moved by that which is holy dies away entirely. The gradation of sin, therefore, appears here conditioned by the development of the internal consciousness and the deeper knowledge of Divine things thereby made practicable. He who has attained to the point of a general knowledge of God, can, therefore, sin only against God the Father, on the contrary, he who through a

---

[1] Hence, a so-called cursing or swearing, and thoughtless misuse of the name of God is here out of the question, for, in as far as this takes place merely in a thoughtless manner, this very thoughtlessness is the sin, which can effect no *such* guilt

more perfect development is in a position to recognise the Son of man, can likewise reject the deeper, more inward revelations of Divine things, that announce themselves in him; he on the contrary, who is able to recognise that which is Divine in its purest and clearest state of revelation, as the Holy Ghost, may, through inward impurity of the heart, harden himself against the clearest voice of truth.[1] Hence, a high development of spiritual knowledge is no warrant against sin, on the contrary, the greatest sin pre-supposes the greatest degree of knowledge.[2] Only purity, uprightness, and humility of heart afford such security in every degree of development But, inasmuch as these very faculties of the mind were wanting in the Pharisees, hence, they were *in the way* to commit the sin against the Holy Ghost.

Without entering, therefore, already here upon a more minute disquisition concerning the doctrine of the Trinity, let us simply regard the Father, Son, and Spirit, as gradations in the revelation of the Divine Being. The knowledge of God as the Father refers to his power and wisdom, that of the Son refers to his love and mercy, and that of the (Holy) Ghost refers to the holiness and perfection of the *one* Divine Being. Whosoever is able to recognise the holiness and perfection of the Divinity, according to the degree of development of his knowledge (and this not only in mere imagination, but in reality), and closes his heart, notwithstanding this, to their influences, nay, calls holiness itself unholiness, such a being demonstrates, that his internal eye is darkness. According to this, the λόγον εἰπεῖν κατὰ τοῦ υἱοῦ τοῦ ἀνθρώπου, "to speak a word against the Son of Man," must not be regarded as signifying merely, "to speak against the unattractive human appearance of the Messiah,"[3] it must be distinctly

---

[1] Moreover, the *resisting* the Holy Ghost (Acts of the Apostles vii. 51,) the *grieving* of the same (Ephes. iv. 30), even the *embittering* and *provoking* of the Holy Ghost, (Is lxiii 10), is still to be well distinguished from the *blaspheming* thereof, which is the mortal sin against the Holy Ghost. *Grashoff* (as already referred to, p. 947,) again considers the blasphemy against the Holy Ghost as a species of the genus sin against the Holy Ghost This is a view, however, which does not seem to be countenanced by our text

[2] The Reformed, i e, Calvinistic, church, asserts that merely on account of predestination, it is impossible for a regenerated person to commit the sin against the Holy Ghost, the Lutheran church, on the contrary, teaches that it is such a person only who is capable of committing it

[3] This view would be on the whole similar to the one above referred

understood, that such a sinner felt an internal impression of the divinity that shone forth in the appearance of Jesus, and that he gave no place to such an impression. Whosoever opposes himself to the intense or melting power of such a revelation, sins heinously; yet, perfect holiness and its impressions, the result of which is fear and dread, may contribute to overcome the obduracy engendered thereby; but wherever it also is rejected, there is spiritual death It is altogether a departure from the point of view for a right understanding of the text, if the πνεῦμα ἅγιον, "Holy Ghost," be applied only to the general power of God that was revealed in the miracles.[1] How, in the non-recognition of such a power, which creates merely an impression of might, a sin can, or is to be, committed, which is never to be forgiven, can be the less conceived, inasmuch as evil miracles also may be performed, which are the results of diabolical powers, and so deceptive, that even the elect, were it possible, might be misled thereby (Matth. xxix. 24); forgiveness, then, here appears in its proper place. The πνεῦμα ἅγιον, "Holy Ghost," is here the highest revelation of God, as of the absolute holy and perfect one. Hence, in so far as the divinity dwelt in the person of Jesus, and as Father, Son, and Spirit were also inseparably connected, the impurity of man, in proportion to the degree of its development, might sin in the person of Jesus against Father, Son, and Spirit, in proportion as they perseveringly withstood the effects of divine power, love, and holiness, which proceed from him. On the other hand, purity of mind, combined with an equally developed knowledge, can receive through him Father, Son, and Spirit. But, wherever the perception for the higher revelation of the divinity in humanity, such as it appeared in Christ, was as yet quite shut out, there a man might fancy he beheld in the person of Jesus a prophet or righteous man in the Old Testament sense,

to, according to which υἱὸς τοῦ ἀνθρώπου, "the Son of man," is = ἄνθρωπος, "man" For, whosoever sees *in reality* in Christ only what is purely human, because he is not possessed of a deeper susceptibility, i. e perception, of what is divine, sins no more in cursing or swearing against Christ, than were he to do so against any other human being. The inward *intention*, which, of course, is known to God only, is the measure of the action

[1] Πνεῦμα ἅγιον, "the Holy Ghost," always refers to things ethical, i e moral, the notion of mere power is here left in the background. On the contrary, πνεῦμα, "spirit," by itself, as for example Matth xii. 28, signifies as much as power, only with reference to its higher origin

and that he received from him the blessing which was needful for him in his position Thus was the Redeemer *all* things to all men, to the pure in heart he was a dispenser of blessings for all the degrees of their development; to the impure he was a reproving judge, in the first place, in order to lead them to repentance, and, in the second place, whenever they had shut up the road thereto by their obduracy, to lead them to judgment (Luke ii. 34). Hence, that according to this, the sin against the Holy Ghost may even now be committed, is clear, for, since the divinity in the person of Jesus reveals itself incessantly in the church, so can sin in individual men, even in the highest points of development, set itself in opposition to his beneficent influences Were it not so, either the time in which such a sin was alone possible would appear to be kept in the background, or the earnestness with which the Redeemer speaks thereof would appear somewhat remarkable. But if, as is frequently the case with persons that are touched by the effects of grace, earnest repentance is accompanied by the idea, that they may have committed the sin against the Holy Ghost, and that they may be in consequence thereof excluded from forgiveness—an idea which may be of highly pernicious consequences in susceptible minds, and may at least keep back for a time consolation through the word of grace; therefore, every man who is charged with the care of souls, or who is asked for advice, may invite all such with a cheerful heart, by faith to cry for mercy For, whosoever grieves himself with the notion that he may have committed the sin against the Holy Spirit, proves already by his grief and self-accusation that he has not done so—He who has really committed it will harden himself against every accusation —but if the sin should have developed itself in a highly critical form in any mind, so that the pain of repentance, as in the case of Judas Iscariot, should degenerate into despair, then is the exhortation to belief in forgiving love still in its right place, inasmuch as the sin against the Holy Ghost is not unpardonable because God *will* not forgive, but because the capability of believing that God *can* forgive has departed from his creature. Therefore, if the announcement of grace retains its hold on the heart, then is the actual conviction that the sin against the Holy Ghost has not been committed borne in upon it.

The text which here occupies our attention, is likewise the chief doctrinal passage to prove the doctrine of everlasting punishment. All other passages or texts which treat of an αἰώνιος κρίσις, "eternal condemnation," are more vague, i e. less precise than this, in which it is expressly added, ἐν τῷ αἰῶνι μέλλοντι, "in the world which is to come." It is true, indeed, that the expression, αἰών, "an age, a period," αἰώνιος, "eternal, endless" (in the phrases, εἰς τὸν αἰῶνα, "to eternity, for ever, never," αἰώνιος κρίσις, "eternal damnation," in St Mark), as also the formula, αἰὼν οὗτος, "this world," and μέλλον, "that which is to come" (as in St Matthew), has a sense capable of various interpretations. The Bible knows nothing of metaphysical definitions, whence it is deficient in an expression for eternity = timelessness (Zeitlosigkeit) absence of time. All the biblical expressions thereof imply, or denote, long periods connected with one another. The formula, εἰς τον αἰῶνα, "to eternity, for ever," is in every respect parallel with the others, εἰς τοὺς αἰῶνας, "for ages, for ever," εἰς τοὺς αἰῶνας τῶν αἰώνων, "for ages of ages, for ever and ever" (Gal. i. 5), expressions which denote the *aeternitas a parte post*, or the *future* conceived as an indefinitely extended period; but the expression, ἀπ' αἰῶνας, "from ages, from everlasting," is = ἀπὸ τῶν αἰώνων, "from all eternity," πρὸ τῶν αἰώνων, "before all ages, before the worlds," which expresses the *aeternitas a parte ante*, or the *past*, conceived as an indefinitely extended period. Αἰων, "an age, the world," is therefore, like עוֹלָם, "for ever, the world or universe" = αἰῶνες, "ages," עוֹלָמִים, as the formula, συντέλεια τοῦ αἰῶνος, "the consummation, end of the world," shows, which is synonymous with συντέλεια τῶν αἰώνων, "the consummation of all ages or times." (Comp. 1 Cor x. 11 on the expression, τὰ τέλη τῶν αἰώνων, "the ends of the world.") But, inasmuch as the same expressions are applied to the eternity of God, as also to a long-enduring period according to the mode of conception of the creature; since the expressions, κρίσις, "damnation," κόλασις αἰώνιος, "eternal punishment," κρίμα, "judgment," πῦρ αἰώνιον, "eternal fire," form the contrast to ζωὴ αἰώνιος, "eternal life," no objections can be raised from a philological point of view against the eternity, or everlasting duration of punishment. But, the sentiment which is expressed by the defenders of an ἀποκατάστασις τῶν πάντων, "the restoration of all things" (of which there has existed at all times, but at no former period so many as at the present one), against the doctrine of the eternity of the punishment of the wicked, may be frequently based on a feeble moral consciousness, yet it has, no doubt, a deep root in noble minds; it is the expression of a heartfelt desire for a consummate harmony throughout creation But, considered from a purely exegetical point of view, we must confess, that no passage in the New Testament affords a clear and *positive* testimony for the consummation of this heartfelt desire. The expressions made use of in Scripture, which denote the resolution of the disharmony caused by sin into harmony, such as ἄφεσις, "deliverance," καταλλαγή, "reconciliation," and ἀπολύτρωσις, "redemption, deliverance from," all imply a being fettered by the power of the evil one, together with a mixed state of good and evil, as we find it in human nature, and which is the result of the fall of Adam. Hence, the above-mentioned ideas are never applicable, according to Scripture doctrine, to the spirits of the kingdom of darkness, or to men that have become the prey of this kingdom, because of their firm and continued opposition to the drawings or leadings of grace. But, were we to say that evil, as a thing created and temporal, must share likewise the general character of that which is temporal (des Zeitlichen), annihilation, cessation (das Aufhoren), and that the ages of the course of this world, even if they bring a lasting punishment to evil, must ultimately have an end; so, it is true, that there is a passage in Scripture which points to this passing away of time itself, with all its temporary phenomena, into the abyss of eternity, as to a timeless period, this text is the obscure or mysterious words contained in 1 Cor. xv. 28 (to which compare the exposition). But, the mysterious character of the passage itself, coupled with the circumstance, that no mention is made therein concerning evil and its dissolution, afford an authority for scarcely more than conjectural inferences to be drawn therefrom, with regard to the endless duration of punishment, the words of the Saviour, as contained in St Matth. xii 32, remain a fearful testimony as to the terrible character of sin and its consequences.[1] But, as

[1] Were we to interpret our text, 1 Cor xv 28, in such a manner that here it may merely mean that the sin committed against the Holy Ghost is forgiven neither in this nor in that world, but, that it may obtain forgiveness after that life· then this would evidently contradict the meaning of the author. For, the οὐκ ἀφεθήσεται, "it shall not be forgiven," of Matth xii. 32, is in a decided manner contrasted with the ἀφεθήσεται, "it shall be forgiven," the addition οὐκ ἐν τούτῳ τῷ αἰῶνι, οὔτε ἐν τῷ μέλλοντι, "not in this world, neither in that which is to come," is only made use of to exhaust completely the οὐκ, "not," hence

they are this, so are the same words in like manner a consolation, inasmuch as they promise the possibility of a forgiveness even of sins committed against the Father and the Son, and hence for very spiritual forms thereof. And certainly the addition: οὔτε ἐν τῷ μέλλοντι αἰῶνι, "neither in the world that is to come," will not be strained too far, if we infer: "that all other sins can then be forgiven in the world to come," of course, as has been already observed, under the general pre-suppositions of repentance and faith. (Comp. on 1 Peter iii. 18 sqq) Texts such as St Matth. v. 26, comp. with xviii. 34, point, indeed, thereto. For, the βληθῆναι εἰς φυλακὴν, ἕως ἂν ἀποδῷ τὸν ἔσχατον κοδράντην, "being cast into prison until he have paid the last farthing," is evidently very distinct from the κρίσις αἰώνιος, "eternal condemnation." (See the observations of Matth. xviii. 34; Luke xvi. 19 sqq.) But, that the doctrine of the forgiveness of some sins in the αἰὼν μέλλων, "the world to come" forms no contradiction with the doctrine of the judgment, is pointed out in the following exposition of the relation of the αἰὼν οὗτος, "this world," to the μέλλων, "that which is to come." For the former expression the New Testament gives also ὁ νῦν αἰών, "the world which now is, the present world," (Tit ii. 12, 2 Tim. iv 10;) καιρὸς οὗτος " this time," (Mark x 30), αἰὼν τοῦ κόσμου τούτου, "the course (cycle) of this world," (Ephes. ii 2), αἰὼν ἐνεστὼς πονηρός, "the present evil world," (Gal. i 4). For αἰὼν μέλλων, "the world which is to come," there stands likewise: αἰὼν ὁ ἐρχόμενος, "the world which is coming," (Mark x. 30), αἰὼν ἐκεῖνος, "that world," (Luke xx. 35), αἰῶνες ἐπερχόμενοι, "the ages (cycles) which are coming," (Ephes. ii 7.) The formula κόσμος μέλλων, "the (visible) world which is to come" is not found. The old dispute concerning the relation thereto of the Rabbinical expression עוֹלָם הַזֶּה, "this world," and הַבָּא, "that which is to come," which was kept up with so much violence between *Witsius* and *Rhenferd*, (Comp *Koppe's* Exc. i on the Epistle to the Ephesians,) as to whether we are to understand by the αἰὼν μέλλων, "the cycle which is to come," the Messianic period, or eternity, is tolerably barren, and does not touch upon the sub-

---

to strengthen, but not to weaken, the sense St Matthew by no means conceives that subsequently to the αἰὼν μέλλων, "the world which is to come," there shall arise another degree of duration of the world (Weltbestand), on the contrary, the same appears as consummated in αἰὼν οὗτος, "this world," and μέλλων, "that which is to come."

stance of the contest; the αἰὼν μέλλων comprehends indeed both, at one and the same time, just as does the βασιλεία τοῦ Θεοῦ, "kingdom of God," (see on Matth. iii. 2), though this certainly does not prevent us from supposing that at one time the one reference, and at another time, the other, predominates in the expression. The αἰὼν μέλλων, "world (cycle) that is to come," forms, in its general acceptation, the contrast to the entire temporal system of this world, the peculiarity of which is that it contains good and evil in a *mixed* state. In so far it stands betwixt and intermediate between the kingdoms of light and darkness, and forms the contrast to the βασιλεία τῶν οὐρανῶν, "kingdom of the heavens," inasmuch as, although that which is good is deeply rooted in the temporal system of this world, yet, does evil, according to appearance, prevail therein, whence the αἰὼν ἐνεστώς, "this present world" is called directly in Gal. i. 4, πονηρός, "evil," a βασιλεία τοῦ ἄρχοντος τοῦ σκότους, "a kingdom of the prince of darkness." With this temporal system of the world is contrasted that which is to come, as one dissolving the mixture of good and evil, and founding the dominion of the former in purity. The expression. αἰὼν μέλλων, "the world which is to come," with its kindred terms, is synonymous, therefore, with the βασιλεία τοῦ Θεοῦ, "kingdom of God," this expression considering the same phenomenon only from another point of view, but in that case, αἰὼν μέλλων is *used* somewhat differently. It has no application to individuals, as we have observed of the βασιλεία τοῦ Θεοῦ, (see on Matth. iii 2); it is nowhere said the αἰὼν μελλων, "world to come," exists *for* some one, or *in* some one in particular. It always refers to the totality of the church, or of mankind The language, on the other hand, entirely corresponds in so far as αἰὼν μέλλων, "the world to come," is conceived like βασιλεία τοῦ Θεοῦ, "the kingdom of God," in a twofold reference to its revelation; in the first place the αἰὼν μέλλων, "the world to come," appears as being already come and in operation; and in the second place, as future. To the view according to which αἰὼν μελλων appears as already existing, belongs, 1 Cor. x. 11; Heb vi 5; ix. 26, in which the συντέλεια τῶν αἰώνων, "consummation of ages (or worlds)," (= τέλη τῶν αἰώνων, "ends of the ages (or worlds)" as the transition of the αἰὼν οὗτος, "this world (age or cycle)" to the μέλλων, "that which is to come" is conceived as being present This must be explained in the same manner, as the similar language when made use of concerning the βασιλεία τοῦ Θεοῦ, "kingdom of God." As the kingdom of God was present in its power with the person of Christ and the foundation of the church, so in like manner did repose therein the next world as present in this one (In the same manner as in St John, where the ζωὴ αἰώνιος, "eternal life, (life of ages)," exists for the believer, not only as that which is future, but as that which is already present. Comp. on 1 John iii. 14.) Generally speaking, however, the idea of the αἰὼν μ. as that which is to come, prevails, and accordingly the appearing thereof takes place only with the συντέλεια τοῦ αἰῶνος, "consummation of the world," (τούτου " of this"), with the manifestation of that which is divine as the ruling and the victorious, and of sin as of that which is excluded. This momentous period the apostles considered as being near, and beyond this, the single moments which might be distinguished therein from one another, especially the first and second resurrection, were as little separated in their minds as such momentous periods appear separately to be defined in the expression βασιλεία τοῦ Θεου, "the kingdom of God." The analogy of the prophets of the Old Testament, who do not separate or distinguish a twofold advent in their prophecies as regards the advent of the Messiah, may serve to explain this phenomenon. (Compare on this subject our further remarks on Matth. xxiv. 1.) Hence, if an ἄφεσις, "forgiveness" in the αἰὼν μέλλων, "world to come" of our text is granted as being possible, there then predominates herein that signification of the expression according to which eternity and the general judgment preceding it is excluded. The αἰὼν μέλλων is here conceived as the world to come, which shall reveal itself at a future period in the victory of that which is good, and sinners in the Sheol (hell) are assumed as belonging thereto. The preaching of the gospel to the unbelieving contemporaries of Noah (1 Peter iii. 18,) involves such a forgiveness in the αἰὼν μέλλων, "world to come" for all those that were inclined to put faith therein.

Ver. 33. What follows seems to be favourable to the opinion of those, who believe that the Pharisees to whom Christ spoke, had committed in their speech (ver. 24,) the sin against the Holy Ghost. Indeed, St Mark seems to speak in favour of this view: ὅτι ἔλεγον πνεῦμα ἀκάθαρτον ἔχει, "because they said he hath an unclean spirit," for, by these words the discourse on the sin against the Holy Ghost is connected with the above blasphemous speech. But, the preceding discourses of Jesus (ver 25, sqq.)

render it in my opinion, as has already been declared above, very improbable, comp. with the texts 1 Cor. ii. 8, Acts of the Apostles xiii. 27, 28; Luke xxiii. 34. For, admitting that the ἄρχοντες, "rulers," herein spoken of, were other than those of our text, as indeed may be assumed, yet can they hardly have been less guilty, inasmuch as they ndeed crucified the Lord of glory, than were these who did not acknowledge his miracles as divine miracles; yet, it is said that they killed him from ἄγνοια, "ignorance." If then, the ἄγνοια was of as guilty a character as possible, yet, can the sin against the Holy Ghost only take place where there is a perfect consciousness, inasmuch as it is to be regarded as the highest degree of development of sinfulness The words in Mark iii. 30 receive indeed their full validity, if the discourse concerning the sin against the Holy Ghost be applied to the conjectural final result of the sin of those Pharisees; for he who, standing in the position of the Pharisees, who were the heads and teachers of the people, and who were in full possession of knowledge, can say of the wonders of the Son of God, who displayed before them all his glory, that they were the operations of the evil spirit, that individual is surely in the way leading directly to the sin against the Holy Ghost, if he be not indeed as yet sufficiently developed to be able to commit the thing itself.

Ver 34, 35. Our Saviour places good and evil in opposition to one another in the contrast of their nature, even as it appears also in physical phenomena; the good tree bears good fruit, the idle or bad tree brings forth that which is bad. (Comp. Matth. vii. 18 sqq —The term ποιεῖν, "to make," ver. 33, is used in a sense analogous to the Latin *facere, ponere;* "to make, to set or plant a tree," &c.) Luke vi 43—45, which must here be compared, is very nearly connected with our text. For, St Luke therein compares in like manner the creative nature of the tree with the internal, i.e. moral productive power of man, (θησαυρός, "treasure," ver. 45,) and adds: that as the fruit expresses the character of the tree, and as we are thus enabled to draw an inference from the one as to the nature of the other, and *vice versa,* so it is likewise with man; wherever the internal source of life has been poisoned, from thence evil actions will proceed. (St Luke gives ver. 45 the very pertinent addition, θησαυρός τῆς καρδίας, "treasure of the heart;" the καρδία, "heart," is here to be viewed as the centre point of the ψυχή, " soul, the principle of life,' consequently of all individual life, of all self-determination [*Selbst-*

I

bestimmung]. Our Lord therefore clearly infers from the general principle: ἐκ τοῦ καρποῦ τὸ δενδρον γινώσκεται, literally: "by the fruit the tree is known,"—that the Pharisees are wicked, and hence that they are in this their state incapable of any good action. He calls them: γεννήματα ἐχιδνῶν, literally "generation of vipers," (see Matt. iii. 7,) and infers from the wicked language which they made use of, as to the state of the inner man, whence it proceeded. (All things external are types of the internal—στόμα, "the mouth," is the counterpart of καρδία, "the heart,"—περίσσευμα, abundance," = θησαυρός, "treasure," the internal fulness of life which is expressed externally in everything, nay, in the feeblest thing existing, in forms the most varied.) But, the whole text, taken independent of the connection with what goes before, possesses difficulties of no trifling character. The parable appears, namely, to sink the moral in the physical, and to assume an internal difference among men, according to which the one are good and the others bad, and according to which, likewise, they *would* of necessity act. And, inasmuch as the Pharisees are here called the bad, it would appear as though the sin against the Holy Ghost is to be ascribed to them as a necessary consequence of the wickedness of their heart, which would refute our view as expressed above. But, in these axioms would be contained that which would contradict the whole doctrine of the Bible, that a necessary distinction is to be assumed among the good as well as the evil, as we cannot assume that any one of the fallen race must, from an indwelling necessity, produce good from out his good treasure, so in like manner must we not assume that any one brings forth in the same manner *only* that which is bad; in *all* fallen human beings good and evil appears in a mixed state. The correct exposition, therefore, of this difficult passage, is, no doubt, that the Redeemer conceived man in his ideal manifestation, in the manner in which He himself represented him, in contradistinction to fallen man, who as the prey of the destructive influence of the kingdom of darkness, without the aid of restoring grace, is a true picture of evil. This forlorn state of humanity was represented by the Pharisees, opposed to the perfect Christ; rejecting the grace and mercy presented to them in his person, they gave place in their heart to the power of darkness, and uttered in their foaming passion the wicked speeches with which they were inspired while under the influence thereof. The kingdom of the devil represents itself as the kingdom of God. Thus the contrast obtains its full keenness, and even the apparently offensive nature thereof contained in the physical necessity which the words of Jesus seem to attribute to the actions of men, assumes its full truthfulness. For man assuredly cannot act out of the element in which his innermost source of life preeminently exists and moves, if this be as yet of a worldly character, man will then act in a worldly manner *in whatsoever he does;* but if the same has assumed a divine nature in consequence of regeneration, his actions will thenceforth be pure and good; the coarse vulgar, *Pelagian* view of freedom is unknown to holy writ. Nor does it indeed recognise aught of an absolute predestination, and a *gratia irresistibilis,* "irresistible grace," whence it is that the contrast in this text is not of an absolute and eternal character. The γεννήματα ἐχιδνῶν, "generation of vipers," which as such *can* do no good. (πῶς δύνασθε, "how can you," of ver. 34, must be taken in the proper spiritual-physical sense of impotency to do good,) may through grace cease to be what they are, and by repentance and faith change their nature. This doctrine the Baptist had already preached, (Matt. iii. 7, 8): γεννήματα ἐχιδνῶν, τίς ὑπέδειξεν ὑμῖν φυγεῖν ἀπὸ τῆς μελλούσης ὀργῆς, which signifies literally: "generation of vipers, who has warned you to flee from the coming wrath?" (that is to say, being such, as you at present are, the old man must die); ποιήσατε οὖν καρπὸν ἄξιον τῆς μετανοίας, i. e. "produce therefore fruit worthy of repentance." And in like manner does Christ here preach, and because he thus preaches repentance to the seed, or generation of vipers, they cannot as yet have committed the sin against the Holy Ghost, for otherwise the preaching of repentance to them would amount to an act of derision practised against them. Hence as the bad tree, bearing in its natural state bitter fruits, can be improved, and be rendered of a superior character by means of a noble graft; so is it in like manner with the natural man, who may be renewed by regeneration to the image of Him, whose heart was overflowing with mercy and redemption.

Ver. 36, 37. The manifest endeavours of the Saviour, to come to the aid of the Pharisees, who were thus precipitating themselves into the abyss of sin, is pointed out in the verses which follow, wherein he places before their eyes the signification of sin in its spiritual form. Inasmuch as they had only *spoken,* and inasmuch as they viewed only *actions* as incurring real guilt hence they might have regarded their sin as a matter of little importance, but Jesus leads them to a higher moral point of view, according to which it is the spiritual intention,—supposing it even to reveal itself in a mere *word*,—which becomes the object of Divine justice. The ῥῆμα ἀργόν, "useless word," (it must be taken as nom. absol.) was evidently chosen in contradistinction to the πονηρόν, " evil word," which they had spoken; ἀργόν, " idle, unprofitable,"=ἀεργόν, " idle, inoperative," ἄχρηστον, "useless, unprofitable, vain," an expression denoting an inferior degree of liability to punishment,[1] but heightens thereby the sense, or meaning. In the λόγον ἀποδιδόναι, " to give an account," is indicated in the first place that even the most secret emotions of evil find their punishment in the eye of God. And the more spiritual the word is the more punishable becomes its abuse; yea, it is the word, which as the expression of the inner man, reveals the whole nature of the man. With the λόγοι, "words," are contrasted ἔργα, "works," these latter appear to the sensual man of greater importance, because they affect more his sensual nature. But every action is in fact an embodied word, or every word may become the mother of an action. It is in this internal, i e. moral sense, that our Redeemer here considers the word, and hence makes it the subject of judgment. As man speaks, so he is; as he is, so he is judged. Hence the λόγοι, "words," are not only outward, or uttered words, but more particularly internal or meditated words, which represent the spiritual emotions of the internal life; whosoever utters, therefore, good words in a hypocritical manner, is also judged indeed according to his words, because they are hypocritical words. (Δικαιοῦσθαι, " to be justified," is the reverse of καταδικαζεσθαι, " to be condemned,"=κατακρίνεσθαι, " to be sentenced, condemned," *pro justo declari*, " to be declared a just man," but under the assumption of being just and righteous, [see Rom. iii. 21.] The passage ἐκ τῶν λόγων, " by words," expresses, or contains, the determinate power of the λόγοι, "words," with regard to the κρίσις, "judgment."

Ver 38 In St Matth this is closely followed by a severe lecture, or admonition, addressed to some Pharisees, who wished to see a sign, of which St Luke contains the elements, and although

---

[1] *Chrysostom* has already pointed this out; he understands by ῥῆμα ἀργόν, not only wicked but also useless words, τὸ μάταιον, τὸ γέλωτα κινοῦν ἄτακτον, " to set agoing idle silly discourse lightly or licentiously."

in a different order, yet do they literally agree with the same. The connection in St Matthew is simple and plain, so that nothing can be said against the introduction of the discourse in this place; the whole description of St Luke, however, bears more the stamp of originality, and hence we shall also do well in giving it the preference here. But whether the τινές, " some," who here demand the sign, were one and the same with the Pharisees, who uttered the blasphemies as above, ver. 24, (of whom St Luke xi. 15, says, τινὲς ἐξ αὐτῶν, " some of them,") or not, matters little as regards the exposition; the expressions made use of by our Lord, in order to dismiss them (ver 39,) show that they occupied the same ethical, i. e. moral, position with the others. St Luke xi. 16, where their request of a σημεῖον, " sign," is anticipated, however, renders the supposition very probable that one party expressed itself in this manner, in order to put him to the test, and the other in another manner. (St Luke xi. 16, ἕτεροι δὲ πειράζοντες σημεῖον παρ᾽ αὐτοῦ ἐζήτουν ἐξ οὐρανοῦ, signifying, " and others, tempting him, sought of him a sign from heaven.") The σημεῖον, " sign," appears at the same time distinctly expressed as one ἐξ οὐρανοῦ, " from heaven." A σημεῖον, " sign," (אוֹת) is to be conceived as a miracle not *per se*, but in its relation to something else, (St Matt. xxiv. 24,); hence as it proves, signifies, and points out something, in this case it is the Messianic character of Jesus. Independent of any miraculous nature, as a mere testimony for the internal direction or tendency of the Spirit, (innere Geistesrichtung), as Dr *Paulus* wishes to have the word applied, it never occurs in the New Testament. The σημεῖα ἐξ οὐρανοῦ, " signs from heaven," (or ἀπὸ τοῦ οὐρανοῦ, " from the heaven," according to St Mark viii. 11, as also ἐν τῷ οὐρανῷ, " in the heaven," Rev. xii. 1,) are the reverse, i. e. form the contrast to σημεῖα ἐπὶ τῆς γῆς, " signs upon the earth," and appear to sensual man to be a requisite of the Messiah, inasmuch as they presuppose a greater power.

Ver. 39. Jesus dismissed them and their demand in a severe and reproachful manner. (Γενεά=דּוֹר, "generation," signifies primarily, "the period of life," and then those living together within a certain period; comp. on St Matth. xxiv. 34.—In the same combination as it does here, μοιχαλίς, " adulterous," occurs also again in Matth. xvi. 4, which passage forms a real and verbal parallel to this one. The expression must here be explained in accordance with the pervading Old Testament manner of speaking, according to which everything of an unbelieving and unholy character is regarded as born of unholy love, implying therefore a separation of the soul from the Lord. This spiritual turning away of the soul from the Creator to the creature is represented as adultery, according to a profound mode of viewing the relation existing between the soul and God, to which frequent references will be made hereafter.[1] Comp. *Gesenius*, Hebrew Lex. sub. verbis זָנָה, זְנוּנִים, "fornication, whoredom, adultery," זְנוּת, "whoredom." The rebuffing of these miracle-sick individuals (dieser Wundersüchtigen,) forms evidently no contradiction with the worth or value which Christ otherwise places on his miracles (John v. 20; x. 25) For, as the objects of the miracles were altogether of a moral tendency, hence they presupposed a disposition of mind susceptible of what was holy or sacred, wherever this was wanting they had so little effect that even miracles of the most astounding character could be ascribed to an unholy power (ver. 24). Hence it is made evident as the curse of sin, that that which is divine in its exalted and blessing revelations is withheld from it; to the wicked race belongs only an invisible sign like unto that of the prophet Jonas.

Ver. 40. In how far the Redeemer will give to the Pharisees a sign of the prophet Jonas, the evangelist himself points out in the words: ὥσπερ γάρ κ. τ. λ., "for like as," &c.[2] There is no doubt but that there exists more than one signification in the parallel here brought forward, between the resurrection of Jesus and the fate of Jonas. In the first place, both concern the person himself, (whence St Luke expresses himself, xi. 30: ἐγένετο Ἰωνᾶς σημεῖον, "Jonas was a sign," he himself *was* the sign); in the second place, the rescuing of Jonas from the fish, was like the resurrection of Jesus, an invisible sign given only to the

---

[1] Comparisons with John viii., 41 are here wholly inadmissible; μοιχαλίς, "adulterous," does not signify begotten of adultery (*spurius*), but practising adultery.

[2] *De Wette* thinks falsely, that St Matthew has explained in an erroneous manner the decision of Jesus, and in the same manner that St John ii 21, has misunderstood a similar decision But, the explanation of St John is as little erroneous (comp the Comment on John ii 21,) as is here the proposition ὥσπερ κ. τ. λ., a false self-made exposition of St Matthew The main reason by which *De Wette* seems to have been actuated in adopting that view, is the opinion, that it is doubtful: "Whether Jesus thus distinctly predicted his resurrection," or declared openly whether he were to arise at all.

faith (of the adversaries); furthermore, the ἐν τῇ κοιλίᾳ κήτους, "in the belly of the whale," together with the ἐν τῇ καρδίᾳ τῆς γῆς, "in the heart of the earth," may serve also as a parallel, in contradistinction to the σημεῖον ἐκ τοῦ οὐρανοῦ, "sign from heaven." But the main signification which forms the mediate link between the whole connection, is this: that as the preservation of Jonas was an invisible one to the Ninevites, so also the greatest miracle which takes place in the person of the Son of man, was to be to the Pharisees one of an invisible nature; the mystery of the glory of the Lord is withheld from the vulgar eyes of the adulterous generation The exposition of this passage attempted of late, according to which the σημεῖον Ἰωνᾶ, "sign of Jonas," is said to be his sermon to the Ninevites, (according to which ver. 40 is turned into a misunderstood interpretation by St Matthew of the words of Jesus,) has proceeded from a total mistake of the whole context, and hence sufficiently refutes itself. Moreover, the reference contained in the words of Jesus to the history of Jonas, contains for the biblical expounder an important hint with regard to the exposition of the Old Testament work, to which it refers. The exposition itself, however, has no further connection with the question here at issue. Jesus makes use of what occurred to Jonas also under other circumstances, (St Matthew xvi. 1 sqq.), in order to compare his resurrection therewith. The τρεῖς ἡμέραι καὶ τρεῖς νύκτες, "three days and three nights," must be explained according to the Hebrew mode of speech. A νυχθήμερον, "day and night," = יום, "day," without twenty-four hours having run exactly three times their course. But the Redeemer rested during three days in the tomb, and hence, he thus fulfilled his prediction. With all the precision to be discovered throughout the Scriptures, we never meet therein with any trivial painstaking and anxious striving, as in nature, so in like manner do we find therein regularity combined with freedom, and hence it is that it affords scope for freedom, that it places and fulfils all the prophecies in such a manner, that they may be believed and yet may be contradicted. The holy Scriptures would fail entirely in attaining their object, were they to *compel* the reader to the adoption thereof, by means of mathematical precision.—We must not overlook the parallel existing between ἐν τῇ κοιλίᾳ τοῦ κήτους, "in the belly of the whale," and ἐν τῇ καρδίᾳ τῆς γῆς, "in the heart of the earth." The former words follow the Septuagint, which renders the words דָּג גָּדוֹל, "great fish" of Jon. i. 17, κῆτος, "a whale." The καρδία = לֵב, "heart" expresses the internal parts in general. The expression, however, does not seem to be proper in reference to the repose in the tomb; nor is the parallel a close one. The question is, whether these mysterious words have not rather a further reference to the state of the soul of Jesus after his death, (comp. 1 Peter iii. 19; Ephes. iv. 8.)? The words bear only a general inferential character, and hence, they may at the time when they were uttered, have been understood neither by the Pharisees nor by the disciples, as was the case with so many other expressions of our Lord, the deep meaning of which became clear to them only at a later period Our Lord, moreover, had not as yet spoken distinctly concerning his death; hence, the whole acquired, as indeed it must, a mysterious character; it was, as it were, a hieroglyph for the time present, which was only to be interpreted by a future generation. It may be said, that in passages such as these, our Redeemer prophesied of and for himself; for, although the whole great process of his work lay, no doubt, clear and distinct before his soul, as soon as he had begun it at his baptism in the Jordan, yet, it is not improbable, that the isolated momentous events therein displayed, especially his death, and the individual points connected therewith, assumed by degrees only a more definite form before his human eye. The history of the transfiguration (Matt. xvii. 1 sqq) seems to speak in favour of this view. (For the particulars, see the exposition of the passage here referred to.)

Ver. 41, 42. The mention of the history of Jonas led our Lord, in the course of his discourse, to another event, whereby he was enabled to point out the fallen state of the generation of his period. Although a visible sign had not been vouchsafed to the Ninevites, yet they believed at the preaching of repentance by Jonas, and the queen of the south (Sheba) hastened uninvited to Solomon, in order to learn wisdom from him. The Pharisees received not even that which was presented to them. The severe admonition contained in the comparison, was the more cutting, inasmuch as it was the *heathen* who, in both cases, gave these proofs of belief, and above whom the Jews were so fond of exalting themselves; just as was the case in the similar parallel at xi. 20 sqq. The judgment and the resurrection is here too again given as the period of final unerring decision, in which all is laid open exactly as it is in the innermost being. Νινευῖται, "Ninevites," = ἄνδρες Νινευί = אַנְשֵׁי נִינְוֵה, "men of Nineveh," according to the well-known Hebraism. Jos. viii. 20; x. 6.—The βασίλισσα νότου, "queen of the south," is the מַלְכַּת שְׁבָא, "queen of Sheba," 1 Kings x. 1. The expression νότος points, in a vague manner, towards the south, to *Arabia Felix*. The πέρατα τῆς γῆς, אַפְסֵי הָאָרֶץ, "ends of the earth," is a well-known expression of the old Testament, borrowed from the popular view of the world. The smaller the splendour was, by which the Ninevites and the Arabian queen permitted themselves to be overcome, the more culpable must appear the struggle against the ideal of holiness itself. (Πλεῖον Ἰωνᾶ, Σολομῶνος ὧδε, "a greater than Jonah, than Solomon is here," compare St Matt. xii. 8.)

Ver. 43. St Luke, who throughout the whole of his eleventh chapter has arranged the elementary parts thereof with peculiar propriety, as we shall see hereafter, and who has introduced at the verses 27 and 28, a little separate story, gives the words which follow (St Matt. xii. 43—45,) in immediate connection with the demoniac and his healing, concerning whom everything has been related also in St Matth. xii 22 sqq. St Matthew, on the contrary, after his usual manner, has introduced these words, which might indeed very properly have taken their place next to the story of the healing, in an independent, and by no means spiritless manner. He places them after the concluding words of ver. 45, οὕτως ἔσται ἐν τῇ γενεᾷ ταύτῃ τῇ πονηρᾷ, "even thus shall it be unto this wicked generation," in connection with the main conversation respecting the γενεὰ πονηρὰ καὶ μοιχαλίς, "wicked and adulterous generation," (ver. 39). It appears here, indeed, singular, how such a thing could be said of the Pharisees, who are nevertheless to be understood as included in the γενεὰ μοιχαλίς, "adulterous generation," ver. 39. For, inasmuch as no demon was cast out from them, it is not possible to see, how such an one could return into them. For, inasmuch as there also dwelt in their hearts neither longing nor faith, so can it as little be perceived how the casting out of a demon could form the question at issue, were we in any way to regard the return of the same as something expected to take place at a future period.

Their ἀπιστία, "want of faith," itself could be regarded as the demon to be driven out, only from a misunderstanding of the text. But, as the Pharisees, representing the *pars pro toto*, "the part for the whole," might very well be regarded as representing the whole nation which had received or adopted their spirit, so in like manner could the Jewish people of that period, regarded in the light of a greater individuality, be taken together with the Israelitish people of former times, and be regarded as an individual personification in different moments, or at different periods of development. That there were always some among the people, as for example the apostles, and other noble-minded individuals, who did not exhibit the general character of corruption, affords no ground why such a view should not be adopted; all these belonged, as such properly speaking, not to the people, but occupied a station that was far above them. The Babylonian captivity appears in the history of the Jewish nation as the period of purification thereof, as a true casting out of the devil of idolatry under fearful paroxsyms. The Jews, indeed, were after their return from captivity much purer than before; but, instead of idolatry, the more pernicious Phariseeism returned, which was in the end the same spirit of idolatry, only under other forms. It was in the fetters of this spirit that our Redeemer found the nation, which would not even suffer itself again to be redeemed, so that it was like unto a maniac, possessed by an evil spirit, who was sunk back into his former state of disease. A profound and significant application of the comparison! The only thing inconsistent therewith, would be the future tense made use of, ver. 45, οὕτως ἔσται ἐν τῇ γενεᾷ ταύτῃ, "thus shall it be unto this generation," inasmuch as all appears as past, according to the description just given. But, the ἔσται, "shall be," evidently only refers to what immediately precedes it: τὰ ἔσχατα χείρονα τῶν πρώτων, "the last *state* (is) worse than the first;" the evil consequences of the relapse of the Jewish people, only revealed themselves indeed very forcibly on the destruction of their independence. Were we to apply the terms οὕτως ἔσται, "even thus shall (it) be," to the *whole* simile, so that the devil being cast out of the man, and his return with seven others should refer to a future period,—the passage then would be quite unintelligible, for neither the Pharisees nor the entire nation itself, furnish events that could be viewed in this light.

In the words of ver. 43, 44, is contained a Jewish popular

idea, and we may say, a common human notion parabolically carried out. Evil, conceived as a disharmonised wilderness, is also to be met with in the physical world, as it were, in the echo, in the impression of the spiritual. The deserts of the earth are the witnesses to the sins of mankind, the practical proof of the vanished paradise Inasmuch as things having a relation to one another appear to man as being connected with one another, hence deserts, or wildernesses, were considered as the abodes of evil spirits; that which was made desolate by sin, becoming also the local abode of evil, (Tob. viii 3, Baruch iv. 35, Is. xiii. 21; xxxiv. 14, Rev. xviii. 2). This simple idea, which has its foundation in the depths of human nature, our Redeemer here makes use of, in order to place before his hearers a lively picture of the nature of evil. The whole of the description bears the impress of a parable, the individual features are therefore, it is true, not to be minutely entered into, yet, the whole comprised therein rests not on an empty accommodation to a national superstition, void of every share of truth, but on the simple truth itself, that in the great creation all the parts form one whole, and that the spiritual is also reflected in the physical. Hence, overcome by the power of good, the evil spirit, according to the description of Jesus, appears to escape to the wilderness (τοπος ἄνυδρος, "a dry (barren) place," = ἔρημος, "a desert," that is אֶרֶץ צִיָּה מִדְבָּר, "a barren land, a wilderness," Is. xxxv. 1; Joel ii. 20), seeking for rest, (ἀπάναυσις, see on St Matth. xi 29), to have lost which expresses, indeed, the nature of him that is evil. But change of place can afford no rest to a spirit; it only rests in God, its primeval source. Hence it is represented as returning to the soul which had constituted itself the abode of evil

Ver. 44. Carrying out the imagery of the dwelling, Jesus now depicts the guilt of a man freed for a time from the power of the evil one The term σχολάζων, "unoccupied," points at the guilt incurred by slothfulness and negligence, which is the source of a relapse into a state of sinfulness; the term σεσαρωμένον, "having been swept, (from σαρόω, "to sweep," Luke xv. 8,) and κεκοσμημένον, "having been adorned," only denote the alluring and charming character of the dwelling, or abode, offered by the purified soul Here likewise the figure is based on the notion, that sin, as moral filth, has its analogy in the visible world; that which is pure and clean is alluring to the unclean, but its communication defiles it. Here all is imagery, but a *deep* truth is contained in the imagery! The soul appears here as the bride, wooed by heaven and hell; it rests with herself to accept the one as freely as the other. The spirit, whom she receives, transforms her into his own nature, and dwells bodily within her.

Ver. 45. Hence, as the good is ever in the process of continued internal development—inasmuch as a standing still, or equipoise, is here altogether out of the question, so does in like manner the evil grow and attain to maturity. The evil man, raised into the element of the good, yet falling back, sinks the lower the higher he has been raised (John v. 14) There are degrees also among the evil ones, ($\pi\nu\epsilon\acute{\upsilon}\mu\alpha\tau\alpha$ $\pi o\nu\eta\rho\acute{o}\tau\epsilon\rho\alpha$, " spirits more evil;" compare Ephes. vi. 12) The discourse finally ends with the general concluding idea, or inference: that every relapse is more formidable than the disease itself. This was likewise evident in Israel. At the time of the Babylonian captivity, the rod of chastisement still produced its effects; but, no sooner did the Creator enter upon his possession, (John i. 12,) than his people that had become estranged from him, received him not ($T\grave{\alpha}$ $\pi\rho\tilde{\omega}\tau\alpha$, " the first or former things," signifying, as it were, the simple state of suffering and $\tau\grave{\alpha}$ $\check{\epsilon}\sigma\chi\alpha\tau\alpha$, " the last, or latter things," the position or situation of relapse)

§ 20.—THE ARRIVAL OF THE MOTHER AND BROTHERS OF JESUS.

(St Matth. xii. 46-50. St Mark iii. 31-35. St Luke viii. 19-21.)

The importance of the Gospel of St Mark for the right understanding of many gospel sections, by the addition of minor features, becomes here very palpable. According to the narration of St Matthew and St Luke, it would be obscure, or perhaps unintelligible, why Jesus does not admit his mother and brothers even into his presence; the declaration itself that his disciples were his true relatives would comprise something startling, were St Mark not to afford us his aid. He relates at the beginning of the section explained on a former occasion, (iii. 20, 21,) that Jesus went with his disciples into a house; this however was surrounded by dense masses of the people, so that they could not even appease their hunger in consequence of their spiritual employment or ministry, (ὥστε μὴ δύνασθαι αὐτοὺς μήτε ἄρτον φαγεῖν, "so that they were not even able to eat bread,") and here then were his relatives, (οἱ παρ' αὐτοῦ, "those belonging to him,") come to take him," (κρατῆσαι, "to seize, to arrest"), in order to place him in a state of safety, for it was said ὅτι ἐξέστη, "that he is beside himself." (On ἐξίστημι, "to be out of one's mind, beside one's self," see on St Matth. xii. 23. Here it is=μαίνεσθαι, "to be mad, furious," the consequence of the δαιμόνιον ἔχειν, "having a devil," of which he was accused by the Pharisees; owing to the inimical power, man himself appears, as it were, dislodged from his self-possession, or government) This notification explains the whole scene. The malicious Pharisees had succeeded by means of their blasphemous assertions in turning the minds even of the relatives of Jesus against him, who thereby had been induced to make an attempt at bringing him back, 1. e, of withdrawing him from his, to their view, pernicious ways. Without this hint we should have to abide by the remark of St Luke; οὐκ ἠδύναντο συντυχεῖν αὐτῷ διὰ τόν ὄχλον, "they were not able to come at him on account of the crowd," (ver. 19), whereby the whole occurrence would acquire a somewhat obscure character. That the unbelieving ἀδελφοί, "brethren," might have been carried away by such a report, may well be conceived according to John vii. 5, but that his mother should give credit to such an assertion, is more difficult to explain; one might have supposed that her faith must have remained unshaken. In the first place, it may be supposed, indeed, according to the gospel narrative, that Mary did not share the views of the brethren of Jesus, but that she only accompanied them on their way, in order perhaps to mitigate their perverted zeal Anything decisive can hardly be brought forward against such a supposition. Yet, it is not so very improbable, on the other hand, that a moment of weakness in the combat of faith, should have occurred in the life of Mary. The long series of years which had passed since the great experiences she had acquired, the so altogether different form in which the ministry of her divine Son revealed itself, from that which she might have herself expected, might well have been a severe trial for her, and have shaken her faith, as it did that of John the Baptist (see Matth xi 2 sqq) Her faith she had certainly not given up, yet, it is possible enough that in accordance with the declaration made to her, (St Luke ii. 35,) it even now had to endure a hard struggle, and hence then came the afflicted mother rather to *obtain consolation* from her Son and Lord, than really to *take him home,* and yet led, nevertheless, by the tormenting public report, asking, "Art thou he that is to come?" Truly, features, or traits such as these instil life in an uncommon manner into the gospel history, it is highly perverse to regard all the heroes thereof, (as has been mentioned already at Matth. xi. 1,) in the light of firm and unwavering characters. The stupendous events of the life of Jesus must have been connected, no doubt, with mighty fluctuations in every one that surrounded him; these form integral parts or traits of this noble picture, which cannot well be obliterated. No detriment is caused thereby to the sacred character of the persons mentioned in holy writ, because of their appearing under such circumstances as internally wavering, no saint ever became holy without severe struggles, wherein the billows may very frequently have passed over his head, and the Son of God himself led the way through all of them

Ver. 46. During the conversation the μητηρ, "mother," and the ἀδελφοί, "brethren," came, (concerning this see Matth. xiii. 35) They stood ἔξω, "without," (see St Mark iii. 31,) before the house, and sent in messengers to him.

Ver. 47, 48. On his receiving information thereof, they met with a rebuff from Christ. This, it is true, is not stated literally, but the form of the language: ὁ δὲ ἀποκριθεὶς εἶπε, "but he answering said," compels us to assume that such was the case. He neither *went out* to them, nor did he *admit* them, on the contrary, he continues his discourse. That he might have seen them *at* the conclusion of the whole, is certainly probable; but not *before,* the point of the whole answer requires this.

Ver. 49, 50. St Mark adds a picturesque trait: περιβλεψάμενος κύκλῳ, literally, "on looking about in a circle," as though Christ called the host of his disciples ἡ μήτηρ μου καὶ οἱ ἀδελφοί μου, "my mother and my brothers." But ver. 50 applies the expression not only to those present, but also in a general way, inasmuch as the doing of the will of God (λόγον τοῦ Θεοῦ ἀκούειν καὶ ποιεῖν, "to hear and to do the word of God," according to St Luke), is brought forward as the criterion of spiritual affinity. Hence, the expression, μήτηρ, "mother," and ἀδελφοί, "brothers," here used in consequence of circumstances, includes the general notion of relationship, this Jesus views in its most ideal form, in its spiritual, moral unity, (Einsseyn) in *one* loftier whole, which is indeed the kingdom of God. The only thing remarkable therein, is that our Lord appears to place himself altogether as a member within this great circle, or community, yea, even as a subordinate one, inasmuch as he speaks of his μήτηρ, "mother." On the one hand, one might herein refer to the usual formula. In such conversations the expressions must not be urged and closely adhered to; on the other hand, however, it might fairly be said, that in this view it is an expression of the lowly Son of man, who said: they are my mother and my brothers, whereas he might have said: they are my children. This, however, could scarcely suffice completely to exhaust the idea, and it would appear as though our Lord would in the words: ἰδοὺ ἡ μήτηρ μου, "behold, my mother," have an especial view to the community, according to which that same community of the faithful, who, considered separately, are his brethren, is, or may be called his mother, when considered as a whole, inasmuch as that which is divine ever assumes a human form in the church, and inasmuch as Christ is continually born anew therein.

§ 21.—A WOMAN ANOINTS JESUS.

(St Luke vii. 36, viii. 3.)

By means of a determinate chronological statement, St Matthew in this instance connects the 13th chapter which follows with the foregoing, in which also St Mark iv. 1 agrees, so that we must consider them as belonging to one another. But, it is for this reason that we consider the present occasion as most suitable to our purpose, in order to introduce a narrative which is only found in St Luke; and which is most closely connected by the evangelist, with the narration of the parable of the sower. To assert a strict order, is here certainly out of the question; for, whilst St Matthew xiii. 1, has ἐν ἐκείνῃ ἡμέρᾳ, "on that day," so that the parable might be attributed together with that which precedes it, to one and the same day, we read after the history of the anointment: ἐν τῷ καθεξῆς, "on the succeeding" (sc. χρόνῳ, "time,") ἐγένετο, "it came to pass," a form which transfers, at all events, what follows to a later period. Hence, this section ought to have been placed according to this before St Matth xii.

provided that all related in that chapter occurred on the same day with the events of chap. xiii. But, as in his dates (Zeitbestimmungen) St Matth. leaves us entirely in the dark as to where the day begins, and in St Luke, moreover, nothing being stated concerning the time of this anointing, hence no fitter, or more precise moment of time could be ascertained, and therefore, we have been induced by the agreement with that which follows, to introduce it here. As regards, however, the occurrence itself, the first question that occurs, is, in what light are we to view it, as connected with a kindred narrative in St Matth. xxvi. 6—13, (comp. Mark xiv. 3 sqq. John xii. 1 sqq.) The long acknowledged and undisputed diversity of the occurrences, has found of late an acute opponent in the person of *Schleiermacher* (Versuch uber den Lukas, p. 110, sqq.), he declares the occurrences to be identical, and is of opinion, that the statement made by St Luke has been misunderstood by the recorder thereof, and noted down by him in the present form. There is much, it is true, which speaks in favour of this view. It appears strange to assume two stories, in which a woman anoints Jesus on occasion of a feast, given at the house of a certain Simon; it appears singular, that a woman of ill-fame, but otherwise unknown to the master of the house, should have intruded upon those assembled at the feast; yet, the whole affair assumes a more unaccountable aspect still, the moment we assume that the occurrence is the same, and that the view given of it in St Luke is only an altered one.[1] In the first place, it is true, it may easily be explained that Mary might freely express herself at the party in such a manner, in regard to her attachment to the person of Jesus, inasmuch as according to the narratives of St Matth , St Mark, and St John, the feast took place in the bosom of the friendly family of Lazarus, and that Simon, ὁ λεπρός, "the leper," who is mentioned by St Matthew and St Mark as the host, must be viewed as a relative, or very intimate friend of this very family. But, hereby indeed it becomes wholly inexplicable, how this same amiable host could have expressed himself in a manner which could even in the remotest degree have been misunderstood, in

---

[1] I place no weight on the circumstance that the occurrence took place, according to St Luke vii 37, in a city or large town, but that Bethany was a κώμη, "small town or village," (John xi. 1). The two indeed, can not be well distinguished from one another

such a way as it must be misinterpreted according to the narrative of St Luke. The very supposition of his having uttered any suspicion against the person of Jesus, is improbable, but yet more so any insinuation of the kind against the sister of Lazarus. Suppose, even, that according to the intention of the person speaking, the expression: ἁμαρτωλός, "sinner, sinful person," was not made use of to signify a female sinner in the common sense of the word, and that this exaggerated view of the word is indeed a misconception, or misunderstanding of the relater, whom St Luke follows, still, it necessarily follows that something was said by Simon the leper, which *could* be thus misinterpreted. But, to a supposition of this kind, the narratives of St Matthew, St Mark, and St John, give not only no occasion whatever, but, on the contrary, all argue against it; her expression of love seems to have had something touching and affecting; Judas alone blamed her for the waste of the precious ointment. Assuming the circumstances so minutely described by the three evangelists, no cause whatever is to be found for all the speeches which are given in St Luke in connexion with this occurrence; on the contrary, everything bears witness against the idea that such conversations were held by our Lord in the bosom of his beloved family of Bethany. Hence, if the occurrence related by St Luke is to be considered identical with the anointment of Mary, the sister of Lazarus, in Bethany, then there is not only to be perceived in St Luke a misunderstood view of the matter, but a *total misrepresentation;* the occurrence is specifically become another. But, this is partly incompatible with the significancy of the Biblical writings, for the furtherance of Christian knowledge, partly also with the position of St John, who, no doubt, also was acquainted with St Luke, as *Schleiermacher* himself assumes. This learned man even pretends to find traces, (no mention being made of the particulars), that St John was acquainted with both narratives; these I have been unable to discover; but this much appears to me as certain, that if a story so totally disfigured could have crept into the gospel of St Luke, St John would not have omitted to designate it as such. Hence, if by the adoption of the identity of the narratives there arise such essential difficulties, it becomes at once more natural to hold to their diversity. For, that something similar should have occurred twice at a feast in the house of a certain Simon, is indeed singular, but it is by no means whatever, either a thing impossi-

K

ble or contradictory, especially since the name Simon was one of so very common occurrence among the Jews. But, the repulsive action apparently expressed in the circumstance of a woman intruding herself at a feast, is at once very much mitigated, partly by the eastern manners and customs in general, and partly as we are totally unacquainted with the particular circumstances of the woman of whom mention is made in St Luke. Had it been, for example, a woman belonging to the circle of those who continually surrounded Christ, her approach to the Saviour might be easily explained. But, finally, that St Luke makes no mention of the anointing in Bethany, a circumstance, which might be considered as a favourable sign for the supposition of the identity of the occurrences,—this can indeed be of little importance, inasmuch as similar omissions occur in all the evangelists, as for example in St John, at the institution of the holy Eucharist [1] According to the opinion of many ancient interpreters, this woman, who, according to St Luke, anointed Jesus, is said to have been Mary Magdalene; but no ground whatever can be brought forward to prove it. Yea, it appears improbable, inasmuch as that person is mentioned soon after, (St Luke viii. 2,) without referring back in any way whatever to the occurrence recorded. In that case we should have to say that Luke designedly did not wish to name her, and that. ἀφ' ἧς δαιμόνια ἑπτὰ ἐξεληλύθει, " out of whom he had cast seven devils," is used to indicate her guilt. Meanwhile, considering the complete want of any precise statements, it will be best to leave the personality undetermined

Ver. 36. This Pharisee had perhaps himself been healed by Jesus, and believed that, without experiencing any true gratitude, he might be able to acquit himself of his debt by means of an invitation, (see on ver. 47.)

Ver. 37 Πόλις, "the city," here has been understood to imply Nain, because Luke vii 11 has preceded it by the history of the raising from death of the widow's son at Nain; but, the transitions in ver. 17, 18, 20, 36, are much too general, to regard this supposition as well founded. The woman is called ἁμαρτωλός, "a sinner," that is, guilty of sexual offences, (John viii 7, 11)—'Αλάβαστρον, "an alabaster," for σκεῦος ἐκ ἀλαβάστρου, " a vessel of alabaster."

---

[1] I give no weight to the circumstance, that the occurrence took place, according to St Luke vii 37, in a city or large town, whereas Bethany was a κώμη, "small town or village," (John xi 1,) the two might not indeed be clearly distinguished from one another.

Ver. 38. The scene must be examined as in accordance with ancient manners, according to which those who were eating lay stretched, (accumbere, "to lie down," ἀνακλίνεσθαι, "to be reclined,") with their feet bare, or covered only with sandals. The impulse of grateful love expressed itself in the most heartfelt approximation, but the feeling of shame and humility only permitted her to approach the *feet* of the Redeemer. The case was different with Mary the sister of Lazarus; her love was not less intense, but it partook less of the character of shame; she anointed the *head* of our Lord. (Comp. Matth. xxvi 7, Mark xiv. 3. Both narrate here probably with more correctness than St John xii 3.)

Ver. 39 The unloving Pharisee, unprepared for the unqualified exhibition of such an expression of love,[1] hereon makes his

[1] I cannot forbear quoting here the words of a noble-minded man, who reproves the uncharitable criticism exercised on his ardent love, and its expressions or manifestations towards the Redeemer by a cold, dead time, as regards the anointing of Jesus. The following words of *Hamann*[*] have been introduced by the excellent *Von Roth*, in the preface to his edition of *Hamann's* Works, (see p. 9 of vol. 1) "Jerusalem, —it is the city of the great king! To this king, whose name, like as his fame is great and unknown, flowed forth the little rivulet of my authorship, despised like the waters of Siloah that go softly, (Isaiah viii 6.) Critical severity persecuted the dry reed, and each floating leaf of my muse, because the dry reed with which the little children who sit in the market-place play, resounded, and because the fluttering leaf tossed and whirled about, filled with the ideal of a king, who with the greatest gentleness and humility of heart, could declare of himself One greater than Solomon is here! As a devoted lover wearies the ready echo with the name of his adored mistress, and spares not even the young tree of the garden or wood with engraving the initials and characters of her beloved name; so was the remembrance of the fairest among the children of men, (Ps xlv. 2,) in the midst of the enemies of the king, like unto an out-poured Magdalene-ointment, and flowed like the precious balsam which flowed from the head of Aaron over his whole beard, down on to

[*] *Johann Georg Hamann,* or *der Magus im Norden,* as he styled himself, is the learned and excellent author of "Golgatha and Scheblimini," "Sybellinische Blatter," &c, &c. H was a most original thinker, a firm adherent to Biblical Christianity, and was one of its stoutest defenders. His writings, edited by *Fr. Von Roth,* (8 vols. Berl. 1821—43,) contain an inexhaustible fund of great and startling truths, and new observations, and were distinguished for a remarkable degree of extensive and tasteful reading, *multum et multa legit,*—to use his own words. But these truths, together with the "balmy fragrance of the ambrosial tables of the ancients," to speak with *Herder,* "are intermixed with a few *vapeurs* of the Gauls and the exhalations of British humour, which have formed around him a mist,"— which requires, in our opinion, no slight powers to dispel it. *Hamann* is the founder of that system of German philosophy, which some Germans call "*Glaubensphilosophie,*" i e. philosophy of faith, or rather ph. founded *on* faith,—a system, which has been more fully developed by *Herder* and *Jacobi* with more or less success.—T.

reflections on the person of Jesus, this is inconceivable under the circumstances, on the occasion of the feast in Bethany; such a person could not have taken his place there. (Εἰπεῖν ἐν ἑαυτῷ, "to say within himself," = אָמַר בְּלִבּוֹ, "he said in his heart.") The notion of a contamination of the pure through a contact with the impure, contains a certain truth as regards earthly purity, (see on Matth. xi. 19); only the overpowering might of Jesus, which the Pharisee did not perceive, rendered it, as regarded him, an untruth. The circumstance, that the appearance of the woman at the feast seems to have excited no astonishment, leads to a supposition of a recognised intimacy with the Pharisee or with Jesus. But, notwithstanding this acquaintance, the Pharisee could well believe that the secret sins of the woman might remain concealed from Jesus.

Ver. 40, 41. The Pharisee, who was less wicked than was usual among them, is instructed by the affectionate φίλος τῶν ἁμαρτωλῶν, "Friend of sinners," by means of a narrative, in which he represents the relation of the woman to God, as also that of the Pharisee himself. (Χρεωφειλέτης = ὀφειλέτης, "a debtor," is only once more found in St Luke xvi. 5. Δανειστής, "a creditor, a lender," = נֹשֶׁה, fenerator, "usurer," 2 Kings iv. 1. In the New Testament it is only to be found in this place.)

Ver. 42, 43. The comparison between the *more* and *less* of love, necessarily leads to a parallel between the Pharisee and the woman; whence the supposition is very probable, that the Pharisee too was indebted to Jesus for a benefit.

Ver. 44—46 The demeanour of the Pharisee is compared with the ardent love of the woman, who did more than was enjoined either by custom or the circumstances. The water for the feet, (Genes. xviii. 4, Judg. xix. 21,) the kiss, (Genes. xxxiii. 4, Exod. xviii. 7,) the offering of ointment, have a reference to well-known Jewish and universal oriental customs; the distinguished Pharisee had abstained from the application of such courtesies, inasmuch as he probably regarded the invitation

his garment. The house of Simon the leper was filled with the odour of the gospel-anointing, certain merciful (unmerciful) brethren and critics, however, were discontent with (what they called) the ordure, and their nostrils were only filled with the odour of death." Precious and profound words, containing abundant hints for those who can *see* and *hear!*

itself as an honour great enough. Jesus rebukes this lukewarmness towards his benefactor, which was coupled with so much self-conceited exaltation above the woman.

Ver. 47. The contrast referred to above, is here once more brought forward, and although the words: ᾧ δὲ ὀλίγον ἀφίεται, "but to whom little is forgiven," present the idea in a general way, it may nevertheless very appropriately embrace, or include the σοὶ ὀλίγον ἀφίεται, "to thee little is forgiven," words that were not spoken out from polite consideration. The first half of this hemistic, or verse, however, is difficult of comprehension; for, according to it, love does not appear as the *consequence* (as we perceive very correctly in the second half of the verse, according to the parable), but as the *cause* of the forgiveness. Both the ὅτι and also the Aorist ἠγάπησε represent the love as the antecedent and as that on which the forgiveness is founded. It has, indeed, been maintained (comp. *Schleusner's* Lexicon II. 325.) that ὅτι stands for the Hebrew כִּי, "because," עַל דְּבַר, "for the sake of," יַעַן, "on account of," in the sense of διό, "wherefore, on which account;" but, neither in the texts of the Old Testament (Ps. xvii. 6, cxvi 10, Deut. xxii. 24, and others) can it be so understood, nor does this signification occur in the New Testament. (We are erroneously referred to texts such as John viii. 44, 1 John iii. 14, by men holding this view.) To evade, however, the difficulty which is contained in the aorist, the word ἀγαπᾶν, "to love," must be taken in the sense of "giving a proof of love," so that the meaning of the verse would be: "thence, thou mayest conclude that her sins are forgiven, because she has given me a great proof of love." The signification of ἀγαπᾶν, "to love," as it appears in the second division of the verse, however, forms a contradiction to this view, for according to these, it signifies a *condition*, not a mere *action*. The meaning, it is evident, is not intended to be that she *has* loved, and that her love was now past, but on the contrary, that she is living *constantly* therein. It is merely thrown back into the past tense in order to place it in connection with the forgiveness. We shall thus have to endeavour the rather to overcome the difficulty of the *idea*. The Catholic church has misinterpreted[1] the latter, in so far as

---

[1] On this text, *De Wette* makes the remark. We are now advanced beyond the polemical contradiction of the Catholic doctrine of sanctification, or holiness by works, (Werkheiligkeit). I very much doubt this.

with her forgiveness is based, or depends on, the performance of meritorious works, since she views the ἀγαπῆσαι, " to have loved," as *active*, i e. in the sense of that activity which is the result of natural powers, upon which forgiveness depends, but which, in accordance with the parable, cannot be the meaning. But, the power and faculty to seek, or rather to receive inwardly forgiveness, pre-supposes of necessity love in the mind as a *receptive* working, which will be the more intense the greater the guilt to be forgiven appears to man. If this receptive love (which is identical with the faith of repentance,) verily apply to itself the grace of forgiveness, or forgiving grace, then it unfolds itself, and reveals itself, in actions, as in the case of this female sinner towards Jesus In the same receptive love, it makes or changes, as it were, the power which enkindles life within it, into the receptive pole of its activity, so that according thereto, love represents itself in these words of our Lord in the wondrous form of its manifestation, according to which it makes itself known, now as active, then as passive, but always as the same. We may, therefore, affirm, that the sense of these words is· that he who is to have faith in the forgiveness of sin, must harbour within himself an analogous fund of (receptive) love; and this then manifests itself, as soon as the forgiving power of love, which is, as it were, the positive pole, approaches it, in the same ratio, as the sin increases, which is being taken away There is comprehended herein, at the same time, a reference to the peculiar decision, or rather disposing power of our Lord, that where sin becomes mighty, or abounding, there does grace reveal itself and abound in a higher degree, (Rom. v. 20); not as though sin could produce any kind of good, but only, because God's mercy reveals itself towards those that are the most miserable, in a manner the most refulgent The Pharisee was not without love, he loved a *little*, conscious that he had received but *little;* but the woman, who had received *all*, hence loved ardently and with all the pulses, or energies of her life [1]

Holiness by works is the natural resort of an unrepentant heart, and manifests itself even within the Evangelical church, in forms not Catholic

[1] Concerning the relation of receptive love to faith, compare the comment on St Matthew xiii 58 The weighty text, Hosea ii. 19, 20, must here be glanced at, for there love and faith pervade each other, and are intimately connected in the words of the prophet

Ver 49, 50. With this is connected a repetition of the solemn forgiveness: ἀφέωνταί σου αἱ ἁμαρτίαι, "thy sins are forgiven," as well as of the astonishment expressed by those present. (Concerning this comp on St Matth. ix 3, wherein also faith and its relation to forgiveness form the point at issue)

A transition, describing in general terms the ministry of Jesus, (Luke viii. 1—3,) introduces us to the parables The Redeemer wandered about visiting cities and villages, preaching the kingdom of God, accompanied by living witnesses of his redeeming power. The persons specially named, are, *Mary* of Magdala (See on St Matth xv. 39) Her situation previous to her restoration is described as having been peculiarly distressing, (ἑπτὰ δαιμόνια, "seven devils." See St Matth. xii. 45), all her powers and capacities seem to have been surrendered to the ministrations of darkness.[1] 2. Chuza's wife, *Joanna*, (ἐπίτροπος = οἰκονόμος, steward) 3. *Susanna*, שׁוּשַׁנָּה, Lily. · The two latter are mentioned in this place only, but Mary Magdalene is known from the history of the sufferings of the Redeemer, (St Matth. xxvii 55), but according to the same text, others also, and among them probably those here mentioned, persevered in their adherence to Jesus, even up to the moment of his being nailed to the cross These women afforded him support out of their private property, (ὑπάρχοντα, *opes*, *facultates*, " wealth, substance," and waited upon him The more rare the glances afforded to us by the gospel-history, into the external circumstances of life in the circle in which Jesus moved are, the more attractive do they prove in the eye of the reader, they throw a peculiar light on his whole life while dwelling on earth The heavenly manifestation which presented itself in his person to the world, is enveloped in all respects in a genuine human garment, his glory shines purely internally, and reveals its brightness externally, only when it is to prove a blessing to others. He, who was the support of the spiritual life of his people, dis-

---

[1] St Mark xvi 9, notices this event in a totally different connection as regards Mary It appears, according to him, as though her liberation from demoniacal influences was to be regarded as something altogether peculiar Her former situation was in the highest degree unfortunate, and therefore the power of the Redeemer was manifested in her in a more dazzling manner, and her love to the Lord became by so much the more ardent Everywhere (compare the narrative of the resurrection) she is the first named among the women

dained not to be supported by them in the body; he was not ashamed to penetrate so far into the depth of poverty as to condescend to live upon the alms of love; he only fed others in a miraculous manner, for himself he lived upon the love of his people.[1] Hence, he loved with a perfect and pure love, and so permitted himself to be loved; he gave all things to men, his brethren, and received all things from them, and enjoyed thereby the pure blessings of love, which is perfect then only when it is at the same time both giving and receiving. What a feature in the picture of the Messiah! Who could invent things such as these! He who feeds thousands by *one* word of his mouth, lives himself upon the bread of the poor. It was necessary to live in this manner, in order that it might be so recorded.

§ 22.—THE COLLECTION OF PARABLES.

(St Matth xiii 1—53; St Mark iv. 1—20, 30—34; St Luke viii. 4—15, xiii. 18—21.

In continuation of the gospel-history of St Matthew, the exposition thereof brings us to a collection of parables. There is something peculiar in this collection, for it does not appear to be in keeping with the nature of this manner of teaching, to accumulate together a number of parables. For since they present truth under a veil, and are intended to induce to reflection and inquiry, their significancy would be weakened by the bringing together many, in one oral discourse. The mind would feel itself rather disturbed and bewildered than excited by the varied references contained in the parables, and hence their end would not be attained. The case is indeed different with written discourses. The reader can reflect on each individual parable at leisure, he can compare the one with the other, and obtain thereby a clearer insight into the peculiarities of each; for Holy

---

[1] It is worthy of remark, that women only are named, αἵτινες διηκόνουν αὐτῷ ἀπὸ τῶν ὑπαρχόντων αὐταῖς, "the which ministered to him of their substance," and who clove to their Lord with an abiding devotion, as is witnessed by the narrative of the resurrection. The weaker half of the human race were the first to arrive at the knowledge of the strength that they possessed in Christ.

Scripture, therefore, a collection of parables is peculiarly adapted. But, although a written collection of parables appears, according to what has been said, partly very important in itself, and partly very suitable to the collective manner of representing events, of St Matthew, yet, the question might be raised, whether it would not appear more consistent to imagine, that St Matthew has here formed, not so much a collection of parables spoken at very different periods, as that, historically faithful, he has delivered them in the same manner in which they were communicated one after the other by Jesus when teaching in parables. For the support of this view we might refer to passages contained in the Gospel of St Luke; more especially to chap. xiv. 28; xvi. 31, wherein Jesus brings forward parable after parable, and yet everything seems to testify that in these passages the original connection has been preserved. To this must be added the bearing which all these parables have in common to the kingdom of God, a circumstance which contributed much to prevent the hearers from becoming bewildered, inasmuch as one simile was calculated to throw light upon another,—and the manner in which St Matthew (ver. 1 sqq) portrays the scene, where Jesus, sitting on the sea-shore surrounded by a vast multitude of people, teaches them, and concludes thus, xiii. 53, his ministerial teaching. Yet, against this view argues *first* the fact, that St Luke must in that case have transposed some of the parables, inasmuch as he brings them forward in chap. xiii. 18—21, spoken in an entirely different, though well-chosen connection; and then *secondly*, the loose manner in which St Matthew avails himself of certain opening and closing formulas; a feature which we have already reflected upon when treating on the Sermon on the Mount. As he evinces no interest whatever in local or chronological data, hence no great stress can be laid thereon. With the scene depicted by St Matthew at chap. xiii. 1 sqq., cannot be brought by any means into unison the fact narrated in ver. 10, viz. of the drawing near of the disciples and their asking him concerning the meaning of the parables; the multitude had evidently nothing to do with this, but it appertained solely to the private circle of the disciples. St Mark iv. 10, shows that this sentiment is very correct; and adds, moreover, that this question was put by the disciples to the Lord, ὅτε ἐγένετο καταμόνας, "when he was alone" Here, then, we at once perceive, that according to St Matthew, everything is not to be supposed as appearing in its immediate or strict connection. He has anticipated the interpretation given by Jesus of the first parable, the Evangelist seeing that this interpretation could only have taken place as soon as Jesus had withdrawn himself from the multitude and found himself alone with his disciples, as is recorded, indeed, on occasion of the second interpretation at ver. 36. Hence, it appears dubious, according to this verse, whether the Lord addressed the last three parables to the disciples alone, or whether they were directed likewise to the people. In either case the discourse must have been interrupted, and the concluding formula, ἐτέλεσεν ὁ Ἰησοῦς τὰς παραβολὰς ταύτας, "Jesus had finished these parables," given in ver. 53, acquires thereby a totally different position with regard to ver. 1, from that which at the first view it seems to have. Under circumstances such as these, it is doubtless best to assume (and this would be, indeed, quite in accordance with St Matthew's usual manner of representing facts) that he here formed a collection of parables in his own way. The circumstances under which the Evangelist introduces them, still retain therewith their perfect veracity. Jesus may have related, no doubt, some parables under these very circumstances, to them St Matthew has added others in order to place this manner of teaching of Jesus more fully before the reader. Both St Mark and St Luke perfectly agree with St Matthew in the order of the first parable; the latter ones alone are arranged differently. The existence of an intimate connection with each other of the parables related in St Matthew xiii is in no way denied in consequence of this manner of presenting them; on the contrary, this becomes evident from the manner in which they are communicated. The seven parables communicated by St Matthew in this chapter are destined to characterise the various relative positions of the kingdom of God. The *first* parable comprehends or views the relative position of the various classes of mankind with regard to the Word of God; the *second* has in view the position of mankind with regard to the kingdom of the evil one; the *third* and *fourth* depict the greatness of the kingdom of God as compared with its insignificant beginning, in the *fifth* and *sixth* the value of the kingdom of heaven is prominently brought forward, and finally, in the *last* is depicted the ever-mingled form or state of the church upon earth which will endure even until the day of judgment

But, with regard to the parable itself, i e , its nature, and the use made thereof in the New Testament, it must be observed that the Greek terms, παραβολή, παροιμία, "parable," and "proverb," altogether correspond with the Hebrew, מָשָׁל, "proverb, a weighty saying." Both expressions are used in a certain indefinite sense. As מָשָׁל, which it is well known, signifies frequently a normal precept, sentence, or decision, so also does παραβολή, namely, whenever a sententious idea implies, or rather comprehends a simile or comparison (St Luke iv. 23; St Matthew xv. 15) But, even common similes with this normal conception, i e mode of viewing, occur under the same designation (St Mark iii. 23; St Luke v. 36, vi 39.) Most commonly, however, this name is used in the three first Gospels, (for neither the expression used in this sense, nor the thing itself, are to be found in the Gospel of St John and in the rest of the writings of the New Testament,) when speaking of a peculiar form of teaching, which has, indeed, some analogous examples in the Old Testament (Isa. v. 1 The *mashal*, i e parable, here made mention of, is used by Jesus himself; [comp. St Mark xii. 1,] Ezek. xvii. 1 sqq ; Judges ix 7 sqq ; 2 Kings xiv. 9, 2 Sam xii. 1,) and which is most closely related to the fable (λόγος, ἀπόλογος, αἶνος.)

The *parable* differs from a *simile* chiefly in this, that the latter does not imply or express any individual subject or fact, which is the case with the parable whenever it appears in a state of perfect development Sometimes, it is true, the parables are merely indicated, as, for example, the parables of the hidden treasure and of the merchantman in St Matthew xiii. 44, 45. But even in such an unfinished form they differ from mere similes, or allegories (far extended similes,) inasmuch as the basis of the determinate simulated fact therein indicated may be always discovered. But it is more difficult to point out the difference which exists between *parable* and *fable*. The ancients, especially *Aristotle* (Rhet ii. 20), who is followed by *Cicero* (De Invent. i 30), and by *Quinctilian* (Inst. v. 11), perceive a difference only in the more or less ample treatment thereof, inasmuch as to them the fable appears as the more finished production, whereas the parable is regarded as the more unfinished. Among recent writers, *Lessing* regards the difference as consisting in this, that the fable represents the individual case as *real*, whereas in the parable it is only *possible;* with *Herder*, however, it consists in this: the fable has recourse to irrational nature, whereas the parable makes use of the rational. Yet, none of these suppositions are without their difficulties; to judge according to the Biblical parable, it also represents the occurrence as a real one, not merely as a possible one, as for example, the very first parable of the sower in St Matthew xiii. 4. This argues against the view taken by *Lessing;* but against that of *Herder* we have the Old Testament parables above referred to, especially Ezek xvii. 1 sqq., wherein the very subject of the action is represented by the inanimate creation, and which nevertheless can be regarded by no one as a fable. The fables of Æsop, however, on the other hand, sometimes represent human persons as the media of instruction. The difference, no doubt, is a purely internal one. The point of view occupied by the propounder or inventor of fables is of an inferior character, and hence, his object also is the more subordinate; the end of the fable is to exhibit earthly virtues or commendable qualities; and inasmuch as the earthly virtues, such as prudence, skilfulness, industry, &c., have their representatives in certain species of animals, hence, the irrational animal creation may be used most advantageously for this form of instruction; if we employ human beings in fables, they must always appear therein in that light or character, according to which they belong to the animal creation. But the parable introduces us into a more exalted, a purely moral sphere, its object is to represent heavenly rules of life, or circumstances decreed by the Deity. Hence is its element more peculiarly conversant with human nature; wherever the parable touches upon irrational elements, there it views them as conditioned by a higher divine power. In the fabulous world, humanity, if it appears therein, is viewed from its subordinate side; in the parable, irrational nature is viewed from its divine side. Fable could find no place in the sacred Scriptures, if we consider their peculiar character,[1] inasmuch as their whole endeavour is to seize upon the divine character of man, and to exalt it. The parable, on the contrary, is their true element. One might say that the Old Testament is a real, matter-of-fact parable, which teaches in its history subjects of a divine nature; in the New Testament, the Son of God veiled the truths of the kingdom of

---

[1] At the most may Judges ix. 7 sqq be regarded as a fable, but even here also there is visibly no higher point of view evolved, which has its foundation in the circumstances connected with the passage.

God revealed in him in parabolic symbols, in order thus to afford instruction for all degrees of mental development and intuition, and thereby to bring it to pass, that the *one* should be as profoundly initiated into the mysteries of the doctrines of the kingdom of God, as the others should be left in a state of darkness with regard to his nature [1]

Ver. 1, 2. From his dwelling-place, (which was probably in Capernaum,) Jesus went to the sea, (the lake of Genesareth,) and in order to withdraw himself from the crowd, he entered into a ship which happened to lie there ready; the people stood on the land (shore), (ἐπὶ τῆς γῆς,) by the sea-side, (πρὸς τὴν θάλασσαν, St Mark iv. 1.)

Ver. 3—9. The parable of the sower is one of the few of which we have an authentic explanation by the Lord, which is not only very important for the right understanding of this single narrative, but which is also of importance, for the deduction of principles for the exposition of all parables. We may particularly infer therefrom what appears to be the most difficult in the exposition of parables, *how far the isolated features of the parabolical discourse frequently have any signification or not* Just as shallowness may on such points make light of all that is profound in the Word of God, by simply exclaiming, this or that is a mere decoration—so can superstition in like manner make a mountain out of every grain of sand. (To the words τὰ πετεινά, "the birds," contained in ver. 4, St Luke adds. τοῦ οὐρανοῦ, "of heaven," according to the Hebrew, עוֹף הַשָּׁמַיִם, "the birds of heaven."—Βάθος τῆς γῆς, "depth of earth," stands =βαθεῖα γῆ, "deep earth."—Καυματίζεσθαι, signifies to be *burnt up by the sun*, or to be scorched, ξηραίνεσθαι, to wither, to dry up altogether. Ver. 7. ἀναβαίνειν, = עָלָה, צָמַח, to spring up. St Mark gives, iv. 8, the numbers inverted yet the same as St Matthew, which points out to us, that nothing further is to be sought for in the position thereof. The well-known em-

---

[1] Modern literature is enriched with some works on the Scriptural parables, which are very full of learning. RETTBERG and SCHULZE composed prize essays for Göttingen University, (both published in Göttingen 1828) A most ample and satisfactory treatise, de Parabolarum Jesu natura, interpretatione, &c "On the nature and interpretation of the parables of Jesus,' was published by Unger, Lips 1828.

phatic formula, ὁ ἔχων ὦτα κ τ λ, "he that hath ears, &c.," invites to examination)

Ver. 18—23 With this parable itself we connect closely the explanation of the Lord, which the disciples, when they were alone, request of him, (καταμονας, "when he was alone," St Mark iv. 10), the important discourses which intervene we shall consider hereafter The expression, ἀκούσατε τὴν παραβολὴν, "hear ye the parable," must not be translated: hear the *exposition of the parable (Schleusner* has even a special number, or cipher, under the word παραβολή, for the explanation, a *parable*), on the contrary, it is only by the comprehending of the narrative that it becomes a parable. Our Lord draws a parallel between the four kinds of fields and four kinds of mental dispositions of those who receive the Word of God which is scattered abroad, St Luke viii. 11) The parable here changes at once into the literal discourse, inasmuch as instead of the seed, which was represented in the simile as developing itself in a different manner, in accordance with the nature of the soil upon which it fell, he enumerates the individuals in whom those developments take place His literal discourse is mixed up in a peculiar manner with the parabolical language, as in St Matthew, in the: ὁ παρὰ τὴν ὁδόν, ἐπὶ τὰ πετρώδη, εἰς τὰς ἀκάνθας σπαρείς, he who was sown (upon) by the way side, upon stony ground, among thorns." In St Luke, only, (viii 14, 15) the neuter gender is several times made use of. With regard to the *first* disposition of mind (heart), this is not represented *per se* in the explanation of our Lord, but only in its consequences, but which however admit a reference to the position itself. An ἀκούειν, "hearing," but no συνιέναι, "having understood," of the word is assumed, but only a losing of the same. Although a positive cause, external to the nature of the described subject is supposed, which is the prince of darkness, who is anxious to prevent the winning of souls, (ἵνα μὴ πιστεύσαντες σωθῶσιν, "lest believing they should be saved," St Luke viii. 12); yet, it is evident, that the possibility of such a ministration of the prince of this world lies even in the disposition of the mind itself The figure (the ὁδός, "public way,") points to a state of hardness of the individual mind, caused and brought to pass by external causes, it is a want of receptive power, an inability to believe, which prevents him from receiving the word; if in such hearts a certain entrance of that which is Divine takes place, (ἐν τῇ καρδίᾳ,[1] St Matthew ver. 19), yet it is not intimately received by his nature (μὴ συνιέντος, "not understanding it,") and thus it does not sink and penetrate deep enough, in order to be saved from the attacks of the inimical principle; the evil power does not penetrate into the γῆ καλή, "good ground," ver. 23, hence the Divine element can there freely develope itself. It is remarkable that the πετεινά, "birds," spoken of in the first part of the parable, (ver. 4), are explained by the πονηρός, "evil one," (σατανᾶς, "Satan," of St Mark, διάβολος, "the devil," according to St Luke),[2] an explanation which, had it not been given by the Lord himself, could have hardly been received, the figure (τὰ πετεινά, "the birds,") would have been solved by means of the general notion, destructive influences. But, here we have evidently a passage, in which, as in ver. 39, the Redeemer speaks of the devil in a *didactic manner*, and this too, without being solicited, in the most contracted circle of his disciples. The description of the *second* disposition of mind or heart, is that of one nearly related to the former, although deviating much in its outward manifestation. There exists in the interior the same want of receptivity of that which is Divine, (τὰ πετρώδη, the stony places,") the exterior alone is capable of being moved and susceptible of what is noble, the beginning of life excites for this reason fair expectations, (μετὰ χαρᾶς λαμβάνει λόγον Θεοῦ, "he receiveth the word of God with gladness,") yet, the plant cannot take deep root, (it wants the ἰκμάς, "moisture," St Luke viii 6, = ὑγρότης, the nourishing moisture), such an one is, therefore, a πρόσκαιρος, "temporal," (which St Luke explains. πρὸς καιρόν πιστεύει, "he believeth for a time,") the contrast to αἰώνιός, "eternal," (2 Cor iv 18). In the hour of temptation, (ἐν καιρῷ πειρασμοῦ), which is characterised more precisely by St Matthew, and St Mark, by the expressions θλίψις, "tribulation," and διωγμός, "persecution,"

---

[1] In the formula ἐσπαρμένον ἐν τῇ καρδία, "sown in the heart," ἐν, "in" does not permit of being interchanged with εἰς, "into," it means, the seed which was scattered abroad, and is now in the heart

[2] It is incomprehensible to me, how *Schleiermacher* (Glaubensl v 1. p. 213, 2d edition), can say, "the expressions are here of double interpretation, and the enmity of mankind against the divine word is as nearly connected herewith as the devil." The expressions ὁ σατανας, ὁ διάβολος (with the article, without anything preceding whereto to refer them) cannot possibly be explained as referring to man

coming from without, they fall off. (St Luke ἀφίστανται, "fall away," St Matthew and St Mark σκανδαλίζονται, "are offended," for what particularly regards σκάνδαλον, "offence," comp. on St Matthew xviii. 8). This application of ἥλιος, "the sun," (St Matth. xiii. 6), as signifying scorching fire, heat, in parabolical language is likewise found in the Old Testament. (Comp. Ps. cxxi. 6, Is. xlix. 10, with Rev. vii. 16).

In the *third* disposition of the heart indifference does not appear, as the thing which prevents the development of the Divine word; but only those foreign elements which become mixed up in the mind with the divine principle of life, which are, so to speak, the thorns that stifle the germ of the young plant. Good and evil are according thereto conceived, as existing in the inward life in a simultaneous process of development, yet in such a manner as to afford the latter a predominance over the former, whereof the growth is thereby suppressed. As that which prevents the development of the heavenly germ, the two forms are brought forward, in which sin reveals itself in this temporal system of the world, (αἰὼν οὗτος, "this world.") Firstly, the μέριμνα, "care, anxiety," the oppressive, heavy portion of earthly life, which causes its falling off, or apostacy from that which is Divine; secondly, the ἀπάτη τοῦ πλούτου, "deceitfulness of riches," the alluring portion of life, which pretends in a delusive manner to appease the desires of the soul. St Luke describes this latter form of the pernicious influences of the worldly principle more fully by adding, (viii. 14,) the words: ἡδοναί τοῦ βίου, "pleasures of life" (Βίος, "life," like *seculum*, here signifies the temporal existence of man, as he appears incorporated with sin,—comp. 2 Tim. ii. 4, whence is derived the expression used by the fathers of the church: βιωτικόν, βιωτικά = *secularia*, "the things of this life or world," implying whatever concerns this world, whatever belongs thereto. Comp. *Suiceri* Thes. s h. v. and St Luke xxi. 34, 1 Cor v. 3, 4.) St Mark uses instead of ἡδοναί, "pleasures," the expression: αἱ περὶ τὰ λοιπὰ ἐπιθυμίαι, "the desires after other things," so that other allurements of the external world are placed on a parallel with πλοῦτος, "riches," as producing a similar effect. These extraneous objects withdraw man's undivided attention from holiness, which requires it, and hence it is prevented from developing itself, in its fulness and power Συμπνίγουσι τὸν λόγον, ἄκαρπος γίνεται, οὐ τελεσφοροῦσι, "they choke the word, it becomes unfruitful, they bring not to perfection," in St Luke. The expression τελεσφορέω, is only to be found in this one passage, (Luke viii 14,) and signifies: to bring to the end, to finish; but the fruit of the spirit is the end of the internal spiritual life, which the word of God ingrafted in the heart, must attain to (Gal. v. 22,) inasmuch as it assumes that it has produced its full effect upon the entire inner man.—That the spiritual fruit, then, grows out of the Divine word engrossed into the heart, is that which forms the characteristic feature of the *fourth* and last disposition of the heart, which the Redeemer figuratively calls the γῆ καλή, "good earth;" a spiritual soil, endowed with the fulness of receptivity, in which the process of development is interrupted by none of those hindrances, above treated of. The various expressions used by the evangelists, render highly intelligible the effects produced by that which is Divine upon such hearts. According to St Matthew, with the ἀκούειν, "to hear," is likewise connected the συνιέναι, "to understand," which is a reception of the Divine thing, in its most true or proper nature and manner, and is thus contrasted with ver. 19 It is according to St Mark a παραδέχεσ- θαι, "receiving," a receiving into ourselves, into the depths of our life, and forms a contrast with the *losing* spoken of at ver. 15. According to St Luke it is a κατέχειν, "holding fast," wherein is implied an activity of will in defence of the divine principle of life which is obtained, and the expulsion of all extraneous influences, it forms a contrast to ver 14. St Luke has, moreover, the marked addition ἐν ὑπομονῇ, "with patience," in order to describe the bearing of fruit, as the result of the gradual process of the internal amalgamation of life with the Divine, which by no means depends upon a mere arbitrary determination of the will. St Matthew and St Mark indicate the various degrees of fruitfulness in language still more figurative. Without enlarging too much on the meaning of the expressions, ἑκατὸν, "a hundred fold," ἑξήκοντα, "sixty fold," τριάκοντα, "thirty fold," we may assert, that the numbers not merely imply the various degrees of endowment with miraculous powers, which forms the condition of the perfection of the fruits, (comp. St Matthew xxv. 14 sqq), or the degrees of care spent in the promotion of their thriving, but that there is likewise brought forward, besides these, the fact that all is distributed, even in this portion of the mighty kingdom of God, *according to rule and order,* hence, that the capacities and powers bestowed on vari-

L

ous individuals are not poured out without rule, but that they are given according to laws and regulations.

In the account by Luke viii. 16—18, and by Mark iv. 21—25, there follow immediately after the explanation of the parable thus given by the Lord, certain words which are awanting in Matthew, but which are not without importance for the deeper understanding of the similitude. The connexion of these verses with the foregoing parable is obvious, if one only keeps in view the circumstance that the Saviour, in passing on to another comparison, is showing how the apostles were the γῆ καλή and therefore called to bring forth seeds and fruits, which in their turn were destined to produce still more extensive results. The light which has been kindled, and which is intended to diffuse its radiance, is thus equivalent to the seed scattered abroad and designed to grow up,[1] and the general idea which follows οὐ γὰρ ἐστί τι κρυπτὸν κ. τ. λ. contains merely the affirmation that every thing wrapped up in the divine word shall gradually unfold and develope itself. To this is subjoined the admonition, βλέπετε ὃυν πῶς ἀνούετε ὃς γὰρ ἂν ἐχῃ δοθήσεται αὐτῷ καὶ ὃς ἂν μὴ ἔχῃ καὶ ὃ δοκεῖ ἔχειν ἀρθήσεται ἀπ' αὐτοῦ The same words stand at Matt. xiii. 12, but are somewhat differently introduced. The original connexion may probably have been preserved by Luke and Mark. For according to them, the words were obviously designed to prevent a possible misunderstanding of the parable, lest it should be supposed that the states of mind described as existing in different men, originated in any inherent *necessity*, or that the consequent variety of effects flowing from the word of God in them, arose from such a source. The admonition βλέπετε κ. τ. λ. and especially the remark ὃς γὰρ ἂν ἔχῃ κ. τ. λ. takes for granted the freedom of choice and the influence of self-determination, amidst all differences of internal organization. For, according to the connexion, the ἔχειν and the μὴ ἔχειν (as conjoined with the δοκεῖν ἔχειν) refers to the fruit which was really produced, or only apparently brought forth. The ἔχειν admits also of being referred to the γῆ καλή to which the fruit stands related simply as effect to cause, but the former view is to be preferred. Thus under-

---

[1] The same intermingling of the two comparisons of seed and light is found also in Philo, ἀθάνατα ἔγκονα μόνη τίκτειν αφ' ἑαυτῆς ὅια τε ἔστιν ἡ θεοφιλής ψυχή σπείραντος εἰς αὐτήν ἀκτῖνας νοητὰς τοῦ πατρὸς αἷς δυνήσεται θεωρεῖν τὰ σοφίας δόγματα. De vita theoret. Opp. v. ii. p. 482. Mangey.

stood, the whole sentence (*Gnome*) affirms that wheresoever that which is divine has once manifested itself in fruit-producing power, it goes on to develope its influences ever more purely and more nobly, but wheresoever it fails of effectual operation, there not merely the old state returns, but the man sinks deeper, and loses even that which he vainly imagined himself to possess. This idea plainly leads to the further conclusion that the states of mind depicted in the parable are not to be conceived of as definitely restricted to separate individuals, but are rather to be regarded as realized in the same person *successively* in different periods and situations of life, so that as well on the one hand may the hard stony heart, by a faithful using of grace, be ennobled into a good and fruitful soil for the Divine word, as conversely may the good ground[1] on the other hand by faithlessness be desolated and destroyed. But this implies no denial of the fact, that in different individuals there naturally exist predominant tendencies towards the one or the other of these mental states, such predominance arising from the blessing of pious, or the curse of impious conduct. Only, every man must be viewed as a free agent, and as the Bible nowhere teaches the existence of a *decretum reprobationis*, according to which, sin concentrates itself of necessity on certain natures, just as little does it teach the existence of a *gratia irresistibilis*, in virtue of which, good concentrates itself of necessity on certain individuals We are rather made everywhere to see that the Divine government of the world, which has its foundation in necessity, is in harmony with a world full of beings who are free agents, and who are never forced by compulsion under the influence of good or evil. The most favoured individuals, if personally unfaithful, can attain not the slightest advancement in good, while the least favoured, if personally faithful, may develope themselves most attractively. By the principle, therefore,—he who has much, of him shall much be required,—the apparent unrighteousness connected with the different positions in which men are born, is fully removed. Only in Mark do we find the statement added

---

[1] All who hold the doctrine of the saints' perseverance with its kindred truths, will dissent, as the Translator does, from this statement and some others which follow If the author really understood this truth as implying that men are not free agents, but driven by force (*durch Zwang*,) to good or evil, he could not have known what the Calvinistic system of doctrine really is —T

(Mark iv. 26—29,) in which the comparison of the seed sown in the field is taken with a modification such as does not occur in the other evangelists. It stands in immediate connexion with the preceding idea, that wheresoever the divine root has entered into a soul, it evermore manifests its blessed influence according to the power which dwells in it, and which developes itself outwardly. The comparison therefore sets forth this indwelling energy (and in this respect it is allied to the parable of the leaven), quite as strongly as it does the inability of him who soweth the seed of the Divine word to effect its growth, that growth proceeding wholly from itself as the general law of all development implies. Mark iv. 26, 27, contains a representation of the gradual growth of the seed without the co-operation of the sower; Καθεύδειν, ἐγείρεσθαι is merely a description of what happens in ordinary life, which excludes any further attention to the seed that has been sown. Independently of the efforts of man, the earth itself [αὐτομάτη] brings forth fruit. What properly belongs to the seed is here attributed to the earth, as that on which the growth of the seed depends, in other respects it is of no importance to the understanding of the similitude The expression αὐτομάτη, that which moves of itself, which grows of itself, does not occur elsewhere, except at Acts xii 10 The mode of growth, by progressive stages, is described by the words χόρτος [the first springing of the corn which is grass-like,] στάχυς [the sprouting of the ears,] σῖτος [the ripened grain] In verse 29th, παραδῶ, scil ἑαυτόν is used after the analogy of the Latin se dare, tradere, as Virgil, Georg. i. 287, writes, *multa adeo gelida melius se nocte dederunt*. Compare also the Hebrew שָׁלַם, the Chaldee שְׁלַם, Ezra vii 19, [see Buxt Lex Talm. p 2422] Δρέπανον sickle stands for the labourers bearing the sickle, the θερισταί. see Matt. xiii 39. There is only one difficulty in this parabolic discourse, as given by Mark, the circumstance namely, that the sower who after scattering the seed goes away, is none other than the υἱός τοῦ ἀνθρώπου, as our Lord's own explanations afterwards show, (Matt. xiii 37,) and as is indeed indicated by the very fact, that the Lord, when the harvest is come, sends the reapers into the field, an act which, according to Matt xiii. 39, must be referred to the time of the κρίσις. But in what sense it can be said of the Lord that he lets the field grow without caring for its advancement, one does not well see, inasmuch as grace is required equally at the commencement and throughout the course of the divine life. Every thing would appear to harmonize better if we could suppose that by the ἄνθρωπος σπείρων is to be understood any and every teacher who may be labouring in the Lord's vineyard, and who certainly after implanting the word in the heart, must, in respect to its future growth, leave it to take its own course. Perhaps, however, such difficulties show that the similitude ought not to be pushed thus far. The very nature of a similitude implies that on some point or other, the thing compared must differ from that to which it is likened, else the two would be identical. Only in this case we feel ourselves shut out from having recourse to this explanation, by observing that the specific point on which the whole comparison turns, is just this very abandonment of all care for the seed after it has been sown. Unless, therefore, the whole is to have the appearance of inanity, meaning and force must be given to this point. Perhaps then, according to Matt. ix. 15, the meaning of the entire parabolic discourse may be taken in this way: although the inner life in man is never, during the course of its development, absolutely without the grace and the presence of the Lord, yet may it be said that there are two special periods when that grace is pre-eminently active. The first is the commencement of the life, (the sowing,) the second is the ripening of the fruit, (the harvest). Between these points lies a period, during which it may be said, that comparatively the soul is without the Lord, the divine life implanted in man developing itself according to its own inherent power, and to this season perhaps, a season of internal struggle and turmoil, the Lord here refers. Thus understood, the comparison gains for itself, at least, a specific meaning, and its connexion is made clear with what had gone before. Nor does this explanation exclude a reference to individual human teachers, only this does not appear as the thing primarily intended.

It is in another sense however, that the words ὃς γὰρ ἂν ἔχῃ κ. τ. λ. are interwoven as part of this discourse, by Matt., in the verses before us, the exposition of which we are now to give. According to ver. 10, sq., the disciples came to Jesus and asked him generally what his purpose was in thus speaking in parables, (διατί ἐν παραβολαῖς λαλεῖς αὐτοῖς;) the Lord replies that he employed them on account of the differences that existed among the various classes of his hearers, some of whom he wished to understand him, others not. In speaking by parables this twofold object would be gained, for every thing that it was needful for him to state would thus be declared, but in a form so veiled that only those understood it who were designed to understand it. Among these the disciples are mentioned first of all, and in this connexion is it said ὅστις γὰρ ἔχει κ. τ. λ., (ver. 12.) The idea thus appears set in a different light from that in which we find it with Luke and Mark. The apostles are represented as the ἔχοντες on whom, for this reason, there flows in the περίσσευμα, the λοιποί, however as the οὐκ ἔχοντες, who lose for this reason what they already have, to whom the appearance of the light tends to bring destruction. Before considering however, this idea, which is further developed in the following verses, we must attend to the expression, μυστήρια τῆς βασιλείας τῶν οὐρανῶν (τοῦ θεοῦ). It marks the general object of the παραβολαί, and in those very parables which follow throughout this chapter constant reference is prominently made to the βασιλεία. The word μυστήριον then, from μυέω to shut up, to conceal, is in the New Testament used to denote the Divine counsels, decrees, doctrines, which, as such, could never have become known to men as such, to men if left to themselves. (So the Heb. רז in the Old Testament.) Nowhere, however, are these decrees, &c. represented as absolutely eternally hid, and incapable of being known; but God, who at the prompting of his own love, reveals himself and all that is in him, is constantly by his ἀποκάλυψις revealing his μυστήρια; yet not in such a way that they cease to be μυστήρια, they retain for ever their divine character, which exalted them above all the powers of discovery belonging to man himself, only instead of hidden, they have become unveiled μυστήρια. (1 Cor. ii. 7. Rom. xvi. 25.) According to this view, the μυστήρια τῆς βασιλείας τῶν οὐρανῶν, denote the whole system of Divine counsels, ordinances, and doctrines, which have been revealed through Christ, and through the new economy which he founded. These stand in contrast, as it were, with the μυστήρια τοῦ νόμου, which, after the fulfilment of the Old Testament economy, had to make way for a new system of μυστήρια. This whole collection of mysteries, however, was made known only to some (ὑμῖν δέδοται γνῶναι,) from others it was hid, (according to Mark τοῖς ἔξω, as opposed to the apostles τοῖς ἔσω.) As to the mode of expression used by Paul in regard to this matter, comp. 1 Cor. v. 12, 13; Col. iv. 5; 1 Thes. iv. 12. In the use of the word δέδοται, it is impossible not to see a reference to the decree of God. It implies first, the positive exercise of divine grace, its communicating or imparting the blessing, and then negatively it implies the inability of man's will to attain of itself the thing bestowed. He uses the expression in the same sense as at Matthew xix. 11; xx. 23, and especially at John iii. 27; vi. 65; xix. 11, with the addition of ἄνωθεν, ἐκ τοῦ οὐρανοῦ. But this idea, that the passage asserts the giving and the withholding a knowledge of the secrets of the divine kingdom, forms precisely the great difficulty that meets us in this and the following verses, (ver. 13—15,) where at greater length it is explained, and founded on Old Testament prophecy.

According to the narrative of Matthew xiii. 13, the idea certainly seems put in such a form as to intimate that Christ's speaking in parables was simply a *consequence* resulting from the blindness and insensibility of a portion of his hearers. For the expression employed is ἐν παραβολαῖς λαλῶ ὅτι βλέποντες οὐ βλέπουσι κ. τ. λ., while Mark and Luke in the corresponding passage give ἵνα βλέποντες μὴ βλέπωσι, words which obviously mean that their failing to understand him was the *object designed* by our Lord in using the language of parables. But that in Matthew's account of our Lord's discourse he meant to convey no meaning different from that of the other evangelists, is shown first by the quotation from the Old Testament, which of itself expresses as strongly the same idea, and in the next place, if we take the ὅτι in verse 13, to denote the *cause* which led to his speaking in parables, it implies something self-contradictory. "For this reason do I speak to them in parables, *because* they do not understand," is a mode of thought which could in no respect be explained or justified.[1] For if they wholly failed to comprehend him, one does not see why the Lord did not speak at once in simple unfigurative terms—that would at least have given a chance of his being understood somewhat better than speaking before men of dull apprehension in language obscure and veiled. And according to this view the possibility of his being understood, must, to a certain extent, be assumed, as otherwise it would have been more to the purpose for him to have refrained from speaking altogether. On the other hand, the idea is a very simple one:—" I speak in

---

[1] The words could only be so interpreted if the parables were to be considered as means for *facilitating* the understanding of the subject referred to. But against this view the passage ἐκείνοις δὲ οὐ δέδοται, (v. 11,) is so decisive that the point admits of no further discussion.

parables *in order that* they may not understand," and this view has been attempted to be got rid of simply on account of the dogmatic difficulties it involves—difficulties which do not concern the interpreter of Scripture. According to the connexion therefore, the words in Matt xiii. 13, should be translated only in this way, "I speak to them in parables, *for* seeing, they see not," so that the result is represented as an effect contemplated and designed. This is plainly shown also immediately afterwards at ver 15, by the expression μήποτε ἴδωσι, in the prophecy of Isaiah (comp. Mark iv 12.) Attempts have been made it is true to put such a meaning on the μήποτε here, and the ἵνα in Luke and Mark as to take away from both particles the idea of *design* And it is not to be denied that μήποτε (as was already remarked in regard to ἵνα on Matt. i. 22,) sometimes in the New Testament, wants the sense of intention, or design. Especially convincing in support of this view of μήποτε, is the passage 2 Tim ii. 25, μήποτε δῷ αὐτοῖς ὁ Θεὸς μετάνοιαν, which it is utterly impossible to translate, "*in order that* God might not grant them repentance," but rather "whether God (εἰ πότε,) will not bestow on them repentance." According to this the passage before us, (ver 15,) might be rendered,—whether they might not see, whether they might not hear. The reference however to the prophecy (Is. vi. 9, 10,) which is also introduced in the same sense at John xii. 39 sqq.; Acts xxviii. 26 sqq., admits no interpretation of the passage except the teleological. Matthew and also Luke in the Acts of the Apostles, follow with some unimportant variations the reading of the LXX., while John on the contrary has given a translation of his own which expresses however the idea of the passage with the closest accuracy. He writes οὐκ ἠδύναντο πιστεύειν, and ἵνα μὴ ἴδωσι, so that the utmost violence must be done in interpreting the passage before the words will bear any other sense than this, that the design was they should not understand. The connexion of the words also as given in the Old Testament clearly shows the same meaning. (Compare Gesenius in his Commentary on the passage Is. vi. 9, 10.) It is represented as the penalty, as the curse of sin, that it prevents man's understanding the revelation of that which comes from God (The βλέπειν and ἀκούειν, as contrasted with the οὐ συνιέναι, οὐκ ἰδεῖν, denote the opportunity which had been given of understanding the Divine, inasmuch as it had been opened up in their immediate presence, while they did not possess the susceptibility necessary for embracing it. This want of susceptibility—the inability to believe—is denoted by ἐπαχύνθη,== הַשְׁמֵן, "*to become fat,*" in the sense of "*to become unfeeling or insensible.*" It stands as parallel to the הַכְבֵּד, and הָשַׁע, which in the Greek are rendered βαρέως ἀκούειν, καμμύειν. Καμμύειν is a barbarous form, for καταμύειν==κλείειν τοὺς ὀφθαλμούς. The verb ἐπιστρέφειν,==שׁוּב, *to abandon a path which had been already entered on,* is here as frequently elsewhere used to denote the inward turning of the soul from darkness to light. In the last clause καὶ ἰάσωμαι αὐτούς, a various reading, ἰάσομαι, is found, which certainly has been transferred from the LXX. in order to lessen the hardness of the passage by giving to the words the sense of "but I will heal them." This interpretation however does not agree with the connexion of the Hebrew, in which וָשָׁב וְרָפָא, holds a position entirely parallel. In Mark accordingly, the whole force of the idea is preserved, only the figure implied in ἰάσομαι, is explained by the words ἵνα μὴ ἀφεθῇ αὐτοῖς τὰ ἁμαρτήματα, a rendering which is also given in the Chaldee version.) According to the connexion then as found in the prophet, the passage Isa. vi 9, 10, refers primarily to the cotemporaries of Isaiah. Matthew sees in it a reference to the cotemporaries of Jesus, not judging capriciously, but taking a profound view of its real import For that which was exhibited in the days of Isaiah did not differ from what occurred in the times of Jesus—making allowance for circumstances—it was essentially the same. The Divine, as set forth in the discourse of Isaiah, was met by the insensibility of the people whom he summoned to spiritual effort, and the curse of their sin lay in this, that they did not even see the Divine as it existed in him. In the time of Jesus the same nation was dealt with in the same way, with only this difference, that in Jesus there was exhibited to the people the purest manifestation of the Divine, a faint reflection of which was all that could be beheld in Isaiah. Inasmuch then, as even this glory of the Divine light remained unperceived by them, the curse of sin in all its magnitude was exhibited to view, and the prophet's words consequently met in this with their entire fulfilment. And as in this instance, so is it generally with the New Testament writers—the phenomena of life in the Old Testament are viewed in the original root whence they sprang, and are seen to have corresponding analogies more fully developed amidst the occurrences of a later period. (As to the bearing which the train of thought in this passage has on the doctrine of predestination, see further what is said in Rom. ix.)

Ver. 16, 17. In contrast to the curse therefore which strikes these hardened hearts, there follows here that blessing which falls to the share of the disciples as men of receptive minds. The ὀφθαλμοί, ὦτα, are mentioned as the organs of reception in general, something corresponding to which belongs to the inner man. At Luke x. 23, these words occur in a quite different connexion, which will afterwards engage our attention. He adds that Jesus addressed these words to the disciples when by themselves (κατ' ἰδίαν=καταμόνας, Mark iv. 10, 34,) a fact which might have been inferred even from their contents. The comparison of his disciples to the προφῆται, and the δίκαιοι, of the Old Testament, (Luke instead of the δίκαιοι, has the word βασιλεῖς, an expression however which must in this case be held as applying to *righteous* kings,) would have been unintelligible to the multitude. Besides, the idea expressed in ver. 17, is simply an exposition of the frequently occurring πλεῖον Ἰωνᾶ, πλεῖον Σολομῶνος ὧδε, (Matt. xii. 41, 42.) All the longing desires of the pious throughout the Old Testament centred in the person of the Messiah. To behold him was the loftiest object of Old Testament hope. This benefit was granted to the disciples, and their whole blessedness, all their glory, consisted in this that they were illumined by the radiance of the Sun of righteousness. The special grace thus vouchsafed is brought to their remembrance by Christ, not in order to exalt them above the Old Testament saints, but to lay them low before the Lord.

Ver. 24—30. From this same comparison of seed-sowing, a second similitude arises, which however contemplates a different aspect of the kingdom of God. Of this parabolic statement also an authentic explanation is given by the Lord, ver. 36—41, which we shall take up at the same time. (The ὡμοιώθη ἡ βασιλεία τῶν οὐρανῶν ἀνθρώπῳ, is an abbreviated form of expression—one point of the similitude is brought prominently forward, and on it the comparison is concentrated. Here it is the man who scatters the seed, and so at ver. 33, it is the ζύμη, at ver. 44, the θησαυρός, at ver. 47, the σαγήνη, at ver. 45, the ἄνθρωπος ἔμπορος. The word παρατιθέναι,=שׂים, is here selected with reference to the enigmatical character of parabolical language—he laid the parable before them, for the purpose of opening it up. In the σπείρει, ἐν τῶ ἀγρῷ, we must beware of supposing that there is any confounding of εἰς and ἐν, he sowed *upon* his field as the place of his labour. The night-time is described as ἐν τῷ καθεύδειν τοὺς ἀνθρώπους, as at Job xxxiii. 15. Ver. 25. ζιζάνια, in the Talmud, זוּנִין. Comp. Buxtorf Lex. Talm. fol. 680, Suid. ἡ ἐν τῷ σίτῳ αἶρα, i. e. lolium [Virg. Ecl v. 37, *infelix lolium,*] *cockle, darnel.* The weed showed itself first at the springing time [βλαστάνειν,] and latterly when the fruit was forming, [καρπὸν ποιεῖν,] and it could not therefore have been stifled by the grain. Ver. 28. ἀπελθόντες συλλέξωμεν. This is represented as spoken according to the analogy of the Hebrew, הָלַךְ, in the οἶκος of the οἰκοδεσπότης, but neither here nor in any other passage where הָלַךְ is used are we to regard it as an empty pleonasm. Ver. 30. θεριστής,= ὁ θερίζων, occurs only here; δέσμη, ıs also a ἅπαξ λεγόμενον,=אֲגֻדָּה. Exodus xii. 22. An Old Testament comparison lies at the foundation of this whole parable of the burning up of the tares. Comp. 2 Sam. xxiii 7, where the same reference had already been made to the final judgment. The ἀποθήκη corresponds to the Hebrew, אוֹצָר, " *granary, storehouse.*")

Ver. 36—43. The explanation of the parable was in this instance also communicated to the disciples when alone, after the people had been dismissed (ver. 36). In brief sentences our Lord expounds the several portions of the comparison, the last point however, the final separation of the good from the bad, on which the whole turns, being more shortly given. But for this express exposition by Christ another interpretation would unquestionably at first sight have suggested itself. Jesus explains the field as being the κόσμος, the good seed as the υἱοὶ τῆς βασιλείας, the ζιζάνια as the υἱοὶ τοῦ πονηροῦ, and consequently the whole human race, good and bad together, are viewed as the corn that is growing up in the κόσμος, a word which here seems like *orbis terrarum,* to denote the universal earth. The generality of this reference does not appear at first sight to agree with the connexion, for the subject of discourse is not the whole world (ver. 24), but rather the βασιλεία τῶν οὐρανῶν. That in the general world evil intermingles itself with good, is obvious at a glance, but it is strange that in the kingdom of God itself, onward to its close, the same intermixture should be seen, for the express design of that kingdom is to represent the good. Beyond all doubt, however, this similitude must be understood of the kingdom of God, which is here termed the world, inasmuch as viewed ideally, it is destined to pervade the whole κόσμος, or conversely, the κόσμος viewed ideally is seen as destined of God to become his kingdom. The derangement of this original purpose by the influence of the kingdom of darkness, the Saviour will here explain, and he undertakes to define the relative connexion of good and evil in the church of God on earth, as well under the Old as the New Testament, down to the final judgment. The υἱὸς τοῦ ἀνθρώπου, consequently appears here again in his ideal dignity (comp. Dan. vii. 13,) as the adversary of the διάβολος, while from the beginning onward he has been working out the victory of good among the human race. This moreover is another passage belonging to the number of those in which Christ refers in his teaching literally and directly to the devil. The disciples had requested here an authoritative exposition of a similitude that was dark to them. In no point of view was this an occasion for conceding to popular prejudice (even if the idea of such accommodation were not essentially inconsistent with the holy character of Jesus,) and still less for having recourse to the use of proverbs or any thing else of the kind. While, however, according to this view, the parable as a whole is clear, yet on particular points, we are met by important difficulties. Thus the way in which the υἱὸς τῆς βασιλείας, and τοῦ πονηροῦ, are set in contrast, seems to point to an absolute severance of individuals, which might again seem to favour the doctrine of predestination. But the prohibition forbidding the rooting out of evil (ver. 28,) at once sufficiently shows that neither are the υἱοὶ τῆς βασιλείας conceived of as entirely dissevered from the evil, nor the υἱοὶ τοῦ πονηροῦ as wholly dissociated from the good. The one class appear only as in a certain respect the concentration of good, (not however as though any *gratia irresistibilis* preserved them from falling back,) the other as the concentration of evil, (not however as though any *decretum reprobationis* forced them into wickedness, and held them back from the possibility of repentance,) drawn by birth, circumstances, education, now more towards the one element, now more towards the other. For though all men are involved in sin, yet are they *not* all in an equal degree under its power; sincerity, uprightness, and susceptibility for everything good being beyond all mistake manifest in some, while others display malice, obstinacy, hardness of heart. It is strange however that this prohibition to separate these elements before their becoming ripe should be the thing *omitted* in the Lord's explanation, whether it be that Matthew has abridged his exposition, or whether it be that the Saviour wished merely to set prominently forth the great final separation, thus sufficiently indicating that until that separation take effect, no arbitrary, and therefore merely pernicious attempt to dissever them ought to be made.[1] It is indeed self-evident that this does not prohibit the severance of what is sinful from that which is good; it is only meant that no *individual person* should be shut out from intercourse with the good *as incorrigible*, there is always the possibility that the beneficent influence of good may awaken up in him the slumbering elements of improvement. At the same time however, it admits of no doubt, that according to the meaning of this parable all *violent* interference with the course of life led by the sinful members of the church (not merely death, but also final excommunication,) as well as every arbitrary effort to realize absolute purity of communion on earth, (Donatism) is forbidden, because the former leads to harshness and injustice, the latter inevitably to pride and blindness. For as *within* man, even the best, there exists a mixture similar to that which prevails *without* him, the effect can only be most pernicious, if, overlooking the sin that is in his soul, he holds himself forth to others as a *pure* member. The view here inculcated leads simply to humility, mildness, and to constant watchfulness at the same time, for the improvement of one's self and others. For there is no intention to prohibit admonition, or appropriate church discipline, or any other methods of dealing with the lives of sinful members of the church, if only *not forcible* in their nature. What man however is unable to separate, that the all-knowing God dissevers finally in the συντέλεια του αἰῶνος τούτου. The meaning of this expression cannot here be very accurately determined, generally and com-

---

[1] The view of this parable recently put forth by Steiger, (Ev. K Z Feb 1833, p. 113, sqq) to the effect that it is simply prophetico-historical, i e that it contains no admonitions intended to guide the conduct of believers, but merely instructs us in the truth that the church shall never on earth be pure, is obviously untenable, for in that case the account of the servant's zeal in wishing to root out the weeds, and the Lord's prohibition, would be mere decorations incidentally introduced to adorn the similitude—a supposition which clearly is most arbitrary, and destructive to the character of the parable

prehensively it denotes simply the conclusion of this temporal course of the world which contains the mixture of good and evil. That this severance is advancing of itself step by step, that it has been going on throughout the course of the world's history, that it was decisively manifested in the founding of a visible kingdom of God, and will be finally consummated in the universal judgment—are truths not touched on in the passage here before us. There is merely presented to us the great principle of biblical theodicy, that one day the holy and the unholy shall be mutually and wholly separated, but up to that period they shall remain ripening together, each according to its own nature. (Comp. in regard to συντέλειά τ. α. what is said at Matth. xii. 31, and xxiv. 1). In the account of the κρίσις, as here given, the βασιλεία τ. Θ. is contemplated as the only thing that exists, that is in being, out of which it is merely required that foreign admixtures be expelled, in order to manifest its real nature. (The sending of the ἄγγελοι, and the whole manner in which the punishment is represented will be found explained more fully at Matth. xxiv. 31; xxv. 30, 31. The σκάνδαλα, be it also observed, and the ποιοῦντες τὴν ἀνομίαν, are not to be taken as synonymous—the former is the more forcible expression, Κάμινος πυρός=πῦρ αἰώνιον. As to κλαυθμὸς καὶ βρυγμὸς ὀδόντων, see on Matth. vii. 12). After the expulsion of evil as the element of darkness, good reveals itself in its pure nature as light. (Τότε οἱ δίκαιοι ἐκλάμψουσι, as children of light— children of God the πατὴρ τῶν φώτων [James i 17] The words are chosen with reference to Dan. xii. 3. Comp Wisdom iii. 7, 4; Ezra vii. 55).

The *third* parable of the mustard seed is at once seen to be far less fully carried out than the two which precede it. It approaches the character of a mere comparison, for it is simply the nature of the mustard seed itself, and of the plant growing out of it, which is employed to illustrate the βασιλεία τ. Θ. In Luke this parable, and the following one of the leaven, also occur, but in another connexion, which we shall afterwards consider more at length. (In the parable the μικρότερον, and the μεῖζον, with the genitive following them, have certainly the force of the superlative, only too much stress in this respect must not be laid on them. The selection of this particular plant is perhaps to be explained from its qualities as a seasoning; which in the parable that immediately follows, forms also the *tertium comparationis*. Λάχανον, = יָרָק, *vegetables, cabbage-like plants* generally. The πετεινὰ τοῦ οὐρανοῦ, appear here in a connexion wholly different from that at Matt. xiii. 4, as representing all those who seek protection and refuge in the kingdom of God, according to Ezek. xvii 23, which passage seems to lie at the foundation of this whole comparison. Inasmuch as in the separate forms which exist throughout creation various characters seem to find expression, they admit also in the parabolic language of Scripture of being understood in a variety of senses.) The idea which this parable is obviously designed to set forth, is simply this—that in the manifestation of what is Divine, the beginning and the end of its development stand related to each other in an inverse ratio. Springing from invisible beginnings, it spreads itself abroad over an all-embracing field of operations As however the kingdom of God may be conceived of at one time in its totality, at another in its speciality, i. e., as manifested in a greater or smaller sphere, in nations, or in private individuals, so also may the parables which set forth particular aspects of the kingdom of God, be viewed. The rich thoughts deposited in them possess the same truth for the whole body as for the private members, because truth is universally alike and consistent with itself.

Ver. 33. The *fourth* parable of the leaven is very nearly allied to the foregoing, illustrating like it the all-pervading power of that which is from God, and the efficiency of which does not depend on the extent of the mass on which it may have to act. The two parables differ simply in this, that, in the former, that of the mustard seed, the divine kingdom is exhibited as manifesting its powers *outwardly*, in that of the leaven as unseen, as working *in secret*. The leaven shows it at the same time acting on another element which it strives to transmute, and draw into the nature of its own being, whereas in the parable of the mustard seed, the only point brought into view is the inherent development of that which is divine viewed by itself. (Ζύμη is used, Matt. xvi. 6; 1 Cor. v. 7; Gal. v. 9, in a bad sense, with reference to the passover feast, Ex. xiii 3. Its pervasive, seasoning power, forms here the single point of comparison with that which is divine; wisdom, the eternal mother of life, having sunk down into human nature in order to hallow it. The word ἐγκρύπτειν, indicates its secret, invisibly-acting influence. "Αλευρον, stands for the substance of the φύραμα, the meal, of which the dough was to be formed. The measure, σάτον, according to Josephus [Antiq. ix. 2,] contains μόδιον καὶ ἥμισυ 'Ιταλικόν. The mention of the particular measure individualizes the comparison as the nature of a parable requires. It were wrong expressly to apply the particular number to spiritual subjects, yet are we not perhaps altogether to deny some reference here to spirit, soul, and body, as the three powers of human nature which are to be sanctified by that which is divine).

Ver. 44—50. The last three parables, which however are given more in the shape of hints than of full detail, exhibit the kingdom of God in a way peculiar to themselves. They bring out the relative positions in which men stand to it, while the preceding parables had adverted partly to the nature of that kingdom in itself, and partly to the relation in which it stands to men. This peculiarity makes it not improbable that, as Matt. ver. 36, had already indicated, these latter parables were spoken confidentially to the inner circle of his disciples, with whose position, relatively to the kingdom of God, they singularly harmonize, as indeed with that of all who are connected with it like them as preachers of the gospel. The first two parables respecting the *treasure* in the field, and the *pearls,* come into contact in the same way as those of the leaven and the mustard seed. They represent the absolute value of divine things as compared with the relative value of every prized earthly treasure, and enjoin the sacrifice of the latter for the sake of the former. The abandonment, for the sake of the Divine, of a man's whole possessions, whether external (property, goods, possessions,) or internal, (opinions, usages, tendencies by which life had been swayed,) the apostles had begun to put in practice, and the Saviour here intimates, that step by step they would be required to carry it out But while the two parables are thus allied, a difference is yet obvious between them In both the precious object (the θησαυρός, or the μαργαρίτη, appears it is true as concealed, but human effort in searching for the concealed treasure is differently represented in them In that of the *pearls* a noble *active* nature is exhibited, which, under the pressure of inward impulse, seeks after (ζητεῖ,) the true, and strives for the exalted till it gets sight of the essence of everything that deserves a wish in the divine, as revealed in Christ its centre, and by complete self-renunciation becomes possessed of it. In the similitude of the treasure in the field, on the other hand, it is a more *receptive* turn of mind in reference to the divine which is presented to our notice It comes unsought, unlooked for, yet has the soul the will and the power, at any price, to acquire possession of it, only the active exertion (the ζητεῖν,) is wanting The history of a Peter and a Nathaniel exemplify these forms in which the principle of life developes itself among men (comp. John I). In the parable of the treasure hid in the field, not only is bold, joyful, self-sacrificing zeal (ἀπὸ τῆς χαρᾶς αὐτοῦ ὑπάγει,) commended, but praise seems also given to prudential management in divine things, inasmuch as the man who finds the treasure hides it again, and then buys the field from the owner without saying anything of the treasure contained it. The singularity of this will be considered and explained when we come to the difficult passage, Luke xvi., respecting the unjust steward. Another thing peculiar to the parable of the pearls is the contrast between unity and plurality. It expresses in a peculiar way the absolute importance of the one thing, and the merely relative value of everything else. Naturally this one thing can be no mere doctrine, no dogma, but something essential; it must be the divine in the human, as exhibited in the person of Christ. That man should in his own experience find God in himself, and himself in God—this is the one pearl for whose acquisition he must, in a peculiar sense, be willing to part with all things that he may win all things. The oneness of the pearl, however, does not contradict the idea that there are a multitude who seek it, for just because it is in itself the divine, therefore may each man seek and find it. It exists everywhere, inasmuch as the divine germ lies slumbering in all hearts, and requires only to be awakened by quickening, and life from on high.

The last similitude of the fishing-net is again closely allied to the second of the tares in the field. In both there is represented the intermingling of good and bad in the βασιλεία τ. Θ. which are to be separated only at the end of the day. For, what in the parable of the tares is denoted by the harvest, is here shadowed forth by the completing of the draught of fishes. In verses 49, 50, the parabolic discourse indeed is explained in such a way as to correspond word for word with verses 41, 42, and our observations on the former passage therefore apply equally to this. The difference between the two similitudes might perhaps be most properly stated thus. In that of the tares the βασιλεία τ. Θ. is set forth in its ideal form as identical with the whole κόσμος, while in this of the fishing-net on the other hand the kingdom of God is taken according to its real appearance, as a smaller whole defined and marked off within the κόσμος but including within itself the tendency to diffuse itself over all This is pointed out by the circumstance that it is from the θάλασσα, which represents the whole, that fishes are taken into the net of God's kingdom. Thus explained, the passage is another evidence to prove that the Saviour himself acknowledged no pure communion in his visible church on earth. It appertains to the wondrous leadings of God's grace that everywhere in the course of this transitory world, evil intermingles itself alongside of good. As in the ark a Ham appears along with Shem and Japhet,—as in the company of the twelve, a Judas,—so has the spiritual Israel, the spiritual Jerusalem, a Babel in its bosom. By this arrangement the opportunity of repentance is everywhere put within reach of the evil, and the child of light, amidst his struggles with the enemy, is carried on towards perfection. Not till the κρίσις ἐσχάτη, will an entirely pure fellowship of saints be exhibited. The parable gives us further an important hint as to the ἄγγελοι, to whom the work of making a separation is entrusted For it is obvious that they are the same persons who first cast out the net, then draw it to shore, and afterwards separate the fishes If we compare then Matt. iv. 19, where the Lord promises to the apostles that he will make them ἁλιεῖς ἀνθρώπων, it appears that by the ἄγγελοι, we are to understand no spiritual beings from the heavenly world, but men whom God has furnished as his messengers and servants, by infusing into them heavenly powers for trying and proving the spirits of others. Thus had the כֹּהֵן already been styled at Mal. ii. 7, מַלְאַךְ יְהוָֹה־צְבָאוֹת. Although therefore the apostles in one sense are themselves fishes (ἰχθῦς,) caught in the net of God's kingdom, yet are they in their renewal and regeneration so transformed, that they take part in the spiritual work of Him who first took them by the might of his love, an intimation which is not without importance for the understanding of other passages, such as Matt xxiv. 31; xxv. 31, compared with Jude ver. 14; 1 Cor. vi 2, 3; xi 31.

Ver. 51, 52. Matthew concludes this collection of parables with the question of Jesus to the disciples, συνήκατε ταῦτα πάντα; If we compare Mark iv 13, we find a word of reproach uttered by Jesus against the little power of understanding possessed by the disciples, and this question may therefore be translated—have ye now then at last comprehended all this? Not as though they should have gained an understanding of it without explanation, but along with it and through means of it. For Mark observes, IV. 34, κατ' ἰδίαν τοῖς μαθηταῖς αὐτοῦ ἐπέλυε πάντα. (The verb ἐπιλύειν, points plainly to what was enigmatical [חִידוֹת] in the parabolic discourses of Christ) On receiving the affirmative reply of the disciples, the Saviour gives under another similitude a view of the peculiar nature and ministry of a γραμματεύς in that more exalted sense in which the character ought to belong to the apostles. The διὰ τοῦτο refers back to the preceding ναὶ κύριε of the apostles, the force of it being—" on this account can ye now fulfil your calling for," &c. &c.,—obviously however the reading τῇ βασιλείᾳ must here be preferred to the other ἐν βασιλείᾳ, or εἰς βασιλείαν, which can have arisen only from a misunderstanding of the passage. For it is not simply the members of God's kingdom who are here spoken of, but those who act as *teachers* in behalf of the members. The expression γραμματεύς τῇ βασιλείᾳ μαθητευθείς is therefore to be explained as meaning a scribe who has been instructed, and who, by means of instruction, has become capable of labouring for the kingdom of God, who therefore himself, in the first instance, belongs to it, and who, moreover, hath penetrated into its deep things that he may be able to lead others the further. Obviously our Lord intends to contrast his apostles with the Jewish סֹפְרִים, the γραμματεῖς τῇ βασιλείᾳ τῆς γῆς μαθητευθέντες. These latter learn earthly wisdom after a human method for earthly ends, the apostles, and by consequence, all who resemble them, draw instruction from the eternal Word (John I. 1,) the fountain of all wisdom and truth, for heavenly objects. The relation in which these spiritual γραμματεῖς stand to the church is compared by the Lord to the relation in which the father of a family stands to the members of the household. He has wisely provided his stores, and out of them divides to every individual according to his wants. (The θησαυρός is here equivalent to the ταμεῖον, in which the new and old supplies lie treasured up The ἐκβάλλειν, is equivalent to הוֹצִיא, promere.) It is probable that something more definite than the mere idea of diversity is denoted by the καινὰ καὶ παλαιά. The most natural course is to refer it to the great distinction between the law and the gospel, in the due apportioning of which lies fundamentally the whole employment of one instructed for the kingdom of heaven, inasmuch as the inner life of the soul is oscillating for ever betwixt these opposite points, as will be further explained in Rom. vii.

Ver. 34, 35. In conclusion, let us now consider the words with which Matthew finally closes those parables that were uttered in the hearing of the people—words, however, which are applicable to the parabolic mode of speaking generally. Matthew, with whom Mark (iv. 34,) agrees, observes that in general Jesus never spoke, χωρὶς παραβολῆς,—that is, never to the ὄχλοι, for to his disciples he expounded these parables In considering this idea, we must in the first place understand the παραβολή in the more general sense of comparison, *similitudo;* only one does not well see, even when it is thus explained, how the position can entirely be made good, that Jesus never spake without similitudes The shortest mode of explanation is to view the negation as merely a relative one, or if this seems inadmissible, it may then be said that the καθὼς ἠδύναντο ἀκούειν of Mark iv. 33, supplies us with a solution, inasmuch as even though the Saviour in a literal sense did not always speak in similitudes, yet was he never understood *aright* by that multitude, so little fitted for the reception of spiritual truths. With this, the quotation that follows well agrees, in which the mystery that runs through the whole ministry of the Messiah is brought forward into view. (In regard to the formula ὅπως πληρωθῇ, see on Matth i. 22. The passage quoted is found at Ps. lxxviii. 2, in a poem by Asaph. According to the account of Jerome [in his commentary on the passage,] the name of Isaiah stood in the passage of Matth. as given in the old MSS, but without doubt it was interpolated because the writer of the Psalms did not seem to the transcriber to be a prophet—a name which it was usual to restrict to the person primarily so called) The first half of the verse agrees with the Hebrew and the LXX., the second, however, varies from both. The words אַבִּיעָה חִידוֹת מִנִּי־קֶדֶם are translated by the LXX., φθέγξομαι προβλήματα ἀπ' ἀρχῆς. The words as given by Matthew are so peculiar that they furnish another argument for the independence of the Greek text. The phrase ἀπὸ καταβολῆς κόσμου, in the sense of ἀπ' ἀρχῆς, does not once occur in the Old Testament; in the New Testament, on the contrary, it is very common, Matth. xxv. 34; Luke xi. 50, John xvii. 24, and often besides. At the foundation of it lies that figure which compares the world to a building whose erection commences with the foundation καταβολή. Only in this passage, however, do we find the verb ἐρεύγω, which the LXX. also employ at Ps. xviii. 2, in translating הִבִּיעַ, and which is very commonly used by the Gnostics to express their emanation-doctrine of the streaming forth of being. The expressions מָשָׁל and חִידוֹת imply the idea of a dark, enigmatical mode of speaking, as an outward covering, and, along with this, the reality of deep thoughts full of profound meaning. The חִידוֹת מִנִּי־קֶדֶם are the eternal mysteries of the world and of human history which Christ unfolds for those who comprehend his discourses, but which remain hid from the multitude. The poet utters the words of the quotation in connexion with the rest of the Psalm, and מָשָׁל and חִידוֹת refer in the first instance to the leadings of God's ancient people. This then is another passage added to those which seem to countenance the idea that the phrase ἵνα πληρωθῇ does not imply the fulfilment of a prophecy. But that Matthew saw in it such a fulfilment—(even if he were wrong in taking this view,) is clearly shown from his translating מִנִּי־קֶדֶם by ἀπὸ καταβολῆς τοῦ κόσμου, while from the connexion of the Psalm it refers primarily to the times of Moses. The expositor therefore ought not in this case to reject the most obvious meaning of the formula—a meaning which the writer himself plainly intended to give it. If we ask however how it is conceivable that the Evangelist can see in these words the fulfilment of a prophecy, the explanation may be given in the following way. What the prophets utter as men inspired by the Spirit of God and through his power, is really spoken by the Logos, the Son, who in all inspired Scripture reveals himself through them. In thus far then it is Christ's part alone to say ἀνοίξω ἐν παραβολαῖς τὸ στόμα μου, for without his power it is impossible for any to find out or reveal divine secrets, and what the poetic writer of this Psalm says respecting wisdom and revelation, he utters only through him.

§ 23. JESUS IN NAZARETH.

(Matth. xiii. 53—58; Mark vi. 1—6; Luke iv. 14—30)

The older expositors (Storr also, and Dr Paulus at the present day,) assume that in these narratives the Evangelists refer to distinct visits paid by Christ to Nazareth at separate periods. According to this view, Matthew refers to a later period when Christ returned and taught a second time in his native town, while Luke records the earlier visit. As to this, the only question is, how to connect Christ's presence at Nazareth on the first occasion with the imprisonment of John, (for according to the parallel passages [Mark i. 14; Matth iv. 12,] the two events seem to hang together,) and next, how to find for the second visit a proper place in the history, inasmuch as Mark puts it in a different connexion from Matthew. Schleiermacher, however, has conclusively proved (on the writings of Luke, p. 63,) that the narratives refer to the same occurrence. For if the narrative of Matthew were transferred to the later years of Christ's life, it is not easy to suppose that the inhabitants of Nazareth could ask πόθεν τούτῳ ἡ σοφία; and still less can it be thought that the events recorded by Luke are posterior to those related by Matthew. In point of internal character both histories are entirely alike, and the single circumstance that countenances the idea of their being distinct, is the chronological succession of events.[1] This very fact, however, is another proof that there is, especially in Matthew and Mark, the absence of any prominent attempt to trace the course of events according to the period of time in which they happened. Matthew, at the commencement and conclusion of his narrative, uses general formulae, xiii. 53, μετῆρεν ἐκεῖθεν καὶ ἐλθών κ. τ. λ.; xiv. 1, ἐν ἐκείνῳ τῷ καιρῷ. Mark vi. 6, breaks off so indefinitely that even if he had in general followed the thread of chronology, he here obviously let it fall from his hand with the words καὶ περιῆγε τὰς κώμας κύκλῳ διδάσκων. The words used to denote the transition of the narrative to a new subject— μετῆρεν ἐκεῖθεν ἐν ἐκείνῳ τῷ καιρῷ are obviously so vague that they do not even amount to anything so definite as *afterwards* or *at the same time*, in however wide a sense these expressions be taken—they are rather, according to the standing-point of the Evangelist, to be understood as meaning generally, "Jesus came

---

[1] Sieffert (p 89, sqq) thinks that the wrong position assigned to this narrative disproves the apostolic origin of the gospel But as the whole of these occurrences at Nazareth happened before the calling of Matthew (comp. Luke iv. 14 sqq.) one does not see how it is precisely as to the events of this period that Matthew must have been so accurately informed. Besides, it is far from his object to trace the chronological course of events.

once upon a time to his native city." In the connexion as it stands in Matthew, the whole narrative is plainly introduced, not for its own sake—it serves simply as a key-stone to the collection of parables. The whole emphasis lies on the words πόθεν τούτῳ ἡ σοφία αὕτη καὶ αἱ δυνάμεις. This σοφία of Jesus was unfolded in the parables here recorded, and the relation in which those around him stood to it, is shown in the following narrative. They knew it well, but took offence at his immediate earthly connexions, and despised on this account the blessing which Jesus was come to bring to them. Luke, on the other hand, relates the occurrence for its own sake, and unquestionably he is in respect of chronology more correct, although the vagueness of the formulæ (Luke iv. 14, 15,) do not admit of an accurate determination of the time—only that the occurrence belongs to the commencement of our Lord's ministry, is more than probable.[1] Him, therefore, we shall follow mainly in our exposition, adding at the end the particulars given by Matthew and Mark.

Luke iv. 16, 17, represents most graphically Christ's entry into the synagogue at Nazareth. The words κατὰ τὸ εἰωθὸς αὐτῷ, (comp. Acts xvii. 2,) do not refer to an earlier period, for, that Jesus previously to the commencement of his public ministry delivered addresses in the synagogues, is improbable even on the showing of this narrative. The narrator rather refers by anticipation to his subsequent course of labour. According to the practice of the ancient synagogue men who were deemed trustworthy, even though not rabbins, might deliver doctrinal addresses to those assembled. They usually stood up during the reading of God's Word (ἀνέστη ἀναγνῶναι, ver. 16,[2]) the servant of the synagogue (ὑπηρέτης, ver. 20,) handed the roll, and the teacher, after reading the section, sitting down delivered his dis-

---

[1] Yet De Wette thinks Luke may have placed the incident at too early a period.

[2] In reference to this custom quotations are given by Lightfoot on the passage In the first it is said,—Non legunt in lege nisi stantes. Imo non licet legenti, alicui rei inniti Unde autem tenetur legens ˈstare? Quia Scriptura dicit: tu autem mecum sta. The reader in the prophets was called מַפְטִיר, i. e. according to Buxt. Lex. Talm. p. 1719, *dimittens*, he who read last and dismissed the people According to this, one may suppose that the reading of the passage from the law was already completed, and that Jesus, as maphtir, now concluded the service of God

course (ver. 20) After a section from the books of Moses, there followed a passage from the prophets The account given in this narrative corresponds closely to the usual practice, the only doubtful point being whether the Redeemer read the passage from the Prophets set down for that Sabbath or not. To me the latter view seems probable. On the contrary supposition, one must assume that first an extract from the law, and next this passage from Isaiah, had been read, but in this way the deep impression of these prophetic words must have been greatly weakened. Besides, the words ἀναπτύξας τὸ βιβλίον εὗρε κ. τ. λ. point not so much to reflection or previous calculation, but to the Holy Spirit himself, as guiding to the discovery precisely of that passage in which the Messiah's appearance was predicted.

Ver. 17 The βιβλίον is to be conceived of as a roll, so that ἀναπτύσσω retains its literal sense of *unfolding* or *unrolling*. The person who presented it was undoubtedly the חזן, the ὑπηρέτης, ver. 20, (comp. Buxt lex p. 730.)

Ver. 18, 19 The passage Is. lxi. 1, is quoted by Luke freely, and therefore with some variations, from the LXX Many changes, however, have been adopted from the translation into our text, as for instance the additional clause ἰάσασθαι τοὺς συντετριμμένους τὴν καρδίαν after the ἀπέσταλκέ με The clause ἀποστεῖλαι τεθραυσμένους ἐν ἀφέσει, on the other hand, is found neither in the Hebrew text nor LXX translation of the passage, and consequently must have been inserted by the Evangelist quoting from memory. The passage, moreover, in its prophetic connexion, belongs to that majestic prediction of the עֶבֶד יְהֹוָה, which fills the second half of Isaiah. It contains under the figure of the prophet and the enlightened portion of the people, who are now spoken of literally, as Israel, and now as an individual person, a prediction of the Messiah, in whom, as its individual representative, the holy Israel is presented to view. In this light does the Redeemer now make himself known while explaining the words of the ancient seer as fulfilled in himself.

The expression πνεῦμα ἐπ' ἐμέ = רוּחַ עָלָי occurs also in the same form at Isaiah xlii. 1. lix. 21. It denotes the exalted character of Him who was sent from God, and furnished with power from on high. The words ἔχρισέ με, refer more definitely to his being furnished with spiritual power for the royal and priestly offices of the Messiah, the separate forth-putting of which powers, the following narrative records. Oὗ εἵνεκεν = יַעַן is nothing more than the simple ὅτι, and assigns the ground of the spiritual anointing, "*for* he anointed me to preach good tidings to the poor." The εὐαγγελίσασθαι πτωχοῖς (לְבַשֵּׂר עֲנָוִים) points out that which was the primary work of the Messiah. The πτωχοί, like the πτωχοί πνεύματι of Matt. v. 3, are those who have been awakened from natural death to anxiety, within whom the felt need of an atonement has been excited. The εὐαγγέλιον was brought to these men through means of the very appearance of the Messiah, of faith in him and his help against sin with all its inward and outward consequences. The ἄφεσις and the ἀνάβλεψις, are specially brought forward as the real results effected by the Spirit-anointed Redeemer. The saving power of the Messiah, which is one and the same, is represented first as breaking the bonds of sin, then as removing the insensibility of the darkened mental eye; so that it is merely two aspects of the same subject which are brought forward, and these have their analogies in the physical world. The expression κηρύξαι (לִקְרֹא) however, implies that the ἄφεσις and ἀνάβλεψις were not set forth as something merely distant and future, but as close at hand, so that the annunciation and the thing announced go together The beautiful idea of the clause ἰάσασθαι τοὺς συντετριμμένους τὴν καρδίαν, in which is expressed the tender act of the Saviour lifting up all who were bowed and bent down, is omitted by the Evangelist, in order that he may, in a seemingly pleonastic form, once more repeat the idea of the ἄφεσις. But the τεθραυσμένοι puts us at once in mind of the συντετριμμένοι, (θραύω, *to break up, to crush in pieces*. θραύεσθαι, *to be in a state of brokenness*, equivalent to the Hebrew רְצוּצִים Is lviii. 6.) And the ἀποστεῖλαι ἐν ἀφέσει, is in the same passage parallel to the שַׁלַּח רְצוּצִים. The ideas of *healing, deliverance, restoration to our original state*, are here intermingled. There is, moreover, something remarkable in the relation between the words τυφλοῖς ἀνάβλεψιν, ἀποστεῖλαι τεθραυσμένους ἐν ἀφέσει, and the Hebrew text of the passage Is. lxi. 1. Both there and in the LXX., the last words are wholly wanting; the first do not accurately correspond to the Hebrew text. The words of the latter run לַאֲסוּרִים פְּקַח־קוֹחַ, and they are rendered τυφλοῖς ἀνάβλεψιν. The expression פְּקַח־קוֹחַ had been read as one word, in the sense of *the opening of closed eyes;* אֲסוּרִים

captives, was seemingly taken to mean, *men with eyes bound up;* but this does not agree with the connexion of the passage in the prophet, which does not admit any other rendering than "*release to those that are bound.*" The words ἀποστεῖλαι τεθραυσμένους ἐν ἀφέσει, which are entirely awanting in Is. lxi. 1, have undoubtedly been taken by Luke from the parallel passage, Is. lviii. 6, and interwoven here with the former. In this expression he again follows the LXX. It thus appears that the writers of the New Testament deal very freely by those of the Old. With memories uncertain and wavering like those of other men, confusing passages, mistaking words, the heavenly Spirit of truth, who inspired and led them, yet so manages all, that nothing untrue, nothing that may mislead has resulted, but the truth itself is rather presented in a new aspect, and its real nature the more completely revealed.[1] Finally, the concluding words, κηρύξαι ἐνιαυτὸν κυρίου δεκτόν, are again taken from Is. lxi. 1. The LXX. have simply rendered לִקְרֹא by καλέσαι The phrase שְׁנַת־רָצוֹן, like the יוֹם which follows it, denotes the whole period of New Testament life, during which they who receive into their souls the mind of Christ the beloved, appear as themselves also through him well-pleasing to God.[2] Ephes. i. 6.

Ver. 20. It may be a doubtful question whether the Saviour read merely these words, or brought forward also the following verses. To me the former supposition seems the more probable He wished simply to proclaim a joyful message, and invite the inhabitants of Nazareth to embrace it,—the immediately succeeding verses, however, contain a threatening of the day of wrath. (Πτύσσω is found only in this passage, *to lay together, to roll up.* Ἀτενίζω, *to look with sharp unflinching gaze*, a favourite word with Luke.)

Ver. 21, 22. The expression ἤρξατο λέγειν, is not by any means to be held redundant; it indicates the solemn and weighty mode in which he entered on his discourse. In the clause ἡ γραφὴ

---

[1] In regard to the quotations from the Old Testament in the New, compare the striking treatise by Tholuck, in the supplement to his Commentary on the epistle to the Hebrews. Hamburg 1836.

[2] It is strange that several of the Fathers understood this passage to mean that Christ preached only one year (and some months). Comp. Clem. Alex. Strom. 1 p. 407. Orig de princ. vol. 1. p. 160.) As to the rroneous nature of this view, see more at length in the Comm. on John ii. 13, v. i. vi. 4

πεπλήρωται, Luke gives shortly the contents of Christ's address That this passage must be specially understood as an authentic exposition of the Old Testament prophecy, can admit of no doubt. (On πληρωθῆναι, see besides at Matt. i. 22.) To suppose that there is here any concession or accommodation to popular sentiments, would be to wound the Gospel to its very foundations. The preaching of Jesus in Nazareth was a preaching of grace; the unbelievers themselves admitted this, but they took offence at his earthly connexions, and squandered without improvement the ἐνιαυτὸν κυρίου δεκτόν. The expression λόγοι τῆς χάριτος, refers primarily to the outward charms of the Saviour's speech, but that must be considered simply as the visible result of the grace which revealed itself in him. He manifested before his hearers the fulness of his χάρις and ἀλήθεια. (John i. 14.)

That it was the well-known family connexions of Jesus against which the inhabitants of Nazareth took offence, is shown both by Matthew and Mark. They recount the names of all his family, and wish, as it were, to mislead themselves into the conviction that he is merely one of them Like all sensual men, strangers to the spiritualities of the unseen world, they look on that which is divine, and for the reception of which they want all perceptive power, as something absolutely unattainable, and they hold themselves far off from it, should it seek, with its transforming influences, to enter the circle of their own life. This is especially true when its influences are brought to bear through means of those whom they see moving amidst earthly connexions analogous to their own. In the phrase ὁ τοῦ τέκτονος υἱός, the prevalent popular idea was embodied, and that impression was wisely permitted, because the idea of the heavenly origin of Jesus could be of use only to believers. Mark, however, in the parallel passage, terms Jesus himself ὁ τέκτων, inasmuch as the Saviour, amidst his earthly connexions, and before his coming publicly forward as the Messiah, undoubtedly followed the calling of Joseph,[1] a circumstance which formed part of his humiliation. Christian antiquity saw, in the facts thus recorded, nothing offensive, for the real life of Jesus was in every respect unseen. Adopting apocryphal additions, Justin tells us ταῦτα γὰρ τὰ τεκτονικὰ ἔργα εἰργάζετο ἐν ἀνθρώποις ὤν, ἄροτρα καὶ ζυγά, διὰ

---

[1] Mark does not name Joseph, he only says of Jesus that he was υἱὸς Μαρίας, which probably indicates that Joseph was already dead.

τούτων καὶ τᾶτῆς δικαιοσύνης σύμβολα διδάσκων καὶ ἐνεργῆ βίον (Dial. c. Tryph. Jud. p. 316. Paris 1636.) As respects the ἀδελφοί here named, and the ἀδελφοί who are left nameless, a question may arise as to whether they were full brothers, or step-brothers, or cousins. The middle opinion, that they were step-brothers, is the least of all supported by proof, having nothing to rest on but the tradition that Joseph, at a former period of life, had been married to a woman named Salome. It may, therefore, be at once set aside. Between the two views which remain, it is hardly possible, owing to the defect of proof, to decide with historic certainty. At first sight, however, everything seems to conspire in favour of the opinion that the brethren and sisters of Jesus were really *Mary's own* children, and great pains have recently been taken to establish this view.[1] 1. Their names are given in immediate connexion with that of the mother. 2. We have no ground for supposing that Joseph's marriage with Mary was a marriage only in appearance, and Matt. i. 25 rather seems to be a positive testimony on the other side. (Compare, however, the Comm. on the passage) Yet a careful examination tends rather to discountenance this, and support the latter opinion, that the so-called ἀδελφοί τοῦ κυρίου were cousins to Jesus. For first of all, it is conclusively proved that none of these four brethren of Jesus can have belonged to the number of the twelve apostles, although among them there were two who bore the similar names of James and Judas. For, according to John vii. 5, they did not believe in Jesus. And at Acts i 14, they are still markedly separated from the apostles, although they appear here as believers.[2] It is expressly stated, however, respecting Mary, the

---

[1] Compare Stier's Andeut. Part i. 404 sq, and Clemen in Winer's Zeitschrift fur wiss. Th. Part iii. p 329 sq. Also Schneckenburger's Beitr. p. 214 sq annot in Iac. epist. p 141. Tubing Zeitschr. 1829, p. 47 sq., 1830, p. 2 sq. If, however, Joseph had been the father of the persons who are termed Christ's brethren, and if Mary, the mother of Jesus, had been their mother, some of them would surely, for once at least, have been styled " the son of Joseph," since it was common for the Jews to use the name of the father in denominating each other. According to our view, the " brethren of Christ" are sometimes also styled " sons of Cleophas."

[2] Those who maintain the identity of the apostles, James and Judas, with the ἀδελφοί τοῦ κυρίου of the same name, appeal especially to the fact that Alpheus, who is mentioned as the father of James, (Matt. x. 3) is the same person with Clopas or Cleophas, the husband of Mary, who was sister to the mother of Jesus (John xix. 25.) According to the

wife of Cleophas, and sister to the mother of Jesus, (John xix. 25,) that she had sons, two of whom, James and Joses, are named to us by Matthew (xxvii 56). According to this, then, the two mothers who were of the same name themselves, must have had sons whose names were also alike Certainly it may possibly have been so, yet the number of persons in the New Testament bearing similar names must in that case be immoderately increased. But how John xix. 26, can accord with the opinion that Mary had sons of her own, it is impossible to see. Beyond all doubt she would have been taken charge of by them, and not entrusted to John, who stood without the circle of the family connexion. When one considers that according to Hebrew usage אָח is the common term for cousin; and that two of the so-called brethren are demonstrably the Lord's cousins; the preponderance of proof unquestionably inclines to the conclusion that Jesus had no brethren of his own after the flesh.[1] If Joseph died young, one may suppose that Jesus and Mary dwelt in the house of her sister, that Jesus grew up along with her sons, and this circumstance would explain very simply how it happens that Mary, the mother of Jesus, and her sister's sons, should sometimes be named together.

Luke iv. 23. Jesus looked at once through the hearts of the men of Nazareth, and saw that they could not penetrate into his real nature beneath the cloud of humiliating earthly circumstances which enveloped his hidden glory He held up, therefore, before them, as in a glass, the likeness of themselves, giving them thus to see that they were incapable of knowing him. For their benefit he quotes from the Old Testament examples to

---

mode in which Greek names are formed from the Hebrew, it was possible that חַלְפַּי may have been changed into 'Αλφαῖος, by leaving out the aspirate, while by laying stress upon it, the name would be formed into Κλωπᾶς. It is inconceivable, however, that the same writer would have constructed the name in both these Greek forms, as we find them in Luke, who now writes Κλεόπας (xxiv. 18,) and now 'Αλφαῖος (vi. 15.)

[1] The opinion that Joseph and Mary had children born to them, I am further led to reject, on the ground that, according to the Old Testament predictions, it is difficult to conceive of any continuation of the stem of David, the line out of which the Messiah was to come forth. We conceive of it as a fitting thing that in Jesus, the everlasting Ruler, who arose from the house of David, the stock was finished What we read of David's descendants at a future period, (compare Euseb. H. E. iii 20,) refers beyond doubt to the children of some collateral line.

show that so early as the times of their fathers, the Divine found no acceptance among those most closely connected with the prophets, and that, impeded in the development of its influences among them, it had to take refuge among the heathen. The Saviour's first words, however, intimate clearly that the inhabitants of Nazareth had desired to see his miracles, and had remarked that he might perform a miracle on himself, changing himself from a poor man into a rich,—from a lowly man into a mighty. This carnal appetite for the marvellous, the Saviour here, as elsewhere, repels. (Compare on Matt. xii. 38, 39, xvi. 1 sq.) He performs no miracle, in order by its splendour to blind, but to heal, and to strengthen the poor, the weak, the needy. (Πάντως ἐρεῖτε, *ye assuredly say to me.* The word πάντως often occurs in Luke, [Acts xviii. 21; xxi. 22; xxviii. 4.] Respecting παραβολή, see on Matt. xiii. 1. Here it denotes like מָשָׁל a proverb.) The meaning of ἰατρέ, θεράπευσον σεαυτόν, is simply this,—show your skill on yourself; are you great—do you allege that as a Saviour you can give deliverance? then deliver yourself from poverty. Thus did the blinded people mock his love when on the cross, (Matt. xxvii. 42,) and thus does selfishness ever manifest itself in the heart that is alienated from God. Pure love, however, set free from selfishness, gives rather than takes, (Acts xx. 35,) becomes poor in order to make others rich, (2 Cor. viii. 9.) Wetstein on the passage, quotes, moreover, from the Rabbins proverbs of the same meaning; for example, from Tanchuma on Genes. p. 61, medice sana claudicationem tuam. In connexion with the things of this world, the idea is in some respects true, in the kingdom of grace it is false.) The concluding words of the verse show further with what latitude the introductory remark at Luke iv. 14, the general formula of transition, must be taken. Jesus had, after his temptation, been to Capernaum, and there performed miracles, (εἰς is the correct reading, and means *in behalf of, for the benefit of* Capernaum,) the report of which had reached Nazareth. This proves that even in Luke the chronology is hard to trace, and that we cannot even in his case conclude from the immediate collocation of events, that they followed each other directly in point of time. In the words ποίησον καὶ ὧδε, the pride and arrogance of the natural man are most plainly expressed. They demand miracles, as though they had, from being his countrymen, a special right to them. Yet do they mock him who claims to be more than they, disparaging themselves in their self-contradictory pride. Meanwhile they cannot subdue the impression which his divine presence had made on them, for they are astonished. (V. 22.)

Ver. 24. This verse forms, in the account of Luke, the climax of the narrative. With Matthew and Mark it rather falls incidentally into the course of the history which is looked at from a point of view entirely different. Most appropriately does Luke introduce this occurrence at the outset of Christ's ministry, and narrate it with such care, for the reception he met with when commencing his official labours in his native town, exhibited to view, as in a mirror, the peculiar experience of his whole subsequent career. Matthew and Mark further add: the prophet is of no esteem ἐν τῇ οἰκίᾳ αὐτοῦ καὶ ἐν τοῖς συγγενέσι. By these words the picture is cut down within narrow limits, but its leading outlines remain the same. As Christ's brethren believed not, (John vii. 5,) so neither did the inhabitants of Nazareth believe, and like the latter, so the whole people of the land disbelieved, εἰς τά ἴδια ἦλθε καὶ οἱ ἴδιοι αὐτον οὐ παρέλαβον. (John i. 11.) The kingdom of God passed over to the heathen, and to them even Luke himself went as a preacher. As, however, after the resurrection, the brethren of Christ were among the believers, (Acts i. 14,) so shall Israel, who at the time of the great resurrection (Rom. xi. 25) turn back to the Lord. That which happened, however, to Christ personally, he applies to *all* prophets, οὐδεὶς προφήτης δεκτός ἐστιν ἐν τῇ πατρίδι αὐτοῦ. For in the case of every prophet, the Divine that is within him comes into conflict with the sinful, as it exists among his cotemporaries, and the more close the connexion in which they stand after the flesh, the more incomprehensible to the worldly man is the distance which separates them after the spirit. The spectacle of the prophet entangled amidst those irritating connexions with this earthly life in which all are involved, rendered it more difficult under this lowly guise, to trace the presence of the heavenly element.

Ver. 25—27 The examples by which the Lord illustrates the working of this divine power, passing by those which are near and acting on those at a distance, are taken from 1 Kings xviii. 1. sq., xvii. 12. sq. The ἔτη τρία καὶ μῆνες ἕξ, are also given at James v. 17, but, according to 1 Kings xviii. 1, the time seems merely to have extended over the second and into the third year. If, however, we compute it, not from the coming of the rain, but from the flight of Elijah, 1 Kings xvii. 9, as Benson has proposed, the difficulty disappears. Σάρεπτα = צָרְפַת a small town betwixt Tyre and Sidon. The whole stress is to be laid on the fact that heathens instead of Israelites saw the miracles of the prophet.

Ver. 28, 29. These parallel cases from amidst the heathen, wounded the vanity of the Nazarenes; they drove out their prophet, and so made the words of Jesus true. Nay, they even intended to take his life, as they wished to cast him down from the hill on which their town was built (Compare on Matt. ii. 23.) ('Οφρύς, *eye-brow, steep precipice*. Hesych. τά ὑψηλὰ καὶ ὑπερκείμενα χωρία)

Ver. 30. The unbelieving Nazarenes, eager to see a miracle, met, in his escape, with a proof of his wonder-working power, of which, however, they took no heed—Διελθὼν διὰ μέσου αὐτῶν ἐπορεύετο the Evangelist records. These words in themselves certainly do not indicate anything miraculous; some fortunate accident might have made it possible for an individual to escape from the inhabitants of a whole city, if the crowd were broken up But any one who holds that nothing happens by accident, and that least of all this could be the case in the history of the Son of God, any one, moreover, who enquires exegetically into the view of the writer, must be forced to confess the meaning here expressed to be this: Jesus departed through the midst of them without restraint or hindrance, inasmuch as being the Mighty One, his divine power held their limbs and senses bound. No one could take from him his life, unless when he freely gave it. (John x 18.) In the same way also is the narrative at John viii. 59, to be understood.

Matthew (xiii. 58,) and Mark (vi. 5,) remark in conclusion, that Jesus performed few miracles in Nazareth. According to the more minute account of Mark, he healed a few sick persons by laying his hands on them. Probably this was *before* his address in the synagogue, for *after* it the scene of uproar immediately broke forth There is no need to suppose that this contradicts Luke iv. 23, if we only assume that these cures had taken place in quiet family circles, for surely the good seed was not wholly wanting even in unbelieving Nazareth The mode of expression, however, employed by Mark, is remarkable, ἐθαύμαζε διὰ τὴν ἀπιστίαν αὐτῶν, (which contrasts painfully with Matthew viii. 10, where Jesus wonders at faith,) and οὐκ ἠδύνατο ἐκεῖ οὐδεμίαν δύναμιν ποιῆσαι. These words strikingly explain the relation of πίστις to the miraculous power of Christ. Faith appears here once more (compare what was said on Matthew viii. 1.) as a condition indispensable to the manifestation of that miraculous power, which as the positive pole requires the negative, demanded susceptibility of mind before it could impart its gifts. The οὐκ ἠδύνατο is therefore to be taken quite literally, as denoting an internal impossibility—obviously not one of a physical kind—but a divine, a *moral* impossibility. Since God *can* save no impenitent sinner, as such, who refuses humbly to mourn over his guilt, so Jesus *cannot* heal where faith is wanting. Hence it appears that the object of the miracles is not to produce faith, they *presuppose* faith as existing, but where it already is they can purify and confirm it, and at the same time awaken the mind to correct knowledge. For, clearness of understanding does not necessarily go together with depth and liveliness of faith. It is not likely that the views of that heroine of the faith, the Canaanitish woman (Matthew xv. 22,) were very clear, but her heart burned with love, and her whole soul was full of susceptibility for the power of the Spirit from on high. Hence was she enabled, as it were, to compel (if I may so speak,) the reluctant Saviour to perform a miracle. (Compare on Matthew xv. 28) Faith, therefore, in all stages of its development, proceeds from the heart, its resting-place is in the immediate sphere of the inner life, it is *receptive* love, as grace is *communicative* love. The operation, however, of that which is divine, (Grace,) which unites itself to faith, seeks to pervade the powers of knowledge and understanding, as indeed it does the whole man, in all his faculties. By mere powers of knowledge, however, no man attains to faith, nor shall any be saved by mental speculation, yet well may a believing heart enjoy salvation, amidst much confusion of ideas. (Compare Proverbs iv. 23.)

§ 24. THE BAPTIST'S DEATH.

(Matt. xiv. 1—12. Mark vi. 14—29. Luke iii. 19, 20; ix. 7—9.)

The chapters in Matthew which here follow, (xiv.—xvii.) no longer resemble, in character, those that had gone before; no thread of connexion can be traced, guiding the arrangement of their several portions. Not till the 17th chapter, does the distinctive peculiarity of Matthew, his method, namely, of combining fragments of various discourses, again appear. The chapters which here immediately follow, I am inclined to regard as supplements of a historic kind to the preceding sections *(Rubriken.)* Although the unchronological character of Matthew still remains, yet in the frequent mention made of Christ's death a disposition may be observed to anticipate the subsequent period. As regards the first incident in chapter xiv., the account of the Baptist's death, it is obviously of a supplementary character,—the fact of his execution is supposed to be long past. Luke (iii. 19, 20,) had anticipated it. The mention of the views current regarding Christ, points, however, to a period when the reports respecting him had already obtained wide circulation, and the fact that the disciples were acquainted with the nature of these rumours is easily explained, if one considers that their mission must have brought them in contact with persons of various kinds. From this point down to the end of the section, the position of Mark relatively to Matthew, is peculiar. He follows him closely and throughout, only in two cases (vii. 32—37; viii. 22—26,) inserting short narratives of cures which Matthew does not give. The account, Matthew xvii 24—27, of the coin in the mouth of the fish, he omits. This can hardly be explained, unless we suppose them to have used the same sources of information, yet on what grounds Mark leaves out particular topics, it would be difficult to tell. The peculiar method, however, with which Mark brings forward his subjects runs unchanged through these sections; particular narratives he presents far more graphically than Matthew, but at the same time he is continually occupied with things external.

Ver. 1. The expression ἐν ἐκείνῳ τῷ καιρῷ is here used in all its vagueness, inasmuch as the preceding occurrence happened at the commencement of the Lord's ministry, while the account of Herod which follows belongs to a later period. (Concerning Herod [Antipas] and τετράρχης, compare on Matthew ii. 22; Luke iii. 1.) The vain worldling seems at first to have given himself little trouble about Jesus, he never heard of him till his fame had been widely spread.

Ver. 2. Matthew merely records the impression which the information about Christ made on the tetrarch; Mark and Luke state, in addition, the various rumours respecting him which were in circulation among the people Subsequently they both repeat the same rumours on an occasion when Matthew also gives them, (xvi 14,) and we will therefore defer the fuller consideration of them till we come to Matthew xvi 14. As to Herod, Mark agreeing with Matthew, relates that he believed Jesus to have been John raised from the dead. He expresses this opinion directly to those about him. ($παῖς = δοῦλος$, עֶבֶד). According to Luke, it was the mere *report* of this which disturbed him, ($διηπόρει$, Luke ix. 7,) yet he wished to see Jesus, (Luke ix. 9,) which would rather lead us to the opposite conclusion, namely, that he himself disbelieved the report as to John's resurrection. (Compare Luke xxiii 8.) This seeming contradiction disappears, however, when we consider how completely this worldly man must have been involved in darkness. At the first hearing of the report his heart would be shaken with fear, for conscience would testify that from a desire to please others and against his better knowledge (see Mark vi. 26,) he had let the Baptist be murdered. A mind so superficial as his, however, would soon pacify itself and become convinced of the improbability of the whole matter. His Sadduceeism would come to his aid (see on Mark viii. 15, compared with Matthew xvi. 6,) and put to flight every idea of a probable existence beyond the grave. A consistent carrying out of their opinions on the part of such sensualists is not to be looked for; they deny the reality of what is divine, yet amidst their very denial their heart quakes with the secret belief of it. With metempsychosis we have here nothing to do, for it is clear they did not believe that John's soul had passed into another body, but that he was himself personally risen from the dead. Not even at John ix. 3, are we to look for traces of a belief in metempsychosis, or the pre-existence of souls, during the times of the apostles. (Compare the Comment. on that passage.)

Ver. 3, 4. The aorists are, according to the connexion, clearly to be understood as equivalent to the pluperfect tense. (Compare Winer's Gram. p. 251.) The place of John's imprisonment was, according to Josephus, (Antiq. xviii. 5, 2,) the fortress of Machaerus. The notorious Herodias, with whom Antipas lived in incestuous connexion, was the daughter of Aristobulus, a son of Herod the Great. The latter married her to his son Philip, (who is not to be confounded with Philip the Tetrarch, see on Matthew ii 22,) who was disinherited by his father, and lived subsequently merely as a private individual. For this reason, his wife, Herodias, preferred the connexion with the tetrarch, Antipas, that she might become a reigning princess. Antipas cast off, in her favour, his former wife, the daughter of Aretas, the Arabian prince. (Compare Josephus Antiq. xviii. 5, 1.) John, the severe preacher of repentance, had dared to rebuke this scandalous union, and drawn upon himself the unmitigated hatred of Herodias. In Antipas himself, it would appear, there often arose feelings of a better nature. (Mark vi 20)

Ver. 5. Mark paints (ver. 20,) Herod in more favourable colours, so that it is Herodias who appears as the special enemy of John. (ἐνέχω, v 19, *to rage, in anger to lay snares for;* Luke xi. 53.) Matthew, however, ascribes to Herod the intention of putting John to death, only, he remarks, that he feared the people. The expression in Mark, εἰδὼς αὐτὸν ἄνδρα δίκαιον καὶ ἅγιον, seems to indicate that his conscience had been roused, and this is confirmed by what follows. (Συντηρεῖν = שָׁמַר means here *to guard as a protector*, to preserve from the machinations of Herodias) The eager hearing of John refers not to the time of his imprisonment, during which any interview between the prince and the Baptist is hardly conceivable, but to an earlier period, before he was shut up. At such a conference John might well have called his attention to the unlawfulness of his union with Herodias, as well as to other things of the same kind. (Compare Luke iii. 19, 'Ηρώδης —ἐλεγχόμενος ὑπ' Ἰωάννου περὶ Ἡρωδιάδος—καὶ περὶ πάντων ὧν ἐποίησε πονηρῶν.)

Ver. 6. It is safer to understand Γενέσια as meaning *birth-day*, than the commencement of his reign, not a single passage can be brought to show that the entry on a reign was usually so denoted. Besides, so early as Joseph's time, the Pharaohs kept the ἡμέρα γενέσεως. (Genesis xl. 20.) Mark employs the general expression ἡμέρα εὔκαιρος = יוֹם טוֹב, *festive day*, and paints the guests at the feast. The expression μεγιστᾶνες, seems of Persian origin. Josephus (Antiq. ix. 3, 2,) ranges them along with the satraps. The LXX. use the word among others for רַבְרְבָן, Daniel v. 1. In the New Testament it occurs again only at Rev vi. 15; xviii. 23. Here it seems to denote the highest civil officers at the court, as χιλίαρχοι does the highest military officers. The πρῶτοι τῆς Γαλιλαίας, would, in that case, mean the wealthiest men of the province. We are doubtless to understand the dancing of the daughter of Herodias to have been the mimic dance, but not exactly or necessarily unchaste. On the part of the step-daughter, (Salome was her name,) this is hardly conceivable

Ver. 7. The verb προβιβάζειν occurs at Acts xix. 33, in its most obvious sense of *to draw forth, to lead out;* figuratively, it means to *instruct* any one, to *train* for some purpose. At Exodus xxxv. 34, it stands for הוֹרָה. The wicked mother directed the maiden to John the Baptist, and she asked for his head. The weak Antipas granted it, though with a reluctant mind (ἐξ αὐτῆς sc. ὥρας, Mark vi. 25.)

Ver. 9, 10. The weak fear of man extracted from the tetrarch the order for the beheading; he was ashamed before the assembly to recal his too hasty promise. The inward state of Pilate's mind was similar when the demand was made that he should suffer Jesus to be led forth to death—only he was overcome by fear, Antipas by shame. Mark vi. 27 uses the Latin name σπεκουλάτωρ, by which the executioner was commonly designated. The mode of writing the word varies between spiculator (from spiculum, a spear with which they were armed,) and speculator—the former seems the preferable.

Ver. 11, 12. As the execution seems to have been so soon carried into effect, the feast must have been held in the castle of Machaerus itself, or in the neighbourhood. The faithful disciples buried the body (Mark vi. 29, has πτῶμα,) of their master as the last token of their respect.

§ 25. FEEDING OF THE FIVE THOUSAND.

(Matt xiv. 13, 21; Mark vi. 30—44, Luke ix 10—17, John vi 1—15.)

This account of the feeding of the five thousand is fixed down chronologically by John vi 4, to a certain date, (see as to the explanation of ἦν δὲ ἐγγὺς τὸ πάσχα the Comment on the passage,) only there is no way of throwing a bridge from John over to the three earlier Evangelists. (See the Introduction, § 7.) Mark and Luke place this feeding immediately after the return of the disciples from their mission. The account of John's execution, which they both interpose, may have been inserted for this reason, that Jesus was first informed of it by the disciples, on their return. By Matthew, however, that mission is placed in an entirely different connexion, (see chapter x.) so that their accounts can only be made to harmonize by supposing, as Dr Paulus does, (see above on Matt. x.1,) that the disciples were sent forth on two separate occasions, which, however, one can hardly imagine to have been the case. The conjoining, besides, of Christ's retirement into the desert, with his receiving the news of John's death, is extremely simple and probable. As his hour was not yet come, he went into quietude, partly that he might avoid all hostile machinations, partly that he might in prayer to God and converse with his disciples, meditate on, and make known those mighty events in the kingdom of God which were steadily approaching nearer. (Compare on Mark i. 35.) As the people crowd thither after him, the scene of his subsequently feeding the multitude rises on our view.

Ver. 13. Matthew informs us in the most general terms Ἰησοῦς ἀνεχώρησεν ἐκεῖθεν εἰς ἔρημον, leaving undetermined what the ἐκεῖθεν refers to, for the last account we have of Jesus (Matt. xiii. 53—58,) mentions no locality. Only the expression ἐν πλοίῳ points to his passing over to the opposite side of the sea of Gennesareth, an inference which John vi. 1, and Luke ix 10, confirm.[1] The latter mentions Bethsaida. This town, however, must not be confounded with the city of the apostles, (John i. 44,) which lay on the western shore of the sea. This second Bethsaida was situated on the eastern bank, close to where the Jordan flows into the lake. At first it was a village, but Philip the tetrarch raised it to the rank of a city, and named it Julias. (Josephus Antiq. xviii. 3; Wars of the Jews ii. 13; compare Von Raumer's Palest., p. 100.) According to Mark, (ver. 31,) this retirement was intended also for the sake of the disciples, that they might rest from the labours (ἀναπαύεσθε ὀλίγον,) which the pressure of the people had caused them. They had even been prevented taking their necessary food. Eager, however, for help, (though it was only outward aid that in the first instance they sought,) the people hastened after them into the uncultivated region whither our Lord had withdrawn, and he had compassion on

---

[1] De Wette (on Luke ix. 10,) thinks that Luke places this feeding in a different locality from Matt , and Mark , he knows nothing of a passage across the sea, and conceives Bethsaida to have been on the western shore. But this is sufficiently disproved by the single circumstance that there was no desert near the western Bethsaida, it was surrounded by the most fruitful land.

them. (See respecting σπλαγχνίζεσθαι on Luke i. 78.) He taught, therefore, (Luke and Mark,) and afterwards performed cures (Matt.). As to the words, (especially as given by Mark,) compare the passage Matt. ix. 36. They contain allusions to Old Testament passages, such as Numbers xxvii. 17; Isaiah liii. 6. Luke (ix. 11,) mentions as the subject of his teaching, the Βασιλεία τοῦ Θεοῦ, under which expression is here comprehended, in an indeterminate and general way, that more exalted heavenly life which Christ was come to render the dominant principle here on earth. (Compare on Matt. iii. 2.)

Ver. 15, 16. In narrating the course of the miracle, John deviates from the synoptical gospels. He states that the Saviour put to Philip the question, how shall we buy bread for so many? while the synoptical writers tell us that the apostles had applied to Jesus to dismiss the people, that they might disperse themselves and find provisions in the villages that lay immediately around. It is easy, however, to reconcile both accounts. As the day was now far gone (Mark vi. 35, ὥρα πολλή, like the expression ἡμέρα πολλή, in the LXX. on Genesis xxix. 7,) some of the disciples enquired of Jesus as to the time when the people would be dismissed. John mentions another circumstance occurring at another moment, either before or after the inquiry of the disciples, the question, namely, put by Jesus to Philip. If, a-Bengel supposes, the charge of providing food had been entrusted to him, the special object in putting the question must have been a moral one. Philip must have his mind awakened (John vi. 6, ἔλεγεν ὁ Ἰησοῦς πειράζων αὐτόν,) that he might be able to understand aright the approaching miracle. Philip, however, appears here as at John xiv. 8, unable to get free from his earthly standing-point, he refers to the sum of money that would be required for feeding them. (200 denarii = 40 rix dollars. This sum is given also by Mark vi. 37.)

Ver. 17. Another difference in the narrative, which it is just as impossible to regard as of material consequence, arises from the circumstance that John vi. 8 expressly names Andrew as the person who mentioned the boy with the five loaves and the two fishes, (ὀψάριον, properly means merely *by-meat*,[1] any thing eaten with bread; the other Evangelists define it by ἰχθύες,)

---

[1] According to lexicographers, however, ὀψάριον was, at a later period, used as precisely equivalent to ἰχθύδιον.

while Matt., Mark, and Luke, make the apostles say that there was no food whatever at hand. These last Evangelists have looked on Andrew as speaking for all the apostles, and expressing their mind. The expression παιδάριον ἕν (the ἕν is not to be taken as having the force of the indefinite article, but as distinctly intimating that none else besides this boy had brought food with them,) forbids our supposing that the five loaves and two fishes were merely the disciples' own supply of food. John immediately places, in direct contrast, the whole number present, (ταῦτα τί ἔστιν εἰς τοσούτους,) with the whole supply of provisions. (The assigning of the number at 5000 is alike in all the narratives, only Matt. and Mark do not mention it till the conclusion. Matthew remarks, enhancing it still more, χωρὶς γυναικῶν καὶ παιδίων. The method of arranging them at the meal facilitated much the reckoning. The agreement of the numbers, as well of those who were fed, as of the provisions set before them, is not to be overlooked. It is a strong testimony to the truth of the narrative, later tradition would have corrupted the numbers.)

Ver. 18, 19. The Saviour causes the crowd to be ranged in regular order, and proceeds to divide the small supply of food. (The ἔρημος, where the Saviour was at this time, was grassy pasture ground, without towns or villages. In the same way מִדְבָּר is used to denote pasturage. We are not therefore to conceive of any thing like sandy wastes, but rather of *steppes*. Συμπόσιον, denotes here the persons who partake of a meal together, like our German word *Gesellschaft, a company.* Luke uses instead, the term κλισίαι, the reclining or sitting together at food; each company of fifty was looked on as forming a party by itself. The repetition of the word denotes, according to Hebrew usage, the separate distribution, instead of the Greek ἀνά. Like a painter drawing from a vivid conception of the scene, Mark calls the separate parties πρασιαί, *spaces separately and carefully marked off,* for example, garden-beds. It is so used by Homer. Mark adds, that some of these parties consisted of 100, others of 50, nay, he does not forget to notice the freshness of the grass. (ἐπὶ χλωρῷ χόρτῳ—χλωρός = יָרָק in the LXX.) These traits originate wholly in his mode of recording events, which seizes chiefly on the externals of the narrative. In detailing the division itself, Mark (41,) adds expressly καὶ τοὺς δύο ἰχθύας ἐμέρισε πᾶσι. These words clearly intimate that, according to the view of the narrator, the two fishes were the object subdivided among

all, Jesus had only this small supply for satisfying the multitude
The words of John, ὅσον ἤθελον, (vi. 11,) exclude all idea of a
merely seeming satisfaction to the wants of the crowd, every one
partook as much as he desired, *that* was the standard of supply
to which, on this occasion, the food was adapted

Ver 20, 21. The command to gather up the fragments admitted of being carried into execution, for our Lord was standing in one fixed position when he broke the bread and the fishes, (fragments of which latter, the minute and accurate Mark informs us were also collected,) at which point they would naturally collect themselves, and means might also be taken before-hand for keeping them clean. The twelve baskets (as to which all the four Evangelists are agreed), show that the fragments that remained over, were of greater amount than the loaves had been at first. Probably each apostle took a basket to complete the gathering of the bread, hence the twelve. The union of this savingness and care with creative power, is something so peculiar, that it impresses beyond all mistake, a heavenly character on the narrative. Never would such a thing have been invented. Nature, that mirror of divine perfections, places before our eyes the same combination of boundless munificence, and of truest frugality in imparting her benefits

The Evangelists close their narratives with nothing certainly like exclamations or expressions of surprise,—John only remarking what an impression the incident had made on the people They concluded from it that Jesus was the prophet who had been promised, and wished to take him by force and make him the sovereign of their outward worldly kingdom. Whether such an ebullition is conceivable, if the multitude (a caravan returning from a festival, as is conjectured,) had satisfied themselves with the provision which themselves had made for the journey, and in the most courteous way, left untouched the small supply of food placed before them by the apostles, we leave intelligent and believing readers to infer for themselves.

In considering the fact itself thus recorded, it obviously belongs to that class of Christ's miracles, the object of which is *nature* In the other, and first class of miracles, there is, for the Christian mind, this facility towards the understanding of them, that we have, in the faith of the individual who (for example in the case of a cure,) is the object of the miracle, a channel for the communication of the wondrous power and its effectual operation. But in cases where physical nature is seen as a simply passive object, the miracle easily assumes the appearance of being *magical*. The best way of escaping from this false impression is, never to view those miracles which refer to the natural world as standing apart from human beings, but as in living union with them. The mere increase of food is not the point on which stress is here to be laid, but its increase for persons who were in a certain state of mind. It is when such miracles are thus conjoined with the wants of human nature, as these were manifested in the individuals actually present, that they appear in the character which really belongs to them. As the Lord, in general, performed no cure save where he found faith, so he generally bestowed no food save where he found spiritual hunger.[1] As regards the fact itself, we pay no attention to those representations, which, in contradiction to the true exegesis, explain away all that is miraculous;[2] but just as little ought we to tolerate any views of it which are positively antinatural. This, however, must be done, if we suppose the materials to have been increased without a real interposition of Divine power. Rather let us believe that the same power which flowed forth from Jesus to heal the sick, here produced, in obedience to his will, another physical effect. In these cures it appeared more as setting in order, as restorative,—in this case more as creative.[3] The most correct view of the matter then is

[1] It is repugnant to common sense when in reply to this Strauss asks, (vol. ii. p. 206,) what was done then with unbelievers? The supposition is, that where Christ performed a miracle *all* were believers.

[2] Pfenninger says of it, "What usually takes place in three quarters of a year between seed time and harvest, is said here to have been done within a few minutes, while the food was being divided. Thus the narrative will have us believe in an increase wondrously hastened forward, *and I could more easily discredit the fact were I the most believing of men, or I could credit it were I the most unbelieving, sooner than really and truly believe that the narrative does not intend to make us believe it.*" The pitiful remark of Strauss, in reply to this profound view of Pfenninger, that for the production of bread, besides the natural process of growing, there is required also the artificial work of grinding and baking, originates assuredly in something worse than mere intellectual incapacity, namely, in his entire disbelief in a living God. But for this he would not have had such difficulty in supposing that the Divine agency had replaced the work of man.

[3] Yet in no gospel narrative is a *pure* exercise of creative power ascribed to the Saviour. As nature, out of the seed corn, evolves a new creation, so Christ turns water into wine and increases the already existing

undoubtedly this, that under the hands of the Saviour, and by his Divine power, an increase of the means of food must be held to have taken place. As, by the touch of his hand, he healed and blessed, so in the same way he *made*. Along with this, however, the idea is still to be firmly retained, that these appearances were merely natural processes, extremely hurried forward in point of time, for real formations must, in every case, be brought about as the result of a course of real developments. These developments, however, we know, are capable of being hastened, and that to an extent which it is impossible for us to limit. The right conception, however, of what a miracle really is, carrying us back to a supernatural causality, drives us to make such suppositions. No phenomenon is conceivable, unless in connexion with powers sufficient for its causation. In the person of Jesus, however, those higher powers which regulate all the processes of nature, interfere with and control natural life, directly and to its innermost centre,—for, supreme and creative, like a God he ranges through all productions or formations of the elements, ordering and wielding them for the high objects he aims at. As regards the increase of the means of food, similar things were seen formerly, under the Old Testament. Elijah, with twenty loaves, (2 Kings iv. 42, sq.) fed one hundred men. Oil and meal increased to the widow at Sarepta. (2 Kings iv. 1, sq., comp. also 1 Kings xvii. 1, sq) Manna and quails nourished the Israelites in the desert. (As to the typical meaning of this, see on John vi.) What was there done by God in heaven and from afar, is here effected by God visible and near at hand. (Ps. cxlv. 15, 16)

bread, but without a substratum to begin with he makes neither wine nor bread. I observe that in these remarks I refer only to the recorded facts; how far it is conceivable that Christ's miraculous powers might have been put forth in a different form, is another question. According to gospel history, the Saviour constantly appears as the *restorer* of creation. He creates no new men, but he transforms the old; he makes no new bodily members formerly wanting, but he restores the old that were useless. The same thing applies to the miracles of the Old Testament, for even in the case of the manna, the supernatural increase of a natural production may be supposed, and not the creation of matter absolutely new

§ 26. JESUS WALKS ON THE SEA.

(Matt. xiv. 22—36; Mark vi 45—56; John vi. 16—21.)

The following narrative of our Lord's walking on the sea is akin to the preceding, in so far as it also manifests Christ's dominion over the natural world, his dominion, however, being exercised in a totally different respect. For it is not so much an interposed influence brought to bear on nature, that is here spoken of, the special difficulty in this case consists in his withdrawing himself personally from the control of earthly natural laws. The difficulty, however, which is commonly found in this occurrence, disappears, or at least is considerably diminished, if, along with that close affinity which connected the body of Christ with those of other men, we clearly recognise at the same time its distinctive peculiarities It is common to conceive of the glorifying of our Lord's body, as effected either at the resurrection or ascension, and as the work of a moment. But if we suppose the Spirit's work, in glorifying and perfecting Christ's body, to have been spread over the Saviour's whole life, (certain periods being still distinguished as seasons of special activity,) much that is obscure will be made clear A body thoroughly of the earth, chained down by unseen bands to earthly matter, cannot shake itself free from its origin, but that a higher bodily frame, teeming with the powers of a loftier world, should rise above the earthly level, is less surprising.[1] This transaction, then, of Christ's walking on the sea, is not to be viewed as a work wrought *upon* him and effected by magic, as though some external power had laid hold on him and borne him up, but as the result effected by his own will, the forth-putting of an energy inherently belonging to himself. If this power was seldom used, it was because the Saviour never did wonders for the sake of doing them, but to serve some useful end. Thus in the present instance, the manifestation of his hidden glory was designed to build up his disciples in the faith. They saw more and more

---

[1] The absurd questions which Strauss (vol II, p 182, second edition,) gets up in reply to this explanation, he might have spared himself, had he been willing to reflect that the freeing of Christ's body from its bondage to earth, is not inconsistent with its being entirely at the disposal of his own free will

with whom they had to do, and perceived that he was the revelation of the invisible Father; (Matt xvi 16,) their Jewish prepossessions, as to the Messiah, were more and more cleared up in his light. The Old Testament representations of Jehovah's glory were in living reality set before their eyes in the life of Jesus. He alone spreadeth out the heavens *and walketh on the waves of the sea.* (Job ix. 8) We will not disturb those heavenly images of a Divine government among men, by reviewing the attempts that have been made, in defiance of just exegesis, to reduce their weighty significancy to the level of every-day generalities Such pictures, taken from the Lord's life, set before us in miniature his whole mighty work and influence on the inner mental world of man, they are full of exhaustless meaning. As respects the form of the narrative, the superiority in vivid and graphic description belongs to Matthew The incident which befel Peter, who wished to come to Jesus over the water, is, for example, recorded by Matthew alone The account by John is short, and like most narratives of events contributed by that Evangelist, is given chiefly for the sake of the discourses which are connected with it. The motive which led to the breaking up of the assembly, and the removal of the disciples, is, however, distinctly assigned by John, who thus confirms the accuracy of the connexion between this and the preceding occurrences as stated in common by the three other Evangelists. The miraculous supply of food excited in these worldly men a desire to make Jesus the Messianic king From their importunities he withdrew by retiring to the solitude of a mountain for prayer, (Matt. xiv. 23,) but he caused his disciples to go before him by ship to the other side of the sea Mark vi 45 specifies Bethsaida, John vi. 17 mentions Capernaum as the point to which their course was directed. As the two places, however, were close to each other, the disciples may have intended first to put in at the one point, and then sail on to the other. (The expression ἀναγκάζειν, in Matt. and Mark, ver. 22 and 45, means merely earnest, impressive exhortation, and this was needed apparently because the disciples were unwilling to separate from their Lord.)

Ver 24, 25. John (vi. 16,) mentions the evening as the time of their setting sail. From his supplemental remark, καὶ οὐκ ἐληλύθει πρὸς αὐτοὺς ὁ Ἰησοῦς, it would appear that they had continued to look for Jesus rejoining them, and it was probably their thus waiting for him which delayed so long the period of their setting sail. As the darkness of night now came on, and a storm arose, the scene became full of terror, which well agrees with the whole circumstances of the narrative. Through gloom and tempest came the Lord, walking onwards over the raging waves, to the help of his disciples in their tossing boat. Matt. and Mark observe that the wind, besides being fierce, was contrary to them, (ἐναντίος,) so that the force of the waves struck the boat more violently. (βασανίζεσθαι.) According to John, they had already rowed a distance of 25—30 stadia, (ἐλαύνειν,) and consequently more than half-way across, (the sea was 40 stadia broad, about one German mile,[1] Joseph. Bell. Jud. i. 3, 35,) when they saw Jesus walking on the sea. According to Matt. and Mark, it was now towards the morning, about the fourth watch. (Φυλακή = אַשְׁמֻרָה.) Before the Exile the Jews had divided the night into three parts, afterwards they adopted the four Roman divisions of three hours each. In the expression ἀπῆλθε πρὸς αὐτούς, the idea of his leaving the place where he was formerly staying, is concisely conjoined with that of his going to meet the disciples.)

Ver. 26, 27. The disciples seeing Jesus walking on the sea took fright; they believed that they saw a φάντασμα. The word πνεῦμα, stands in a similar connexion at Luke xxiv. 37. The term is to be understood in all its latitude like our word *gespenst, apparition*, which, according to popular notions, means any sort of incorporeal appearance, without very accurately defining the idea of it. That any thing of a bodily nature could walk on the sea, was inconceivable to the disciples, and there came upon them, therefore, the terror which usually accompanies all unwonted spiritual appearances. The word uttered by Jesus, ἐγώ εἰμι, again reassures the disciples. In him they had already recognised what was unusual, they saw in him the ruler of the invisible world, his friendship they themselves enjoyed, and knew that he ever came to their aid in moments of danger. The expression ἐπὶ τῆς θαλάσσης or ἐπὶ τὴν θάλασσαν, (in Matt.) and afterwards at Matt. xiv. 28, 29, ἐπὶ τὰ ὕδατα, certainly *may* mean *beside* the sea, inasmuch as the bank of the sea or river is conceived of as elevated above the level of the water. (2 Kings ii. 7; Dan. viii. 2; according to the LXX.) Of itself, however, ἐπί never means *ad, juxta*, (compare Fritzsche Comm. in Matt. p. 503,) but unquestionably it denotes *to* or *towards* any thing, *versus*.

---

[1] One German is equal to about 4¼ English miles.

(Acts xvii. 14.) The parallel passage, John xxi. 1, is very accurately explained by Fritzsche, ἐφανέρωσεν ἑαυτὸν ὁ Ἰησοῦς τοῖς μαθηταῖς ἐπὶ τῆς θαλάσσης, (δῦσιν) in such a way that the formula bears its usual meaning. But that in the passage before us there is no evading the obvious meaning of the words as denoting that Christ walked over the waves of the sea, appears plainly from the narrative taken as a whole. If differently understood, it becomes either trivial or deceptive. The opinion which would hold it a myth is sufficiently refuted by the calmness of the narrators. Least of all can Matthew's account of Peter's walking on the sea, be reconciled to it. Obviously it stands forth as a naked fact.

Ver. 28—31. The special feature in the conduct of Peter, the account of which is here contributed by Matthew, is quite in keeping with that disciple's character. In the same way something of a similar kind is also told of him after the resurrection of Jesus (John xxi. 7, sq) Fiery and ardent, full of burning love for the Lord, he cannot wait patiently the moment of his near approach, but hastens to meet him with most daring courage As John is called the disciple whom the Lord loved, ὃν ἠγάπα ὁ Ἰησους, John xxi. 7,) so might it be said of Peter that he loved the Lord. In other words, as the nature of John was pre-eminent for being receptive and profound, Peter's was distinguished for activity and energy. As however this power of love wherewith he embraced the Saviour was not yet freed from selfishness, it betrayed him into mistakes of very different kinds. Once more in the case before us, his over-hasty impetuosity brings about a fall. The whole of this little history is a rich picture of the inner life—a commentary on the words of the prophet, the heart of man is a froward and timorous thing (Jer. xvii. 9). Without the command (not the bare permission) of the Lord, Peter ventures himself out of the ship. Trusting to the ἐλθέ, he walks forth, but at sight of the hurricane, he sinks. (Καταποντίζεσθαι occurs again at Matt. xviii. 6, in the sense of sinking, or being sunk into the πόντος.) Yet faith remains so far firm that he only seeks aid from Jesus. (Here he already calls him κύριε, with reference to his higher nature, the knowledge of which had previously been revealed to Peter [see on Matt. xvi. 16]. So also, on seeing this dominion exercised by Jesus over the powers of nature, the other disciples take occasion to make the confession at ver. 33, ἀληθῶς Θεοῦ υἱὸς εἶ Comp. on Matt. xvi. 16). Christ gave him help along with a word of rebuke, ὀλιγόπιστε, which, however, is a different thing from ἄπιστε. The point of reproof was merely that the faith which existed in him was not beyond being shaken. (Διστάζω occurs again at Matt. xxviii. 17. Literally it means to turn in two different directions, hesitating and undetermined which to follow. Whence it denotes in general *to be in doubt*, and is equivalent to ἀμφισβητέω) In this case it once more plainly appears, as in all the miracles of Christ, that faith was the intermediate element, through means of which he performed them on men. So long as the inner soul of Peter was purely and simply turned towards the person of the Lord, he was capable of receiving within himself the fulness of Christ's life and Spirit, so that, what Christ could do, he could do, but so soon as his capacity for receiving the Spirit was contracted by his giving place and weight to a foreign power, the result was that the latter entered his heart, repressed the influence of Christ, and thus the sea-walker fell back under the dominion of earthly elements. Analogous to this is the way in which faith on the Lord's strengthening and upholding power conducts us securely over the agitated sea of a sinful life, but assuredly it only too often happens that the weakness of this faith sinks down into the waters The peculiarity of the gospel narratives, which makes them capable of such an application to the inner life, does not belong to them by accident, nor is it to be viewed as a capricious or arbitrary thing actually to apply them thus. Far rather is it true that founding on the significancy and importance of the Saviour's position as the centre of all spiritual life, everything in him and with him rises into a higher significancy.

Ver. 32, 33. According to Matt. and Mark, the disciples, in the strongest terms, express their astonishment (Mark vi. 51, λίαν —ἐκ περισσοῦ—ἐξίστασθαι,) and adoration. (The meaning of προσκυνεῖν, which had otherwise been vague, is at Matt. xiv. 33, accurately defined by the confession which follows that he was the Son of God. See as to this more at length on Matt. xvi. 16.) Christ, along with Peter, stepped on board the ship, the wind calmed down, (ἄνεμος ἐκόπασε, see above, Mark iv. 39,=γαλήνη ἐγένετο,) and they gained the further shore. The account given at John vi. 21, ἤθελον λαβεῖν αὐτόν, seems to differ from the others, as though the disciples had intended taking him on board when they suddenly found themselves already at the land. Read by itself the statement of John would leave the impression that the εὐθέως τὸ πλοῖον ἐγένετο ἐπὶ τῆς γῆς, seemed to him to imply something miraculous. But as the disciples had in the first instance sailed half the distance before they saw Jesus, as they had the wind against them, and as during the scene between Christ and Peter, they assuredly forgot their oars, they cannot well have very speedily reached the shore. The meaning of εὐθέως however, is vague, and none of the narrators give marks to fix the time; we can therefore conceive of a rapid rowing forward of the ship through the calm, and an immediate landing thereafter The only difficulty that remains is the ἤθελον λαβεῖν, in so far as it is usually held to imply the non-fulfilment of the purposed intention, in which case there would result an open contradiction to the two other narrators. We might certainly at once, in this as in other cases, admit that a contradiction really exists, inasmuch as the Gospel history makes no claim to exemption from trifling and unimportant irregularities. At all events, we would rather do so than either hold ἐθέλω to be here redundant, or that it means *to do a thing eagerly and joyfully*, (so that the sense should be—they took him eagerly and joyfully on board,) a construction for which there is no support in the usage of the New Testament [1] The following, however, appears to me a simple way of escaping from the difficulty. The disciples were afraid that they saw a spirit, which naturally they wished as far as possible from their ship. Jesus, however, explained to them that it was he Thereupon it is simply added that on receiving this explanation they strove to take him in, with the natural ellipsis, and they took him in accordingly—after which they directly gained the land. (The verb θέλειν then retains in this case its literal meaning of *active volition*, see Passow in Lex sub voce. For, in order to take in Christ while the ship was on her course, certain preparations were needful, such as the taking down of the sail, &c. The whole of these operations are denoted by the ἤθελον λαβεῖν, and the expression consequently implies the effectual carrying out of these preparations. The clause therefore, if completed, would run thus, ἤθελον οὖν λαβεῖν αὐτὸν εἰς τὸ πλοῖον καί ἔλαβον.)

Ver 34—36 Both evangelists conclude this narrative with the general remark that immediately after the return of Jesus many sick persons applied for his help, and strove simply to touch the

---

[1] In profane writers, especially in Xenophon, (Cyrop I, 1, 3, 1, 5, 19 Anab II 6, 6, and 11,) this use of ἐθέλω frequently occurs.

hem of his garment   (Compare what is said on Luke viii. 44.) Mark is more copious in his language, but without adding any new ideas, only that when he passes on to relate their arrival at the opposite shore, immediately after stating the astonishment of the disciples at Christ's walking on the sea, he adds οὐ συνῆκα ἐπί τοῖς ἄρτοις, (elliptically for ἐπὶ τῷ θαύματι ἐν τοῖς ἄρτοις γενομένῳ.) Mark means to say that they might have been sufficiently enabled from that miracle of feeding the multitude to see his Divine nature, if their capacity for receiving the truth had not been so weak. (Respecting πωροῦσθαι, [callo obduci, then *to become hardened, insensible,*] see Mark viii. 17; Rom. xi. 7. It is parallel to παχύνεσθαι, Matt xiii. 15. The verb προσορμίζεσθαι, Mark vi. 53, from ὅρμος, to land, occurs only here.)

§ 27   OF WASHING THE HANDS.

(Matt. xv. 1—20.   Mark vii. 1—23.)

As to the connexion of this event chronologically with that which precedes it, little can be said, owing to the vagueness of those forms of expression which are used to unite them. It would be rash to draw any inference from the presence of the Pharisees and Scribes who came down from Jerusalem. For the fact that they came from Jerusalem does not prove that they *belonged to* Jerusalem, and just as little that they were sent for the purpose of watching him   One can only infer from the form of Christ's discourse against the Pharisees, that the occurrence belongs to the latter period of his ministry, for during his earlier labours he did not usually express himself so strongly against them as he does here.

Ver. 1, 2. It was so completely in keeping with the true spirit of Phariseeism to rebuke every deviation from that external ritual which they counted holy, that the question of these Pharisees may be accounted for without supposing that they were designedly lying in wait for Christ. Such scruples arose from the peculiar character of their minds. The παράδοσις τῶν πρεσβυτέρων is the same with the δόγματα ἄγραφα, which gradually under the learned men of the Jews formed around the Mosaic law a new and holy circle of traditions. Mark feels himself called on, for the sake of his non-Jewish readers, to explain more particularly the practice of eating with the hands washed. (κοινός=טְמָא Acts x. 14, conjoined with ἀκάθαρτον, here it is equivalent to ἄνιπτος) He observes that among the Pharisaic Jews it was the general custom (πάντες οἱ Ἰουδαῖοι is to be taken in connexion with κρατοῦντες τὴν παράδοσιν, for the Sadducees did not observe such ordinances) The meaning of πυγμῇ νίψονται τὰς χεῖρας is uncertain. Undoubtedly, however, πυγμή is to be taken in the usual sense of *hand, fist*, so that the method in which the Jews washed before eating is here pointed out. The hands seem to have been used alternately, the one in washing the other. The Syriac translators have rendered it *frequently, generally*, as though they had read it πυκνῇ. Either the translator had heard the word wrong, or he did not know how to translate πυγμῇ. Mark, after explaining the practice of washing the hands, next proceeds to other usages of the same kind, for ablutions of all sorts, (among the rest those applicable to the priests, Exod. xxix. 4; xxx. 18, sq., compared with Heb ix. 10,) were common among the Jews. He confines himself, however, to those washings which accompanied meals. The term βαπτίζεσθαι is different from νίπτεσθαι; the former is the dipping and rinsing, or cleansing of food that has been purchased, to free it from impurities of any kind; the term νίπτεσθαι implies also the act of rubbing off, such as takes place in all forms of washing. In precisely the same way do the Rabbins distinguish between נְטִילָה and נְטִילַת יָדַיִם. (Compare Lightfoot on the passage. βαπτισμός is here, as at Heb ix. 10, *Ablution, washing* generally) The words ποτήριον, ξέστης, χαλκίον, are different names for vessels. Ποτήριον denotes a drinking vessel, ξέστης, corrupted from the Latin sextuarius, means a vessel for holding or measuring fluids; χαλκίον means a vessel of brass, the nature of which we cannot more accurately determine. The κλιναί here, must, according to the connexion, be referred to the couches on which the ancients were wont to recline at meals. (Compare Mark iv. 21.)

Ver. 3, 4. In recording the following discourse, addressed by Jesus to the Pharisees, (down to ver. 11,) Mark varies from Matthew, inasmuch as he makes the Saviour begin at once with the quotation from Isaiah, while in Matthew it forms the conclusion The latter is unquestionably the more natural position. Appropriately the description of the Pharisees stands first, and then follows the passage from the prophet, in confirmation as it were, of what had been said. The leading idea of the whole passage, however, is neither more nor less than the opposition of their human institutions to the commandment of God. The real test of a spurious faith is the substituting of the former of these for the latter, or the placing it above the latter. In this way the Spirit is withdrawn from the service of God, it becomes a mere human service. This corruption of the Divine by means of the human, the Saviour explains by an example, showing how the Pharisaic hypocrisy subverted a holy precept of God by an ordinance calculated to promote their own earthly selfish advantage Jesus quotes Exod. xx. 12; xxi. 17, in order to show what, according to the Divine ordinance, is the true relation in which children stand to their parents. The Mosaic regulation, the Lord (Mark vii. 10,) here acknowledges as one which proceeded directly from God, because God spake through Moses and his ordinances possessed Divine authority The verb κακολογεῖν, (= βλασφημεῖν,) stands in antithesis to τιμᾶν, in the same way that μακροχρόνιος γίνεσθαι in the first (not fully quoted) passage, does to the verb ἀποθνήσκειν. According to the standing-point of the theocracy, the highest curse and the highest blessing were thus conceived of in a form level and obvious to the senses.

Ver 5, 6. This holy commandment the Pharisees taught men to evade by the ordinance,—"Temple offerings take precedence of all gifts in behalf of parents." As to the construction, we observe *first*, that the clause δῶρον (sc ἔστι,) ὃ ἐάν ἐξ ἐμοῦ ὠφεληθῇς, is obscure. The idea is that the parents are making a request, and the children are refusing it, with the explanation that the thing which it would have been becoming (ἐάν stands for ἄν, compare Winer, p. 285,) in them to grant, they had already decided to give to the temple (Δῶρον = קָרְבָּן, applies as well to bloody as to unbloody offerings.) On this they found the inference that it is not incumbent to give them anything. Probably it is to be presumed either that the priests took a small portion of the gift instead of the whole, or that they knew how to instil it into the children that they would acquire special merit by those temple offerings. It is not conceivable otherwise that any child could have been induced to act thus towards his parents. The *second* difficulty lies in the expression καὶ οὐ μὴ τιμήσῃ. Mark guides us here to the right meaning In the first place, the future τιμήσει is a false reading; it does not agree with εἴπῃ. In the next place, the καὶ οὐ corresponds to וְלֹא, and introduces the supplementary remark—"if any one says your property is consecrated to the temple, it is then unnecessary for him to honour his father and his mother." The verb τιμᾶν, (in the sense of giving bodily support,) is thus chosen simply to bring out more markedly the contradiction to the Divine commandment. It is needless, however, to suppose that any thing requires to be understood, as, for example, ἀναίτιός ἐστι. Hence our Lord deduces the inference that by means of what is human they subvert what is Divine, (ἀκυρόω is used especially in regard to laws. Gal iii 17.)

Ver. 7—9 After this Jesus applies the prophetic words of Isaiah xxix. 13, to the piety of the Pharisees The two evangelists agree, word for word, (only instead of ὁ λαός οὗτος, Mark has οὗτος ὁ λαός,) in the quotation. The LXX. deviates from the original much in its expressions, although the idea is the same. This agreement of Matt. and Mark in a passage containing a deviation, and which is quoted from memory, would lead to the inference that the one had used the other's gospel, or that they had drawn from some common source. (The text of Matt. in this quotation is in many MSS corrected after the LXX. Mark being less read and less expounded is free from such interpolations.) The simple idea then expressed by the prophet is this,—the outward service of God, unless the whole inner man take part in it with the living energy of mind and will, (both being comprehended by the term καρδία = לב) is in the highest degree offensive to God. Isaiah spake these words to the Jews of his day, as the connexion of the passage shows, yet both evangelists remark that Christ observed καλῶς προεφήτευσε περὶ ὑμῶν, an expression which may serve as a commentary to the words ὅπως πληρωθῇ. An explicit reference in these words to the cotemporaries of Jesus, the Saviour, and also the evangelists, in this passage, must have discovered, in thus far, that as Christ was the central point of all life and being under the theocracy, every mental tendency and aim, even though embodied in representatives who had existed previously, yet gathered round *Him* in the full development and display of their inherent qualities. The whole Old Testament history was prophetic of Christ and of those around him in this respect, that everywhere in the continually recurring contrast between light and darkness, between truth and error, there were displayed the types of that which in its highest energy developed itself in and around Christ. (As to ὑποκριτής, see on Matt. vi. 2.)

Ver. 10, 11. The general idea which throughout this conversation impressed itself on the Saviour's mind, namely, that purity is to be sought for within the soul and not in externals, he puts forward before the great mass of the people, as the germ of many other fruitful thoughts, (ὄχλος in contrast to the μαθηταί,) for the benefit of all those who were able to penetrate its meaning and properly to apply it. As the idea, however, was expressed figuratively, (in reference to the words ἐν παραβολῇ, see on Matt. xiii. 3) Jesus at a later period, after he had dismissed the people, (Mark vii. 17) prompted by a request from the disciples, whose organ, (according to Matt.,) Peter once more was, gives an exposition of it. (Matt. xv. 17—19.)

Ver. 12—14. Matthew adds, however, a parenthetical remark explanatory of the Pharisees and the relation in which they stood to the kingdom of God—a remark which may have been called forth by the anxiety of the disciples lest the Pharisees should have taken offence at his discourse, and lest this should have led to fatal results. (As to σκανδαλίζεσθαί, see on Matth. xviii. 6) The words of Christ in which he allays their anxiety on this point, refer also to the parable of the field and the different kinds of seed, to the end of the bad seed and of the plants which spring from it. (Matt. xiii. 24 sq especially ver. 30, συλλέξατε τὰ ζιζάνια κ. τ. λ.) The term ἐκριζωθήσεται therefore expresses the idea of the final judgment, and the Saviour chose for the statement of this idea a figurative form of expression already familiar to the disciples. It is a false interpretation, however, to refer the φυτεία to the doctrine of the Pharisees, and not to themselves personally. (Literally the φυτεία is the act of planting itself, then, the thing planted = φύτευμα.) That were a false attempt to weaken the idea of the κατάκρισις, (the total cutting off from all communion with what is good,) which is openly announced here as formerly it was at chap. xiii. 30. Undoubtedly the Pharisees are God's creatures as well as other men, but in as far as the falsehood of their mental tendencies consequent on a state of soul alienated from God had become amalgamated with their innermost personal identity, and only in such identification do such tendencies exist at all, in so far do they belong not to God but to the devil. The expression ἣν οὐκ ἐφύτευσεν ὁ πατήρ μου ὁ οὐράνιος must therefore be completed by supplying, as the evangelist intended, ἀλλὰ ὁ διάβολος, who according to Matt. xiii. 25, 38, casts in the bad seed. (The τέκνα διαβόλου mean the same thing, see on John viii. 44.) An absolute predestination or material difference (in the Manichean sense) between the good and the evil is not to be understood here; no one is by birth a τέκνον διαβόλου, he becomes such only by his corrupt will and continued striving against grace. But what applies to the leader, Jesus attributes also to the followers (see on Matt. xxiii. 15). The perverted suffer along with the perverter, obviously according to the principle laid down at Luke xii. 47, 48. The figurative form of the expression is besides intelligible by itself. Luke vi. 39, inserts it amidst the contents of the sermon on the mount. (As to βόθυνος see Matt. xii. 11.)

Ver. 15, 16. Hereupon follows the request of the apostles, (Peter being their representative,) that he would explain the figurative discourse (παραβολή, see on Matt. xiii. 3). Jesus rebukes their defective powers of comprehension (σύνεσις, *understanding*, νοῦς, *reason*, comp. on Luke ii. 47,) and then explains to them the similitude. (The expression ἀκμήν literally means *on the moment* in the Greek profane writers, and comes also to be used as synonymous with ἔτι). Even the explanation itself, however, is still very difficult.

Ver. 17. In the sentiment formerly stated, (ver 11,) it must have appeared at the very outset a difficulty to the disciples that Christ's explanation τὸ εἰσερχόμενον εἰς τὸ στόμα οὐ κοινοῖ, seemed to contradict the Old Testament, which taught the distinction between clean and unclean meats. As Christ acknowledges the divinity of the Old Testament, (Matt. v 17,) he must see something important even in its laws respecting food. That these, however, were wholly void of meaning, the Saviour, in explaining the words, does by no means say. He only gives prominence to the contrast between what is external and internal, and calls attention to the circumstance, that food as being external (ἔξωθεν εἰσπορευόμενον εἰς τόν ἄνθρωπον,) could never reach or pollute the *inner* soul. He does not however say, that what is *outward* may not cause *outward* pollution, or that it is thus of no consequence what a man may eat. This was hint enough to the disciples that our Lord left to the Jewish laws all their significancy as to externals, (and as types of what was spiritual,) and only intended to rebuke the Pharisaic transposition, which put the external in room of the internal.[1] Mark, who here formally paraphrases the words of Matthew, gives a correct view of the first half of the thought. The food taken into the outward organ for its reception (the mouth) enters not into the inner man, ($καρδία$ = לב,) but goes into the $κοιλία$ in order to nourish the bodily organism. The additional clause $καὶ εἰς ἀφεδρῶνα ἐκβάλλεται$, is partly intended as the climax of those explanations, which show how thoroughly external the process of taking food is, and partly designed to intimate that nature herself has already assigned the means by which that which is nourishing in food may be separated from that which is impure. Mark, in his explanatory way, expresses this in the words $καθαρίζον πάντα τὰ βρώματα$. The neuter gender (the readings $καθαρίζων, καθαρίζει$, are the corrections of transcribers to diminish the difficulty,) refers to the whole of what precedes, in such a way that $τοῦτό ἐστι καθαρίζον$, must be supplied

Ver. 18, 19. The internal however is here set in contrast over against that which is outward, and the defilement of man properly so called (the soul of man) is pointed out. To this impurity of soul the Pharisees gave no heed while carefully avoiding that which was external. In this second idea here propounded, however, there are also internal difficulties. For in the *first* place it does not appear that it is the mere $ἐκπορεύεσθαι$, (the manifestation of feeling by word or deed) but the very presence of corrupt feeling itself which pollutes, and assuredly (as Matth. v 28, shows,) the Saviour was far from wishing to exclude the belief of this. But *secondly*, the $καρδία$ is represented as the source of evil actions, (ver. 19, $ἐκ τῆς καρδίας ἐξέρχονται διαλογισμοὶ πονηροί$,) yet one does not see how in that case man can be made unclean, for, to his innermost soul he is unclean already. Only that which is pure admits of being defiled, not that which is already unclean. This leads us more closely and accurately to define

---

[1] It is unquestionably wrong to look on this as containing an abrogation of the Old Testament laws respecting food such as we afterwards find at Acts x 10 The Old Testament, as typical and external in its ordinances ($σκιὰ τῶν μελλόντων$, Heb x. 1,) could effect only outward purification (Heb. ix 13, $τὴν τῆς σαρκὸς καθαρότητα$,) but this the Pharisees, according to their usual mistake of the outward for the inward, confounded with spiritual purity, and to point out this error is the object of Jesus

the meaning of the expression ἐκπορεύεσθαι ἐκ τοῦ στόματος, (the opposite of the foregoing εἰσπορεύεσθαι,) an expression which seems intended to mark the relation in which the will stands to these evil thoughts. The general fact that evil thoughts enter into the mind of man, is a consequence of the universal sinfulness of the race, but that any particular evil thoughts gain power over him sufficient to manifest themselves in outward act, is the result of the will, and its voluntary choice. By peccata actualia, however, the habitus peccandi is strengthened, and thus also the noble germ of human nature is defiled. The καρδία here, therefore, is not the *source* of evil thoughts, but the canal, as it were, through which they flow, and through which in like manner the Spirit of grace pours good thoughts into man.[1] In no respect is man the absolutely free and independent *creator* of his own thoughts and inclinations, (which Pelagianism would make him,) but he possesses the power equally of rejecting what is bad and admitting what is good into his soul, or the reverse. It is very obvious therefore what value is to be put upon the opinion of those who infer from these words that the heart produces at will evil thoughts (or good,) and that these do not originate in the kingdom of darkness. " Doth a fountain send forth from the same opening sweet water and bitter?" James iii 11. (Comp. as to καρδία and διαλογισμός at Luke i. 51; ii. 35; Matth. ix. 4) In the enumeration of the several forms of evil propensities which is given also by Mark more at length, ἀσέλγια is not to be referred to sexual impurity as elsewhere at Rom. xiii. 13; 2 Cor. xii. 21; Gal. v. 19, al. freq.) for it stands quite apart from πορνεῖαι and μοιχεῖαι. It is best understood as denoting an evil-disposed wilfulness of mind, and its results. The expression ὀφθαλμὸς πονηρός, however, corresponds to the Hebrew עַיִן רָע, Prov. xxiii. 6; xxviii. 22; which denotes an envious, malicious glance. It is connected with the idea that such a look is capable of inflicting injury. (Comp.

---

[1] Krabbe (On Sin and Death, Hamburg 1836, p 131, note,) thinks that " καρδία is here the innermost will in so far as it, acting unconditionally, cooperates for the production of actual sin." But that is what I doubt —whether the human will can act unconditionally and independently of every thing beyond itself A good action has for its condition the influence of God, an evil action that of the kingdom of darkness and its prince How this does not subvert the true freedom of the will, is shown in our remarks on Rom ix. 1.

Matt. xx. 15.) The last expression ἀφροσύνη=ἄνοια, refers to forms of sin and wickedness in which stupidity is prominently exhibited—"senseless wicked acts."

§ 28. THE HEALING OF THE CANAANITISH WOMAN'S DAUGHTER.

(Matt. xv. 21—31; Mark vii. 24—31, [32—37; viii. 22—26.])

Without marking accurately either time or place, Matthew (and Mark also, who follows him,) proceeds to the narrative of a cure, in which however, our interest is awakened, not so much by the act of healing itself, by the antecedent circumstances. Mark once more distinguishes himself by giving minute traits which illustrate the outward action, but he leaves out also essential features, for example the statement at Matt. xv. 24, as to the relation of the heathen to the people of Israel, which casts so much light on the whole transaction.

Ver. 21. The μέρη Τύρου, Mark describes more definitely by μεθόρια. The Lord *approached* these boundaries, but that he really passed over them, is at once rendered improbable by the idea stated at ver 24.[1] The woman, however, came to meet him (Ver. 22. ἀπὸ τῶν ὁρίων ἐκείνων ἐξελθοῦσα.)

Ver. 22. The woman is called by Matthew (in the true phraseology of Palestine,) χαναναία, but by Mark ἑλληνίς συροφοινίκισσα, (the better manuscripts have this form instead of συροφοίνισσα, which certainly is a more correct Greek form of the word, but on this very account is less deserving of being admitted into our text.) The addition of τῷ γένει obviously marks her descent from the inhabitants of that region; ἑλληνίς refers to the language she spoke and her education, which, as was usual in those countries about the time of Christ, were Grecian.

Ver. 23, 24. She prays in behalf of her daughter who was possessed of a devil, but the Lord refuses her as an heathen with the words οὐκ ἀπεστάλην κ. τ. λ. (comp. on Matt. x. 5, 6) Inten-

---

[1] De Wette asserts (on the passage) "it is not said here that Jesus entered on foreign ground with a view to exercise his ministry." But after commencing his official career, he continually exercised it, and he did so specially in the present case It is thus, to say the least of it, not probable that he crossed the boundary.

tionally and wisely did the Saviour confine his ministry to the people of Israel. Only on certain heroes of the faith from amidst the heathen world did Jesus bestow grace as the representatives of nations who as yet were far from the covenants of promise.

Ver 25, 26. To the woman who still impressively repeated her request, Jesus again addressed the same reply, but in a sharper form. Representing himself as the steward of the mysteries of God and dispenser of all the heavenly powers of life, he compares the Israelites to the children of the family, and the heathen to the dogs (κύνες is used contemptuously as at Philip. iii. 2. Neither the Old Testament nor the New recognises the noble nature of this animal. Comp. on Luke xvi. 21. The diminutive certainty has a milder sense. Still the thought remains very sharp and bitter, and he *designs it to be so.*)

Ver 27. The woman's faith, however, humbly receives the reply in all its bitterness, and child-like she takes the position assigned her, claiming no place within the temple; she is content to remain standing as a door-keeper in the outer court, and pleads simply for that grace which was fitting for the occupant of such a station. (Taking up the comparison she entreats an gift of the ψιχία. The expression occurs again only at Luke xvi. 21, in regard to Lazarus the sick man, and in a similar connexion. It is from ψίω, to *rub down, to crush in pieces*)

Ver. 28. Overcome as it were by the humble faith of the heathen woman, the Saviour himself confesses μεγάλη σου ἡ πίστις, and straightway faith received what it asked. This little narrative lays open the magic that lies in a humbly-believing heart more directly and deeply than all explanations or descriptions could do. Faith and humility are so intimately at one, that neither can exist without the other, both act as by a magic spell on the unseen world of the spirit, they draw the heavenly essence itself down into the earthly. In this cure faith is again obviously seen not as knowledge, not as the upholding of certain doctrines for true, but as an internal state of the mind—the tenderest susceptibility for what is heavenly—the most entire womanhood of the soul. When *yearning* faith, by coming in contact with the objects it longs for, becomes *seeing* faith, out of such a mental state there certainly spring beliefs and doctrines of all kinds, which, as being the product of this inward and immediate operation, may themselves be termed πίστις. Usually, however, the Christian mind finds more difficulty in understanding the conduct of Christ than in the depth of this heathen woman's faith. It would seem as if he who knew what was in man (John ii. 25,) must have been constrained at once to help *this* woman, as her faith could not have been concealed from him, and even although for wise reasons he was led to confine his ministry to the Jews, yet as in other instances he made exceptions, (comp. on Matt. viii. 10), so might he have done in her case *at once* without laying on her the burden of his severity. Nay, the severity seems so very severe, that it were difficult to find a place for such a trait in the beauteous portraiture of the mild Son of man. It is Christian experience alone which opens our way to the right understanding of this. As God himself is compared by our Lord to an unjust judge who often turns away the well-grounded supplication (Luke xviii. 3, sq.), as the Lord wrestles with Jacob at Jacob's ford, and thus exalts him to be Israel (Gen. xxxii 24, sq.) as He seeks to kill Moses who was destined to deliver his people (Exod iv. 24), so faith often in its experience finds that the heaven is of brass, and seems to despise its prayers. A similar mode of dealing is here exhibited by the Saviour. The restraining of his grace, the manifestation of a treatment wholly different from what the woman may at first have expected, acted as a check usually does on power when it really exists, the whole inherent energy of her living faith broke forth, and the Saviour suffered himself to be overcome by her as he had when wrestling with Jacob In this mode then of Christ's giving an answer to prayer we are to trace only another form of his love. Where faith is weak, he anticipates and comes to meet it; where faith is strong, he holds himself far off in order that it may in itself be carried to perfection.[1]

Ver. 29—31. According to both evangelists, Jesus after this left the western boundary of Palestine, and turned back to the sea of Genesareth. (As to Δεκάπολις, see on Matt iv. 25). Without marking more closely the connexion, local or chronological, the narrative ends in one of those general concluding formulae, which plainly show either that the author never intended to produce a historical work closely cohering in its several parts, or that he embodied just as they stood certain separate narratives which were complete in themselves. To me it seems not unlikely, from the frequency with which such forms of conclusion occur

---

[1] As to the faith of the woman in behalf of her daughter, see on Matt xvii 14 sq

in Matthew (comp. iv 23—25; ix. 8, 26, 31, 35, 36; xiv. 34—36,) and their mutual resemblance, that he interwove into his work minor treatises of this kind which had perhaps at an earlier period been written down by himself. There is a peculiarity in the use of κυλλός which occurs in this passage in the enumeration of the sufferers who assembled around Jesus. The same word is found at Matt. xviii 8, conjoined as in this case with χωλός, and there it obviously means *one maimed*. But never in any other case is it recorded as an express fact that Christ really restored bodily members which had been cut off, and a cure of this kind would ill accord with his usual mode of healing It is better therefore to take κυλλός here in the sense in which the word is usually employed by profane writers, as meaning, *bent, crooked, bowed down*. As the denial of Christ's higher, heavenly, miraculous power is an error, so it contradicts the gospel narrative to hold that this miraculous power put forth its energy without internal law or order, to guide its manifestations. Never does the Lord create members to replace those which had been cut off, but he certainly heals those which had been injured; never does he create bread without a substratum to begin with, but certainly he increases that which previously existed. The question, then, whether he was not able to have done such things, must be cast aside, as not to be entertained, it is enough for us that he did them not. Still the principle stands fast which is implied in the very idea of Christ's divine nature, that boundless as was his power, it was yet fully regulated by laws, inasmuch as the Spirit himself is law, and all spiritual manifestations are included in a cycle of high and heavenly laws, in the course of which cycle they form the system of nature (*das naturliche*). This is confirmed by the short narrative of the healing of the man who was deaf and dumb (κωφὸς μογιλάλος, i. e., *hard of hearing*, and for this reason as not hearing his own voice, speaking unintelligibly. According to ver 35, therefore, he at once spoke on his hearing being restored,) which Mark here inserts (vii. 32—37,) and which he alone records. Minute and circumstantial in his narrative, he recounts here, as in the similar account of healing the blind man, (viii. 22—26,) many particulars as to the external form of Christ's cures which bring them vividly before the mind's eye. With these notices may be compared both the account of the disciples performing cures with *oil* (which Mark vi. 13 alone gives,) and also the narrative in

John ix. 6, according to which Christ applied *spittle* in the same way when healing one born blind The *oil* is to be regarded as merely an ordinary outward means of cure (Luke x. 34,) which the disciples, disbelieving, as it were, the full efficacy of their miraculous powers, (Matt. xvii. 20,) applied at the same time. It is a wholly unscriptural view that Christ, *along with* their heavenly miraculous power, had *enjoined* his disciples to employ the expedients of domestic medicine, he rather permitted them the use of the oil in accommodation to their weakness. Leaving this out of view, there remain in these narratives the following peculiarities. (1.) It is a new thing that Jesus should take those who are about to be healed *apart* by themselves (Mark vii 33, ἀπολαβόμενος αὐτὸν ἀπὸ τοῦ ὄχλου κατ᾽ ἰδίαν; viii. 23, ἐξήγαγεν αὐτὸν ἔξω τῆς κώμης). It is not to be thought that this was done out of anxiety lest the people on seeing his treatment of the sick should be led into all sorts of superstition. This would have applied as much to the sick themselves who belonged to the people, and shared their views. A single word, moreover, would have been enough to provide against such superstition It is better to seek the ground of it in something *belonging personally* to the sick themselves. As their moral healing was the ultimate end of their physical cure, the Saviour ordered every thing external so as to contribute to that object Amidst the outcry of popular tumult beneficial impressions could with far more difficulty be made on them. And with this also agrees the command given to both that they should preserve silence as to their cure. (Comp. vii. 36; viii. 26. See what is said on this at Matt. viii. 4.) (2.) The mention made of the gradually advancing process of cure in the blind man's case is peculiar. According to Mark viii. 24, after the first touch of Jesus he saw darkly and obscurely. "I see men as trees (the power of measuring extension by the eye was probably as yet awanting,) walking." After the second touch he was wholly restored. Obviously, therefore, the cures performed by Christ were no magical transactions, but real processes. In the case of the blind man the course of the cure may have been retarded for this reason, that his disease was deeply seated, and a too rapid process of recovery might have been injurious. We remarked something of the same kind in dealing with the history of the Gergesene (Matt. viii 28,) from whom the demon did not depart till the command of Jesus had been twice given (3.) The application of *spittle* is peculiar to these narratives, which is also mentioned again at John ix. 6. In regard to this, we must at once reject, as unworthy of the dignity of Christ, the opinion which holds that he was himself misled by the popular notion that attributed to the spittle healing virtues, and which, further, infers from this that the thing here recorded must be understood even in cases where it is not mentioned, and so would transform Christ into an ordinary physician, acquainted with the use of certain remedies. That other opinion is also to be rejected according to which Christ employed this means in order to aid the weak faith of those who were to be healed.[1] For on the one hand the Lord does not make use of this means in cases where weakness of faith really existed (Mark ix. 24,) and on the other, it is incongruous to endeavour by a thing so wholly external to remove the inner want of the soul. We must therefore have looked on the employment of the spittle as a thing that exercised real influence, even though we had been unable to show any link of connexion in regard to it But as we already observed that the laying on of Christ's hands (so here the holding of his finger to eye and ear) must, as it were, be considered as the medium of conveyance for spiritual power, (it is only in singular cases that this power imparts itself from afar, and without the means of communication being visibly interposed. See on Matt. viii. 10), so it is in a way analogous to this that we are to look on the use of *his own* spittle. (Mark vii. 34, gives in Aramaic the exclamation of Christ, ἐφφαθά—διανοίχθητι. It is the authoritative summons of Christ adapted to the present case, it is the expression of his Divine will, of whose fulfilment that Son who had called on the Father [εἰς τὸν οὐρανὸν ἀναβλέψας ἐστέναξε, ver. 34,] was fully assured. The form of the word is the imperative of the Aramaic conjugation Ethpael, ἐφφαθά=ἐθφαθά [in Syriac אֶתְפְּתַח from the root פְּתַח,]—ver. 37. The exclamation καλῶς πάντα πεποίηκε, almost reminds us of the history of creation, where it is said πάντα, ὅσα ἐποίησε, καλὰ λίαν, Gen. i 31. The ministry of the Messiah seems to be viewed as a καινὴ κτίσις = בְּרִיָה

---

[1] In the case of the deaf and dumb, however, it is not to be overlooked that the actions of Christ, (the touching of his ears and tongue, the looking up to heaven,) were obviously calculated to make him aware of what was about to be done with him in order to rouse his faith, which could not be done in his case by words.

הַחֲדָשָׁה.—According to Mark viii 22, the healing of the blind man took place at Bethsaida [see as to it on Matt. xi. 21,], by which we are here probably to understand the place of that name on the eastern shore of the sea of Genesareth. Yet is the description of the locality even in Mark indefinite, so that we cannot with certainty decide where the cure took place.—Ver. 25. The expression ἐποίησε αὐτὸν ἀναβλέψαι, is not to be referred to the restoration of the sight, that is afterwards expressed by ἀποκαθίστασθαι, in integrum restitui. Rather is the ποιεῖν ἀναβλέψαι equivalent to the Hebrew Hiphil, " he caused him, after laying his hands on him the second time, to look up," and then he saw τηλαυγῶς. That word, which is found only here, literally means "*shining from afar, radiant,*" from τῆλε, *in the distance.* Here according to the connexion, it means *plainly, distinctly.*")

§ 29. FEEDING OF THE FOUR THOUSAND

(Matt. xv. 32—39; Mark viii. 1—10)

The account which follows of feeding the four thousand is conjoined by Matthew to the preceding context without any mark to determine the time when it happened, and by Mark with the indefinite words ἐν ἐκείναις ταῖς ἡμέραις. The latter gives us once more separate minute traits, which make the narrative more graphic, as for example, ver. 3, τινὲς αὐτῶν μακρόθεν ἥκουσι, and in ver. 1 the amplification of Matthew's laconic expressions. The latter alone informs us that the number of four thousand is reckoned apart from the women and children (ver. 36). The narrative itself certainly contains no new points when compared with the first account of feeding the five thousand, Matt. xiv.13 sq. The single circumstance to be inquired into, therefore, is whether we are to regard this whole occurrence as distinct from the other, or whether, by a mistake of Matthew, (and after him of Mark,) the same instance of feeding has been twice recorded. This latter view has been put forward by Schleiermacher (on Luke, p. 137, and Schultz (on the Lord's Supper, p. 311) De Wette also and others see in this second account a repetition of the first fact drawn from tradition. The chief ground for this supposition is thought to lie in the circumstance that one cannot conceive how the disciples, if they had once had experience of such a miracle, could ever in similar circumstances have asked unbelievingly πόθεν ἡμῖν ἐν ἐρημίᾳ ἄρτοι τοσοῦτοι ὥστε χορτάσαι ὄχλον τοσοῦτον; (ver. 33). But there is the less weight to be laid on this remark when we find that on various occasions the disciples forget things which it should have been impossible for them to forget. For example, the plainest declarations as to Christ's sufferings and death they seem never to have heard when the event really took place. If we suppose then that some considerable time elapsed between these two miraculous entertainments, that meanwhile they had frequently met with analogous cases when the disciples and those around them were for the moment in want, (one may call to mind the plucking of the ears of corn,) when the Lord however did not see it right to help them in this manner, it will then be very conceivable that on the instant of their feeling want it did not suggest itself to the disciples that the Saviour would here be pleased in this form for the second time to put forth his might We are all the more disposed to declare in favour of this explanation, as there is otherwise not the least improbability in the same fact having occurred a second time under analogous circumstances, just as the narratives of cures are repeated in similar cases. To admit, on the other hand, that the narrative in this case is not authentic is to open the way for consequences affecting the authority of the gospel which the Christian mind could never admit, unless they rested on certain historic proofs which are here wholly wanting. A new and fully detailed history of events which did not really take place could be given neither by an apostle of the Lord nor by an assistant whose gospel rested on the authority of a second apostle Still less could both narrators at a subsequent period (Matth. xvi. 9, 10, Mark viii 19, 20,) put into the mouth of our Lord an allusion to a fact which really did not take place.[1] If the narrative forced us

[1] The passage here quoted is also of importance for our object in this respect, that the remark of the disciples, ὅτι ἄρτους οὐκ ἐλάβομεν (Matth. xvi 7), shows that even *after* the second miraculous feeding the disciples could not imagine that their being in the company of the Son of man made it needless for them to take provisions for the body. Jesus finds it necessary to rebuke them for this unbelief, and remind them of *both* miraculous entertainments. One can hardly conceive a stronger proof that the second feeding is authentic. Meanwhile superficial modern criticism knows how to set it quite easily aside by the cheap assertion that it was only after the formation of the two fabulous reports as to the feeding, that this whole conversation was—invented. At this rate any fact one chooses may be struck out of the narrative

to such assumptions as this, the authority of both gospels would be overthrown. The supposition that a fully detailed narrative of fact is a pure invention is quite another thing from the admission of some trifling historical oversight—for example, whether there were one or two blind men. To this it must be added, that on closer examination the invention of the fact by tradition is wholly improbable. For in the first place, if this second narrative of feeding the people had owed its origin to tradition, many things would have been added by way of embellishing it. The unadorned style in which the second incident is told, precisely as was the former even as regards the separate words, vouches for its apostolic origin Nay, this narrative, so far from any effort to display the fact in brighter colours, sets it forth as of less importance. In the former case there were 5000, here only 4000, and yet there are here seven loaves while formerly there were only five, although the less the number of loaves the more marvellous must the miracle appear. It is precisely in these little circumstances that the handiwork of tradition would most easily be detected. What could any one gain by inventing the account of Christ's having fed 4000 men, when in fact he had already fed 5000? It is not thus that the fictions of tradition run. If we had read here of Christ having fed 10,000 men with one loaf, the probability of forgery had been greater.[1] Is any one ready to say that this second fact may be the real one while the former is the fictitious in which the number of the fed is increased and of the loaves diminished? This however is the most improbable of all views of it—that any one should place last the real fact as being the less important and put first the false. Obviously an unconscientious narrator will overdo the truth itself, and for this reason he places last the invented fact as being the most striking. We can discover then only proofs for the authenticity of this second feeding as narrated, none whatever to show that it is spurious; for, in regard to the disciples, we can easily admit that previously to their being furnished with power from on high their me-

[1] With great *naïveté* Strauss (vol ii p. 203), describes these as " eager remarks into which one had better not enter." By all means, for this wanton critic had nothing to allege against them, except that the first feeding was a myth as well, i e a lie. Thus, with this man, one lie is built upon another. One who, like myself, honestly calls things by their right names, which certainly makes a fatal impression, does not, Strauss thinks, know how to penetrate the depths of the mythic view.

mory was often weak, indeed they themselves state quite plainly that it was so with them. They walked in a new world full of spiritual and bodily wonders, amidst which they could not find themselves at home until the Spirit came upon them, and brought to their minds all things that the Lord had said to them and done. (John xiv. 26.) (As to Magdala [Matth. xv. 39,] and Dalmanutha [Mark viii. 10,] see on Matth. xvi. 5.)

§ 30. WARNING AGAINST THE LEAVEN OF THE PHARISEES.

(Matth. xvi 1—12; Mark viii. 11—21.)

Along with his narrative of the first miraculous feeding, the evangelist conjoins the account of an incident which shows the weakness of the disciples. When Christ used the words προσ-έχετε ἀπὸ τῆς ζύμης τῶν Φαρισαίων, they thought they were reproved on account of having forgotten to take bread, while the Saviour was thinking only of the spiritual influence put forth by the Pharisees. Every thing in this section is connected with Christ's words of rebuke and warning against the Pharisees, but since neither in the preceding nor following context are they further spoken of, it is rendered probable that the evangelist merely points out the occasion when those words, so intimately connected with the account of the feeding, and on which he laid such peculiar stress, were spoken. It can moreover excite no surprise that the Pharisees, when they demand of Jesus a sign (and a sign from heaven too, Luke xi. 16,) should have been rebuked in terms similar to those at Matt. xii. 38, sq. by a reference to the sign of Jonas. There is nothing to justify the assumption (which Schulz defends loco citat.) that Jesus had spoken the words only once, but that the narrator, drawing from impure tradition, had twice recorded them. It may be that portions of the addresses here incorporated by Matthew were originally spoken in another connexion, (for example, verses 2, 3, which are given by Matthew alone, but which yet appear to me to be quite as appropriately placed here as at Luke xii. 55, 56, on which passage see the exposition of the words,) but the whole is to be viewed as a new occurrence. For if the Pharisees more than once eagerly desired a sign from heaven, and this from their entire devotedness to externals may easily be supposed, it is also conceivable on the other hand that the Saviour more than once addressed them as a γενεὰ πονηρα καὶ μοιχαλίς, and alluded to the great Jonah-sign (For the exposition of Matth. xvi 1—4, see on Matth xii 38 sq)

The peculiar essence of the narrative Mark, as one plainly sees, has rightly seized. He brings everything relating to the conversation of Jesus with the disciples, which is the main point, very carefully forward (viii. 13 sq) They pass together across the sea to the further shore This points us back to Matth. xv. 39, Mark viii. 10, where Magdala and Dalmanutha are mentioned as the places to which Christ betook himself The latter of these places is mentioned only here, but it lay probably in the neighbourhood of Magdala, which is named by Matthew. Μαγδαλά (from מִגְדָּל *a tower*, for which reason it is not to be written μαγαδάν or μαγεδάν,) lay on the eastern shore of the sea in the district of the Gadarenes. One of the Marys, (with the surname *of Magdala*,) was undoubtedly a native of this town. On their voyage across, the conversation here recorded took place, and to their accounts of it both evangelists prefix the remark that the disciples had forgotten to take bread. (The careful Mark even adds that they had *only one loaf,* εἰ μὴ ἕνα ἄρτον οὐκ εἶχον μεθ' ἑαυτῶν Such traits indicate the extreme accuracy of the sources of information employed by Mark; it is not thus that myths are formed. It would ill accord also with the idea that the second narrative of feeding the multitude is fictitious) The remark of Jesus, ὁρᾶτε καὶ προσέχετε ἀπὸ τῆς ζύμης τῶν Φαρισαίων, must be accounted for, for this reason, did the narrators prefix the request for a miracle which shortly before the Pharisees had addressed to Jesus.

An apparent contradiction seems to arise between Matth. xvi. 6 and Mark viii. 15, inasmuch as the former conjoins the Sadducees, the latter Herod with the Pharisees. Herod however stands merely for his party (Matth. xxii. 16; Mark iii. 6,) in which the laxity of the Sadducees in point of opinion both religious and moral, was mixed up with political objects. (Comp. on Matth xiv 2, which passage does not contradict this view.) If therefore the Sadducees be not precisely identical with the Herodians, yet are they nearly akin,—doctrine holding the more prominent place with the former, politics with the latter. Against their whole tendency and aim does the Saviour mean to give warning. Then, although ζύμη is immediately explained at

Matth. xvi 12, as διδαχή, yet is this not to be looked on apart from the whole circumstances amidst which it stands, for outwardly considered there was much truth in the doctrine of the Pharisees (Matth. xxiii. 3). The διδαχή was merely that which came forth from them, and consequently it was that which, as it were, infected others and spread the plague of these men At Luke xii. 1, therefore, it is said most correctly ἡ ζύμη τῶν Φαρισαίων ἐστὶν ὑπόκρισις, for with them the danger lay in their hypocrisy, with the Sadducees in the Epicurean pursuit of enjoyment—on the part of both in their alienation from God and mental idolatry. The term ζύμη belongs to those figurative expressions in Scripture which may be applied in either of two opposite ways. (See on Matth. xiii. 33.) That application of it according to which it denotes the corrupting (fermentation-causing) element of evil, is the original one It rests even on Old Testament usage, the purification of the house from leaven, for the paschal feast is the symbol of inward purification and sanctification (1 Cor. v. 7)

Ver. 7. The disciples who lived as yet more in the outer than the inner world mistake the connexion of Christ's remark with the conversation formerly held with the Pharisees. They do seek for some connexion, but permit themselves at once to make a transition from the ζύμη to the bread. They attributed to Jesus doubtless their Jewish prepossessions as to food, (that Jews ought not to eat with heathen,) and looking to the hostile relation in which he stood to the Pharisees, they deemed that he meant to prohibit their receiving food from them. This took place within their mind (διελογίζοντο ἐν ἑαυτοῖς,) and found utterance in the words (ταῦτά ἐστι ἃ λέγει) ὅτι ἄρτους οὐκ ἐλάβομεν. The whole is so drawn from the life that any thing like a fiction derived from later tradition is not to be thought of. This occurrence also supports most decisively the second account of feeding the multitudes.

The Saviour rebukes their weak faith and reminds them of the two visible proofs of help received from him in time of need Outward bread, the Saviour means to say, would not fail them, only let them not slight the enjoyment of the true and pure bread of life,—*that* would be the surest preservative against hankering after the ζύμη of the Pharisees. (Mark expands the discourse further, Matthew gives shortly and concisely its essence. One should say that Mark rather rewrote and expanded than epitomised Matthew.)

§ 31. CONFESSION OF THE DISCIPLES. PROPHECY OF JESUS RESPECTING HIS OWN DEATH.

(Matth. xvi. 13—28; Mark viii. 27—ix. 1; Luke ix. 18—27.)

Matthew and Mark transfer the scene of the following narrative into the region of Caesarea Philippi. (The town is not to be confounded with Caesarea Stratonis, which lay on the sea. [Acts xxiii. 23 sq.] Caesarea, called Philippi from the tetrarch of that name who enlarged the city, lay on the north-east side of Palestine [Joseph. Antiq. xviii. 2, 1]. It was not far from Magdala and Gerasa. Originally the town was called Paneas. Philip, in honour of the emperor named it Καισάρεια, as Bethsaida was, in honour of the emperor's sister called Ιουλίας [Joseph. ibid.]) Luke gives no note to mark the time, but subjoins this incident immediately after his account of the first feeding of the multitude. Schleiermacher (loco citat. p. 138,) draws from this an inference unfavourable to the genuineness of the narrative of the second feeding as given by Matthew and Mark. Could we cut out it and all connected with it, he remarks, Matthew and Luke would appear quite to harmonize in respect to the chonography. The supposition that the second feeding must be transferred to the western side of the sea (while the first took place on the eastern shore, certainly appears according to Von Raumer's remark (Palestine p. 101,) to be untenable. Meanwhile what has been already advanced should be sufficient to show the impossibility of identifying the two, and thus no weight is to be laid further on the circumstance to which Schleiermacher has drawn attention. In the important narrative which follows, moreover, Matthew comes forward as the leading historian. He informs us (xvi. 17—19,) that after the confession of the disciples through Peter as their organ a remarkable declaration was added by the Lord, as to which the two others are silent.[1] Mark, it is true, once more subjoins in his account several

[1] It is remarkable that Mark, whose Gospel, according to the tradition of the ancient church, rested on the authority of Peter (comp. Introd.

minute and peculiar traits (for instance ver 27, that the conversation was carried on even during the journey) but into the essential meaning of the transaction he gives us no deeper insight.

Ver. 13, 14. The conversation on the road to Caesarea (ἐν τῇ ὁδῷ Mark viii. 27,) begins with the question of Jesus, τίνα με λέγουσιν οἱ ἄνθρωποι; (some manuscripts have falsely left out με, it was omitted simply because of the following expression, τόν υἱόν τοῦ ἀνθρώπου, which contains more closely the definition of με. The whole clause is to be taken thus, ἐμὲ τὸν υἱὸν τοῦ ἀνθρώπου [ὡς οἴδατε] ὄντα. Then would the disciples be led forward from the idea of the υἱὸς τοῦ ἀνθρώπου, to that of the υἱὸς τοῦ Θεοῦ. [v. 16.]) The question itself undoubtedly had its ground in the special circumstances as they stood at the time. Its object, however, was to awaken the disciples to a deeper consciousness of the dignity of Christ. According to the disciples, then, some merely saw in Jesus John the Baptist, (risen from the dead,) others Elias. (Compare on Matt. xiv. 2, and the parallel passages, Mark vi. 15. Luke ix. 8.) These men therefore did not see in Jesus the Messiah himself, but certainly they saw a person who stood in close connexion with his (speedily to be expected) advent. (According to Malachi iv. 5, the appearance of Elias was expected before the Messiah. See more particularly as to this, on Matt. xvii. 10 sq, and Luke i. 17) There were, however, still others who held Jesus to be Jeremiah, or some one of the old prophets, (προφήτης τις τῶν ἀρχαίων, Luke ix. 8—19.) All viewed him thus as a remarkable phenomenon, and placed him at least in close connexion, according to their several prevalent ideas, with the coming Messiah. They did not declare their belief in him as the Messiah himself, doubtless for this reason, that the whole ministry of Christ appeared to them to stand in contradiction to their Messianic expectations. The opinion that one of the ancient prophets had re-appeared in Christ, is undoubtedly to be understood in such a sense that the Jews believed really in their resurrection, but not as though they believed that their

§ 5,) should be the writer who omits to notice the important place which Peter held. One might have attributed this to modest reserve, were it not that in the passage parallel to Matth xiv 29—31 Mark has also passed over in silence a special communication respecting Peter, which, however, is not to his praise. The supposition that Mark in writing his Gospel used that of Matthew can in truth with great difficulty be reconciled with these facts souls had anew made their appearance in the person of Jesus (according to the doctrine of μετεμψύχωσις or μετενσωμάτωσις). For since, according to Jewish opinion, the *first* resurrection (see on Luke xiv. 14, compared with Rev. xx. 5,) was connected with the appearance of the Messiah, (his first appearance in humiliation not being dissevered from his second in glory, but associated with it as the prophets do,) and the setting up of his kingdom, so the idea very readily suggested itself that forerunners of the resurrection would precede that mighty period. From no express statements of the Old Testament, except in the case of Elias, did this opinion derive any support, for unless violence were done to it, the reference to the passage, Isaiah lii. 6, sq, is inapplicable. In the New Testament also there is nothing to favour it, (see however, on Moses and Elias at Matt. xvii. 4; and we can attribute it therefore only to Rabbinical legends. Around the person of Jeremiah especially there had gathered a circle of traditions, (comp ii. Maccab. ii. 7, 8, xv. 14,) they termed him, by way of eminence, προφήτης τοῦ Θεοῦ. Isaiah was also named among the forerunners of the Messiah, iv. Esra ii. 18 (Compare on all connected with this, Berthold Christ. Jud. § 15, p 58, sq)

Ver. 15, 16. Alongside of these opinions of the people respecting the person of Jesus, there is here set forth the judgment of the disciples They declare him to be the Χριστός = מָשִׁיחַ himself, and thus dissever themselves from the popular views, according to which Jesus was held to be a forerunner of the Messiah In how far, however, it may have been, this confession of Jesus as the Messiah which gave occasion to the following words of Christ, μακάριος εἶ κ. τ. λ. is not very obvious, for already had they been spoken respecting the disciples when they first attached themselves to Jesus. (John i. 41, 42) The whole relation in which Christ stood to his disciples, which must be viewed as implying an ever-advancing development, requires that in this case, the confession of the disciples should have been fuller and more complete than before. For the understanding then of this remarkable passage, Matthew is specially important, for with all his deficiency in outward and graphic descriptive power, he yet, amidst his simplicity and plainness, often shows great depth of insight Thus, after Χριστός, he adds, by way of explanation, ὁ υἱὸς τοῦ Θεοῦ τοῦ ζῶντος. This remark is most important in tracing the meaning of the expression ὁ υἱὸς τ. Θ. For obviously, the expression cannot be precisely identical with χριστός, since in that case there would arise a tautology Rather must the idea of the υἱὸς τοῦ Θεοῦ be viewed as intended to fix more closely the sense of the first expression The meaning, therefore, which most naturally results is this,—at first the disciples in acknowledging Christ as the Messiah, had merely, according to their Jewish prepossessions, seen in him a distinguished man raised up and furnished by God for special objects[1] In closer intercourse with the Saviour there was, through the working of the Spirit, opened up to them a view into his higher nature, they recognised in him a revelation of God, and without thinking of any theory as to the generation of the Son, they termed this revelation, in that personal manifestation in which it stood visibly before them, *the Son of God.* (Comp on Luke i. 35) The article points to the definite, Divine, central manifestation which they perceived in Jesus having been by the prophecies of the Old Testament instructed as to its real nature We must conceive of the disciples as living in this, and step by step advancing in their knowledge of it. When Matthew expressly adds υἱὸς Θεοῦ ζῶντος, this epithet (אֱלֹהִים חַי) obviously has reference not to idols, there being no reason for here contrasting the true God with them, but to the reality of the Divine manifestation in Christ The image of the Divine, as reflected in him, was so strong and powerful, that through it the Father, as his original, was for the first time properly revealed in his wondrous essence All former life-revelations of the living one, were dead when contrasted with that fulness of life which the appearance of Jesus sent forth in streams (John i. 4)

Ver. 17. According to this view, the import of the blessing pronounced by the Saviour on hearing this confession becomes obvious For, if this confession of Jesus as the Son of God were

---

[1] The common opinion among the Jews as to the Messiah, is exhibited by Justin Martyr, (Dial c Tr. I. p 266, 267,) when he lets him be called ἄνθρωπον ἐξ ἀνθρώπων, and be chosen of God to the Messiahship κατ' ἐκλογήν, because of his virtues Probably the disciples, during the first period of their intercourse with the Saviour, saw in him only the son of Joseph, until it gradually became clear to their minds that the Redeemer of the human race must of necessity come forth in a strength mightier than theirs whom he was to redeem, and the direct accounts of Mary, who, not without a reason, was detained till all Christ's work was finished on earth, must then have converted their presentiment into a certainty, by the report of the historical events

genuine, it necessarily implied that divine things had been experimentally manifested to the soul itself, since no man knoweth the Son but the Father, and he to whom the Father will reveal it. (Compare on Matt. xi. 27; 1 Cor. xii. 3.) But the revelation of the Divine within the soul as that which giveth life and being from on high, of itself imparts blessedness. (The μακάριος εἶ, is as at Matt. v. 4, not a mere expression of praise, but an express assurance of that eternal and blessed existence which the preceding confession implies.) The confession leads our Lord back, by way of inference, to an antecedent ἀποκάλυψις, for the Divine glory of Christ was concealed under an outwardly mean appearance, and could therefore become known only through an inward manifestation. This revelation he expressly refuses to ascribe to σὰρξ καὶ αἷμα, but traces to the πατήρ. (The addition ὁ ἐν τοῖς οὐρανοῖς = ἐπουράνιος, stands in contrast to the ἐπίγειος, which is implied in σὰρξ καὶ αἷμα.) That formula denotes what is human abstractly considered, which, as such, is transitory and vain. The phrase corresponds to the Hebrew בָּשָׂר וָדָם which is very common among the Rabbis, [comp. Lightfoot on the passage,] and had previously occurred also in the Apocrypha, [Sir. xiv. 18,] and in the New Testament, Gal. i. 16; Heb. ii. 14; 1 Cor. xv. 50; Ephes. vi. 12) The reference here therefore is to other men as well as to the natural human powers of Peter himself, so that the sense here is "nothing human, no power or faculty of man, has been able to impart to you this knowledge, only the divine can teach us to know the divine." This declaration was made by the Saviour to Peter, along with the address Βὰρ Ἰωνᾶ. It is exceedingly probable that this is intended to form a contrast to the foregoing Ἰησοῦς υἱὸς Θεοῦ. *Simon* denotes here, as does *Jesus*, the human personality of the individual; *son of Jonas* is probably used here in a figurative sense. Primarily indeed it is a genealogical designation, (see on John i. 43; xxi. 16, 17,[1]) but as Hebrew names generally are descriptive, Christ here looks to the import of the name. Perhaps he referred it to יוֹנָה *a dove*, and in that case this meaning would arise, "Thou Simon art a child of the Spirit, (alluding to the Holy Ghost under the symbol of a dove,) God

---

[1] Βὰρ Dan. vi. 1, vii. 13, = Heb. בֶּן. It may be presumed that Jesus in this conversation with his disciples spoke Aramaic. Ἰωνᾶ, contracted from Ἰωαννᾶ, (comp John i. 43) = יוֹחָנָן according to the LXX at 1 Chron. iii. 24, Ιωανάν.

the Father of spirits, Heb. xii. 9, hath revealed himself to thee." Where God reveals himself there is formed a spiritual man.

Ver. 18, 19. Here follows a new installation of the Apostles. After they had in a true sense acknowledged Christ, the Lord could open up to them also the real import of their own office. Let us first examine into the true meaning of the words, that we may be able to fix in our view more closely their reference to the person of Peter. The symbolic name which the Saviour gave to Peter immediately after his first reception as his disciple, (comp. on John i. 43,) he here renews with a definite explanation of its meaning. Peter was to be the πέτρα of the building of the church. (The church is represented as a ναός, a common figure, compare 1 Cor. iii. 9; 2 Cor. vi. 16; 1 Peter ii. 5. The Old Testament temple is viewed as the type of the church, and so also is the σκηνή regarded in the epistle to the Hebrews, chap. viii.) The church, as a spiritual structure,[1] must rest naturally on spiritual ground; it is Peter, therefore, with his new inward spiritual properties, who appears as the supporter of Christ's great work among mankind. Jesus himself is the creator of the whole,—Peter, the first stone of the building. (Compare 1 Pet. ii. 5.) The firmness of the building shows itself in sustaining the onsets of assailing powers. (Mat. vii. 24, sq.) These are here termed πύλαι ἅδου.[2] Hades (שְׁאוֹל) the abode of dark destructive powers, is often represented as a palace, with firm and close confinement, in order to mark the power of its bulwarks and the greatness of its strength. (Job xxxviii. 17; Ps. ix. 14; Isaiah xxxviii. 10.) This war-palace stands opposed to the holy temple of God, (comp. on Luke xi. 21, 22,) and appears with all its powers as assailing it, but not overcoming it, for against ᾅδης there is arrayed οὐρανός in the fulness of its power. Still retaining the same figure, then, the Lord of this temple names Peter as its guardian; he receives the key of it

---

[1] In the gospels this is the only passage where the ἐκκλησία stands as = βασ. τ. Θ. In another sense the expression occurs at Mat xviii 17. In the writings of Paul, on the other hand, ἐκκλησία is the usual expression for the visible communion of Christians Βασ. τ. Θ. is used by him rather for the ideal, heavenly fellowship. In the Hebrew קָהָל corresponds to ἐκκλησία

[2] Compare Euripides Hecuba v 1, where it is said of the lower world, σκότου πύλαι ἵνα ᾍδης ᾤκισται

with full authority to use it,[1] and consequently to grant admission or to shut out. (Isaiah xxii. 22; Rev. iii. 7, explain this symbolic expression,—That the same Peter is first termed the πέτρα, then the מִפְתָּח [see Isaiah xxii. 22,] of the building is to be explained from that free treatment of figurative expression which, with all their accuracy, prevails in the discourses of our Lord. The terms δέειν and λύειν, for *shutting* and *opening*, are to be explained from the ancient custom of simple antiquity to fasten doors by tying The passage, John xx 23, which is in fact parallel to this, has, in explaining the comparison, used the terms ἀφιέναι and κρατεῖν) The representation thus given exhibits the earthly and the heavenly as united in the Church Inasmuch as heavenly powers are acting within the church, it is not dissevered by its perfected organs from the heavenly, rather has it its sanction in the heavenly. Obviously it is only the ideal church which is here spoken of with its ideal representatives.[2] In so far as a sinful element exists in the external church, (Mat. xiii. 47,) the words admit of no application to it. Of the real everlasting church, however, they are for ever true. Further, the power which here is merely *promised*, is, at a later period, (John xx 23,) in point of fact, imparted.

It remains for us, however, to speak of Peter's position relatively to the other disciples That which at ver 19 is spoken to Peter is at Matt. xviii. 18, John xx. 23, addressed to all the apostles The contents of ver. 18 are again found at Rev. xxi. 14, and Gal. ii. 9, applied to all the apostles. One cannot therefore find in these words any thing that is *peculiar* to Peter; he merely answers as the organ of the college of apostles, and Christ acknowledging him as such replies to him and speaks

---

[1] Jeremiah i 10, forms a striking parallel to the prerogative of forgiving or retaining sins here imparted to the disciples For the Lord there says to the prophet, " I put my words in thy mouth, see I set thee this very day over nations and kingdoms that thou shouldest root out, break in pieces, throw down, and destroy, and build and plant " What in the Old Testament is given in an outward, is in the New Testament given in an inward form

[2] It is certainly true at the same time that the ideal church exists nowhere else than in the real, as the kernel within the shell If this be overlooked we are lost in empty idealism But certainly the outer form is not the same thing with the higher being which animates it, just as the soul is not without the body, yet the body must not be taken for the soul itself.

through him to them *all*. Only this ought never to be overlooked, that Peter is and was intended to be really the representative *actively* of the company of apostles, (of John the same thing may be said in a *passive* point of view, comp on John xxi. 21) For it is impossible to conceive that the same thing which the Lord here addresses to Peter could have been spoken to Bartholomew or Philip; no one save Peter could have been called the representative of the apostles. The personal difference between the apostles individually and the pre-eminence of Peter has been denied merely on polemic grounds in opposition to the catholic church, which certainly deduced inferences from it for which there was not in Scripture the slightest ground. (comp. on Matt. x. 2, and John xxi. 15.) But that which is through Peter bestowed on the apostles, was again through the apostles conferred on the whole church, as is obvious from the real nature of its inner being, according to which it follows that the existing representatives of the church (i. e. the really regenerate) exercise the powers granted by the Lord to that church, not, however, in any way which they may themselves think proper, but according to the intimations of that same Spirit whom to know and to obey is essential for the believer. That the apostles then and their true successors in the Spirit turned with the word of truth towards one place and away from another, that they followed up their labours on one man and not on another, in this consisted the binding and loosing. The whole new spiritual community which the Saviour came to found took its rise from the apostles and their labours. No one became a Christian save *through them,* and thus the church through all time is built up in living union with its origin. Christianity is no bare summary of truths and reflections to which a man even in a state of isolation might attain, it is a life-stream which flows through the human race, and its fountains must reach every separate individual who is to be drawn within this circle of life The gospel is identified with, and grown into union with, the persons. That which lies wrapt up in Christ Jesus as the centre or germ of the new life, first spreads itself forth in the company of the twelve, (comp. on Acts i. 16 sq.) and from them into the widening circle of life, which gradually expanded over the church. Already, however, have we referred to the fact, that the Lord's words to Peter were spoken to him as a new man, and are true only when viewed with reference to this new nature. That the old man in Peter was incapable of labouring for the kingdom of God—to say nothing of its being a rock—is shown by the following context, v. 22 sq. The usual explanation, therefore, of the passage which the Protestant Church[1] is wont to oppose to the view of the Catholics, according to which the *faith of Peter, and the confession of that faith*, is the rock, is entirely the correct one,—only the faith itself and his confession of it must not be regarded as apart from Peter himself personally. It is identified with him—not, however, with the old Simon but with the new Peter. (Peter as the new name being understood as denoting the new man. Rev. ii. 17.) Hence the power of binding and loosing can be affirmed only of that which is divine in Peter (and the other disciples) for God alone, (in so far as he works through one man or in the whole church) can forgive sin, (see on Matt. ix. 4, 5.) Although, therefore, the forgiving of sins is a prerogative of the church in all ages, yet since the power of the Holy Ghost in the church is manifested no more in its original concentration, that forgiveness is imparted only conditionally, *on the supposition, namely, of true repentance and living faith*, whose existence it is not possible for spiritual or clerical men to discern, since the gift of trying the spirits has ceased, (1 Cor. xii. 10.) It is for the Lord alone to do this.

Ver. 20, 21. On this advance in knowledge the Saviour immediately founds their introduction to a closer acquaintance with his work as the Redeemer, he openly declares to them that he, the Messiah, the Son of the living God, must suffer, but that in these sufferings he would be perfected. He wished to accustom them by degrees to bear this thought. The former prohibitions forbidding them to speak of his dignity, (see on Matt. viii. 4,) had reference undoubtedly to the people who were accustomed to associate with the term "Messiah" a series of external ideas which would only have been obstructions in Christ's way. For fuller details as to ἀρχιερεῖς, γραμματεῖς and πρεσβύτεροι, see on Matt xxvi. 57, John xviii. 12) Respecting the prophecy of Christ which he here utters in regard to himself, we remark, that a figurative exposition of his words which would make them mean, "I shall to appearance sink, but soon and gloriously shall

---

[1] This explanation some of the fathers of the church had already given. Gratz, following Du Pin, (de antiqua ecclesiae disciplina) has brought together the passages in his work on Matt. part ii p 110 sq.

my cause make itself good," is too shallow to claim our approval. Christ speaks too often, and in circumstances the most varied, of his death and his fate generally, (see on John ii 19, Matt. xxvii. 63, according to which last passage, the Pharisees place a watch at his grave, for this reason that he had spoken of his resurrection,) to permit our thinking of any thing but death literally as such. In the δεῖ παθεῖν, however, the death of Christ is viewed as a necessary one At the parallel passages, Matt. xx. 18, Mark x. 33; there stands the simple future παραδοθήσεται κ. τ. λ. What this δεῖ was intended to mean is shown plainly by Luke xviii. 31, (parallel to the last quoted passages) where it is said τελεσθήσεται πάντα τὰ γεγραμμένα διὰ τῶν προφητῶν τῶ υἱῶ τοῦ ἀνθρώπου (Comp. Luke xxiv. 26, 27, 44, 46. In the last passage it is said οὑτω γέγραπται καὶ οὑτως ἔδει παθεῖν τὸν Χριστόν). The prediction of Messiah's sufferings in the prophets was not, however, arbitrary, but proceeded from the internal necessity of the divine counsels. Only for the sake of the disciples does the Lord go back to Scripture, explaining it to them authoritatively, and comforting them by the fact that the Old Testament also knows of a suffering Messiah It might, however, possibly appear as if the disciples had, *post eventum*, put all these statements in more specific detail into the mouth of Jesus, for example, the chronological reference in the case of the resurrection. The same view might be taken of Matt. xx. 18, 19, and the parallel passages in Mark and Luke, in which all the particulars of Christ's sufferings are fore-mentioned, that he should be reviled, spit upon, scourged. The character of the gospel history would not in its *essentials* be altered indeed, even if we were to suppose that the Evangelists after the event had more fully and particularly filled up our Lord's shorter declaration as to his sufferings, only if one considers how already in the Old Testament, especially at Ps. xxii. 17, 19; Is. 'l. 6; liii. 4 sq., the Messiah's sufferings had been stated in full detail, no offence can ever be taken at the speciality of Christ's predictions. It is, however, a thing wholly and entirely inadmissible to raise a doubt as to whether the Saviour possessed generally a fore-knowledge of his own death. To draw from the disconsolate state of the disciples on the death of the Lord, an inference against his having previously mentioned the resurrection, is incompetent for this reason, that the doctrine regarding a suffering Messiah was, among the Jews of Christ's time, forced very much into the back-ground. (See on John

xii. 34. Comp Hengstenberg's Christology, p. 252 sq) When Christ therefore died, the disciples who were still influenced by popular opinion, thought not of his resurrection, for in regard to *every thing* they were staggered. The contrasts through which the life of Christ passed before their eyes, were so dreadful that they were stunned and confounded.

Ver. 22, 23. If however we find on the part of the disciples an incapacity to penetrate in thought the mysterious contrasts presented by the life of Christ even after our Lord's crucifixion, previous to which they had yet to experience so much, far more must it have been impossible for them at the period here referred to They could not endure that the Son of God should be a sufferer. The manner in which our Lord however casts back the declaration of Peter, who again speaks as the representative of all the apostles, points to something more than simple deficiency in the comprehension of an idea hard to be understood Peter wholly misunderstood the relation in which he stood to the Lord, he came forward to admonish and correct Him, and that which Christ had represented as necessary (for his work,) he seeks to put far from Him. (The ἵλεώς σοι, scil εἴη ὁ Θεός = חָלִילָה לְךָ, 1 Chron. xi. 19) But even this does not exhaust his meaning. The expression σκάνδαλόν μου εἶ, which follows, points to the idea that Peter's remark was not merely sinful as respected his own standing-point, but formed a temptation to the Lord. Peter, we find here, perhaps from having his vanity excited by the praise which had been bestowed immediately before, sunk back to the standing-point of the natural man—and along with him the other disciples whom Jesus here rebukes through Peter, just as, at ver. 18, 19, he had conjoined them with him in praise. (Mark viii. 33, indicates this by his expression ἰδὼν τοὺς μαθητὰς αὐτοῦ). It is the part of the natural man however, τὰ τῶν ἀνθρώπων φρονεῖν, and of the new man τὰ τοῦ Θεοῦ φρονεῖν. It is not the ἄνθρωπος πονηρός who is here spoken of, but only the ψυχικός (1 Cor ii. 14), who, incapable of receiving the Divine in its real nature, draws it down to the level of his low human sphere But in a case where the co-existence of the old and the new man (in those who are regenerate but not yet perfected,) is admitted as intelligible, and the alternate predominance now of the one and now of the other, it is also clear how Jesus can here rebuke that same Peter whom he had just praised For this difference of expression was dependent on the varied prevalence of the new or the old man in the same individual. It only remains for us to say something more particularly of the ὕπαγε ὀπίσω μου, σατανᾶ. These words are to be explained by the expression which follows σκάνδαλόν μου εἶ, by the addition of which Matthew greatly facilitates our understanding the whole of this remarkable narrative, and again furnishes proof of how accurate he is in the setting forth of events, even though he does overlook their external features. For, unquestionably the Saviour must be conceived of as having maintained one *continuous* conflict with temptations. The great periods of such temptations at the commencement and termination of his ministry, exhibit merely in a concentrated form, what ran through his whole life Here then for the first time, there meets our view a moment in which temptation assails him by holding forth the possibility of escaping sufferings and death. It was all the more concealed and dangerous that it came to him through the lips of a dear disciple, who had just solemnly acknowledged his Divine dignity. What we remarked in the case of the history of the temptation (see on Matth. iv 1 sq) must in this instance also be faithfully kept in view. From the clear and pure fountain of Christ's life no unholy thought could flow, but inasmuch as he was to be a conqueror victorious over sin, it had to draw near, that in every form he might overthrow it, and upon his human nature, which only by degrees received within itself the whole fulness of the Divine life, sin, when it drew near, did make an impression. Such a holy moment have we here. With the glance of his soul the Saviour at once penetrated the source whence sprang this ἵλεώς σοι, and killed in their very origin the evil roots that were springing. From this it is at once obvious, how we are to understand the address σατανᾶ, which was directed to Peter, (στραφεὶς εἶπε τῷ Πέτρῳ). The opinion that Peter is here termed an evil counsellor, or rather an adversary,[1] (from שָׂטָן,) stands completely self-refuted; the rock of the Church cannot possibly be at the same time an adversary, and yet Peter did not, by having spoken these words, cease to be the rock of the Church. Satan is none other than the ἄρχων τοῦ κόσμου τούτου, who has his work in the children of unbelief (Ephes. ii. 2,) and also in the children of

---

[1] As regards the mere usage of the words, this explanation may be justified by referring to such passages as 1 Kings xi 14, 2 Sam xix. 22 In the New Testament however σατανᾶς never occurred in the sense of *adversary*

faith, in so far as the Spirit of Christ has as yet not sanctified them, *i. e.*, in so far as the old man, still exposed to sinful influences, yet lives in them. This influence had Peter (as the organ of the others, who are to be conceived of as under the same guilt) admitted into his heart without knowing what he did. Our Lord however brings him to the consciousness of what he was doing, by naming the element out of which sprang the thought which he had been weak enough to express. And thus, even as in the foregoing confession (ver 16,) the Divine was seen as predominant in the mind of Peter, so evil now asserts its power over him, and here therefore, we have in his case an exhibition of that ebbing and flowing of the inner life, which every one experiences within himself who has felt in his heart the atoning power of Christ. Where sin is powerful there does grace excel in power (Rom. v. 20); conversely however, where grace is mighty, there sin also puts itself mightily forth.

Ver. 24—26. Immediately after these words, Jesus, transferring his discourse from the narrower circle of his disciples to a more extensive audience, (according to Mark and Luke) subjoins an admonition on the subject of self-denial. The thoughts themselves we have already unfolded at Matth. x. 37, sq , and the only point for inquiry here is, what association of ideas connects these verses with the foregoing. The fact that Christ must die, does not seem to imply as a necessary consequence, the death of his disciples, for indeed Christ died expressly to the end that we might live. Of *bodily* death this is undoubtedly true, but the life and death of Jesus is a pattern for his church (1 Peter ii 21). What the Saviour experienced, that must all his redeemed ones also experience *spiritually;* they taste the power of his resurrection, but previously also that of his sufferings (Phil. iii. 10). To be made alive in the new man (in the $\psi v \chi \tilde{\eta}$ $\pi v \epsilon v \mu \alpha \tau i \varkappa \tilde{\eta}$,) necessarily implies the dying of the old. (Comp. the remarks on Matth. x. 37, sq) The expression of Peter (ver. 22,) had flowed from the natural dread of conflict, sufferings, and death, and hence does our Lord exhort all who would follow him to undertake these willingly, and for the sake of heavenly things to sacrifice all the earthly. The gain of the $\varkappa \acute{o} \sigma \mu o \varsigma$ with its sensuous enjoyments (ver. 26,) could never satisfy man's immortal part. Is the world then the object of his efforts? He loses in that case his real happiness The sacrifice of what is heavenly alone brings real pain, the sacrifice of what is earthly pure joy. The latter may be compensated, the former never.¹ In the words τι δώσει ἄνθρωπος ἀντάλλαγμα there is an implied declaration that only God could have found an ἀντάλλαγμα for the souls of men. (Comp on Matt. xx 28.) 'Αντάλλαγμα is nearly allied to λύτρον, although not entirely synonymous. It denotes the *purchase-money*, the object for which a man exchanges any thing, as Sir vi. 15, φίλου πιστοῦ οὐκ ἔστι ἀντάλλαγμα. Thus, while the ἀντάλλαγμα proceeds on the idea of *possession*, λύτρον refers to a state of *slavery*, out of which the λύτρον gives deliverance. In this respect, the expression ἀπάλλαγμα would correspond to λύτρον, but it does not occur in the New Testament The verb ἀπαλλάσσειν, however, in the sense of *to set free*, occurs at Heb. ii. 15. To this admonition to self-denial Mark and Luke subjoin the corresponding threatening. (As to the contents of the verse compare the parallel passage Matth. x. 32, 33) The shunning to enter into conflict and suffering, is in fact to be ashamed of the Lord, and to sacrifice the eternal for the sake of the temporal And this will, at the day of judgment, display its fatal results. (As to the formula ἔρχεσθαι ἐν δόξῃ μετὰ τῶν ἀγγέλων τῶν ἁγίων, see on Matth. xxiv.)

Ver. 27. From what has gone before, it is plain, that the formula ἀποδώσει ἑκάστῳ κατὰ τὴν πρᾶξιν αὐτοῦ, must be understood in such a way, that the πρᾶξις denotes not individual works of this or of that kind, but the whole inward course of life (the τὸν κόσμον or ψυχὴν κερδαίνειν,) which flows from faith or from unbelief, and shows itself in the fruits of the one or of the other.

Ver. 28 In order to render his mention of the ἡγέρα κρίσεως more impressive, the Saviour sets forth its threatening nearness. As at Matth. x. 23, I here refer once more to the leading passage Matth. xxiv, inasmuch as this same idea, that the day of the Lord's return was near at hand, must be understood in the same way all through the New Testament. Here, the death (θάνατον γεύσασθαι = טָעוּם מָוֶת,) of some who were present—as the longest livers, is assigned as the period of the Parousia. (The words ὧδε ἑστῶτες are to be understood of the whole multitude who surrounded him, the apostles as well as the others.) One involuntarily calls to mind here the enigmatical words at John xxi. 22, on which compare the commentary. The parallel pas-

¹ The same thought was expressed formerly at Ps. xlix. 7—9.

sages in Mark and Luke refer not so much to the coming of Christ, as to the coming of his kingdom, (Mark adds ἐν δυνάμει,) and these expressions may be understood as describing the powerful manifestation of living Christian principle, without reference to the personal return of Jesus. But the immediate connexion of those words with the foregoing context, in which the ἔρχεσθαι ἐν τῇ δόξῃ refers so unmistakeably to the Parousia, does not admit of this explanation. The coming of the kingdom falls at the same period with his coming personally.

§ 32. THE TRANSFIGURATION OF JESUS.

(Matth. xvii. 1—13, Mark ix. 2—13, Luke ix. 28—36.)

In regard to the following important occurrence, some preliminary remarks are necessary, that we may gain the right standing-point for correctly comprehending it—all the more necessary from the great diversity of opinions respecting it which have been put forth. At the outset, we summarily reject those views which reduce the fact itself to a dream or an optical delusion, and we deal in the same way with the views as to thunder and lightning, and passing mists, which some would substitute for the voice of God, and the light-cloud. Other explanations, however, which find here either a myth, or a vision without any outwardly visible fact, must be more closely examined. *Primarily*, then, as respects the mythical hypothesis, it has historical analogy to support it. But he who finds it impossible to place the Judæo-biblical history on a level with the development of history among other nations, must be precluded, as was formerly observed, by this general character of the Bible narrative, from admitting in any case the slightest mythic element. In it, we have a history of God amidst the human race, in which every thing appears really carried into effect, which human fancy, springing from the real longings of the soul, has arranged in mythic forms, and as a beauteous garb around the histories of other nations. Besides, in this narrative of the transfiguration, particulars are given which directly contradict every idea of a mythical construction. That which is mythical, as being the offspring of fancy, is everywhere from its very nature obscure and indefinite, but here, as everywhere, the evangelists maintain their historic calmness. Contrary to their usual practice, they narrate with one voice, that the transfiguration took place six days after what was previously recorded. If we consider that the evangelists wrote thirty years at least after the event, it is obvious how deeply the solemn occurrence must have imprinted itself on their memories, from their so accurately retaining the time. According to Luke ix 37, the healing of the sick boy, which all the evangelists agree in placing directly after the transfiguration, took place the following day.[1] A thing of this kind ill agrees with the mythic structure. The history obviously reads like the simplest narrative of a fact. As respects the view however, that it is a vision which is here recorded, the occurrence is certainly styled an ὅραμα (= חִזָּיוֹן, מַרְאָה,) at Matth xvii. 9, only the expression does by no means always imply a purely inward mental contemplation, it is often used also in cases where an object outwardly visible, was present. It merely denotes, in general, objects which become known to us by the sense of sight, in contradistinction to those made known to us verbally (comp. Acts xii. 9). And further, the view which holds the occurrence before us to have been a vision, is wholly untenable, for this reason, that no instance exists of such an inward vision having been revealed in one and the same way to many individuals at once, and these separate individuals also, occupying standing-points so very different as was the case with Christ and the three disciples. We take our stand then, on the simple literal sense of the narrative, which in the first place was assuredly that intended by the narrators; and in the next place, admits, in the view of the Christian mind, of being thoroughly defended. For if we assume the reality of the resurrection of the body, and its glorification, truths which assuredly belong to the system of Christian doctrine, the whole occurrence presents no essential difficulties. The appearance of Moses and Elias, which is usually held to be the most unintelligible point in it, is easily conceived of as possible, if we admit their bodily glorification. In support of this idea, however, Scripture itself gives sufficient intimations, (Deut. xxxiv. 6 compared with Jude 9; 2 Kings ii. 11, compared with Sir. xlviii. 9, 13), which men have accustomed themselves to set down as belonging to biblical mytho-

[1] Gratz (Part II p. 166,) appeals also to 2 Pet i 17 As however the genuineness of the epistle cannot be certainly established, we must not bring forward this interesting passage *in the character of a proof*. Yet ought it assuredly to be read.

logy,—but what right they had to do so is another question.

Taken then as literally true, the incident has a twofold meaning. *First*, it is a kind of solemn installation of Jesus into his holy office before the three disciples, chosen for the purpose of being present at it. It was intended that they should be confirmed in the truth of the foregoing confession (Matth. xvi. 16,) and more fully enlightened as to the dignity of Jesus. In this point of view, the Old Testament furnishes, in the history of Moses, a parallel to the transfiguration. Along with Aaron, Nadab, and Abihu, he ascended Mount Sinai, received there the law, and shone to such a degree that he had to cover his countenance. (Compare Exodus xxiv with xxxiv. 30 sq.; 2 Cor. iii. 7 sq) So also Christ was here installed as the spiritual lawgiver, inasmuch as the voice said αὐτοῦ ἀκούετε (Matth xvii. 5.) His word is law to his people. But *secondly*, the fact is applicable to Jesus himself. For, the transfiguration takes its place along with the baptism, the temptation, and other occurrences in which Jesus is himself the object of the event, and his inner life is exhibited in the course of its development. Throughout the whole of his earthly ministrations, the Saviour appears in a twofold point of view; on the one hand as the Redeemer already making reconciliation, and so as active, and on the other as inherently advancing his own perfection. Heb. x. 12, ἔπρεπε τῷ Θεῷ τὸν ἀρχηγὸν τῆς σωτηρίας διὰ παθημάτων τελειῶσαι) Only by degrees, did the human individuality of Jesus receive into itself the Divine universality. The transfiguration then, formed one period in the course of this development. It was a representation prefiguring the kingdom of God, in which the risen saints shall dwell around Jesus, and the heavenly messengers opened up to him more fully and deeply the counsel of God in the work of redemption (Luke ix. 31). Should we conceive of the transfiguration as not effected instantaneously, but as a thing gradually prepared for, it would be even in this view not without important meaning. (Compare the Commentary, Part II)

Ver. 1. With perfect unanimity, which runs with trifling exceptions through the whole narrative, the evangelists relate that the transfiguration took place after six days, reckoning from the occurrence which precedes it. (The ἡμέραι ὀκτώ in Luke are merely to be counted according to another way of enumerating the days) The mountain they describe in the most general terms, (ὄρος ὑψηλόν,) and we are left therefore merely to conjecture in determining where the event occurred.¹ The preceding incident took place at Cæsarea Philippi (Mark viii. 27), and there has therefore been a disposition to seek the mountain on the eastern side of the sea of Gennesareth. But it is impossible to show that, during the six intervening days, Christ had not changed his locality. The early fathers of the church conceived it to have been Mount Tabor, (Hos. v. 1, in the LXX. Ἰταβύριον,) for no other reason assuredly but that it is the highest mountain in Galilee. It seems strange, however, that in this case Jesus takes only three disciples with him, for it would appear that the same confirmation of their faith was equally necessary for the others Already, however at Matth. x. 1, we remarked, that the disciples held distinct positions in reference to the person of Jesus. The three disciples here named seem obviously in the Gospel narrative, to have formed the circle which most nearly surrounded Jesus. As they here beheld him glorified, so at a later period (Matt. xxvi. 37), they witnessed his deepest sufferings. The ground of this distinction which the Saviour made among the twelve, was obviously no arbitrary one, but arose from the difference in their dispositions and vocation. And this consequently made a different training necessary. An esoteric, secret course of instruction communicated by the Lord to these three is not to be thought of. Everywhere, stress is laid by Christ, not on the imparting of a doctrinal system, but on the renewal of the whole man.

Ver. 2, 3. While Jesus then, was engaged in prayer, (Luke ix. 29,) there took place a change in his person—his face and his dress shone brightly. It is not said by the narrators, whether this glory shone from within or came upon him from without

[1] It is remarkable that the most important incidents in the life of our Lord, (the transfiguration, sufferings, death, ascension,) took place on *mountains*, as also that it was his custom to ascend mountains for prayer. In the same way, in the Old Testament, sacrifices were offered on mountains, and the temple also was built on a mountain This is connected with the Scriptural system of symbols, according to which mountains were compared to the vault of heaven. Hence so often in the Old Testament does the expression occur "mountains of ascent, everlasting hills" (Gen. xlix 26, Deut. xxxiii. 15; Ps. xi 1, lxxii 3, cxxi. 1, Hab. iii 20, Rev xiv 1.) It is interesting to observe the parallelism of this with the idol-mountains of ancient natural religions (compare Baur's Theology, Part I. p. 169). The learned man we have named compares even the German name Himmel (*heaven*,) with the Indian Himalayes of the primeval idol mountains of the Hindoos.

But as Moses and Elias are mentioned in immediate connexion with it, and as they also shone (according to Luke ix 31), so it is probably the design of the narrators to represent the whole scene as illumined by a bright light (δόξα, כָּבוֹד,) for it is ever in this form that men conceive of what is exalted. One may therefore conceive of the two things as both united in the person of Jesus, he was irradiated by light shed on him from without, and he himself shone from within. Mark paints, after his manner, the outward brightness of the clothing (ix. 3), the indefinite term however, μεταμορφοῦσθαι, employed by Matthew, is paraphrased by Luke, with the words τὸ εἶδος τοῦ προσώπου αὐτοῦ ἕτερον ἐγένετο. According to the intention of the narrator, these words might merely mean to say, that his countenance wore an unwonted, an elevated expression. The characteristic shining or radiance Matthew brings forward with special prominence (comp Dan xii 3; Rev. x. 1) It is a natural symbol, to conceive of that which is Divine as light, in no nation and by no individual is the heavenly presented under the emblem of darkness. The fulness of the radiance betokens very naturally the degree of purity in the revelation from on high. In these figurative forms of speech, do mankind throughout all their tribes express themselves, for it corresponds to that essential existence which reveals itself inwardly to every mind. (Paul uses the word μεταμορφοῦσθαι in describing the internal processes of regeneration, Rom. xii 2, 2 Cor iii 18) It is strange that any question should have been raised as to how the disciples could have known Moses and Elias, partly because of the obvious answer, that in the conversations as to the occurrence which immediately follow, Jesus may have informed them, and partly because to any one living in the spirit of Scripture, such characters as Moses and Elias must be conceived of as bearing a peculiar impress that could not be mistaken

Luke ix. 31, 32 gives some additional particulars, which are of the highest importance for our understanding the whole occurrence. He remarks, first, that Moses and Elias had spoken of the decease of Jesus (ἔξοδος in the sense of *the end of life, death*, as at Wisdom vii 6; 2 Peter i 15,) which awaited him in Jerusalem. The peculiarity here is the contrast, which a myth never would have hit on, implied in uniting the act of transfiguration with the deepest humiliation It would seem, however, as if the Saviour's glory had in reality been exhibited to him in order to strengthen him for victory. Yet even after this, his soul faltered, even although he here tasted the glory. (The expression ἔλεγον ἔξ-οδον, it may be added, is unquestionably to be understood as referring not so much to the fact of the death itself, as to its more immediate circumstances and relations. Moses and Elias appear merely as ἄγγελοι, as messengers from the higher world.) Luke however relates further, that Peter and his two companions were heavy with sleep, and had in the act of rousing themselves (διαγρηγορήσαντες,) beheld the glory of Jesus and of the two men. Even in the same way did sleep overcome these three disciples amidst the sufferings of Jesus at Gethsemane, (Matth. xxvi 40,) where Luke relates (xxii. 45,) that they slept from grief (ἀπὸ τῆς λύπης) Great mental agitations, whether of joy or sorrow, are fatiguing. Their solemn situation amidst the loneliness of night upon a mountain—with the Saviour apart,—all this must have taken hold of their souls, and physically worn them out. Nothing however can be more incorrect, contradicting both history and Scripture, than to conclude that owing to this drowsiness they were unable correctly to observe what passed The accuracy of their narrative rests obviously not so much on their own observations as on their subsequent conversation with Jesus Had the disciples fallen into any mistake, the truthfulness of Jesus would at once have undeceived them. Far rather does the simple narrative of the circumstances as they happened, even of such as seemed unfavourable to themselves, vouch for their honesty and straight-forwardness.

Ver. 4 Peter, the speaker, breaks silence (ἀποκρίνεσθαι = עָנָה, see on Luke i 60,) and expresses his astonishment at this spectacle. Elsewhere, fear is the feeling awakened by apparitions from the higher world (see on Luke i. 12), as indeed in this case also it immediately shows itself at ver. 6 on the part of the disciples, when they heard the voice. To account then for what is so strange in this declaration of Peter, Mark and Luke immediately subjoin the words μὴ εἰδὼς ὃ λέγει These words refer not by any means to the drowsiness of the disciples, but to their inward state of ectasy The elevation of the scene hurried them away; they were lifted, as it were, above themselves. (The expression κύριε in the address is explained more clearly by the parallel terms ῥαββί[1] and ἐπιστάτα in Mark and Luke. It has not

---

[1] As to the name ῥαββί compare on Matth xxiii 7

here as yet the pregnant meaning which it has acquired in the writings of Paul, who uses κύριος =יְהֹוָה.) Among the evangelists it is Luke who already here and there (xi. 39; xii. 42; xiii. 15,) makes this use of *ὁ κύριος* in contradistinction to κύριος. (Compare however on Matth xxi. 3) The meaning of the expression σκηνάς ποιήσωμεν obviously is merely this—would that for a lenghthened period we might remain in this place and in this company! (Compare the remarks on ver. 10) The words express his inward longing after the kingdom of God, in which the saints and those who are raised from the dead shall be for ever around the Lord. Inasmuch as Peter speaks of three tents, he places himself and his two companions humbly in the background as the servants of the three. The whole form of the address however shows that Peter acknowledged Jesus as the primary figure in the picture; the representatives of the old covenant appear to him as merely subordinate, as messengers from the heavenly Father to the Son.

Ver. 5. Again however the scene suddenly changes; even the three disciples who were admitted to see Jesus in his glory, were shut out by a bright cloud from the company of the other three Most graphically is the scene presented to us by Luke. The two messengers Moses and Elias made a movement to one side, went apart (Luke ix 33, ἐν τῷ διαχωρίζεσθαι αὐτοὺς ἀπ' αὐτοῦ,) while Peter was yet speaking the bright cloud came, and Jesus with the two entered into it. All the three were thus enclosed as in a sanctuary, the disciples stood without On this, they became greatly afraid, partly because they felt themselves alone, dissevered from their Lord, and partly because the new appearance of the light-cloud terrified them. (I prefer with Griesbach the reading νεφέλη φωτός, although the most numerous and best MSS. have φωτεινή. For, φωτός was probably changed into φωτεινή because of the apparent contradiction with ἐπεσκίασεν. It seemed impossible that a cloud of light could darken or overshadow, while it was easy to conceive of a bright cloud casting a shadow. The reading φωτεινή consequently better admits of the usual sense of νεφέλη being retained. According to the view of the author, however, the words ἐπεσκίασειν αὐτοὺς are used in regard to the light-cloud, only in so far as it prevented the disciples from seeing. The most intense light is = σκότος Hence, in the language of Scripture the expressions are used synonymously, God dwelleth in φῶς ἀπρόσιτον and in darkness, 1 Tim. vi 16, Exod xx. 21 The voice then, which spake from the midst of the cloud, leaves us in no doubt what we are to think of it. It is the voice of the Father who installs the Son (Ps. ii. 7, בְּנִי אָתָּה,) as the governor of his kingdom, and commands that he be obeyed (Compare as to αὐτοῦ ἀκούετε, the passage Deut. xviii. 18, in which the first Lawgiver promises a second and more exalted) The cloud was the Schechinah (compare Buxt. Lex. Talm. s. h. v. Bertholdt. Christ jud. p 111,) the symbol of the Divine presence, into which Moses entered on Mount Sinai (Exod. xx. 21), and which descended upon the tabernacle and in the temple (Exod. xl. 34; 1 Kings viii 10). As regards the voice and the words uttered, all that is necessary will be found in our remarks on Matth. iii 17. We must not however overlook here the additional clause αὐτοῦ ἀκούετε, which is wanting on the occasion of the baptism (It is taken from Deut. xviii. 15, אֵלָיו תִשְׁמָעוּן.) By these words is the peculiar character of the scene marked out. The Messianic Son of God, who has already laboured and taught under the Divine commission, is now formally appointed the Lord and Ruler of the earth, in presence of the representatives of the heavenly and earthly world. What the tempter had set before the Lord (Matth. iv. 8,) πάσας τὰς βασιλείας τοῦ κόσμου,) is here conferred on him by the Creator of all things, and indeed not merely the dominion of earth but that also of heaven. To this solemn transaction does the Saviour look back, when he says ἐδόθη μοι πᾶσα ἐξουσία ἐν οὐρανῷ καὶ ἐπὶ γῆς (Matth. xxviii. 18) The gospel history thus enables us to follow plainly the separate periods in the τελείωσις of the Son of God, Here, at his appointment to his everlasting kingdom, it is at the same time showed to him how he must by his own blood purchase his church.

Ver. 6—8. Now the disciples lost all consciousness, they sank on their faces, and saw Jesus alone. (Compare as to the sinking down of the disciples, Dan. x. 8, 9; Rev i. 17. In both cases the touch of the hand acts restoratively, it infuses power into men disabled by the sight of the Divine Majesty.)

Ver 9 In a historical point of view this verse is specially remarkable, from the fact that it forms primarily the basis on which rests the credibility of the occurrence which precedes it. The conversation respecting it with the Saviour precludes every suspicion of a misunderstanding which must otherwise have been raised.[1] Further, the prohibition forbidding them to say anything of what had taken place, gives indication of the fact, that Jesus did not impart the same information equally to all the disciples, but that he had as it were a smaller circle of fellowship within the circle of his followers. Certainly, however, we should mistake the matter, did we infer from such an indication that there was any system of doctrines which Jesus communicated to some and withheld from others. That is the error of the Alexandrine fathers and Gnostics But not less were it an error, to deny that there was any distinction in the communications made by Jesus to his different disciples. It is difficult however to assign here the ground of the prohibition (compare on Matth viii. 4) Any abuse or misunderstanding of such a fact, of which there was obviously a risk only in the case of the general multitude, might, so far as the disciples were concerned, have easily been guarded against, by correct information To me it seems probable that this prohibition rested on no other ground than the exclusion of the *other* disciples from being present at the occurrence—they could not as yet bear everything. (At John xvi 12, the same thing is, in regard to other events, applied to the whole apostles) According to Luke ix 36, the disciples obeyed. Matthew himself therefore received his information of the event only after the resurrection. We must obviously conceive of the disciples as engaged at that time in the liveliest interchange of all their experiences. Mark remarks (ix. 10,) that this word sank deeply into the hearts of the disciples ($\varkappa\rho\alpha\tau\epsilon\tilde{\iota}\nu$ = הֶחֱזִיק, *to seize on, to hold fast*, as something important. Compare at Luke ii. 21, the verb $\delta\iota\alpha\tau\eta\rho\epsilon\tilde{\iota}\nu$,) and occasioned also separate conversations among them. It was the $\dot{\alpha}\nu\dot{\alpha}\sigma\tau\alpha\sigma\iota\varsigma$ at which they stumbled The idea they were accustomed to form of it they could not reconcile with the person of the Messiah whom they had just seen in heavenly glory, for it pre-supposed his death This little trait singularly confirms the truthfulness of the narrative.

Ver. 10—13 Luke here closes the narrative, but Matthew and Mark give an extract from a most important conversation which arose in consequence of the occurrence just recorded. It referred to the person of Elias, whom the learned among the

---

[1] The idea, that the prohibition was given merely to prevent these disseminating their misapprehension, stands self-refuted

Jews usually associated with the appearance of the Messiah. There is an obscurity however in the introduction to the discourse, which commenced, according to Matthew, with the question of the disciples, τί οὖν οἱ γραμματεῖς κ. τ. λ. The οὖν points back to something that had gone before, and the whole inquiry leaves the impression that the disciples believed the opinion of the learned Jews to have been incorrect, for which reason Christ confirms it as right. It is most natural certainly to view the reference as pointing back to ver 4, where Peter hoped that Elias would now remain with them, and enter on his labours. Instead of that, he at once disappeared, and for this reason he asks what they were to make of the above opinion Jesus declares it, according to Mal iv. 5, to be wholly correct, and defines the kind of labours in which he was to engage by the words ἀποκαταστήσει πάντα = הֵשִׁיב, in the passage referred to) For as the Tishbite once laboured of old as an *emendator sacrorum*, so shall he also come forth at his second appearance He is no creator of a new order of things in the spiritual life, but, (by legal strictness and earnestness,) he stems the course of sinful confusion, and re-introduces a state of order Into this scene the Messiah steps forth as a Creator. Christ however intimates that one had already exercised for him this office, but the γραμματεῖς had put him to death The disciples understood (according to earlier notices, see on Matth xi 14,) him to mean the Baptist. What is expressed however so decidedly here, ὅτι Ἠλίας ἤδη ἦλθε, must be modified according to the statement of Matth. xi. 14. (Compare the remarks on the passage referred to) For, the appearance of Elias at the transfiguration as little exhausted the prediction of the prophet, (Mal. iv 5,) as did the sending forth of the Baptist. Each was merely a prefiguration, adapted to Christ's first appearance in his humiliation (which the Old Testament never plainly marks as distinct from his second coming in glory.) but the prophecy itself remains awaiting its fulfilment at Christ's future appearance (compare on Rev. xi. 3 sq [1]) While Jesus, at Matth. xvii 12, draws a parallel between the fate of John and his own coming down, Mark reads the prophecies of the Old Testament as predicting the sufferings of John. Καθὼς

---

[1] As to the history of the interpretations which have been given of the passage in Malachi, compare Hengstenberg's Christology, vol iii. p 444, sq

γέγραπται ἐπ' αὐτόν, he writes at ix 13 Now nothing of the kind is expressly predicted of John, nor does the history of Elias admit of being typically referred to him, for Elias did not die in the persecution[1] It is probable therefore that the evangelist brings together here (as at Matth. ii. 23,) in one collective quotation, all the passages of Scripture in which the persecution of prophets and pious men is spoken of. Besides, the answer of Christ in Mark, acquires, through the peculiar collocation of the thoughts, a character quite different from that which it bears in Matthew. It has been conjectured that the text is corrupt, but without any ground for the idea Obviously, according to Mark, the Saviour sets over against the inquiry of the disciples another question, in order to rouse them to reflection. And in this way the following is the meaning, "The Scribes say Elias must first come;" Jesus replied, "Elias certainly cometh first ($\pi\rho\tilde{\omega}\tau o\varsigma =$ πρότερος,) and setteth all in order, but how in that case can it stand recorded of the Son of man that he must suffer much and be rejected?" By the question thus retorted, Jesus wishes to rouse his disciples to the conviction, that the prediction respecting the preparatory ministry of Elias is not to be understood *absolutely*. He certainly setteth all in order, but the sins of men prevent his efforts taking effect And in conclusion, the assurance is subjoined, that Elias is already come in the person of the Baptist (i. e. of John working ἐν πνεύματι καὶ δυνάμει Ἡλίου. See on Luke i. 17).

§ 33. HEALING OF THE LUNATIC.

(Matth. xvii. 14—23, Mark ix. 14—32; Luke ix. 37—45)

The three evangelists are still parallel in this narrative, and the indication of the time given by Luke, ἐν τῇ ἑξῆς ἡμέρᾳ, again conjoins the narrative so introduced in the closest way with what had gone before. Mark exhibits himself once more in this history in his well-known character. The epileptic boy

---

[1] Hengstenberg (Christol. vol in p. 478,) is of opinion indeed that Jezebel had *intended* to kill Elias, and that although her purpose did not, like that of Herodias, take effect, yet no weight is to be laid on this difference. But in this opinion I cannot share A type demands in every case facts, not mere intentions

he paints like a master, and the whole situation in which the cure was wrought. One sees as it were the people continuously streaming together, and the paroxysms amidst which the beneficent power of Jesus overcame the evil influences by which the child was possessed The narrative of this cure demands in itself only some short remarks, for the analogous passages already met with, make it sufficiently intelligible. Only some things peculiar to this cure will require extended remarks.

Ver 14, 15. Matthew calls the sick boy (he was his father's only child, Luke ix. 38,) a σεληνιαζόμενος. According to ver 18, however, he, like Luke and Mark, viewed the disease as brought by an evil πνεῦμα. Now the representations of Mark and Luke agree perfectly with epilepsy,[1] which, as is well-known, being founded on a diseased excitement of the nerves in the lower part of the body, is connected with the changes of the moon. It is not unlikely that the secret sins of the boy (comp on ver. 21,) had destroyed his health. Mark and Luke plainly intimate that the disease was not continuous, but that the child fell into paroxysms. Mark ix. 18, ὅπου ἂν αὐτὸν καταλάβη Luke ix. 39, μόγις ἀποχωρεῖ ἀπ' αὐτοῦ, i. e., the paroxysms endure unusually long) The gnashing and foaming, (τρίζειν καὶ ἀφρίζειν,) and the dying away, and the wasting of the sick, (ξηραίνεσθαι,) most graphically represent his condition. (The ἄλαλον of Mark refers only to articulate speech, which in such moments would be suspended; it does not therefore stand in contradiction to κράζειν [to utter in inarticulate words] as employed by Luke)

Ver. 16, 17. The disciples had not been able to heal the sick child. It is altogether an unfounded conjecture to suppose that not all the disciples, but only certain of their number (and those the weakest in faith,) are here alluded to. The words of reproof are general,—so general indeed that not only may they have included all the disciples, but the people at the same time, and especially the father of the sick boy. The apostles appear here merely as the representatives of the whole, but on them the rebuke certainly falls most heavily. Jesus, however, did stand there for the sake of the apostles alone, not with them

---

[1] I agree substantially with the view given of this narrative in the very successful exposition of Dr Paulus (Comment Part II p 571 sq) with only this difference, that he has missed here, as elsewhere, the fact, that the evangelists mean to refer the origin of the disease ultimately to the spiritual world.

alone had he to deal, the burden of all rested on him. (The verb ἀνέχεσθαί = סָבַל, *to bear the load of sin.* The expression γενεὰ διεστραμμένη agrees with Deut. xxxii 5, where LXX. give it as the rendering of דּוֹר פְּתַלְתֹּל)

Mark ix 20—27, alone sets clearly before us the course of the cure with living graphic power As the boy drew near to Christ, a paroxysm overtook him Jesus upon this began a conversation as with the Gergesene (compare Mark v 9, sq), but here only with the father, owing to the unconsciousness of the son. The object of this conversation was, by means of the peace and security which it breathed, to still the raging element and inspire confidence The father now obtained an opportunity of recounting the sufferings of his miserable child; the convulsions, he states, often threatened in a moment to destroy even his life, by casting him into fire or water which might be near. The hostile influence awakened within him an impulse to self-destruction Jesus thereupon commends to him the all-prevailing power of faith, (see as to this subject on Matth xvii 20,) and calls upon him to believe. The unfortunate man exclaims, (almost with spasmodic impulse,) πιστεύω, βοήθει μου τῇ ἀπιστίᾳ. Thus the Saviour first shows himself here to the father as a μαιευτὴς πίστεως before he heals the son. Amidst the struggles of anxiety, the power of faith is by the help of Christ produced in the unbelieving soul, and then the deliverance is vouchsafed. This passage is one of the most important to our understanding the nature of πίστις, as laid down in the Gospels It is not the acknowledgment of certain doctrinal truths that is here spoken of (that is merely a *consequence* resulting from it), Jesus is not here imparting instruction, and the disciples also supposing they had healed the sick child, would assuredly not have prefaced that cure by any doctrinal discourse on the Messiahship of Jesus Rather is the πίστις an internal state or frame of soul,—we have termed it receptivity, (compare on Matth viii. 10,) into which that which is Divine may find admission Here, however, we see that this state of soul is not to be looked on as altogether independent of man's own efforts. Earnest striving and prayer is fitted to call it forth. Both these imply, it is true, that the germ of faith already exists, (there must always be an ὑπόστασις ἐλπιζομένων in the soul if man is to be able to pray,) but no one is to be regarded as by nature wholly destitute of the germ of faith; only by a continued course of sin could it be destroyed, and so a man be brought to the πιστεύειν τῶν δαιμόνων (James ii. 19,) which, properly speaking, is no faith. (Compare Neander's small Gelegenheitschr. p. 31, sq). There is yet, however, a difficulty here in the circumstance, that the faith of the father seems to benefit the son. (In the same way, already, at Matt. viii 5, sq where the officer believes and the servant is healed, and at Matt. xv. 22 sq , where the mother's faith stands in a similar relation to the cure of the daughter). As it has been established that ἀπιστία is the ground of a refusal to heal, (compare on Matt. xiii. 58,) so it may naturally be presumed that the persons cured *also* exercised faith. Hence one might hold the opinion that two transactions perfectly distinct from each other, must in these cases be supposed to have taken place. *First*, there is the healing of the sick person, whose faith Jesus perceived, though he did not then himself express it; *next*, there is the awakening of faith in the parents or the masters, which was not connected with the cure. Yet a connexion precisely of this kind seems to be asserted here. At Mark ix 23, the cure of the child appears to be expressly conjoined with the faith of the father. It thus seems that a separate and special bond of union here found place between them. If we ask ourselves, then, whether the child not grown up could be conceived of as exercising faith on behalf of his parents, as well as the parents on behalf of the child, the inquiry would hardly meet from any one with an affirmatory reply, and consequently it seems not improbable that the child is here viewed as in a state of union and dependence on his parents from whom he received his being, such an union as is again in infant baptism supposed to exist between the child and the sponsors, as the representatives of the church. It occurs to one here very naturally to suppose such an union of posterity to their parents as is expressed in Heb vii 5, and which also lies at the foundation of the whole account of the connexion in which Adam and Christ stand to the human race (Comp. on Rom v. 13, sq) Something analogous also seems, according to the passage Matt. viii. 5, sq., to be pointed out in the relation between the master and his servant; only, it is self-evident that in this union the relation is merely to be viewed as something accidental, for it may even be conceived of as reversed. After this conversation with the father, there follows immediately the cure itself, which again, as in the case of th Gergesene, calls

R

forth a violent paroxysm, ending in the entire prostration of all his powers. (Comp. Mark v. 15). The boy was so exhausted with the fierceness of the reaction, that they thought him dead, (Mark ix. 26,) but the touch of Jesus again inspired the powers of life.

Ver. 19, 20. After the cure the disciples came to Jesus, and within their more narrow circle, (κατ' ἰδίαν, Matt. xvii. 19,) inquired why it was that *they* could not heal the sick child. Luke wholly omits this important conversation. Mark so curtails it that its essential meaning cannot be perceived, and it seems to bear on its surface a somewhat different sense; and here again then his graphic power of conception shows itself rather in what is external. Matthew, on the contrary, goes into the *essence* of the matter, especially in regard to the discourse of Jesus, and one forgives him therefore willingly that want of exactness with which he treats the outward features of the incidents recorded. Such points speak decisively enough for the apostolic origin of his gospel. On the part of the apostles, also, Jesus now reproves the ἀπιστία, and plainly charges them with guilt in the want of πίστις. They, too, might have cried out βοήθει τῇ ἀπιστίᾳ ἡμῶν. The position of the apostles (as of men in general,) relatively to that which is Divine, thus appears here as not essentially different from that of the person who was to be healed. Does man wish to receive heavenly powers? he must stand passively to await their coming. Yet was the faith of the apostles an active principle, compared with the simple act of reception on the part of him who was to be cured. Thus we plainly see here *different gradations of faith.* (Compare what is said more in detail on Rom. iii. 21.) Along with the reception of the principle of life, there comes an increase in the soul's susceptibility of it, and thus faith goes on to perfection in itself. The apostles had already for a long time been in communion with Jesus, and never had been without faith on him, yet Christ marks here within them the want of the germ of real faith, (κόκκος σινάπεως,) or as one might call it, of *creative* faith, for in this character it ought to show itself *in them.* Faith is thus a living internal state, inherently developing itself, as that which is Divine gradually becomes predominant and effectual within the soul, but in all stages of its development the fundamental condition of the καρδία (in which faith dwells, [Rom. x. 9,] and not in the νοῦς) continues one and the same. (Compare on Matt. xxi. 21,)—

Jesus now presented to their view the portraiture of perfect faith, whose effect it is that to men οὐδὲν ἀδυνατήσει (Compare Mark ix. 23, πάντα δυνατὰ τῷ πιστεύοντι.) Nothing could be a greater mistake than to make shallow the deep meaning of these words by the explanation that they are spoken hyperbolically. We read at Matt. xix. 26 respecting God, παρὰ Θεῷ πάντα δυνατά (compare the parallel passages Mark x. 27; Luke xviii 27) These words guide us to an understanding of the true meaning of this eulogium on faith. Just because faith is a susceptibility, a receptivity for that which is divine, it communicates to the individual in whom it is developed the very nature itself of that which is divine, and under the guidance of the Divine power which animates the believer, he is brought, according to the degree of development imparted to him, into those circumstances in which he must through faith come off victorious. The πάντα, therefore, is to be taken in its widest sense, only not to be referred to every kind of fanciful caprice (which might originate with forward unbelieving men,) but to be restricted to the real wants of the believer. Such a case of need the believers had encountered, but they had neglected earnestly to supplicate that help from on high which they required in the circumstances. The description of the omnipotent power of faith is moreover figurative. First, faith is conceived of as in its minimum state, and then the maximum of effectual power is ascribed to it. (See as to the κόκκος σινάπεως on Matt. xiii. 31. The overturning of mountains is an expression selected unquestionably in allusion to passages of the Old Testament. Compare Job ix. 5; Zech iv. 7. In the New Testament, Paul repeats the statement at 1 Cor. xiii. 2. Another similar figure to denote what is impossible for man, but possible for God in believers, is seen at Luke xvii. 6. In the passage Matt. xxi. 21, [Mark xi. 23,] the figure of the overturn of mountains is repeated).

Ver. 21. The connexion of the following verse with the preceding context is obscure. "This kind (scil. τῶν δαιμόνων,[1] according to what goes before,) goeth not out but by prayer and fasting." (The fasting being viewed as an accompanying means of cure along with prayer.) The immediate connexion of the

---

[1] Sieffert (ut supra, p. 100,) wishes to refer τοῦτο τὸ γένος to the unbelief of the apostles themselves. But I know of no instance in which unbelief, which was something negative, could be compared with demons who must be driven out This view of the passage seems to me inadmissible.

words, with the reproof administered to the apostles for their unbelief, leads obviously to this meaning, " this obstinate enemy was not to be overcome in the same way that many others are. It was needful for you, with prayer and fasting, earnestly to strive after more of the power of faith, and then might you have been victorious." The προσευχή and νηστεία relate thus to the disciples themselves And yet both may be referred also to the person cured, ye ought to have enjoined on him similar duties, and then ye would have been enabled effectually to heal him. The reference in this view to Luke ix. 42, ἀπέδωκεν αὐτὸν τῷ πατρὶ αὐτοῦ is certainly most correct, it is not unlikely that the Saviour had exhorted the father to a wise treatment of his son. According to the connexion of ideas in Mark, this reference of prayer and fasting to the cured boy, who probably had by sins of impurity plunged himself into this nervous disorder, obviously preponderates. In Matthew it is perhaps best to combine both references.

Ver 22, 23. In the concluding verses the evangelists are entirely agreed in introducing a new mention of the Saviour's sufferings (compare on Matt. xvi. 21) The words stand without any visible connexion with what goes before. It is however not improbable that from time to time the thought of his approaching sufferings struck Jesus, and then, as the narrative here presents it to us, he suddenly expressed what he felt to his disciples, especially when, leaving the larger sphere of public labour, he retired more into solitude and the private circle of his nearest friends. (This is indicated at Mark ix. 30, by the words οὐκ ἤθελεν ἵνα τίς γνῷ [sc αὐτόν]). This declaration, however, must only have been at the time of a fragmentary nature, for the disciples could not reconcile themselves to the idea of their Messiah's sufferings, that Messiah from whom they expected the end of all suffering (Mark ix. 32; Luke ix. 45, ἠγνόουν τὸ ῥῆμα τοῦτο.) Meanwhile the expression of that deep and painful emotion carried them away involuntarily (Matt. xvii. 23, ἐλυπήθησαν σφόδρα), but the lofty and serious majesty which was seen diffused around the whole nature of Jesus, deterred them from asking further as to the transaction he had alluded to (ἐφοβοῦντο ἐρωτῆσαι in Mark and Luke,) and so there remained for them only the dark impression of some mighty event which must be expected.

§ 34. THE COIN (STATER) IN THE FISH'S MOUTH.

(Matt. xvii. 24—27.)

Before proceeding to consider the occurrence itself which is here recorded, we must cast a glance at the connexion. Mark ix. 33, as also Matthew, makes the Lord come to Capernaum, but connects immediately with his arrival the narrative of the conversation as to who should be the greatest in the kingdom of God. He relates most minutely that this conversation took place in the house, and was introduced by a question put by Jesus, as to what they had talked of by the way. Now according to the view of Dr Paulus (Comment. Part ii. p. 621,) Peter had not been present at the commencement of this conversation, but had come in subsequently while it was going on, (Matt. xviii. 21,) and it is simply to account for his absence that this narrative of Peter's taking the fish, is inserted by Matthew. But, for this conjecture the whole account gives not the slightest occasion, nay, Mark ix. 35 rather mentions the twelve as all present at the commencement of the conversation. The expression $\pi\rho οσελθὼν\ αὐτῷ$ at Matt. xviii. 21, merely means that Peter came close to him when addressing Jesus. If the evangelist had distinctly intended to represent Peter as absent, he would have stated so in plainer terms. It is far more natural to suppose that Matthew added in conclusion this little narrative of Peter's taking the fish, because it happened just at the time, and in order that he might introduce once more in chap. xviii a more lengthened collection of various fragments of discourse which he did not wish to interrupt Moreover, Christ's conversation with Peter as to the census, might have been considered of importance in respect to the discourse which follows, as will be afterwards shown. The nature of the discourses, as they are given in Matt. xviii., by no means demands, as will afterwards be shown, the absence of Peter, even if they were spoken the one after the other, in the same order in which we read them in Matthew. Peter's taking the fish was undoubtedly (owing to the proximity of the sea,) the work of a few moments, and we may therefore justly suppose him present at what follows.

As regards the incident itself, however, the account of which we read at Matt. xvii. 24—27, it is not to be denied that the natural explanation which Dr Paulus (ut supra,) has given of it, brings forward points that deserve consideration. Taking the narrative in the usual sense, there is much in it that strikes one as strange. First, it is at the very outset, a strange thing that the coin should have been in the *mouth* of the fish. It seems more to the purpose to conceive of it as in the κοιλίᾳ, especially as the fish was caught by an ἄγκιστρον (*hamus, fishing-hook,*) the use of which presupposes the opening of the mouth. In the next place, however, the object aimed at seems to stand in no fitting connexion relatively to the miracle. The miracles of Jesus have always a definite relation to the well-being of man, or they are designed to authenticate the Messiahship of Jesus, and prepare the way for faith in it. Here it does not appear that we can trace a connexion with any of these objects, for the occurrence referred to Peter personally, and to him alone, yet was he already convinced of the Messiahship of Jesus; the address of Jesus (ver. 25,) presupposes faith as already existing in him. Besides, as Jesus was in Capernaum, even if his bag was empty, (John xii. 6; xiii. 29,) he might in this place have obtained the small sum in a more simple way. Thus the proposal to explain the expression εὑρήσεις στατῆρα (ver. 27,) as meaning " thou shalt obtain the coin (stater) for the fish" (by selling it,) will appear as not so entirely inadmissible. For, even according to this very explanation, the transaction taken in a symbolical point of view bears a beautiful meaning, as showing how Christ, as the Lord of nature, caused to be taken from the great treasure-house of the Father what he required. One feels at first sight all the more tempted to accede to this view, because it appears to be in any case a strange thing that at the close of the history the usual conclusion of miraculous narratives is wanting —namely, that Peter at the command of Jesus both did and experienced what had been said to him. But looking now without prejudice or prepossession to the narrative, one certainly ought not to conceal the difficulties presented by this explanation of Dr Paulus. If at ver. 27 we take the words as we find them, καὶ ἀνοίξας τὸ στόμα αὐτοῦ εὑρήσεις στατῆρα, it must be confessed that the narrator means to say that the stater (coin) would be found in the mouth. It must be granted indeed that εὑρίσκειν *may* mean *to acquire, to obtain*, (without defining the way in which a thing is obtained,) but the fact that the acquisition of this piece of money is connected so closely with the *opening* of the *mouth*, unquestionably is in contradiction to the opinion that the money was to be raised from *the sale* of the fish. The remark of Paulus on this point, that the opening of the mouth refers merely to his taking the fish off the hook, and that this was needful because it would otherwise have died more speedily, and so would have been of less value, is obviously too far-fetched. It is clear that this mode of explaining away what is supernatural is suggested not by the text itself, but by reflection In the next place, it is not to be overlooked, that plainly only *one* fish was intended to be caught. Paulus will have it that ἰχθύς is to be taken collectively, but the addition of πρῶτος altogether forbids this. (Compare Fritzsche on the passage.) But in poor Capernaum, where fish were common, the sum of money here named could not possibly have been obtained for a single fish. As it is however the primary duty of an expositor to render the meaning of his writer's text, so must we here maintain, that Matthew means to relate that Jesus commanded Peter to take a fish, and foresaw that it would bear a stater in its mouth. Fritzsche is quite right in saying, that, according to the opinion of the narrator, there were two things of a miraculous nature; first, the foreknowledge of Jesus; and next, the fact that the fish had the coin in its mouth, not in its body. Such, however, being the result yielded by the interpretation of the passage, we cannot leave it standing in opposition to the character of Christ; and it thus becomes a question whether, contrary to the above remarks, the fact can be placed in harmony with the whole nature of Jesus. The main question here requiring to be settled is this, whether such an exertion of miraculous power as we find set forth in the passage, was opposed to the principles of Jesus; the other observations offered will then disappear of their own accord, or will lose their weight. It must ever be maintained as a leading principle, that every miraculous act of Christ had an object which stood connected with his whole Messianic work. What can have been the object of this miracle of Jesus? We must naturally suppose that He was without money, when the tax-gatherers made their demand. Now *to receive* gifts if they were offered him, was in no way against the decorum of his position as the Messiah; it rather formed one part of that peculiar appearance which he presented, that without possessions of his own, he went about here below in perfect poverty, in order that he might receive bodily sustenance from those whom he nourished with the bread of life; nay, what men gave, God gave through them (see Luke viii 2). But it is altogether a different thing to suppose that Jesus, even when destitute of money, could have been reduced to *borrow it* of any one;[1] that would have been against the *decorum Divinum*. It belonged to the form of his office that *his heavenly Father* should nourish him from day to day by working on one and another, and inducing them to furnish everything needful to supply his necessities. But among *men* the righteous never could be left to beg (Ps. xxxvii. 25). Accordingly, the matter may be conceived of in this way. The tax-gatherers came at a time when no money was at hand; Peter over-hastily promised payment; and Jesus, though he rebuked this rashness, deemed it proper here, as in other cases, to fulfil all righteousness; an opportunity was in this way given him of taking from the full treasure-house of his heavenly Father To send Peter a-fishing with a view to sell the fish caught, would have been to prosecute a calling and trade to which the Son of God was not appointed; and so this which was here adopted, remained, as the only form of taking from the fulness of the Father At the same time I cannot decidedly declare in favour of this explanation; and I acknowledge that I hold this to be the most difficult miraculous narrative in Gospel history. Hence, the simplest course that remains, is merely to bring the miracle into immediate connexion with Peter, who, at particular moments, certainly acknowledged the higher powers that dwelt in Christ, but who also soon lost again the vivid impression of his Divine nature. Christ might have been able in another way to obtain the money; but in order to convince Peter of his higher nature, and freedom from all earthly laws, he causes him to seek it in this way. In Peter's answer to the collectors, that the Lord would pay the contribution, there was implied a mistake as to his peculiar position; and although Jesus might appeal to his Divine Sonship, which, at a former period, Peter had already confessed, yet the Saviour seems to have wished still more deeply to impress on his mind a view of his exalted dignity

---

[1] It will excite no surprise that the feelings of Dr Strauss give a different response He sees, as in many other things, nothing offensive in this, that the Son of God is made to contract debt to man In such a case there is no difference between begging and borrowing Compare, moreover, 2 Kings iv. 1, sq, where Elisha also performs a miracle in order to discharge a debt

GOSPEL OF ST MATTHEW XVI. 24—26   249

Ver. 24. As respects the relative value of the money which this narrative refers to, the στατήρ is = 4 drachmas or Roman denarii. These formed a Jewish shekel. The δίδραχμον is therefore = half a shekel, i. e., to about 10 good groschen. The stater thus amounted to 20 good groschen.[1] This sum of itself,[2] and still more, the conversation which follows, shows that it is not a civil tax but a temple tax that is here spoken of. According to Exodus xxx. 13, sq., every Israelite was required to pay such a contribution; and in the time of Josephus (Antiq xviii. 9, 1,) even the foreign Jews paid it. The question put by the collectors of this assessment, whether Jesus would pay it, assuredly arose from the circumstance of these persons believing that as a theocratic teacher he would regard himself as free from such an impost. But Peter, to whom the question was addressed in the absence of Jesus, believed, that with his strong religious feelings, he would make it a point to pay such holy taxes, and answered affirmatively

Ver. 25, 26. Jesus perceived at once that on the part of Peter this arose from unconsciousness. In his answer he had contemplated Jesus rather under the aspect of legal piety than in that of his ideal dignity, and Jesus therefore anticipated his remark (προέφθασεν αὐτόν) by the question τί σοι δοκεῖ, Σίμων, he awakens by this inquiry the feeling of his own higher position, as well as that of Peter himself, above the constitution of the Old Testament temple. Jesus here runs a parallel between earthly kings and earthly tribute (τέλη, *customs-duties on goods*, κῆνσος, *head-money on persons*,) and the heavenly King, and spiritual contributions; as with the kings their own are free from taxes, so also in the things of heaven. For, what God's children possess belong to God,—they have no property exclusively their own,— they contribute out of and into their own purse,—they are therefore free. Jesus places himself here on a level with Peter, but it is obvious that from this figurative mode of speaking nothing can be inferred affecting our idea of the υἱὸς τοῦ Θεοῦ The meaning is simply this,—we belong to a higher order of things than that to which the commandment in question (Exod

---

[1] The good groschen is equal to rather more than 1½d   The Mariengroschen is of less value.
[2] The double article also οἱ τὰ δίδραχμα λαμβάνοντες, indicates a reference to certain appointed persons entrusted with the collection of the temple offerings.

xxx. 13,) applies; not for us did God give it, we pay to the temple not a poor tax, but we ourselves belong to it wholly, with all that we are and have. Jesus thus elevates Peter, and places him on his own standing-point,—a position for which he certainly was not yet fully trained, but to which, in as far as he was a renewed man, he already belonged. The Lord's words at the same time clearly prove that Jesus acknowledged and honoured the Old Testament order in general as a Divine institute,—unless this be assumed, the words have no meaning. Only he contemplated the whole temple service in its preparatory character, and led on the disciples so to view it.

Ver. 27. While thus conscious that he stood above the Old Testament economy, (comp. xii. 8,) the Saviour yet subjected himself to it, as in general, up to the time when his work on earth was finished, he in no respect assailed or withdrew from the existing order of the divine service. Only at Christ's atoning death was the law completed and finished, and a new form of religious life arose in the church, in which the laws of the Old Testament acquired their true spiritual meaning. Here, in this subordination to the law, does Jesus make obvious the weakness of those around him (see as to σκανδαλίζεσθαι on Matt. xviii. 6); he wished neither to give them offence nor lead them to believe that he did not reverence the law of the Old Testament. It is certain, also, that the basis laid down here is the general principle πρέπον ἐστι πληρῶσαι πᾶσαν δικαιοσύνην. (Comp. on Matt. iii. 15).

§ 35. ON THE CHARACTER OF THE CHILDREN OF THE KINGDOM.

(Matt. xviii. 1—35; Mark ix. 33—50; Luke ix. 46—56)

The words ἀναστρεφομένων αὐτῶν ἐν τῇ Γαλιλαίᾳ (Matt. xvii. 22,) again seem to unsettle the whole chronological connexion by their vagueness; nor do the parallel passages in Mark and Luke give any more certain data. The contents, however, of the succeeding context, make it probable that no great interval in this instance elapsed between what had preceded and what now follows. The conversation as to pre-eminence in the kingdom of God in which the disciples were engaged on the way to Capernaum (Mark ix. 33,) may have been occasioned by the transfiguration, and the preference there shown for certain of their number, and as all the three narrators give exactly the same connexion of events, this supposition being of itself possible, ought to be received as probably true. It is true at the same time that each of the evangelists contributes to the narrative something different from the others. Luke is the shortest;—he has merely the admonition to humility. Mark gives also the warning against offences in an extremely expanded form, as his manner is. Matthew, however, adds still further particulars. It is not impossible so to conceive of the antecedent circumstances, that all these different points may on this occasion have been made by Christ the subjects of conversation, simply on account of what had fallen out among the apostles. The evangelists themselves give details according to which we may infer the following to have been the course of events. The disciples not merely conversed as to their pre-eminence in the kingdom of God, but fell into a sharp contest on the point. (Hence the admonition at Mark ix. 50, εἰρηνεύετε ἐν ἀλλήλοις). In the altercation, they not merely boasted the one over the other, but by hard words wounded each other's feelings; nay, the disciples by this gave such offence to each other, or to any individual who might be present, that their faith might have been shaken in the reality of any higher life as existing within the circle that surrounded Christ, or in the more exalted vocation exercised by himself personally This would explain how Christ should successively have discoursed of humility, of offences, of grace towards sinners, of being reconciled. This view, however, rests simply on conjecture as to the contents of that conversation between the disciples. It is also possible that Matthew, according to his custom, has again assembled together portions of different discourses relating to kindred topics.[1] The tie which in this chapter connects the different portions, is the endeavour to depict the true character of the children of God in the words of Christ. Much had already occurred which might be viewed as attributing to the disciples something of outward importance; especially might Christ's very address to Peter as to the temple-taxes, (Matth. xvii 25,) be so misunderstood.[2] Against this error Matthew now places a representation of the inner spiritual nature of discipleship as standing in direct contradiction to all

---

[1] Compare here the remarks on Matt. xiv 1, and the introductory observations to chap xix 1
[2] So we find it in Clemens Alex. quis dives salvetur, chap 21

earthly domination Yet Christ does not deny that there is a difference in the places which shall be occupied in the future kingdom of God; he merely sets forth that frame of mind by which all abuse of these is obviated.

Ver. 1. Most graphically does Mark ix. 33, sq. again depict the scene. The conversation as to who should be the greatest had taken place by the way In the house our Lord questions the disciples on it, and they, conscious of guilt, are silent, whereupon, by a symbolic act, He sets clearly before their view the nature of God's kingdom. First, however, it is to be carefully marked here, that the Saviour by no means denies that the apostles possess special dignity in the kingdom of God; which indeed he could not do, for it is promised them by himself (comp on Matt xix. 28). Further, he does not deny that there is a distinction between his different disciples, for in the same way he gave ground for making that distinction, (see on Matt. xvii. 1.) Thus the error of the disciples did not consist in believing that a difference exists among the members of the kingdom, or in cherishing the consciousness that God has called them to something great, but in this, that they viewed their calling in a worldly, earthly light, and regarded supremacy in the kingdom of God as resembling supremacy in an earthly kingdom. The very idea of a kingdom, it is true, presupposes, necessarily, government and subordination; but in the kingdom of God the government is specifically different from earthly rule. This distinction the Saviour here developes, inasmuch, as according to Mark ix. 35, he represents the $\pi\rho\tilde{\omega}\tau o\varsigma$ in the kingdom of God as the $\text{\textgreek{ἔσχατος}}$, the $\text{\textgreek{κύριος}}$ as the $\text{\textgreek{διάκονος πάντων}}$. (Comp. on Matt. xx. 28). Thus in the Divine kingdom the power of self-sacrificing, devoted, self-abasing love, (which, in the Saviour himself, is seen in its glorious perfection,) is the only turning-point on which all pre-eminence depends; while conversely, in the world, he who rules is wont to make use of the governed simply for himself, his own benefit, his reputation and glory The fleshly minds of the disciples, therefore, mistaking the idea of God's kingdom, had induced them in the future manifestation of Christ's glory to look for the gratification of selfish hopes. These the Lord destroys, inasmuch as he intimates that only he who has divested himself of all self-seeking, and who lives in pure love and lowly self-renunciation shall there reign, or exert commanding influence. (The words here $\tau\iota\varsigma\ \mu\varepsilon\iota\zeta\omega\nu\ \varepsilon\sigma\tau\iota\nu$ clearly express the idea that all the disciples were on a level in this respect that they, as standing immediately around the Lord, were called alike to exercise the most important influence in the kingdom of God—only on this point did they dispute as to who among themselves should be the greater, the more influential. The occurrence related at Matt. xvii. 1, might easily occasion such reflections)

Ver. 2—4—Very naturally according to the account of Matthew, is there subjoined here the symbolic act of Jesus in placing a child, (παιδίον is not = עֶבֶד *a slave* or *servant*, but with reference to regeneration *a child*, one who is new-born) in the midst of them, and in him setting forth the character of those who should have influence in the kingdom of God. That it is not the character of this individual child that he here speaks of, (according to the legend it was the martyr Ignatius) is shown at once by the immediately following words γίνεσθε ὡς τὰ παιδία. Jesus merely brings forward in this individual child the general character of children, as a model for the members of the kingdom of God. For, although the general sinfulness of human nature certainly shows itself at once in children, yet does humility and an unassuming disposition peculiarly distinguish the child's nature, the king's son is not ashamed to play with the son of a beggar This unassuming disposition is here the point of comparison. Certainly it is exercised by children unconsciously, while on the part of believers it is to be deliberately cherished The comparison therefore does not on all points hold good, which it could not possibly do, for this reason, that nothing in the earthly sphere could be found perfectly analogous to the spiritual man who is the subject of the comparison. Into such an unassuming frame does the Lord now exhort that the disciples turn their minds (στρέφεσθαι to change their spiritual tendency, instead of walking on high they must go forward in lowliness), then would they find entrance to the heavenly kingdom. The passage is thus wholly parallel to the important verse, John iii. 3, for the γίνεσθαι ὡς παιδίον is nothing else than the new birth, in which alone such an unassuming child-like feeling can be implanted. By the resolutions and efforts of the natural man it cannot be produced As an evidence of this child-like feeling Christ brings prominently forward the ταπεινοῦν ἑαυτόν (in opposition to the ὑψοῦν ἑαυτόν); as the child, in whatever circumstances placed, will unassumingly be content with a lowly position, so should also the new-born saint, instead of climbing to high stations, step down to the secure valley of humility. The expression ταπεινοῦν ἑαυτόν retains here its widest meaning, inasmuch as even in the regenerate, constant and positive effort is needful to keep down the old man as the source of pride The term ταπεινοῦν may therefore be viewed as a special and stronger expression for becoming a child, and the μείζων εἶναι ἐν τῇ βασ. may be regarded as contrasted with the simple εἰσέρχεσθαι εἰς βασ.

Ver. 5.—Matthew who alone had given the preceding verses, shows himself here again exceedingly accurate in the setting forth of our Lord's discourses According to Mark and Luke, who do not give these verses, it is not so easy to understand the presenting of the child, nay, it acquires with them a different meaning. They both speak directly of the receiving of the child, as to which also Mark (ix. 36,) can even add ἐναγκαλισάμενος αὐτό, an act which, in the first instance, would not agree with the representation of Matthew; for since, according to him, the child was simply a symbol of humility, it must in these circumstances have been a meaningless act to embrace him. (In Luke ii. 28, the term ἐναγκαλίζεσθαι = δέχεσθαι εἰς ἀγκαλας refers to *little* children, in whom alone the character of humility is purely developed. The verb προσκαλέσασθαι at Matth. xviii. 2, does not contradict this; it is only necessary that we do not understand it exactly as meaning sucklings) This, however, agrees well with the connexion as given in Mark and Luke, according to which the παιδίον expresses mainly the idea of a beloved, a dear one. But it may be asked here, how shall we trace the connecting links of thought; for if Matthew, in the first instance, gives another application to the setting forth of the child, he goes on at ver. 5, to use the term δέχεσθαι, and follows this up at ver. 6, by the opposite of δέχεσθαι, so that from this agreement of the three Evangelists we must hold that these words were spoken on the occasion referred to. It certainly seems from the connection here, most natural to consider the δέχεσθαι as an act of unassuming self-humbling love, so that it connects itself with the declaration πρῶτος πάντων διάκονος (Mark ix. 35.). But with this view, the last clause at Luke ix. 48, ὁ μικρότερος ἐν πᾶσιν ὑμῖν κ. τ. λ. little harmonizes, for it is there apparent that the disciples are themselves the μικροί who are to be received, not the recipients. (Compare also Mark ix 41, from which this plainly follows.) Accordingly the connection may better be understood in this way, Be ye eager to become lowly, little-noticed as this child, for the little ones (the regenerate who have the true child's feeling) are very dear and precious to the Lord, so that he regards what is done to them as done to himself. According to this chain of ideas, then, that which Matthew relates must be held as having previously occurred; for it is this which contains the ground of Christ's attachment to them. The expression παιδίον = μικρός ver. 10, is then the symbol of the regenerate. (See on Matth x. 42.) The only thing still remaining obscure is how the expression ὅς παιδίον δέχεται, ἐμὲ δέχεται should precisely in this discourse be used to denote God's fatherly love for his spiritual children. The simplest explanation is, that this description of i is occasioned by the preceding admonition (set forth clearly by Matt.) to enter into the kingdom of God. With this, as something future, stands closely connected the δέχεσθαι, as that which is present, so that the meaning is—"he who thus humbles himself in true lowliness, is great in the kingdom of God; nay even already amidst those connexions with the world in which the regenerate appear as sufferers, they are so precious to the Lord that he holds what is done to them as done to himself," (as to the thought itself, compare Matth. x. 40, sq. where it already occurred in another connection.)

In Mark (ix. 38—41.) and Luke (ix. 49, 50.) there follows here a question by John with the answer of Jesus, which Matthew has omitted, as not belonging to the main scope of the discourse, but as rather interrupting it. The shortness with which Luke touches this intervening question of John, would have left many things obscure, if the more exact account of Mark had not enabled us to trace the connection. For the preceding words of Jesus, in which he speaks of the δέχεσθαι of the little ones, plainly refer to the relation in which the disciples stood to those around them. John, who may not have been able to penetrate fully into the meaning of our Lord's words, brings forward a circumstance which had perhaps occurred at the time, and had particularly struck himself, and he lays it before the Saviour. Some one, it would appear, who doubtless had seen our Lord's miracles, or those of the apostles, had himself made the attempt to heal in the name of Jesus. The disciples, in their selfish exclusiveness, saw in this an infringement on their spiritual jurisdiction, and inasmuch as he did not habitually attach himself to the company of Jesus, had interdicted him [1] This the Saviour re-

---

[1] A narrative precisely similar is recorded at Numbers xi 27, sq

proves, and refers his disciples to that comprehensive love and humility of the true τέκνα τοῦ Θεοῦ, who child-like receive and acknowledge all that is akin to themselves, under whatever form they find it. The individual referred to is thus viewed as one befriended by the benevolent Saviour of men, and represented to the disciples as one from whom they might expect support, it being at the same time implied that he would not be left without a blessing Thus understood, then, this incident takes its place most fittingly in the context; it is, as it were, an example of how the Lord does good to those who *favour* his disciples, even when these latter cannot understand aright the proofs of love The Gnome, the sententious phrase in which Jesus expresses the doctrine which he wished on this occasion to teach his disciples, ὅς οὐκ ἔστι καθ᾽ ὑμῶν ὑπὲρ ὑμῶν ἐστι, is parallel to the statement at Matt. xii 30, ὁ μὴ ὢν μετ᾽ ἐμοῦ κατ᾽ ἐμοῦ ἐστι, which is found also at Luke xi 23. Both are equally true of different persons and grades of vocation. He whose calling is to a sphere of spiritual labour, is already *against* the Lord and his cause, if he do not positively further them; he whose vocation is of a lower grade, who may be placed in a state of spiritual dependence on others, (as the people were ruled by the Pharisees,) is already *in favour of* God's cause, if he keep himself free from the generally prevailing hostile influences, and so continue susceptible of the divine. It must, however, ever remain a singular circumstance, that, even in Christ's own times, persons should have used his name for the working of miracles without attaching themselves to his circle; it is a proof of the general notice which the works of Jesus had attracted. At a later period, we find, in the history of Simon Magus (Acts viii.) and the seven sons of Sceva (xix 13, sq) something of the same kind. If, however, the apostles judge of these men in a way wholly different from what the Saviour does here, the cause of the difference must assuredly be sought in the *motive* from which such a use of the name of Jesus proceeded It might, as in the case of the person here mentioned, flow from faith—perhaps an unconscious faith—in Christ's heavenly power, and was therefore to be borne

---

When Elded and Medad prophesied in the camp, Joshua said to Moses, "My lord Moses, forbid them" But Moses replies, "Enviest thou for my sake? would God all the Lord's people prophesied, and that the Lord would put his Spirit upon them"

with, (although the declarations of Jesus respecting him certainly do not exclude the necessity of his being further instructed, and made to know that the special object of Christ's coming was not to impart the gift of working miracles, but to change the human heart); but on the other hand it might proceed from motives wholly impure, as with the sons of Sceva, and must in that case be unconditionally resisted. For, these men used the name of Jesus as a peculiarly powerful form of adjuration, just as they would other formulæ of their art, for their selfish objects. Thus, it is not the outward act itself, but rather the *feeling* from which it flows, that determines its being admissible or not.

Ver. 6 The idea which follows of the σκανδαλίζειν ἕνα τῶν μικρῶν, connects itself most appropriately with the δέχεσθαι of ver. 5. He merely expresses the opposite thought, so that the sense of these words is, " the little ones are so precious to the Lord, that whatever good is done them he looks on as done to himself, and rewards it, whatever evil is inflicted on them, he most indignantly punishes." The peculiar form, however, in which this thought is brought out by Matthew, and more especially by Mark, does not seem to suit the context, one does not see in what connection it stands with the strife among the apostles. This might render it probable that there are inserted here portions of discourses originally spoken in another connection. (Comp. on Matt. v. 29, 30, where something similar occurs). But at Matt xviii. 10, 14, we again find marked references to the antecedent μικροί, and at Mark ix. 50, also the clause εἰρηνεύετε ἐν ἀλλήλοις again points back to the strife among the disciples, from which the discourse took its rise. We must then hold it proved that these words respecting the σκανδαλίζειν really stand connected with the rest of the discourse. For, even granting that these words had originally been spoken in other circumstances by the Lord, this much is clear, that both evangelists meant here to place them in a fitting connexion. It only remains, then, that we regard the sense of μικρός as modified in such a way that the expression here forms the counterpart of μέγας. Usually the New Testament employs the term μικρός to denote *believers,* the *regenerate* in general, (see more fully on this point at Matt. x 42,) but again we also find a distinction drawn between the great and the small in the kingdom of God, (see at Matt. xi. 11, and v 19) Applying this distinction here,

s

the connection of the passage admits of being taken in this way. The strife among the disciples as to their place in the kingdom of God might have given offence to the other believers, so that they might have been perplexed as to whether the truth dwelt within that circle where such things could occur. This led the Lord to declare his mind as to the guilt of those who gave offence, even to the weakest among the believers. The seventh verse, in Matt however, seems to be in opposition to this view of the connection, for the σκάνδαλα are there ascribed to the κόσμος. In reference to this, however, we must observe, that the disciples, in so far as they gave offence to believers, did themselves belong to the κόσμος, and thus the Saviour here passes over from the particular to the general, just as at Matt. xvi. 23, he traces Peter's declaration at once to the origin of evil from whose influence he was not yet wholly free. With this, also, ver. 8 well agrees, where he is speaking of ἑαυτὸν σκανδαλίζειν, man being thus viewed as presenting an inward conflict between the New and the Old in his heart.

As to the meaning of σκάνδαλον, the old form of the word σκανδάληθρον properly denotes *a trap* for ensnaring animals, then in general, *a noose, a snare,* laying of nets. In the New Testament it is transferred to spiritual things, and under σκάνδαλον everything is included which can hinder the development of spiritual life, or deter men from faith in the Divine = πρόσκομμα, in Hebrew מוֹקֵשׁ, *a cord, a noose,* or מִכְשׁוֹל, *offence.* (On this account also in the New Testament, παγίς, θήρα stand connected with σκάνδαλον, see Rom xi 9). The verb σκανδαλίζειν consequently means, *to give* offence, to prepare spiritual obstruction, σκανδαλίζεσθαι, *to take* offence. There is a peculiarity, however, in the meaning of σκανδαλίζειν in ver. 8 of this passage, according to which the σκανδαλίζων and the σκανδαλιζόμενος appear as united in the same individual This internal conflict in man himself is to be explained, as has been already said, from regeneration, through means of which that new man is made alive who wrestles with the old man, and struggles for the victory. The greatness of the guilt involved in giving spiritual offence, or in deterring the little ones from a life of faith, is depicted by the Saviour in a form which addresses itself to the senses, inasmuch as he represents the sin of these delinquencies as greater than those crimes on which the heaviest political punishment is inflicted. (The συμφέρει αὐτῷ expresses a stronger, namely, a spiritual and eternal punishment.—The sinking into the sea was not practised among the Jews, but it certainly was in use among other nations. See for example Sueton. August. c. 68. Instead of the less usual expression μύλος, ὀνικός in Matthew and Luke, Mark has λίθος μυλικός. Μύλος = μύλη denotes properly *the mill itself*, and in a secondary sense the *mill-stone*. The word ὄνος is commonly used of the lower mill-stone, which does not move. The adjective form, ὀνικός, is not in use as applied to it. The words μύλος ὀνικός therefore cannot well mean the lower and heavier mill-stone. We do better to continue taking it in the sense of *set in motion by asses*, as expressing the size of the stone. The ass mill-stone is contrasted with the stone of a mill driven by the hand of man).

Ver. 7. The same thought again meets us at Luke xvii. 1, where we shall more closely consider it. Here it stands only in an incidental form, and unconnected with the rest of the discourse. (Κόσμος the counterpart of βασ. τ. Θ. See in regard to it what is said more at length in the exposition of John i. 9).

Ver. 8, 9. After speaking of offence given to others, Jesus passes on to that inward offence which he who is born again may give to himself. The general meaning of the words lies clear to our view The cutting off hand and foot, the plucking out of the eye, is intended to denote the denying ourselves to what is dearest and most indispensable to the outward life, when through those sinful influences which act from without, it endangers the spiritual life. But here, as at Matt. v. 29, 30, a difficulty is raised by the additional clause καλόν ἐστί σοι εἰσελθεῖν εἰς τὴν ζωὴν (sc. αἰώνιον) χωλὸν, κυλλὸν μονόφθαλμον[1] For, to regard this as a mere embellishment, which has no meaning of its own, is what I cannot consent to. The sense of the whole comparison rather seems to be this. The cutting off of hand or foot, can, as is self-evident, be only taken as denoting something spiritual, since the outward act were meaningless, (compare on Matt. xix. 12,) unless the inward root of sin were destroyed. Hand, foot, eye, here appear to be used by the Saviour to denote mental powers and dispositions, and he counsels their restraint, their non-development, if a man find himself by their cultivation, withdrawn

---

[1] Compare as to μονόφθαλμος Lobeck's Phrynichus, p 136. The pure Greek form is ἑτερόφθαλμος

from advancing the highest principle of life. The *every-sided* development of all our faculties, the inferior, as well as the more elevated, is certainly to be regarded as the highest attainment, yet he who finds by experience that he cannot cultivate certain faculties,—the artistic for example,—without injury to his holiest feelings, must renounce their cultivation, and make it his first business, by pains-taking fidelity, to preserve entire the innermost life of his soul, that higher life imparted to him by Christ, and which, by the dividing and distracting of his thoughts, might easily be lost, nor must it give him any disturbance if some subordinate faculty be thus wholly sacrificed by him.[1] Assuredly, however, we must add, that this loss is only in appearance, for, in the development of man's higher life, everything of a subordinate kind which he had sacrificed, is again restored with increase of power. But in the first instance, he has the real experience of such a sacrifice, and it still remains true that it is a more elevated and better thing to succeed in learning how to cultivate even the lower faculties in harmony with the higher life. Only, where that cannot be, man ought to choose the safer course. Mark gives, moreover, a very lengthened version of this discourse, without, however, adding anything to the thought. The simple πῦρ αἰώνιον of Matthew is in Mark paraphrased by γέεννα, πῦρ ἄσβεστον ὅπου ὁ σκώληξ αὐτῶν οὐ τελευτᾷ καὶ τὸ πῦρ οὐ σβέννυται. The words are taken from Isaiah lxvi. 24, whence they had already been quoted at Sir vii 19, Judith xvi. 21. They depict the ἀπώλεια by imagery taken from death and putrefaction, inasmuch as ζωή is contrasted with θάνατος αἰώνιος. (See as to κρίσις αἰώνιος the remarks on Matt xii 32.) The expression σκώληξ = תּוֹלַעַת, denotes properly the worm that devours the dead body (Ps. xxii 7; Sir. x. 13); here standing in parallelism with πῦρ, it must be understood as inflicting pain The seeming tautology in the passage τὸ πῦρ ἄσβεστον ὅπου τὸ πῦρ οὐ σβέννυται disappears when we supply αὐτῶν to the πῦρ as

---

[1] Thus also had Origen arleady spoken (Comm in Matt Tom xii ed de la Rue, vol iii 603) When Tholuck remarks (Comm on sermon on the mount, p 234,) in opposition to this that my exposition bears a modern character, inasmuch as the distinction of the various mental faculties belongs to modern metaphysical philosophy—his objection appears to me ill-founded, for men have always perceived the distinction between different powers of mind What people ever wholly confounded memory with reason—the fancy with the will?

in the case of the antecedent σκώληξ, which stands so placed also in Isaiah. For in that case the first expression is a general description of the place of punishment, the second, the special infliction of its agonies on these guilty ones.

The remark is interesting which stands at the conclusion of these words in Mark, ver. 49, 50, πᾶς γὰρ πυρὶ ἁλισθήσεται καὶ πᾶσα θυσία ἁλὶ ἁλισθήσεται. This thought closes very appropriately the foregoing discourse, for it concentrates into one general principle, as it were, what had previously been set forth. The πᾶς πυρὶ ἁλισθήσεται neither refers simply to the πῦρ αἰώνιον, nor merely to the exhortation to self-denial, but it includes both, so that the πᾶς is to be understood in a literal sense as denoting the whole human race. The sense of the expression therefore is this, because of the general sinfulness of the race, every individual must be salted with fire, either on the one hand, by his entering of his own free will on a course of self-denial and earnest purification from his iniquities, or on the other hand, by his being carried against his will away to the place of punishment. The πῦρ appears here first as the cleansing, purifying element, (so it often does, for example, Malachi iii. 2, Sir. ii. 5) and then, as that which inflicts anguish. But, for him who submits in earnest to the pain which is necessarily associated with the overcoming of sin, it works beneficially. (1 Pet. iv 1) The term ἁλίζεσθαι is well chosen to express the effect of fire, first, because of the succeeding quotation, in which salt is spoken of, and next, however, because it is in the highest degree an apt description of fire, for the operation of salt is closely allied to that of fire. From this it is, that according to the deep and true system of Scripture symbols, salt derives its peculiar meaning, especially as applied to sacrifices According to Lev. ii. 13, all sacrifices must be seasoned with salt That passage is here referred to in such a way that one might supply the words ὡς γέγραπται. The Old Testament practice, therefore, of seasoning sacrifices with salt, is here regarded by our Lord in its deeper meaning. As every sacrifice is on the part of him who offers it, a type of his inwardly devoting himself with all that he is and has to the eternal source of his being, so the salt was intended to show that such a sacrifice could never be well-pleasing to God without the pain of self-denial, and the quickening influences of the Fire-Spirit from on high. The fire-baptism (Matth. iii. 11) is just this act of purification in the saints through the salt of self-denial, and even the Son of God himself submitted to it, though he was sinless, in order that he might in the fire of suffering perfect and glorify the human nature which he had assumed. According to this view then the grammatical connection of the clauses must be so explained that the expression καὶ πᾶσα θυσία ἁλισθήσεται bears no meaning different from the πᾶς πυρὶ ἁλισθήσεται which accompanies it, but must be taken as presenting a visible type of the spiritual transaction which the former words describe. It is not necessary, however, on this account, to give to the καί the meaning of sicuti, quemadmodum; we have only to supply διὰ τοῦτο so that the sense should be, " and for this reason (as it stands written) must every sacrifice be salted with salt." We have, therefore, in this passage, an authoritative explanation of the meaning of a sacrifice, and of what was implied in the rite, the ceremony of presenting them to the Lord sprinkled with salt.[1] Among the manifold other explanations of this passage, we are specially bound to reject as contrary to the use of the language, that which takes ἁλίζεσθαι = נִמְלָה in the sense of being *annihilated*, referring to Is li. 6 For in the latter passage the word מָלַח has a meaning wholly unconnected with the term מִלָה *salt*. (Compare Gesen. in Lex sub voc) Certainly the connection of ver 50 with the preceding context is difficult. For, the discourse makes a transition to the nature of salt in general, and brings forward the circumstance that if it have lost its strength there is no means by which it may be regained. The same thought occurred at Matth v 13, Luke xiv. 34, but in such a connection that the disciples are themselves called the ἅλας τῆς γῆς in so far, namely, as they are the seasoning, quickening element, acting on mankind. Here the import of the thoughts is somewhat modified, but not essentially changed. For, in the disciples themselves, a distinction is drawn between the natural life by which they were allied to the κόσμος (Compare Matth. xviii 17,) and the heavenly higher principle of life which animated them. It is here enjoined on them to preserve this last, and so to per-

---

[1] Hamann has already said in allusion to this passage, "the anxiety which prevails in the world is perhaps the only proof of our heterogeneous constitution. For were nothing wanting to us we should act as the heathen, and the transcendental philosophers who know nothing of God, and are enamoured of lovely nature. This impertinent disquietude, this holy hypochondria, is the fire by which we are salted sacrifices." (Works, Part vi p 194)

vade with salt from heaven, step by step, all their faculties and dispositions of mind. In the passage, Matth v. 13, they are called ἅλας τῆς γῆς in so far as they, compared with the great mass of men, were prevailingly filled with the power of heavenly fire. In both passages, however, here as well as at Matth. v. 13, man's own faithfulness is represented as called for to guard the salt of the Spirit. To *call forth* that higher life, is what man cannot do, it is a pure gift of grace, but he can *stifle* it, or he can *protect* it as a mother can secure the child that is under her heart, to a certain extent, from harm and mischance, though she has not the power of calling it into existence. In this exhortation, therefore, ἔχετε ἐν ἑαυτοῖς ἅλας, there lies an admonition to earnestness in self-denial and perseverance, as the means by which the gift bestowed may be preserved. And this admonition is sharpened by recalling to their minds the impossibility of seasoning salt which lost its powers (ἐν τίνι αὐτὸ ἀρτύσετε;). The closing words καὶ εἰρηνεύετε ἐν ἀλλήλοις point back to the commencement of the discourse at Mark ix. 33. Perhaps the expression ἅλας ἔχετε is intended to form a contrast to the εἰρηνεύετε. The former seems to describe a sharp, biting mode of action, the latter, one that is mild and soft; both are to be conjoined in the regenerate; in regard to the ungodliness that is in the world he must reprove and rebuke, and in so far he must, like Christ himself, (Matth. x. 34), bring in strife, but in regard to all that is congenial and kindred in the children of God, gentleness must prevail. As therefore salt cannot season salt, but only that which is unsalted, so the living energy of the children of God should not be expended in contests among themselves, but devoted to the awakening of life in the world. The closeness with which the last verses in Mark connect themselves both with the preceding context and with the commencement of the whole discourse, makes it to my mind very unlikely that they had originally stood in any other connection, and here, therefore, we have an instance in which Mark also contributes to the train of thought something peculiarly his own.

Ver. 10.—While hitherto Matthew has had Mark to give a parallel account, he is left now to recount the discourse alone down to the end of the chapter. The connection of thought between the first clause and the preceding context is simple, inasmuch as the καταφρονεῖν ver 10 refers back to the σκανδαλίζειν of ver. 6. It is not necessary to remark, that in this case also the μικροί are the regenerate, and consequently anything like a special connection between angels and children we are unable here to discover. The ground is a peculiar one of which our Lord here avails himself to enforce the exhortation against despising the little ones. He brings forward their preciousness in the view of his Father in heaven, (who is also their Father, for believers bear within them the life of Christ, see ver. 5,) in the remark which he makes, "their angels continually see God's face." Here then in the first place as respects the words βλέπειν τὸ πρόσωπον τοῦ πατρός, this expression is by no means to be reduced to a mere piece of oriental phraseology, it rather describes simply the reality of the existing relationship. The degree of their nearness to God marks the degree of holiness in their nature, and the meaning, therefore, designed to be conveyed is this, that the regenerate, (even the most insignificant members of the kingdom of God) as being the representatives of the highest holiness on earth are also themselves, in the heavenly world (in which all the phenomena exhibited on earth have their root) represented by the holiest beings. Any existing analogies to this, which political arrangements may exhibit, are merely a more or less intentional imitation of the original relationship. (Compare 1 Kings x 8; Esther i. 14, Jerem lii 25) The idea of angels who take their stand in immediate proximity to the Father often meets us amidst the teachings of Scripture, (Dan vii 10, Rev. i. 4, iv. 4.) but in no passage elsewhere do we find that *these* angels particularly are placed in such a connection with believers as is here indicated by the words ἄγγελοι αὐτῶν. Although, however, in a certain sense this passage stands alone, and is also not peculiarly of a didactic character, yet must we not conceive that it formed any accommodation to Jewish myths There was not the slightest occasion to bring forward this idea here unless it had possessed an internal truth That every individual had his angel, according to the sense in which the idea is taken by the fathers of the Church, (Compare Schmidt de Angelis tutelaribus[1] in Illgen's Denkschrift, Leipsig 1817) this passage does not expressly state In Daniel, angels are spoken of as the representatives of whole nations, (x. 20; xii. 1.) and according to this we may conceive that one angel represents many persons Yet on the other hand, Acts xii. 15 counte-

[1] Meyer gives an extract from this treatise in the Blatt. f hoh, Wahrheit, Th. 1 S 183 sq.

nances the idea that there is a representation of individuals. In any case the passage contains something obscure, for there are no others by comparison with which light may be cast on it. Perhaps in regard to these angels we may be reminded of the pre-existent ideal of man himself, so that the angels would correspond to the *fervers* of Zoroaster. Often is the angelic world moreover viewed in Scripture as standing connected with believers, (Ps. xxxiv. 8; Ps. xci. 11, Heb. i. 14) while the development of the church appears as the central point of the whole, (1 Peter i. 12).

Ver 11—14—In some MSS (B. L and others) verse 11 is wanting; it might have been taken from Luke xix. 10, where he has also the following verses in connection with kindred topics. But first, it is improbable that this verse from a passage of Luke's gospel, and that assuredly not parallel, should have been thrust in here; and in the next place, it agrees too closely with Matthew's context to prevent our believing this much, at least, that Matthew had himself inserted it in this passage, even though we must certainly leave it matter of doubt whether the words may have been spoken originally in the precise connection in which we find them here. For the υἱὸς τοῦ ἀνθρώπου stands beside the ἄγγελοι as one exalted above them, and the fact that the μικροί are the object of the mission of the Son of man, is a new proof of their preciousness in the sight of God. The term ἀπολωλός plainly points already to the following parable of the lost sheep, whose fuller exposition will find a place at Luke chap. xv. Here I only observe with reference to its connection with the rest of the discourse, that the contrast between the strayed sheep and the ninety-nine which did not stray, would stand wholly isolated, unless, as was remarked above, we keep fast hold of the distinction between the μικρός and the μέγας which runs through the discourse. The parable thus acquires in this passage a modified sense foreign to it in Luke, where it is rather employed to represent the δίκαιοι and the ἄδικοι in their relation to Divine grace.

Ver 15—17.—It was already mentioned in the general remarks on this chapter, that the following thoughts on forgiveness may also belong to the discourse as integral parts of it, if we assume that the strife among the disciples had led to offences, that Peter had been the person offended, and on this very account, therefore, the one exhorted to forgiveness. But although the following parable (ver. 22—35,) certainly agrees very well with this supposition, yet to my mind it is rendered improbable, by the connection of the ideas in ver. 18, 19, with the rest of the discourse. Had the disciples been themselves both the offenders and the offended, these verses would hardly have formed part of the exhortation, for they are better fitted to lift up the disciples than to humble them. I can more easily suppose that Matthew, as his manner is, has conjoined kindred elements with the thoughts that form the basis of the discourse. In this instance he wished to depict the character of the children of the kingdom in their humility and meekness. After having in what goes before, warned believers against offending weaker brethren, the discourse brings to view the opposite point of the contrast, and describes how a believer should conduct himself if injury be inflicted upon him, (ἐὰν ὁ ἀδελφός σου ἁμαρτήσῃ εἰς σέ) and specially if it be done by a fellow believer (ἀδελφός is here a brother Christian, a member of the kingdom of God). This instruction, however, is conceived in terms so general, that it at once stands forth as a precept for the whole church, and it rests on the spiritual character of the disciples of Jesus and the everlasting presence of Christ in the midst of his church. This makes it improbable in the highest degree that these words were occasioned by a strife among the disciples themselves, otherwise ver. 18 must be held as meaning "if one of you exclude another from the communion of God's kingdom, that exclusion is held as effectual in the sight of God," an idea that is obviously untenable. The disciples were not to exclude one another; but they are here viewed as the real and the pure germ of the church, which no power of evil should overcome, but if room was left for their being sinned against by their brethren less enlightened than themselves by Christian principle, they must in that case act on the rule here laid down. Thus the βασ. τ. ουρ (ver. 23,) by no means appears in this passage as a communion absolutely perfect, (compare on Matth. xiii. 47,) but as one in which the good exerts a predominating influence, repressing consequently, and restraining the evil, so that this passage once more plainly shows that the Saviour intended to found an *external* church in which, as a kernel in its shell, the ideal kingdom of God should be developed. The disciples are set forth as representatives of this kernel of God's kingdom, to them is entrusted the guiding and ruling of this community, they are the ἅλας and have to care for the preservation of the whole body in the strength of Him who is unceasingly amongst them If they (through unfaithfulness) were to lose their power, the kingdom of God would fall to pieces; the sin even of others should be repressed by them. It must, however, here again be carefully observed, that these injunctions of the Saviour do not apply to the form of the outward church at all times, (Compare as to this on Matth. v. 39, sq.) but are valid only in reference to true believers. For, the external church, since the fourth century, exists in an Old Testament form, and to persons who stand wholly on the legal footing, such distinctions as the above have no meaning; against the injuries of the world a Christian has the protection of the magistrates, and he errs if he believes that owing to this ordinance of Jesus he may not call in their aid. This admonition at every step, first apart, then before certain witnesses, and finally in presence of the church, presupposes a state of mind not hardened against the power of the truth, even where no threat is used to enforce it. The complete carrying out of it, would overset the order of civil society, as completely as if each man were to give his coat to any one who had demanded of him his cloak. For the unawakened unconverted man it is wisdom to act on God's precept, "Eye for eye, tooth for tooth," (Matth v. 33.) Fritzsche's remark (on the passage) is most correct, that it is better to place the interpunctuation after $αὐτοῦ$ than after $μόνου$. The phrase $μεταξύ$ $σου$ $καί$ $αὐτοῦ$ is perfectly sufficient by itself, and the $μόνου$ $ἐάν$ $σου$ $ἀκούσῃ$ is fittingly conjoined into a distinct clause, for thus the idea of individuality stands here in contrast to the plurality subsequently mentioned The leading principle of the whole line of conduct prescribed is mildness, long-suffering, and an earnest endeavour to give ascendancy to the Divine in the mind of a brother The dialogue, therefore, does not deal merely with the isolated fact of the offence given, but refers to the whole state of the offender's soul from which that act proceeded. The point it concerned them to aim at, was to change this frame of mind, and to this reference is made by the term $κερδαίνειν$ scil. $εἰς$ $ζωὴν$ $αἰώνιον$. Every $ἁμαρτάνειν$, especially against a brother, is an act of tolerance to the dominion of the sinful principle, (1 John iii. 8.) and this I would lead to the $ἀπώλεια$ of the brother. When,

---

[1] In this way must 1 Cor. vi. 1, be understood, in the exposition of which further details will be given

therefore, any one, by the gentle power of love, wins a brother for their kingdom, he κερδαίνει = σώζει αὐτόν by the power, as is self-evident, of Christ working in him. Love, after being once repulsed, would put more strength into a renewed effort, the admonition is made more impressive and solemn by the presence of others. The Saviour here refers to Deut. xix. 15. (The ῥῆμα corresponds here to the Hebrew דָּבָר in the sense of cause, *a cause in law*, στόμα is put for oral testimony, in which the deponent is himself produced in evidence.) He here applies this Mosaic ordinance in an elevated form, suited to the higher circumstances in which it is used. For it is not evidence *against* an erring brother that in the first instance is here spoken of, but simply an impressive mode of working *on* his mind. If this produced no impression on him then the presence of witnesses, certainly took the form of evidence against him, inasmuch as his case was laid before the whole church. This appears as the final attempt to call forth the influence of a Christian spirit in the brother who had erred and who clung to his error. The ἐκκλησία here, like קָהָל, is the assemblage of the whole believers in one place, to which assembly the separate individual belonged as a member) If he also refuse to follow this most emphatic rebuke, then the only means of help, as well as the sole punishment, is to exclude him from the community. Where the higher life has left a soul, the withdrawal of fellowship with kindred minds is often the surest means of rousing its slumbering aspirations. (The expressions ἐθνικός and τελώνης denote that sphere of life generally, which is outlying beyond the Christian circle).

Ver. 18.—As to the thought contained in this verse, compare on ver. 16, 17. Here the only question is, in what way the Evangelist wishes the words to be understood, as connected with the context. Plainly, the ὑμεῖς must be held parallel with the ἐκκλησία of the foregoing verse, so that the sure and binding nature of the church's decision is here intended to be affirmed. " What in such a case the church ordains, is no mere human decision, but inasmuch as the Divine is here on earth manifested in the church, the conclusion at which the church arrives takes effect in a higher sense."

Ver. 19, 20. The connection of the following verses with the preceding is simply this; the spiritual power of the church to bind and to loose depends on the operation of the heavenly Father in it; that operation, however, is not dependent on the extent of the congregation, or on the place (one might add, according to Matt. xxviii. 20, on the *time*); God in Christ is universally present in his church (The πάλιν ἀμήν gives no incongruous meaning; the authority of manuscripts favours the omission of the ἀμήν) The ἐκκλησία is here contemplated in the narrowest form in which it appears (δύο ἢ τρεῖς); an individual can form no communion, but any plurality of persons who bear within them the same principle of higher life, constitutes a κοινωνία τοῦ πνεύματος (1 John i. 3,) and consequently a church. From the κοινωνία, therefore, may proceed a συμφωνία, (an harmonious agreement of will for some special end,) and this the Father hears. To the expression ἐπὶ τῆς γῆς corresponds the πατὴρ ἐν τοῖς οὐρανοῖς, so that the church appears as united to the Father by the πνεῦμα, and the latter carries into effect the wishes of the former. The general expression, περὶ παντὸς πράγματος, is usually so restricted, that the meaning is held to be—every thing fitted to advance the welfare of the church, or that belongs to the sphere of Christian life. This is certainly correct, in thus far, that things spiritual form the sole object of a believer's labours, an object in which for him everything else terminates, in so far as it is in itself good. But just because every thing does so terminate, must the πᾶν πρᾶγμα be taken in a literal sense, inasmuch as *every thing*, in so far as it stands connected with the wants of the church, *may* form the object of a believer's prayers. The possibility of abusing this command, or rather, this high *permission*, given by the Saviour to his own people, is excluded by the fact, that it is only the Spirit of the Father in Christ Jesus himself who creates and calls forth the κοινωνία τοῦ πνεύματος with the thence arising συμφωνία, and the prayer in the peculiar case. When, then, all this does not really exist, or is set forth in mere deceptive show, the words of the Lord find no application, but wherever it in reality is found, there his words are eternally true. It is wholly independent of time and place; wheresoever (οὗ scil. τόπου,) the believers may be assembled together if they meet in the name of Jesus (and pray in his name,) there the Lord is in the midst of them [1] (And, according to Matt xxviii. 20, the

---

[1] Interesting allusions to this truth, that the divine is present in the

time is also of no importance, ἐγὼ μεθ' ὑμῶν εἰμὶ πάσας τὰς ἡμέρας.) What defines the thought in these words is the expression εἰς τὸ ἐμὸν ὄνομα. (The εἰς here is not to be confounded with ἐν. In the formula εἰς ὄνομα, the name is as it were, the point of union, so that it corresponds to the German *auf seinem Namen, upon* his name. In the formula ἐν ὀνόματι, the name is the uniting power by means of which the conjunction is conceived of as effected and maintained. Compare on Matt xxviii 19). Ὄνομα, however, = שֵׁם (compare on Luke i 35,) denotes the person, the Being himself, not indeed as incapable of being known, or as actually unknown, but as manifested. The assembling, then, in the name of Jesus, and the praying in his name, presupposes the life of the spirit of Jesus as already existing in those so meeting together. It is no isolated act which every one in all circumstances is able, by the self-determining power of his own mind, to do; it requires rather as a necessary condition, that man should be under the power of living Christian principle. But, as even the believer has dark moments within his soul, he may, from negligence and want of watchfulness, be present in the assemblies of believers, but not in the name of Jesus, so that this makes a watchful, self-conscious state of faith necessary; for the object to be aimed at in our advancement as Christians, is, that we never be without prayer (Luke xviii. 1, sq), never without the name of Jesus, either when alone, or in the company of others. (Compare further as to prayer in the name of Jesus on John xiv. 13, 14, xvi. 24) If, moreover, the Father be spoken of at ver 19, and the Son be at ver. 20 represented as the Person present in the assembly, (and consequently, as the person who acts and who fulfils prayer,) this is explained simply by the relation of the Father and the Son. For, in so far as the Father manifests himself only in the Son, and the Son works out only what the Father prompts, (John viii 28,) the operation of Father and Son is the one and the same agency of the living God To assemble in the name of the Father, and to pray in him, apart from the Son, is an impossibility, it is merely to pray in one's own name, which is no prayer, for, whosoever denieth the Son, hath not the Fa-

---

human assemblies of those who seek it, are to be found among the Rabbins. Thus in the Treatise Pirke Aboth, iii 2, it is said, duo si assident mensae et colloquia habent de lege שְׁכִינָה, (the symbol of God as acting, of the Son, compare on John i 1,) quiescit super eos secundum Mal iii. 16

ther. These last verses, also, have once more an elevated tone like that of John's Gospel, and seem to have been spoken in moments of holiest exultation The parable which follows, at once sinks again into a lower region, for this reason, however, assuredly, because Peter's question proved that he, (and with him, certainly the other disciples also,) was not then prepared to enter into the full understanding of the foregoing thought.

Ver 21, 22. If Peter in what follows speaks of forgiveness, there had yet been no express mention made of that subject by Jesus in the preceding discourse, but the whole precepts, (ver. 15, sq.) as to the treatment of erring brethren, had proceeded necessarily on the supposition of forgiveness. The man who, in his own heart, gives way to anger, will continue to cherish a sense of the individual offence; but the man who forgives will strive as an εἰρηνοποιὸς (Matt. v. 9,) to remove the ground of the sin from the heart of his brother. The state of Peter, however, so little advanced, did not admit of his understanding even the fundamental idea of forgiveness. Mistaking the nature of pure love, which never can do otherwise than love, he conceives of some limit to forgiveness, being apprehensive, as is usual with natural men, that boundless forgiveness must be a thing impossible. (The ἑπτάκις, as also the following ʽεβδομηκοντάκις ἑπτά, contains merely the idea of the limited and the unlimited, expressed according to the Jewish practice, by the number seven. Compare Gen. xxxiii. 3, 1 Kings xviii 43).

Ver. 23. The Saviour, having perceived from Peter's question how far his discernment was here at fault, proceeds to explain to him in a parable the grounds on which a member of God's kingdom must ever stand ready to grant forgiveness, for, only through forgiveness extended towards himself could he have obtained entrance into that kingdom. To every individual, even to such as took their stand on the footing of the law, this must have formed a decisive motive to forgiveness. It was only the law of recompense to which expression was thus given. While, therefore, the enquiry of Peter seemed to presuppose a *right*, according to which man might act at his own discretion in bestowing forgiveness or withholding it, the Saviour explains that nothing of this kind existed. He who was himself in debt for *his all* could advance a claim for *nothing* (As to the formula ὡμοιώθη ἡ βασιλεία τῶν οὐρανῶν ἀνθρώπῳ, compare Matt. xiii. 24.—Λόγον συναίρειν. rationem conferre, *to take account* The δοῦλοι are, as the summing up shows, the servants to whom the disciples are here compared).

Ver 24—26. The sum of 10,000 talents is very great. If it were the Hebrew talent, (כִּכָּר = 3000 shekels, see Exodus xxxviii. 25, 26,) it would amount to fifteen millions of dollars.[1] The magnitude of the sum, however, agrees well, on the one hand, with the management of a king, and on the other hand, with the idea which the parable is intended to express, namely, that the sinner's debt to God is too great for him to discharge. According to ancient custom, the family of the debtor was considered as all belonging to the creditor. In the Old Testament, however, this custom is seen as mitigated by the wise institution of the jubilee year, in which the debtor must, along with his family, be set free (Comp Levit. xxv 39, sq) The wish of the debtor to see the payment postponed, ($\mu\alpha\kappa\rho o\vartheta\upsilon\mu\epsilon\tilde{\iota}\nu$, in construction with ἐπί, as well as with εἰς, means in the New Testament to exercise forbearance, to give a respite,) and his hope of discharging the debt, are merely an expression of anxiety and care, but the thing is to be viewed as in itself impossible, and for this reason, also, the king compassionately forgives him the debt.

Ver 27—30. The severity of the debtor towards his own subordinates contrasts most strikingly with the mildness of the king. (As to $\sigma\pi\lambda\alpha\gamma\chi\nu i\zeta\epsilon\sigma\vartheta\alpha\iota$ see on Luke 1. 78 —The verb ἀπολύειν, as denoting deliverance from personal confinement and slavery, is distinguished from the remission of the debt.—Δάνειον, *borrowed money*, occurs only in this place). The σύνδουλος is not to be conceived of as standing on the same footing with the first, the intention merely is to bring out the equally dependent relation of both to the king, in order to mark more prominently the severity of the debtor On the same ground also, so small a sum (100 denarii = 12 dollars,) is mentioned.

Thus, then, in that idea which the parable is intended to exhibit, this point stands prominently forth, that every debt or sin of man against his fellow-man, (his σύνδουλος,) is unimportant when compared with his sin against God, and never therefore can he enforce his demand against man, while conscious of his own greater debt towards God. This hard-hearted servant, whose feelings the graciousness of the king

---

[1] Taking the dollar at 3s 6d this would amount to L 2,625,000 sterling —T.

failed to soften, permits himself to inflict even bodily violence on his debtor, which the customs of antiquity allowed him to do. (The verb κρατεῖν is not pleonastic, it is the necessary antecedent of πνίγειν = ἄγχειν. In ver. 28, the reading εἴ τι ὀφείλεις is to be preferred to ὅ τι. This last plainly betrays its real nature as a correction of the εἴ τι, which is not to be understood as implying that the debt is in any way doubtful, but merely as a courteous mode of expression. The formula ἕως οὗ ἀποδῷ τὸ ὀφειλόμενον, reminds one of Matt. v 26. As to its meaning in connection with the idea of the parable, see on ver 34).

Ver. 31—33. It is not undesignedly that λύπη and not ὀργή is mentioned as the feeling of the rest of the δοῦλοι, for, the former denotes the nobler emotion as cherished by men standing on the same footing with the offender, (compare ver. 34,) and by it are the rest of the servants contrasted with the single hardhearted fellow-servant. If we suppose that Peter had been the offended party in their contention, and so corresponded to the creditor, while some one else was the debtor, and that not directly forgiveness, but revenge, sprung up in his heart, the parable certainly gains a very special application But we have already called attention to the difficulties of this supposition. In our Lord's rebuke the *reception* of ἔλεος is set forth as a motive for the *exercise* of it towards others, and it is precisely in this circumstance that the whole point of the parable lies.

Ver. 34, 35. Against the hard-heartedness, however, of the sinner, ὀργή manifests itself on the part of the Lord. Where man cherishes compassionate sorrow for the sins of his fellow-men, (λύπη, see ver. 31), wrath reveals itself on the part of God. For, in the case of man, conscience testifies that he has within him the roots of that same sin which he sees in his brother, but in God there is the pure hatred of evil. The idea of the Divine ὀργή does not contradict God's love, (whose manifestation in mildness is χάρις,) but rather, the wrath of God is nothing else than the manifestation of himself as love, in opposition to evil. According to his righteousness, therefore, which gives to every one his due, and which naturally cannot be conceived of as dissociated from the essence of the Divine love, God does good in his grace to those akin to him, but inflicts woe in his wrath on those alienated from him. Since man, however, is not evil itself, but only in one or another respect admits it within him, God's anger is directed merely against the evil that is *in him* In the Divine wrath, therefore, there is displayed only another form of God's sanctifying agency. When his operations *in mercy* are misunderstood or abused, as by this servant, his *punishments* come into action. The punishment is here explained as a παραδιδόναι τοῖς βασανισταῖς ἐν τῇ φυλακῇ. The βασανισταί are, according to the connection, the guardians of the prison, who, also, were certainly employed to inflict torture. There were, however, no special racks or tortures provided for debtors. It is precisely this punishment which verse 35 denounces against the hard-hearted, who refuse to forgive as they have been forgiven. The additional clause, ἀφιέναι ἀπὸ τῶν καρδιῶν, (Ephes. vi. 6, ἐκ ψυχῆς,) expresses more clearly the nature of true forgiveness, which is here intended to be put forward as a characteristic of the children of the kingdom. It is no mere *outward* act, but presupposes a state of mind which only true repentance can produce. Of this inner state the outward act of forgiveness, by word or deed, is merely the corresponding expression. (The words τὰ παραπτώματα αὐτῶν, I am disposed, with Fritzsche, to hold as genuine, in opposition to Griesbach and Shulz; for, as ver. 35 contains the application and short exposition of the parable, it is very much to the purpose to explain the δάνειον by the term παραπτώματα. The verb ἀφιέναι is also commonly conjoined with an object, comp. Matt. vi. 14, 15; Mark xi. 25, 26.) The formula παραδιδόναι εἰς φυλακὴν, ἕως οὗ ἀποδῷ πᾶν τὸ ὀφειλόμενον, still demands here our special consideration in its connection with the creditor. Already at Matt. v. 26, we remarked that it could not denote everlasting punishment; in the words ἕως οὗ it is implied obviously that a limit is fixed. For, should it be said that in any event the punishment must be viewed as an endless one, inasmuch as the debt could never possibly be liquidated, it is undoubtedly true, that the creature never can get free from his obligations to the Creator. But since, according to the representation in the parable, the hard-hearted servant is not devoid of repentance, (he willingly admits his debt,) he is also susceptible of the Divine forgiveness, and this cannot be conceived of as existing without manifesting itself.[1] The purport of the whole, then, clearly seems to be this, that when love shows itself in a way so imper-

---

[1] The translator may perhaps be allowed to say that this view is one to which he cannot assent If the amount of repentance implied in the sinner's merely admitting that in point of fact he *is* a sinner, be sufficient to ensure ultimate salvation, few indeed can fail of reaching heaven.

fect, that it is seen merely in the *receptive* form, not in the *communicative*, there is, in that case, no fitness for the kingdom of God. The man devoid of love is committed to the φυλακή, that the conviction of his real state may be brought home to him. Thus it is plain that it is not the standard of the law which is here applied, (for, according to law, it is not unrighteous to take violent measures in enforcing debt,) but that of the gospel. He who wishes, however, to be meted by this measure, must himself apply it to others. (Matt. vii. 2.) As the hard-hearted servant did not so act, the severity of the law fell on his own head. The φυλακή here is thus = ᾅδης = שְׁאוֹל, the general assembling-place of the dead who did not die in the Lord, but all of whom, it does by no means follow, shall on this account sink into eternal condemnation. (Compare more at length on Luke xvi. 19, sq). According to 1 Peter iii. 19; Matt. xii. 32, there is plainly such a thing after death as deliverance from the φυλακή in behalf of some, and, according to the connection of the parable, we must avail ourselves of that fact in explanation of the circumstances here presented to us. Absolute exclusion from the face of the Lord is made to depend on the entire want of active and receptive love, and so, on the want of faith, without which there can be no love in the soul. (See on Matt ix. 2; xiii. 58.

In that case broad were the way leading to life! But how the parable can fairly be so construed, it is impossible to see. The consignment of the servant to prison is done in the way of punishment, it is done in wrath (ὀργισθείς), and the period fixed for terminating that punishment is, confessedly, one which can never come In the parable these points seem essential and distinctive They ought not to be explained away, even though they land us in a doctrine so solemn as that of eternal punishments. The reader who wishes to investigate the truth of Scripture on this subject, may consult with advantage the " Miscellaneous Observations" of President Edwards,—the more lengthened work by his son, Dr Edwards of Newhaven, entitled " The salvation of all men strictly examined, and the endless punishment of those who die impenitent, argued, &c.," and Fuller's Eight Letters to Vidler on the doctrine of Universal Salvation
T.

IV.

PART FOURTH.

OF CHRIST'S LAST JOURNEY TO JERUSALEM, AND CERTAIN INCIDENTS WHICH TOOK PLACE THERE.

(Luke ix 51.—xxi. 38; Matt. xix. 1.—xxv. 46; Mark x. 1.—xiii. 37.)

FIRST SECTION.

REPORT OF THE JOURNEY BY LUKE.

(Luke ix. 51.—xviii. 14.)

HITHERTO, we have been able to make the Gospel of Matthew the ground-work of our exposition, as it was easy, in the course of his narrative, to take up the little that was peculiar to Mark or Luke. In this fourth part, however, we find ourselves compelled, throughout the first section, to take Luke for our guide, as he records incidents and discourses of the Saviour which none of the other Evangelists touch. Since Luke, in recording this series of communications, which are peculiar to himself, proceeds on the fact of a journey to Jerusalem which seems to be described as the last; and since the Saviour on various occasions throughout this section is described as engaged in travelling (ix. 57; x. 38; xiii. 22; xvii. 11,) it is not improbable that we are in it furnished with a *report of the journey*. Certainly, however, it is difficult to say *what* journey this report is intended to recount. For, should we hold that the section contains a report of the last journey of Jesus from Galilee to Jerusalem, an opinion which one might adopt on comparing Luke xviii. 35; xix. 29, with Matt. xx. 17, 29; xxi. 1, then the account of Luke would come into direct contradiction with that of John. For, according to the latter evangelist, the Lord left Galilee to attend the feast of dedication, (x. 22,) and never returned to Galilee, but remained in Peræa. (John x. 40, where is found added the statement καὶ ἔμεινεν ἐκεῖ) From Peræa the Saviour came back to Bethany in order to raise Lazarus (John xi.) After this miracle, however, he went to Ephraim in the neighbourhood of the desert, (John xi. 54,) and stayed there with his disciples. It thus appears that, according to John, the journey of Jesus to the last passover did not begin exactly at Galilee; there intervenes, it would rather seem, his stay at Jerusalem during the feast of dedication, and at Peræa and Ephraim in the interval Luke, on the other hand, makes it appear as if Jesus went directly from Galilee to the passover. If, however, to escape these difficulties, we understand the account as applying to the journey from Ephraim to Jerusalem, our view would well harmonize with the passage Luke ix. 51, for the lifting up of the Lord is there expressly spoken of, which stands in direct connection with his journey from Ephraim to the passover. But in that case the passage Luke x. 13 sq., in which the guilt of the cities, Chorazin and Bethsaida, is treated of, would be altogether away from its proper connection, for Jesus had left Galilee long before. Further, Luke x. 38 could not be reconciled with this view, for, according to that passage, Jesus is already in Bethany, while at xvii. 11, he again appears on the boundaries of Samaria and Galilee, and not till Luke xix. 29, (compare Matt. xxi. 1; Mark xi. 1,) makes entry into Jerusalem. Besides, in that case there would, according to the narrative of Luke, be too great a space left vacant in the life of Christ. Hence, must the chronological series of events be at once and wholly abandoned, and the idea of our having in this section a journal of travel must be given up, unless it be possible to remove these differences between this account and that of John, for to him undoubtedly the preference is due where the accuracy of chronological or topographical statements is in question. This, however, seems to be effected most simply by the hypothesis of *Schleirmacher*, (on the writings of Luke, p. 158, sq.,) that the section before us should be considered as made up of the narratives of two journeys.[1] This

---

[1] Care should be taken that we are not tempted to confound this hypothesis with De Wette's view of this section, which he thus expresses:—
" We shall have to notice in this section an unchronological and unhis-

acute and learned man observes most correctly, that, not Luke xviii. 14, must be regarded as the conclusion of the section, but Luke xix. 48, where the entry into Jerusalem is recorded.[1] With this, the account of the journey fittingly ends, while at Luke xviii. 14, no termination is to be found. The whole of this report, then, according to Schleirmacher's view, Luke inserted without change, and it again owed its existence to some one who made use of two smaller imperfect reports of two different journeys of Christ, and incorporated the one with the other, not knowing that between the two he abode for a time at Jerusalem. The conjoining of the narratives of these two journeys Schleirmacher does not ascribe to Luke himself, for this reason, that his practice is to insert into his narrative the compositions of others unchanged. Now although this last opinion seems to me unsupported by proof, and that Luke is rather to be considered as having elaborated the materials presented to him, (it is by no means improbable that Luke rewrote certain passages, even though he did insert into his work others unchanged, ex. gr. the family histories [ch. i. ii.] as holy relics,) yet on the whole this view is satisfactory. For, according to it, Luke can be completely reconciled with the more precise account of John. The circumstance that at Luke x 38, Jesus is already at Bethany, while at xvii. 11, he is again on the borders of Galilee and Samaria, is easily explained, if the former passage be referred to the time of Christ's presence in Jerusalem at the feast of dedication, the latter to his presence at Ephraim (John xi. 54). The expressions used by John regarding the Lord's stay at Ephraim ($\delta\iota\acute{\epsilon}\tau\rho\iota\beta\epsilon$ $\mu\epsilon\tau\grave{\alpha}$ $\tau\tilde{\omega}\nu$ $\mu\alpha\vartheta\eta\tau\tilde{\omega}\nu$ $\alpha\vec{\upsilon}\tau o\tilde{\upsilon}$,) allow very well the idea that short excursions were made from that point, or that he had gone out of the direct road in travelling up to Jerusalem at the last passover. This being presupposed, the only difficulty that remains in the section, is, that nothing should be said of Christ's

torical collection, which was occasioned probably by the circumstance that Luke found a good deal of gospel material which he could not elsewhere arrange into its place, and which, consequently, he here threw together."

[1] If, nevertheless, in our exposition, we keep to Luke xviii. 14, as the conclusion of the section, this is done simply because our leading object is not criticism so much as the full understanding of the facts in themselves To facilitate this, however, we must, after Luke xviii. 15, again take Matthew as our groundwork, because his Gospel, subsequently to that point, becomes richer in detail.

coming to Jerusalem, and his stay there. What is recorded in Luke x. 25, sq.; xiii. 1, sq , *might* certainly have happened in Jerusalem, but there is no distinct intimation to that effect. This *argumentum a silentio*, however, is the less calculated to overturn the entire hypothesis, because the circumstance easily admits of being explained from the general want of topographical references. The feast journeys are entirely omitted in Luke, as also in Matthew and Mark, and consequently it is not surprising that he does not give his readers fuller information as to the minuter incidents after the last journey from Galilee.[1] It is enough that on matters of fact there is not the slightest contradiction between the account of John and that of Luke.

For the rest, with respect to the *mode of treatment*, Luke's peculiar way of rendering the *discourses* of Jesus, is in this section very manifestly displayed (Compare the Introduction, § 6). With great delicacy and truth does he give the *nuances* of the dialogue This accuracy is certainly due in the first instance to the original author of the report which Luke made use of, only the evangelist shows that he knew how to appreciate such a report, by not defacing such peculiarities; and besides, in the Acts of the Apostles, Luke displays in his own writing a similar skill.

§ 1. JAMES AND JOHN ARE INCENSED AGAINST THE SAMARITANS.

(Luke ix. 51—56.)

The words with which Luke's lengthened account opens, can only be understood as applying to the Saviour's last journey, which ended in his being offered on the cross and exalted in the resurrection. The expression ἀνάληψις (the substantive is found only in this passage, the verb, on the contrary, is often used, of Christ's exaltation to the Father's right hand. Acts i. 2, 22; 1 Tim. iii. 16,) denotes here Christ's elevation to the Father, which necessarily presupposes his humiliation. That it is not his being lifted up on the cross which primarily we are to understand, is shown by the expression ἡμέραι τῆς ἀναλήψεως, in which

[1] The same thing applies to Matthew and Mark, who speak in terms quite as general of Christ's last journey to Jerusalem. (Comp on Matt. xix 1, and xxi 1)

the whole process of his exaltation, from the resurrection to the ascension, is included. (Only figuratively, according to the analogy of John xii. 32, 33, could the expression refer to the crucifixion.) The period of this exaltation is regarded as fixed by a higher necessity, and the lapse of passing time down to that point as a blank which must be filled up. (Whenever the words πληροῦσθαι or συμπληροῦσθαι, [the two expressions are used synonymously,] are applied to time, we must always thus assume that some definite period has been fixed, either by human [Acts ii. 1,] or Divine [Gal. iv. 4,] determination). But, it may be a question how far this fixed period can be said to have already come on the occasion of Christ's departure from Galilee, when, according to John, so much was to intervene before the passover. The expression employed, ἐν τῷ συμπληροῦσθαι τὰς ἡμέρας τῆς ἀναλήψεως, seems more applicable to the journey of Jesus from Ephraim to Jerusalem (John xi. 54,) than when he was leaving Galilee for the feast of dedication. But, looking at the circumstances simply from the standing-point of a Galilean, and such we must suppose the narrator to have been, it is easy to explain how the Saviour's last departure from Galilee must stand in direct connection with his end, and all that intervenes be passed over in silence. In his view, the scene of all Christ's mighty labours moved between Galilee and Jerusalem; and so soon, therefore, as he had finally left the former place, Christ's work, in the view of the writer, seemed finished. The formula πρόσωπον στηρίζειν, corresponds to the Hebrew, חֻשִׁים פָּנִים לַהֲלוֹךְ, Jerem. xxi. 10. The LXX. indeed so translates it. Gesenius [in Lex. sub. voc. פָּנִים,] compares with it the phrase at Ezek. iv. 3, הָכֵן פָּנִים אֶל, which, however, the LXX. translate ἑτοιμάζειν πρόσωπον.)

Ver. 52, 53. In order to prepare a lodging, and provide the necessary supplies, the Saviour sent messengers forward to a Samaritan village, but the inhabitants turned them away.—Σαμαρείτης in the Hebrew שֹׁמְרוֹנִי, (from שֹׁמְרוֹן, the Capital of the district,) denotes, as is well known, an inhabitant of that province of Palestine, in which, after the Babylonian exile, there arose a mixed population formed from the Jews left behind, and the foreign tribes transplanted thither. (2 Kings xvii. 24.) They arrayed themselves against the Jews who returned from the exile, and at a later period they set up on Mount Gerizim a peculiar form of worship modelled on that at Jerusalem. (Compare the fuller account this in Winer's Bible Reallex. p. 597, sq.[1]). The opposition continued down to the time of Christ and after it (John iv. 9, οὐ συγχρῶνται Ἰουδαῖοι Σαμαρείταις), although, as was natural, it did not show itself alike vehemently in all individuals (John iv. 30,) nor at all times. At festival seasons, when the religious life among the Jews and Samaritans was in its fullest vigour, their hostility was most powerfully developed, the more especially that a leading point of difference between them was the place of Divine worship. Hence, in this instance, it is mentioned as the ground of their unfriendliness; ὅτι τὸ πρόσωπον αὐτοῦ ἦν πορευόμενον εἰς Ἱερουσαλήμ. (In regard to this use of πρόσωπον compare 2 Sam. xvii 11. פָּנֶיךָ חֹלְכִים בַּקֶּרֶב. The term δέχεσθαι includes, as at Matt. x. 14, and the parallel passages, all the friendly services of hospitality in its widest sense)

Ver. 54. That James and John, who are here introduced as speaking, are the two brethren, the sons of Zebedee, is in the highest degree probable, even though Mark iii 17, as will be immediately shown, cannot be adduced in proof of the fact. In their fiery zeal against the churlishness of the Samaritans, they are inclined to bring down on them a destructive judgment, and only await the command of their Lord (θέλεις) to be themselves the instruments of carrying such a judgment into effect. A bold faith reveals itself in these words, and a powerful conviction of the Lord's majesty, and of the relation in which they stood to him. Thus far there was nothing blameworthy in the spiritual position which they occupied. But the form in which it was manifested bore altogether an Old Testament type, they spoke from the standing-point of the *Lex Talionis*. On noticing, therefore, the expression of disapprobation in the look of Jesus, they sought to ground their declaration on an example from the Old Testament, appealing to what is related in the history of Elias, (2 Kings i. 10, 12). (The omission of the words ὡς καὶ Ἠλίας ἐποίησε in some MSS. is assuredly a false reading. The following words plainly contrast the disciples with Elias, the Old Testament with the New).

Ver. 55, 56. As Jesus saw that this fiery zeal of his disciples was not a mere outburst of feeling, but arose from their confounding the relation of the economy of the Old Testament with the New, he in a few words guides them to a right view of the point. After his

---

[1] Or in the second and enlarged edition, vol. ii. p. 435 —T.

lengthened intercourse with them, he might have taken it for granted that the distinction between the two economies was not only clearly known to them, but that in the inner life of their souls, they were familiar with it.¹ The simple mention of it was sufficient to recall them to the conviction that the compassionate love of the gospel had been forgotten by them in the justice of the law. The term πνεῦμα, therefore, in these words of the Lord, is to be understood in its usual sense, for between the ὑμεῖς and the Elias there is a contrast in respect of the principle that animates the two. This principle is the πνεῦμα. Both principles were pure and from God, but that which is Divine in its forward course of development among men, stands forth in its perfect form, in the πνεῦμα of the gospel, whose essence is grace and mercy, which were personified in the Saviour (John i. 17). Elias, therefore, does nothing wrong when he commands fire to fall from heaven, he rather, as the ἄγγελος of God, exercised justice. But Jesus did *better*, inasmuch as he exercised mercy, which he had come to render supreme amidst the human race. The disciples therefore sinned only in so far as they who ought to have received into their hearts the perfect spirit of forgiving love, permitted still the Old Testament spirit of avenging justice to prevail over them. As *they* were aware of the distinction, and had access to the spirit of pure love, they sinned in that very act which on the part of Elias was right. (At Heb. xii. 24 the same contrast is denoted by Christ and Abel. Abel's blood demands *vengeance*, as representing justice, the blood of Jesus pleads for *forgiveness*, for in him dwelleth grace) Many are of opinion that it was in consequence of this occurrence, that the sons of Zebedee received the name of Βοανεργές, (Mark iii. 17.) As regards, first, the etymological explanation of the expression, it has already been rightly given by Mark, inasmuch as he adds ὅ ἐστιν υἱοὶ βροντῆς = בְּנֵי רְגֶז. (The βοανε, βανε is probably the Gali-

¹ The most numerous and best MSS, (particularly A, B, C, E, G, H, L, S, and others, see the New Testament of Griesbach—Shulz on this passage,) even omit the words of the textus receptus, καὶ εἶπεν: οὐκ οἴδατε οἵου πνεύματός ἐστε ὑμεῖς, as given by the Cod D and others. In any case, the longer recension of the words of Jesus, ὁ γὰρ υἱὸς τοῦ ἀνθρώπου οὐκ ἦλθε ψυχὰς ἀνθρώπων ἀπολέσαι, ἀλλὰ σῶσαι, is an unauthentic addition, and even the shorter form of it is not beyond suspicion The supplementary clause, however, corresponds perfectly with the whole connection, and the origin of the gloss is easily explained, inasmuch as the ἐπετίμησεν seemed to call for a closer definition.

lean form for βενε, רָגַז however, and the kindred רָגַשׁ in the sense of to *quake*, to *tremble*, to *roar*, expresses most accurately the idea of the βροντή). The only thing remaining obscure is, what this name *refers to*. The older Christian expositors found the point of resemblance in the majestic and exalted impressions which thunder makes, so that the name, sons of thunder, was used not in the way of blame but of *praise*, as expressing the strength of that holy zeal which animated the sons of Zebedee. Modern expositors, however, for the most part refer to the fact before us, and understand it in the way of *censure*, and as intended to characterize a false and merely natural zeal. (See further details in the learned treatise by *Gurlitt* in Ullmann's *Studien*, vol. ii. part iv. p 715, sq). Were it proved that the name referred to this passage, the latter explanation would undoubtedly recommend itself as the more probable, for the term ἐπιτιμᾷν, in Christ's discourse, could not easily be reconciled with any name of praise. The disciples, therefore, could only have been *put in mind of* the name, (already on a former occasion bestowed on them) so that the connection would stand thus, " know ye not that ye ought to be led by another spirit, inasmuch as ye are the sons of zeal " But, even supposing this connection to be the right one, it seems to yield no thought that suits the context, for there is nothing contradictory between the name of the disciples and their conduct, inasmuch as they showed no want of zeal but of mildness. A contradiction of this nature, however, is assuredly required by the connection. Besides, on other grounds, it seems to me improbable, that the name υἱοὶ βροντῆς is to be associated with the occurrence here recorded. For, *in the first place*, it is unexampled in Bible history, and stands opposed to the idea of the new name, that a second designation should be given to any one in the way of punishment. In this way, his sin would be, as it were, immortalized. *Secondly*, the position in which the name stands at Mark iii. 17, is against the idea that the title υἱοὶ βροντῆς implies censure. It stands quite parallel to the name Peter which was given to Simon, and it is therefore hardly credible that the first name is one of praise, marking the spiritual character of the first apostle, while the second was a bye-word conveying blame. This is the less to be thought when we consider that the three apostles first named at Mark iii 17, and furnished with surnames, are precisely those who stood nearest to the Lord This circumstance leads us to conclude that the early fathers of the church were wholly right when they saw in the name υἱοὶ βροντῆς a description of the spiritual character of the two sons of Zebedee. Thus the bestowal of these names acquires in the case of the apostles the same significancy which the new names (Abraham for Abram, Israel for Jacob) have in the Old Testament. They characterize the new men, and are, as it were, symbols of the new nature. (Is. lxii. 2; lxv. 15; Rev. ii 17.) How far the name υἱοὶ βροντῆς agreed with the personal dispositions of James and John, cannot be shown in regard to the former, for no detailed account of him is given. In reference to John, however, it appears very doubtful how far the name is appropriately chosen, as it has been usual to conceive of him as very soft But as has already been often remarked, to look on John as a man of weak character, is wholly to mistake his nature His whole writings show that with all his mildness and gentleness there existed in him great elevation of thought and keenness of zeal against evil,[1] and it was this which the surname in question was intended to denote, for it was the union of energy with humility, (in Peter) of decision and keenness with gentleness, (in James and John) which formed the basis of their new nature [2]

§ 2 OF FOLLOWING JESUS

(Luke ix. 57—62; Matt. viii. 19—22.)

The short passage which here follows, flowing directly from the contemplation of the immediate circumstances, appears to hold its place most appropriately in the narrative of the journey. Some one (according to Matthew he was no less than a γραμμα-

---

[1] Let John's first epistle especially be read It is full of Divine βροντή as well in its descriptions of the true spirit as of the false, (comp. iv. 1, sq.) He who considers the Apocalypse to have been written by John will not fail to trace in it also the character of spiritual power.

[2] A doubt as to this view may be raised by the circumstance that the name Sons of Thunder never elsewhere again occurs. Had it been intended as the designation of their new nature, one may suppose that like the name Peter it would have been generally used. As it was, however, bestowed on two persons at once, it could not like the name Peter come into general use, and this sufficiently explains its being passed over in silence.

τεύς) who had been mightily attracted by the Saviour, expressed by the way, a wish to accompany Jesus, and Jesus sets before his view the difficulties attending his life and labours. In Matthew a portion of this passage stands amidst a collection of the miracles of Jesus, and consequently in a less appropriate connection. Nay, in the account of Matthew there is wanting that very point which with Luke stands prominently forth as the connecting link with the preceding narrative. For, as the sufferings which his enemies were preparing for the Saviour had been there described, so the following history states how it stood between Jesus and those friends whose affections his appearance and his words attracted. One portion of them pressed most hastily forward, but a single word as to the difficulties caused them to withdraw; another portion of them were called by the Lord himself, but their anxiety on the subject of the world deterred them from at once embracing the call. In Luke then, we are not to overlook the contrast between εἶπέ τις πρὸς αὐτόν and εἶπε δὲ ὁ Ἰησοῦς πρὸς ἕτερον, ver. 59, by which the several positions of Christ's different friends are marked.

Ver. 57, 58. The address ἀκολουθήσω σοι ὅπου ἂν ἀπέρχῃ plainly implies a certain consciousness already of the difficulties involved in being the companion of Jesus. The ὅπου ἂν ἀπέρχῃ cannot refer merely to the change of locality, but denotes dangers, for example those attending the journeys of Jesus to the feasts, in which every one acquainted with the circumstances (and that this well-disposed γραμματεύς was acquainted with them we must believe) must have seen peril both for the person of the Saviour and those about him. The words then are akin to the exclamation of Thomas, ἄγωμεν καὶ ἡμεῖς ἵνα ἀποθάνωμεν μετ᾽ αὐτοῦ, (John xi. 16,) and with Peter's declaration, Matth. xxvi. 35, inasmuch as both these exclamations, like that of the Scribe before us, came from the natural man, who failing to weigh the greatness of the self-denial required, soon started to the path but soon fell. According to the connection, the term ἀκολουθεῖν refers primarily to an external companionship, but it also involves at the same time a spiritual following, *i. e.* the choice of that path of life which Christ opened up, a conversation in righteousness and truth, and consequently the undertaking of a contest with unrighteousness and falsehood. The Lord, acknowledging indeed the good intentions of the suppliant, but perceiving his weakness, sets before him in the strongest terms the difficulty of following him. The want of necessaries, which are provided by the Creator even for the lower animals, of personal property and the shelter of a roof, must be encountered in following the Son of man. (The expression φωλεός occurs only in this passage. Hesychius explains it as τόπος οὗ τὰ θηρία κοιμᾶται.—Κατασκήνωσις = מִשְׁכָּן). The proper sense of οὐκ ἔχειν ποῦ τὴν κεφαλὴν κλίνειν is that of the entire renunciation of every thing which man can call his own, which was exhibited even externally in the life of the Saviour, but which in a spiritual sense must be repeated in the life of all his followers, as we are taught at 1 Cor. vii. 29, sq. Although it is not expressly recorded what effect this admonition of Jesus produced, yet from the following narratives we may infer that probably it had deterred the γραμματεύς. The remarks of the two persons whom Jesus asked to follow him lead us to conjecture that they could not as yet resolve to abandon *everything* in order to embrace Christ, for the necessity of so doing is brought forward as the main idea of the short narrative. (See on Matth xix 27.)

Ver. 59, 60. As in the preceding case, the Scribe had volunteered to follow the Saviour, Jesus in this instance himself gives the invitation to do so. While the former, however, was deterred by difficulties, the latter were apparently held back by sacred duties. The truth of greatest importance to be drawn from the following narrative, and to which most prominence should be given, is this, that not merely sins and crimes (which call first for forgiveness through that repentance and faith which the following of Christ presupposes) but even legal righteousness, nay, attentions to the noblest duties of earthly relationship, may keep man back from the following of Jesus. The θάψαι πατέρα and the ἀποτάξασθαι τοῖς εἰς τὸν οἶκον must be held, when viewed even from an earthly standing-point, to denote noble and tender duties. (The verb ἀποτάξασθαι ver. 61, in the sense of to take leave. The relatives are to be considered as at a distance, so that he means to stipulate for a journey home) We have here, therefore, a commentary of fact on Matth. x 37. In obeying the command of Christ all other duties are absorbed; not that they are thus depreciated in importance or neglected, but that every act of man is put into its right place relatively to the final end of the individual himself, as well as of the whole body. From this standing-point then, can the Saviour ask the the son to abandon to others even the last duties he owes to a deceased father, the point of time favourable for turning the whole of his life into a higher course of action must be seized at once. This man having already become a believer, must now decide on consecrating his life to the preaching of God's word, (διάγγελλε τὴν βασιλείαν τοῦ Θεοῦ). The expression ἄφες τοὺς νεκροὺς θάψαι τοὺς ἑαυτῶν νεκροὺς, has here assuredly no reference to the Jewish opinion that he who touched the dead became polluted. Jesus merely wished to bring immediately to a decision the man whom he had called to follow him, and induce him to give up for his sake every thing in itself lawful, nay, even that which was considered necessary. Just as little ought the νεκροί to be referred to the *grave-diggers*, a view which enfeebles the whole sense of the passage. The Saviour rather regards the call given as a call to ζωὴ αἰώνιος, and demands that the person called should unconditionally resolve in favour of it, and that he should leave everything of an external nature, (even such acts of piety towards a deceased father after the flesh) to those who were as yet wholly occupied with externals, instead of which occupations he should yield obedience to the call of his Heavenly Father. Thus the word νεκρός must in one of these instances be understood as used figuratively of those who have not yet been awakened from the death of natural life, (Rom. vii 8 sq.) The dead, who are to be buried, are naturally those deceased in a bodily sense; but inasmuch as it is said θάψαι τοὺς, ἑαυτῶν νεκροὺς it is unquestionably intimated that the deceased were in a condition in no respect essentially different from that of the living who were to bury them,

Ver. 61, 62. To the last, who like the others presents himself as a follower, the Saviour replies with the statement of a general principle which rebukes his declaration, and conveys the idea that an unconditional determination was necessary for having part in the kingdom of God. The expressions χεῖρα ἐπιβάλλειν ἐπ' ἄροτρον and βλέπειν εἰς τὰ ὀπίσω, denote figuratively, a state of indecision, irresolution. (Gen. xix. 26.) In opposition to this we are to look on the entire determination of the will as a necessary requisite to labouring in the kingdom of God, (εὔθετος *well ordered, fitting, suitable.* See Luke xiv. 35,) which lays claim to all the powers of man. This sentence, however, as well as the preceding ἄφες τοὺς νεκροὺς κ. τ. λ. contains a truth of permanent importance for all times and circumstances of the church, for never can any one be a disciple of Christ save he who renounces all that he has, (Luke xiv 33,) and strives to love God with all his powers (Mark xii. 30); since Christ's call to follow him is the call of God, and man must serve no master *beside* God, (Luke xvi. 13).

§ 3. THE SENDING FORTH OF THE SEVENTY DISCIPLES, WITH THE ADDRESS OF JESUS TO THEM.

(Luke x. 1—24, [Matt. xi. 20—27.])

The sending out of the seventy disciples stands in immediate connection with the special object of Luke's gospel. Matthew and Mark, who wrote merely for Jews, record only the mission of the *twelve;* Luke for the sake of the heathen, narrates the sending forth of the *seventy,* and in the following discourse omits all ideas that might bring to mind Jewish particularism, ideas such as are mentioned at Matt. x 5, sq. (Compare Eisenmenger's entd. Judenthum, Part ii. p. 3, sq. respecting the notion of the Jews that there were seventy distinct nations on the earth). The passage, Num. xi. 16 sq. regarding the seventy elders to whom Moses imparted of his spirit, may be compared as parallel. To this corresponded the Sanhedrim of seventy assessors with the president (נָשִׂיא) who represented Moses. From the idea that the members of the Sanhedrim were seventy-two in number (i. e. twice six times six, or six times twelve), arose the reading ἑβδομήκοντα δύο, which is supported certainly by some good MSS. (as B. D.) but must yield in authority to the common one. Strikingly, however, as this fact agrees with the whole scope of the gospel of Luke, it seems little accordant with its immediate connection as it stands in this journal of travel. The sending forth of the disciples when they were all on the road, appears unsuited to the circumstances. It would seem to us, therefore, as if in the information thus given, a passage from some earlier period of the narrative had been inserted into the account of their last journey. Perhaps, the Saviour, shortly before his final departure from Galilee, having given up all hope of Chorazin, Bethsaida, Capernaum, sent forth once more the seventy messengers into some other region. This well agrees both with the mention of the fall of these cities (x 13–15), and also with the remarkable declaration (ver. 18) which

U

expresses the confident assurance of the triumph of his cause notwithstanding all opposition and unbelief. The μετὰ ταῦτα (ver. 1) however, cannot strictly be taken in its chronological meaning, but must be understood generally somewhat in the sense of *moreover* (Schleiermacher on Luke, p. 169). The address of the Lord to his departing disciples as given by Luke, closely resembles that in Matthew (chap. x.), only this latter evangelist gives every thing more completely and at greater length. Similar circumstances assuredly led most naturally to similar ideas, but closely as the different clauses agree, changes and transpositions are not improbable. The mention of the unbelieving cities, however, connects itself fittingly with the context in Luke, while it stands only very loosely in its place at Matt. xi. 20—24. For, if the Lord had closed his preaching in Galilee, and knew that never more should he set foot within it, this would give, as nothing else would, its full meaning to the reproof in which he rebukes the unbelief of those who so long had listened to him and seen his works.

Ver. 1. The word ἀνέδειξε points to a specific act of election, such as, according to Matt. x. 1 sq., took place in the case of the twelve, to a formal ἀναδείξις (Luke i. 80). The verb ἀναδείκνυμι is to be understood in the sense of " to appoint," with the accessory idea of a solemn and public setting-forth of the dignity bestowed. (Compare 2 Macc. ix. 23, 25; x. 11; xiv. 12; 3 Esr. ii. 3.) The disciples were moreover sent out two and two (ἀνὰ δύο) that they might mutually support each other, and might in the places which Jesus intended to visit, prepare men's minds beforehand for his coming.

Ver. 2. Luke here places at the outset of the discourse of Jesus, the same thought which at Matt. ix. 37, 38, precedes the choosing of the twelve; though certainly the connexion in Matthew is more loose, inasmuch as the words with him, primarily refer to the sight of the people without leaders or teachers. At the foundation of the expression θερισμός, there obviously lies that comparison according to which the divine word is likened to seed, and mankind to the field. (Compare Matt. xiii. 4, sq.) According to this the Old Testament period is to be considered as the time during which the Divine Word had been in operation, whose great result was that lively sense of the need of atonement which showed itself among the people. This is viewed as a θερισμός when compared with what had gone before, but as compared with what was to follow, it appears as merely the given possibility of a new and nobler seed, whose harvest was to be expected in the end of the day at the coming of the Son of man in his glory. The apostles and all the ἐργάται in the first instance stand forth simply as witnesses of the θερισμός; but in another respect, in so far, namely, as they have 'themselves received the higher element of life imparted by the gospel, they appear as those who are called to disseminate it more widely abroad, and indeed this is referred to by the admonition δεήθητε τοῦ κυρίου κ. τ. λ. The fervent prayer of those who have themselves already been received into the kingdom of God, and who labour in the spirit of it, is the means of procuring its ever wider extension, by the stirring up of living labourers for it. The very sending out of the seventy was of itself an answer to the prayer, which on the occasion of sending forth the twelve Jesus urged his disciples to offer.

Ver 3, 4. According to Luke, the discourse, immediately after the command to go forth, begins with the mention of threatening dangers. Matt. x. 16, where our more detailed observations may be seen, gives the same thing at a later period. This remark, respecting the relation of believers to the world, seems to be contradicted by what follows, μὴ βαστάζετε κ. τ. λ. For, while the allusion to the λύκοι seems to awaken fear and anxiety, the subsequent admonition to go forth without the preparation of human foresight, bespeaks believing confidence. But this contrast is the very thing here intended. "Without considering such danger, go forth free from care, every thing shall be provided for you." (As to particulars, compare my remarks on Matt. x. 9, 10.—Βαλάντιον = צְרוֹר [Job xiv. 17] in translating which it is used by the LXX. is allied to πήρα, *crumena*.) The μηδένα κατὰ τὴν ὁδὸν ἀσπάσησθε still remains obscure, even though in seeking an explanation, we call to our aid the oriental practice of saluting each other by tedious forms of courtesy, and so causing detention; for, the injunction—ye must not linger[1]— agrees neither with what goes before, nor what follows. It is better to understand ἀσπάζεσθε as meaning to *salute, to receive, or welcome as a friend*, with the secondary sense of *seeking for*

---

[1] Compare the parallel passage 2 Kings iv. 29, where Elisha enjoins on Gehazi the greatest haste, and says כִּי תִמְצָא־אִישׁ לֹא תְבָרְכֶנּוּ וְכִי יְבָרֶכְךָ אִישׁ לֹא תַעֲנֶנּוּ׃

favour. In this way the expression stands on the same footing with those which precede it, which all denote preparations for the journey, measures of human foresight.

Ver. 5, 6. As to the conduct which Jesus exhorts his messengers to pursue towards those with whom they sojourn, compare Matt. x. 13. The Spirit seeks what is akin to itself, and where that is wanting, finds no abode. The expression given by Luke, υἱὸς εἰρήνης, in some respects conveys a meaning peculiarly its own, in others it is a clearer and closer statement than hat of Matthew, who merely speaks of the οἰκία ἀξία or μὴ ἀξία. According to Luke those minds disposed to receive the gospel, must be distinguished from those in the same house, who were resolved to reject it. To the former the blessing of God's kingdom is promised, to the latter, not.

Ver. 7. The exhortation, that in the house where they had taken up their quarters, they should content themselves with what the inhabitants had to give, (τὰ παρ' αὐτῶν) is connected in Luke so closely with the μὴ μεταβαίνετε ἐξ οἰκίας εἰς οἰκίαν, that the latter idea is more completely modified by it, than is the case at Matt x. 11, where this connection is wanting. It seems, according to the representation of Luke, that our Lord had intended to warn them against leaving the cottages of the poor, and seeking instead the dwellings of the rich. The ἐργάτης in the field of God, receives his μισθός (Matthew has τροφή x. 10,) i. e. his bodily nourishment, and the supply of his necessities. The seeking for more than this, cometh of evil.

Ver. 8—11. According to the connection in Luke, the cures, and the preaching of the kingdom of God, appear in the light of spiritual rewards for bodily services. In Matthew the same ideas are brought forward in another connection. (Compare Matt. x. 8.) As to their conduct towards those who resisted them, compare Matt. x. 14. (Ἀπομάσσεσθαι is found only here. It corresponds to the ἐκτινάσσειν in Matthew.) As to the former the ἤγγικεν ἡ βασ. τ. Θ is a message of joy, so it is to these a message of terror, implying for the one the possibility, for the other the impossibility of their entering it.

Ver. 12—15. The woe which the Lord utters against such an unbelieving city, is most appropriately followed by a curse on the places which had been the witnesses of his greatest glory. The connection here seems to be that in which the passage originally stood, at the close of the labours of Jesus in Galilee, although Matthew (xi. 20—24) has inserted the words not unfittingly into his context. (As respects the exposition, see the details in Matthew *ut supra*.)

Ver. 16. According to Luke, the address of Jesus to the seventy concludes with the general idea, that he, the Saviour, was himself conscious of such living union with his own, that what was done to them was done to him. (Compare on Matt. x. 40, where the same thought, but only as viewed from one side, is expressed).

Ver. 17. The circumstance, that in the following passage the return of the disciples is anticipated, goes to prove the correctness of the opinion that it is impossible in this section of Luke to keep hold of the chronological thread. The discourses of Jesus connected with this return, form a well compacted whole, so that here again the account of Luke possesses more the character of originality than that of Matthew. First, the evangelist makes the disciples on their return express to Jesus their childlike joy for the deeds which in his name they had been able to perform. (The δαιμόνια ἐκβάλλειν is one of the many miracles which they did. This might appear to them of special importance, as it presupposed a control over the mighty kingdom of evil.) Most deeply is this representation drawn from the life. A secret joy seizes a man when he finds that he acts with an energy more than human, for example, that through him the spiritually dead are awakened. In this joy there is the implied testimony that man is called to act with power from on high, but there lies in it also a temptation so dangerous, that the Saviour, though he acknowledges the joy as right and well-founded, yet warns them at the same time against giving themselves up to it without watchfulness, and exhorts them to keep fully in view the foundation of that real joy which can never lead astray.

Ver. 18. Singularly remarkable is the declaration of the Lord, which, according to Luke, follows immediately after the expression of joy on the part of the disciples. Inasmuch as he makes a transition from the δαιμόνια to Σατανᾶς himself, without any occasion for it, and in the most private circle of his own disciples, we must say that here again is a passage belonging to the number of those (compare on Matt. xiii. 39) 'from which it may be rightly inferred that the Saviour himself teaches the existence of a prince of darkness, and that this is by no means to be looked on as a Jewish superstition. Here would have been the place, even on the supposition of Christ's accommodating himself to the views of the multitude, in which to point out the unfounded and ruinous nature of such a belief, and to advise the use of the idea (as some think it should be used) only from extreme necessity, and in the way of accommodation. As to the thought, however, which the expression of Christ ἐθεώρουν τὸν σατανᾶν κ. τ. λ. contains, the θεωρεῖν is naturally not to be understood of bodily sight, but of spiritual contemplation, for the object seen was itself of a spiritual kind. The nature of spiritual vision, however, involves the conception of the future as present. We may, in explanation, compare the parallel passage, John viii. 56, where Jesus says of Abraham, εἶδε τὴν ἡμέραν τὴν ἐμήν. As here in prophetic vision Messiah and the whole messianic future is represented as present in spirit to Abraham, so the Saviour in this passage says that he beheld as a present event the throwing down of the dominion of evil. The preterite tense ἐθεώρουν, therefore, must be referred not merely to the period during which the seventy were absent, but to past time in general, so that the meaning would be,—long ere this have I seen in spirit the power of evil as a thing overthrown. For, the cures wrought by the disciples, are obviously to be considered not as the *causes*, but as the *effects* of the overthrow. *Because* the power of evil was broken by the Saviour's appearance in the midst of mankind, and through him the energies of a higher life were imparted to the disciples, *therefore* could they do such deeds. It was impossible, however, for the deeds of the disciples *to effect* that which was the object of Christ's whole appearance. But being the *results* of the overthrow of evil, their actions were at the same time the *evidences* of that great victory, and thus far was their joy well-grounded, and the transition made by Christ from their deeds to the overthrow of Satan himself, sufficiently accounted for. The figurative expression πίπτειν ἐκ τοῦ οὐρανοῦ, is assuredly chosen after the remarkable passage, Is. xiv. 12, in which the king of Babylon, (as the type of the prince of darkness) is represented as by proud effort scaling the heavens, that he might set his throne above the stars of God, but cast headlong from his self-chosen exaltation. (The LXX. translate it πῶς ἐξέπεσεν ἐκ τοῦ οὐρανοῦ ὁ ἑωσφόρος. Compare as to this the expositors of Isaiah). The addition ὡς ἀστραπήν depicts (as at Zech. ix. 14,) the swiftness of the fall. The whole passage consequently expresses the same thought which lies in John xii.

31, ὁ ἄρχων τοῦ κόσμου τούτου ἐκβληθήσεται ἔξω (according to another reading it is even κάτω βληθήσεται, to which consequently the ὑψωθῆναι of the Saviour forms an appropriate contrast) namely this, that, *in* Christ and *with* Christ, evil is seen as overcome, and good is displayed in all its glory. We may compare also on this point the peculiar representation given in the Revelation of John, where, however, the casting out of Satan (xii. 7, sq.) is distinguished from the complete chaining up of his power (xx. 2, sq.).

Ver. 19. This verse mentions exemption from all liability to personal injury, as a new *result* of the victory thus won by truth, —of that victory which our Lord, in the spirit of prophecy, beheld as actually wrought out. As the Saviour's power sets the captives free, so does it preserve his people from the assaults of hostile force during their subsequent progress. Ὄφεις καὶ σκορπίοι are mentioned, as being amongst animals the representatives of the kingdom of evil, in which poison is collected, and through which it inflicts, on contact, physical injury. (Compare Ps. xci. 13). The expression originates in that profound view of natural life pervading all Scripture, (compare further on Rom. viii. 19, sq.) according to which sinful disturbances in the spiritual world express themselves also in the physical. What follows καὶ ἐπὶ πᾶσαν δύναμιν (צָבָא, στρατιά) τοῦ ἐχθροῦ, fills up the first expression, and extends it so as to comprehend *every* form of assault from the world of evil. The mightier power of Jesus gives security against the influence of these in every shape. Such passages as Mark xvi. 17, 18; Acts xxviii. 5; show that here we are by no means to exclude all reference to what is external. Only, in general this reference is associated with the continuance of the Charismata as the manifestations of the Spirit of Christ exhibited externally. After these Charismata have ceased, the *spiritual* application of the words alone stands prominently forth. (Ἀδικεῖν stands as = βλάπτειν, as at Rev. vii. 2, 3. Compare Mark xvi. 18).

Ver. 20. To these words, which acknowledge as well-founded the triumphant declarations of the disciples (ver. 17), there is now subjoined a warning. According to the connection, therefore, the words μὴ χαίρετε—χαίρετε δέ, are not to be understood as an absolute prohibition of joy over the power of the Spirit in them, but only as forbidding them to rejoice even over that as an isolated fact. For, in that case, should the believer make the effects of God's Spirit through himself the only or the leading object of his attention and joy, he is in danger of withdrawing his view from the *source* of this higher life, and no sooner does he cease to draw from that fountain, than life dries up, and self-indulgence, vanity, pride, spring up in his soul. For this reason does the Saviour here bring forward as the true and abiding object of a Christian's observation and joy, ὅτι τὰ ὀνόματα ὑμῶν ἐγράφη ἐν τοῖς οὐρανοῖς. At the foundation of this remark, there lies the figure of the βίβλος τῆς ζωῆς, in which the names of believers are inscribed, a figure which, in the Old Testament, had already been frequently used, (Exod. xxxii. 32; Ps. lxix. 28; cxxxix. 16). The inscribing is conceived of as the act of God (ἐγράφη ὑπὸ τοῦ Θεοῦ), so that the election of grace by which the saints are chosen, and which they have themselves certainly to make sure (2 Pet. i. 10), is thereby denoted. Hence, in contrast with human agency authoritatively gifted with higher powers, there is set forth a Divine agency in connection with and acting upon man; the former is a very doubtful object of joy, for by means of it self-pleasing and vanity easily insinuate themselves, inasmuch as the will is seldom delivered from self. Divine grace on the other hand, and its manifestation, the calling of man, is clearly the object of holiest joy, for God's will is as pure as it is unchangeable, and in his election of grace therefore, of which he can never repent (Rom. xi. 29), the ground of all salvation and all blessedness to mankind is laid. Even, therefore, if he cannot perform any great spiritual deeds (2 Cor. xii. 9), this remains as the joy of the believer, which, as being personally his own, he can never be deprived of, that he lets his soul satisfy itself in the grace of God.

Ver. 21, 22. With singular appropriateness, there is here added this expression of *holy* joy on the part of our Lord, which stands in strong contrast with the joy of *sense* (ver. 17) as felt by the disciples. The latter exulted over the glorious exterior of the work, the Saviour drew his delight from its hidden glory, from this, namely, that God's true wisdom was revealed by the Father, not to the prudent and wise ones of the world, but to the νήπιοι, in whom, amidst the concealed circle of his new creation as it flourished unseen, he had his quiet and humble joy. Rightly, then, did the Divine consciousness rest in this lowliness and self-humiliation Conscious of his dignity as God, he acknowledged himself as the *Organ* of every true revelation of

God, and at the same time as its object. (For the more minute details compare on Matt. xi. 25—27, where the same words occur but in a more loose connection).

Ver. 23, 24. These verses were already explained more in detail at Matt xiii 16, 17, where they stand in a wholly different connection. Here, the leading idea of both verses, that superabundant grace had been manifested towards them (the disciples) unites them closely to what goes before, for *they* namely were the chosen ones to whom the Lord revealed more than to the saints of the Old Testament. Only, in this connection the στραφείς πρὸς τοὺς μαθητὰς κατ' ἰδίαν εἶπε occasions some obscurity. The στραφείς may easily be understood as referring back to ver. 21, where the Saviour in his discourse addresses himself to God, but the κατ' ἰδίαν remains a difficulty, inasmuch as the whole preceding discourse had already been spoken in the most private circle of his disciples. As the common text, however, has the words στραφείς πρὸς τοὺς μαθητὰς εἶπε before ver. 22, the κατ' ἰδίαν may best admit of being explained thus. While the discourse was going on, some hearers had gathered around him, (as the following 25th verse sq. immediately shows); on their account Jesus spake the last words in a low tone to those more immediately about him, uttering the rest aloud in the hearing of all. In this case, the reading of the common text (ver. 22) would be the correct one, and that view ought to be at once adopted for this further reason, that the omission of the clause may easily be explained owing to the parallel words which follow, but the addition of it can hardly be accounted for. Whether the words, however, were originally spoken here, or in the connection in which Matthew gives them, or whether the Saviour, as in the case of such a declaration may well be conceived, more than once gave utterance to them, it is in this case hard to decide.

§ 4. PARABLE OF THE TENDER-HEARTED SAMARITAN.

(Luke x. 25—37.)

The following narrative appears likewise very appropriate in a journal of travel; it is drawn as from the life. A lawyer comes up to Jesus on the road, in order to hold conversation with the renowned prophet His purpose does not seem to have been precisely bad; it was rather the mere love of novelty which induced him to try how Jesus would express himself. The Saviour's way of dealing with him, does not permit us to suppose that he was a Sadducee who put the question, one who himself believed in no ζωὴ αἰώνιος, and who was now only asking in irony after the way to Utopia. He seems rather to have held the views common among the Pharisees, and only to have been desirous of discovering what more or better knowledge than his own, Jesus possessed. The ἐκπειράζειν, therefore, here has no connection with the laying of snares for Christ, to make him politically suspected,—an attempt which, according to the gospel history, the Pharisees frequently permitted themselves to make, (compare Matt. xxii. 15, sq.) This narrative rather is parallel to Matt. xxii. 35, sq. The question regarding ζωὴ αἰώνιος was not suited to a design that was simply wicked. With amazing wisdom does our Lord on the present occasion treat this blind lawyer. Entrammelled in his Rabbinical particularism, he asks some outward rule by which to set bounds to the duties of love, and not lie under the necessity of exercising that affection on all hands. Instead of giving him such a wished-for rule, the Saviour relates a narrative, in which nothing more is said of the *object* of love, which properly the νομικός had asked after, but of those who exercise love. A Priest, a Levite, members of the same order with the enquirer, and persons on whom the observance of the law was especially incumbent, pass heartlessly by, reckoning that the sufferer might probably be no neighbour. The Samaritan, whom they deemed a heretic, exercised the law of love.[1] In every point from which it can be viewed, reproving, rebuking, demanding repentance, this parable must have arrested the questioner. He must have felt that not merely was his question false, but so also was the whole state of mind from which it could have proceeded. To the man who was asking after a law for the exercise of love, it must have become obvious that he had it not himself, and knew it not, inasmuch as its single law is this, that it is a law to itself. Love loves, and asks not when, how, where; it is the primordial, innermost life, which ignores the whole world of reflections and prudential rules, and blesses the enemy even though he pierce its heel. Into this world of pure love which the heart of Jesus contained, (for who-

---

[1] According to the view which refers this gospel especially to the heathen, this putting forward of one not a Jew as the model of pure love, possessed something peculiarly attractive.

soever exercises it has it only through him) he opens up a glimpse for the benefit of the νομικός, hardened in his legal subtleties, and that was the only means by which he could be helped out of his heartless state. Thus Jesus exercised towards even him that very love, the knowledge of which he was teaching him; he blessed the ἐκπειράζων.

Ver. 25—27. The expression νομικός is not essentially distinct from γραμματεύς and νομοδιδάσκαλος, and the words therefore are unquestionably interchanged. Compare Matt. xxii. 35 with Mark xii. 28; Luke v. 17 with verse 21. Luke employs for the most part the term νομικός as more intelligible to his readers, (Luke vii. 30; xi. 45, 46, 52; xiv. 3), while the Hebraizing Matthew uses γραμματεῖς = סוֹפְרִים. It is the more generic term while Φαρισαῖοι, denotes a particular party among the νομικοί. A Sadducee might also be a νομικός. (Compare on Matt. xxii. 35.) The question as to eternal life, being the final object of all theological enquiry, is put forward by the lawyer, under the conviction that in replying to it, Jesus must bring out whatever was peculiar in his opinions. (The formula κληρονομεῖν ζωὴν αἰώνιον, or βασιλείαν τοῦ Θεοῦ [1 Cor. vi. 9, 10; xv. 50] has, without doubt, its foundation in the comparison of the land of Canaan [as the outward type of eternity,] and of rest in it, to eternal life. The expression κληρονομεῖν τὴν γῆν at Matt. v. 5, refers to this.) The Saviour, however, refers him to the old well-known word of God, saying, as it were, what thou askest has lain from of old expounded in the revealed word; take it thence for yourself. The lawyer now brings forward most correctly the passages Deut. vi. 5 in connection with Numb. xix. 18, (which passages are in a similar way conjoined by another lawyer at Mark xii. 33), wherefore, it only remained for him to translate into living fact the contents of these deep words, which, rightly understood, involve the whole New Testament. That this had not as yet been done by him, the result of the conversation shows. It is further remarkable, in regard to the quotations of this passage, here as elsewhere in the gospels, to observe the way in which they deviated from the Hebrew text and from the LXX. In Hebrew there stand the expressions מְאֹד, נֶפֶשׁ, לְבָב. The LXX. translate these, διάνοια, ψυχή, δύναμις. In the quotations of the evangelists, however, the words run thus.

Luke x. 27. καρδία, ψυχή, ἰσχύς, διάνοια.
Mark xii. 30. καρδία, ψυχή, διάνοια, ἰσχύς.
Mark xii. 33. καρδία, σύνεσις, ψυχή, ἰσχύς.
Matt. xxii. 37. καρδία, ψυχή, διάνοια.

This constant difference of the gospel quotations from the LXX. in the rendering of לֵבָב and מְאֹד leads almost to the conjecture that the evangelists either followed another reading, or that this version of it had been taken by one of them from another. For, it is inconceivable that this deviation should have taken the same form in the three evangelists, if they had written independently of each other. To me it seems most probable, that in this instance the mutual agreement originated with Luke, and passed over from him to Mark and the Greek Matthew. (As to the meaning of the synonyms in the passage, compare my Program on Trichotomy in the Opusc. Theol. p. 143, sq., and on Matt. xxii. 37.) The exalted idea, however, of loving God with all our powers, and loving Him also *wholly* with them all, embraces at once the whole both of religion and morality.[1] For, the addition καὶ τὸν πλησίον σου ὡς σεαυτόν, is at bottom only an unfolding of the contents of the first commandment as Matt. xxii. 37 sq. shows. In love to God, which, on the part of the creature, can only take the form of receptive love, there lies the love of his will, and consequently the implied love of one's neighbour. To draw, however, from the command thus to love God, the inference, that man must therefore be able to do it in his own strength, would be wholly out of place. Since only that which is divine knoweth God, (compare on Matt. xi. 27,) so only that which is divine can love God; and when God commands us therefore to love God; it involves for the creature an injunction to receive the Spirit of God, in whom alone he can be loved. This Spirit, however, the New Testament imparts, and consequently this command of the Old Testament, (as indeed the whole law) for its fulfilment, presupposes the gospel. This same Spirit, who teaches us to love God, wholly and entirely with all our faculties, alone enables also us to love our neighbour aright. As pure love to God loves God more than it does self apart from God, so it also loves God more than our neighbour apart from God; but self and our brother being looked at as in God, and God in them, true

---

[1] As to this and the following thoughts, compare the fuller discussion on the passage Matt. xxii. 37, sq.

self-love and genuine brotherly love are then at one with the love of God. Hence does the Lord say that the *second* commandment is like unto the *first* (Matt. xxii. 39), for this reason, that it is *the same thing* with it. Love to one's neighbour, if it be genuine love, that is, if the creature be loved not merely as a creature, (for in that lies the distinctive character of natural love), is nothing else than love to God. This even the following parable shows.

Ver. 28, 29. The answer of the lawyer was in itself satisfactory to the Saviour, but he directly urged him to follow out the command into action, remarking that life lay in the practical fulfilling of it. But it was by this precisely that the corruption within him was brought out to view; his knowledge wanted that decision of the will fitted to carry it out into life, and this want of moral power again obscured his discernment. He asks, feeling himself struck,—who then was his neighbour? a question which in his own mind he must have felt himself able to answer, if he had sought to exercise perfect love. (Δικαιόω has no peculiar meaning here; it merely refers, through the word ἑαυτόν, to the person wishing to justify himself.) Just because of his want of experience, Jesus transfers him into the midst of the realities of life, and makes him behold love actually loving. (The term ὑπολαμβάνειν = ἀποκρίνεσθαι, excipere, is in the New Testament found only here. It occurs frequently in the LXX.; Job ii. 4; iv. 1.)

Ver 30—33. The traveller whom the robbers assaulted is perhaps to be conceived of as a Jew, for in that case it would on the one hand be more striking that the priest and Levite refused him their help, and on the other hand that the Samaritan gave him assistance when he might so easily have availed himself of a sophistical excuse. But it may be said that the priests would have aided a Jew, and perhaps therefore it is best to view the sick man as a *heathen*. ('Αντιπαρέρχεσθαι is not different from παρέρχεσθαι. It is found in the New Testament only here. Συγκυρία also occurs only here in the New Testament. It denotes an accident. Among profane writers also this form of the word rarely occurs; συγκύρησις is more usual.)

Ver. 34, 35. Most carefully is the compassionate treatment which the despised Samaritan bestows on the suffering stranger, delineated. From the impulse of love he does even more than was incumbent. (Wine and oil, well-known means of cure in the

East. The πανδοχεῖον is the Caravanserai of the nearest place, that at Jericho perhaps, in the neighbourhood of which Jesus might then be staying.) It is a fine trait, that he cares also for the subsequent wants of the sick man, and promises to repay the outlay.

Ver. 36, 37. The enquiry now had certainly changed sides. The lawyer asked, ver. 29, who was the neighbour to whom support should be given. Jesus enquires who was the neighbour,—was it the man who exercised or who refused to exercise love? Even here, however, lay the great doctrine, that love is not determined by its object, but has inherently in itself its own standard. Pure love however loves even an enemy, as here the Samaritan does the sufferer who is a stranger, and one who from difference of creed might have appeared hostile. The acknowledgment, therefore, that true love dwelt in him, involved an answer to the question, and thus it only remained to impress upon his mind the admonition ποίει ὁμοίως. It was an obvious suggestion to trace in the compassionate conduct of the Samaritan a figurative representation of the Saviour's work. The wounds of the sick, (Is. i. 6,) which they who sat on Moses' seat left undressed, he whom they reviled as a Samaritan (John viii. 48) bound up with oil and wine.

§ 5. MARY AND MARTHA.

(Luke x. 38—42.)

Equally appropriate to a journal of travel is the following little narrative, which at once transports Jesus to Bethany in the neighbourhood of Jerusalem (John xi. 1), for which reason, as was formerly remarked, it cannot be the mere journey from Ephraim to Jerusalem, of which a history is here given, as in that case it would be inexplicable how Jesus should again, at the passage Luke xvii. 11, make his appearance on the borders of Galilee. That Martha and Mary, however, are to be sought for nowhere else than in Bethany, is certain from gospel history; in this passage Martha is described as possessing a house of her own in the κώμη. Whether she was a widow, or lived unmarried with her sister and Lazarus, cannot be determined. The evangelists are remarkably sparing in their historic notices of the persons mentioned by them. They confine themselves to what is barely necessary, and devote themselves rather to the delineation of their spiritual life. Hence the account of the two sisters here given, marks them, though in few touches, so strikingly and clearly, that they are often chosen as exemplars of the peculiarities of two distinct religious tendencies. We find in Martha the type of a life busily devoted to externals, such as is frequently exemplified in this passing world; in Mary, the type of quiet self-devotion to the Divine as the one thing needful.[1] To a certain extent both tendencies will be combined in each believer, but it is not to be overlooked that there are different vocations, and many are better fitted for busy outward labour than an inner contemplative life, although the most active must be from the depths of his soul given up to the Lord, and the man of contemplation must consecrate his energies to the advancement of God's kingdom. Hence, even the Saviour's word of rebuke to Martha (ver. 41), is no absolute censure, and is rather occasioned by her own antecedent remark, (which shows that she had mistaken her own place as well as Mary's) than called forth by her conduct itself. Martha serves, as it were, only as a foil to the figure of Mary, in whom appears a mind wholly and undividedly given up to the influence of God. She is another example of the complete fulfilment of the command ἀγαπήσεις κύριον τὸν Θεόν του ἐξ ὅλης τῆς καρδίας σου (x. 27). The Samaritan practised it in an active, Mary in a receptive form.

Ver 38—40. Probably Jesus had enjoyed opportunities of becoming acquainted with the family at Bethany during his former yearly journeys to the festivals. Mary sets herself confidingly at his feet to listen to the words of her Lord; Martha busies herself to provide the best outward entertainment she could for the beloved guest. (We are to view the παρακαθίζειν παρὰ τοὺς πόδας as denoting merely Mary's staying beside Jesus, and certainly in an attitude fitted to catch his instructive and life-awakening words). Martha was zealous meanwhile about externals, which certainly were necessary in part, but with self-gratification she gave herself up entirely to them. (Περισπᾶσθαι, distrahi, in the New Testament occurs only here, in the Old Testament frequently; also the substantive περισπασμός = עִנְיָן Eccles. i. 13; ii. 23, 26. The word διακονία includes here all domestic services in

---

[1] Among the apostles, Peter corresponded to Martha, John on the other hand to Mary.

which Martha lost herself with needless bustle). From this satisfaction in her own occupations arose the reproving speech directed against her sister; perhaps conscience stirred her up and testified that Mary had more of Jesus than she. But as her craving for the heavenly was not sufficiently strong and pure, she suffered herself to be fettered by external activities, which in reality were more agreeable to her, and out of this state of mind arose her speech. Jealous of Mary, she wished her to be as she herself was. The verb συναντιλαμβάνεσθαι, to *support*, to *help*, occurs again only at Rom. viii. 26.)

Ver. 41, 42. The address of Jesus to Martha refers less to household activity in itself (for that must be cared for) than to the state of mind in which she went about it, and the comparison she instituted in this respect between herself and Mary. He rebukes first the μεριμνᾶν and τυρβάζειν, (the word occurs only here in the New Testament, it corresponds to the Latin *turbare*) that is, her restless spirit of action, as moved by the impulses of creature-affection; and he next contrasted the πολλά with the ἕν, along with an intimation that for the sake of the former she was losing the latter, while yet this latter, not the former, (compare on Matt. iii. 14, 15,) was of essential necessity[1] (χρεία). It is one of the peculiarities of the Saviour's discourses, that they often in few words say all that is necessary to bring everlasting truth, in some special view of it, home to all times and circumstances. Standing on the spiritual central-point, he without violence entwined the minutest and least important circumstances of the present, with the loftiest eternal verities. In the efforts of the two sisters the Lord places together the nothingness of all love and care for the creature, in comparison with care for what is everlasting. The one thing must so be laid hold of by the soul, that no striving after any thing else must similarly rouse it; and having begun with the one thing it will be able to deal not merely with many things, but with all things else—not in such a way, however, that these shall have the ascendancy

---

[1] The clause ἑνὸς δέ ἐστι χρεία is wanting in Cod. D. Other MSS. read ὀλίγων or ὀλίγων ἢ ἑνός. On these readings J. D. Michaelis founds his translation—one dish is enough for us. Certainly the reading ὀλίγων seems to be grounded on some such idea. The common text, however, is sufficiently established by critical authorities, and the reference of the passage to a dish of food is altogether excluded, as well by the δέ as also by the subsequent expression ἀγαθὴ μέρις.

and take captive the mind's life, but that it shall itself bear sway and bring every act into harmony with the main design of life. This pure and holy effort after the one and the Eternal portion, had Mary chosen. The expressions μέρις and ἐξελέξατο mutually determine each other's meaning. The former points to the election of grace, the latter to man's free determination to embrace it. By the combination of the two (2 Pet. i. 10) spiritual life is rendered complete, inasmuch as the individual then lays hold of the gift as his own, and in doing so, places it beyond the reach of loss. Without the free decision of his will to embrace it, a man may lose his calling, (Matt. xxv. 29). For Martha, the thought thus expressed includes also this warning, to care for the one thing first, and in that way to make her calling (which certainly was a different one from that of Mary) equally firm and imperishable.

§ 6. DIRECTIONS RESPECTING PRAYER.

(Luke xi 1—13.)

That the following discourses belong to the last passover-journey is by no means unlikely. Only, the indefinite ἐν τόπῳ τινί shows that a close adherence to localities formed no plan of the writer, and he may, therefore, often have been guided in his arrangement more by the connection of the matter than by local association. Although, however, portions of this section are placed by Matthew in the sermon on the mount, yet must we grant, that they hold in Luke a better position, for, on the one hand, the sermon on the mount bears generally, as is obvious, the manifest character of a collection, and on the other, what is here imparted suits better the close of Christ's labours than their commencement. Especially does this apply to the Lord's prayer, which, spoken at the end of the Saviour's public ministry acquires the character of a sacred legacy left behind him to his church. The subsequent exhortations to prayer also, and instructions as to its efficacy, appear peculiarly fitted for the time when the Lord's visible presence was to be withdrawn from the apostles, on which account John (xvi. 23, sq.) introduces similar passages into the last chapters, which contain the parting discourse of Jesus.

Ver. 1—4. As to the detailed exposition of the Lord's prayer compare Matt. vi. 9—13. It only remains for us to speak here of the particular form it bears in the text of Luke, for it is not to be doubted that the text in this gospel has been interpolated from the more lengthened recension of Matthew. First, in the address, the words ἡμῶν ὁ ἐν τοῖς οὐρανοῖς are undoubtedly genuine in Matthew, but like the entire petition γενηθήτω τὸ θέλημά σου κ. τ. λ. which is the firmly established reading of Matthew, they are in Luke of questionable authority. The same thing applies also to the concluding words ἀλλὰ ῥῦσαι ἡμᾶς κ. τ. λ. It is true that by these omissions the prayer is in no respect rendered specifically different, for the γενηθήτω κ. τ. λ. is merely a further carrying out of the ἐλθέτω σου ἡ βασιλεία, in the same way that the ἀλλὰ ῥῦσαι κ. τ. λ. contains a filling up of the antecedent idea μὴ εἰσενέγκῃς ἡμᾶς εἰς πειρασμόν. But the beautiful inner harmony which the prayer exhibits as given by Matthew is wanting in the shorter recension of Luke, for the first half of it (compare on Matt. vi. 9), comprising only two clauses, is disproportionately curtailed. The recension of Matthew should therefore be considered as the original form of the prayer, for what is peculiar to him cannot possibly be a mere amplification originating in later traditions, that of Luke on the other hand should be viewed as an abbreviated form, inasmuch as he is found dealing in a similar way with many of those passages which Matthew has included in the sermon on the mount. (Compare the beginning of the sermon on the mount.)

Ver. 5—8. After the prayer has been imparted, there are fittingly subjoined admonitions as to the use of it. Especially is persevering earnestness of supplication urgently enjoined. In the first verses this is done in the form of a parable, in the last (9—13) by figurative expressions. The latter verses have already at Matt. vii. 7 sq. been explained; the parable of the benighted traveller who by continued entreaty prevails with his neighbour and causes him to fulfil his desire, is peculiar to Luke. It has no difficulties beyond the single circumstance, that, as appears from this comparison, the *impure* motives as well of the supplicant, (the ἀναίδεια) as of him who suffered himself to be persuaded, form the point of comparison connecting them with the most exalted relations. (Of the same nature is Luke xviii. 1 sq., which passage also treats of prayer, and in it God is compared to an unjust judge). But first as respects the ἀναίδεια of the suppliant, it is not to be overlooked that he is here pleading not for himself but for his guest; his pressing importunate petitions acquire thus a nobler motive, he entreats bread that he may not be compelled to violate the holy rites of hospitality. From him who suffers himself to be prevailed on, it is impossible to dissociate an unworthy motive; the nobler one of love is expressly excluded, and he grants what is asked, only that he may get rid of the suppliant—and yet this is applied to God. Here, however, we must have recourse to that usage in regard to parables, (compare on Matt. ix. 16) according to which the likeness is often expressed, not in conformity with the objective truth, but as modified to meet the subjective position of him for whose understanding and instruction it is designed. Here the Saviour places himself on the standing-point of the man who knows from experience that God often delays long the fulfilment of prayer, delineating him as one directly unrighteous (see on Luke xviii. 1), in doing which he merely sets forth fully the impression which in such circumstances a petitioner weak in the faith feels made on himself, and he adds the requisite exhortations according to this impression. Thus do the parables constantly present the appearance of having proceeded from the liveliest conceptions of man's circumstances, and they furnish a true reflection of spiritual things as seen in connection with our every-day earthly condition. How far the interpretation of individual traits in the parable, (for example here the μεσονυκτίου as denoting the time of deepest inner darkness and need) should be carried, must certainly remain somewhat uncertain. In the parables of Jesus, however, which proceed upon powers of conception so rich, it ought on the whole to be maintained as a rule that no single trait is lightly to be overlooked, unless obviously the keeping hold of it does violence to the similitude as a whole.

§ 7. THE HEALING OF A DUMB MAN. THE DISCOURSES OF JESUS THEREUPON.

(Luke xi. 14—28.)

What is contained in this paragraph has already been considered in detail at Matt. xii. 22—30, and 43—45. We simply observe here, in regard to the arrangement, that the position in the history assigned to the occurrence by Luke, merits undoubtedly the preference. The fearful out-break of hatred on the part of the Pharisees and lawyers in the accusation that Jesus cast out spirits by the power of the prince of darkness, seems to belong to the end of his ministry. The words also, (Luke xi. 24—26) as to the return of the evil spirit, stand immediately after the cure in a connection more appropriate than in Matthew, who inserts before them the subsequent discourse, (Luke xi. 29, sq.) as to the sign of Jonah. From the account of this cure, besides, down to Luke xiii. 9, everything hangs closely together, and confirms the conjecture that Luke in this section made use of a journal of travel furnished by an immediate eye-witness. Many things betray such an origin. The only thing in this section peculiar to Luke is the narrative (ver. 27, 28,) of the woman who blessed the mother of Jesus for her son's sake. This little history distinguishes itself so remarkably for naiveté and originality, that it gives no slight evidence for the correctness of Luke's narrative. The invention or inappropriate insertion of it is hardly conceivable. Without doubt we owe to some eye-witness the account of this conversation conducted by Jesus on the occasion of his healing the dumb man. As respects further the contents of this narrative, it is not unimportant on account of the striking answer of Jesus in which the practical aim of all the Saviour's efforts is made apparent—that he cared not to excite wondering astonishment, but only to bring about a saving change of the whole life. The woman was certainly, as her exclamation shows, struck with the power and wisdom of Jesus, but, without taking the words home to herself and applying them to her own salvation, she is lost in contemplating his glory, and extols his blessedness through his mother, to whom she is led as a woman first to refer. This want of practical interest the answer of Jesus reproves, but in such a way that the woman, who had meant well in her remarks, could not feel herself offended, while both she and the others present must have yet been led to observe what was essential in the appearance of Christ. (In the word μενοῦνγε, there is on the one hand an implied acknowledgment of what was true in the woman's exclamation, but on the other an intimation that the ἀκούων καὶ φυλάσσων τὸν λόγον τοῦ Θεοῦ stood still higher. The passage might be translated thus:—he who lets the word of God operate spiritually within him, and is thereby born again, stands higher than her who after the flesh was the mother of the Messiah. This spiritual blessing, however, is open to you all—appropriate it to yourselves).

§ 8 CONTINUANCE OF THE DISCOURSE OF JESUS.

(Luke xi. 29—36.)

What was needful for the understanding of ver. 29—32 has been given already at Matt. xii. 38, sq. In regard to the place assigned to it, however, the narrative of Luke deserves a preference; as was already observed in our exposition of Matthew, (*ut supra*), partly because we find on the part of Luke greater originality, especially as respects the arranging of Christ's discourses, and next because in this very section the accuracy of his narrative is clearly manifest. According to Luke, the Saviour directed his rebuke expressly to the mass of the assembled people, and the allusion to the people of Nineveh agrees well with this. In the closing verses of this section, two thoughts are subjoined by Luke to the discourse of Jesus, which at Matt. v. 15; vi. 22, 23, were already explained in the sermon on the mount. It is of itself very possible that such gnome-like[1] sentences may have been spoken by Christ on many occasions, just as the first passage Luke viii. 16 again occurs in another connection. Meanwhile the connection especially of the latter idea in Matthew is not so simple as to give it the appearance of being there in its immediate and original place. Here, on the other hand, the admonition to care for the purity of the inward sight, connects itself so with the preceding ideas, that its very peculiarity seems proof of its originality. But the whole connection of ideas (from ver. 33—36) requires careful development, for it is not at first obvious. To those who asked a sign from heaven the Lord had held forth the example of the Ninevites and the queen of the East, who were prepared to acknowledge the Divine in far less glorious manifestations of it, in Jonah, namely, and Solomon. From this thought Jesus makes a transition to the object of all revelations of the Divine among mankind, namely, ἵνα οἱ εἰσπορευόμενοι (εἰς τὸν οἶκον τοῦ Θεοῦ) τὸ φέγγος,

---

[1] Axiomatic, pithy.—T.

βλέπωσι. The perfect revelation of God in Christ himself, is so constituted that its glory radiates far and wide, striking every eye. The eye itself certainly must be sound and clear if it is to take in purely the impressions of the truth. Hence the admonition to bring the eye into a rightly constituted state. What here seems strange, however, is that at ver. 33, the λύχνος being that which giveth light, denotes the Saviour himself as the φῶς τοῦ κόσμου, while again in ver. 34 it means the ability to take in the light—to see. Already, however, at Matt. vi. 22, 23, it was remarked that a light itself was needful for the reception of the light, (as a negative pole for the positive) and the darkness here is not to be considered as simply the absence of light, but as that which resists every reception of the light, and consequently as the moral impurity which flies every discovery of itself by the power of light. In order to receive the light of Christ, therefore, the eye must be ἁπλοῦς, and then does it work with an influence so quickening and light-giving, that the φῶς ἐν ἀνθρώπῳ completely and entirely pervades the man. The figure here is only distinguished from that brought forward at Matt. vi. 22, (where the particulars may be compared) by the additional clause ver. 36. There seems, however, a tautology implied in this additional statement, εἰ οὖν τὸ σῶμά σου ὅλον φωτεινόν—ἔσται φωτεινὸν ὅλον. The ὡς which follows, however, indicates very naturally a silently implied ὄντως, by means of which the following sense would arise. "The enlightenment of man (owing to the similitude having been taken from the outward eye, the body stands for man's inner being) by the reception of the Divine light through means of a single and clear eye, brightens him so entirely (amidst the darkness around) that he shines (inwardly and spiritually) as when outwardly (under night) a light irradiates one with its beams." It is not, therefore, a merely ideal knowledge of God and divine things that is here spoken of, but the communication of a higher life-principle, which has the power of forming in him to whom it is imparted a fountain of similar life (John iv 14). The whole passage, therefore, pourtrays believers as men transformed by the influence of Christ, (of the φῶς τοῦ κόσμου) into φωστῆρες ἐν κόσμῳ, (Phil. ii. 15,) enlightening what lies around them.[1] (In ver. 35 σκοπεῖν, as elsewhere βλέπειν, is used in the sense of *to take care, to guard oneself* In the New Testa-

---

[1] Compare also Dan. xii. 3, (Matt xiii 43) 1 Cor. xv. 41, 42.

ment this meaning occurs only here—ver. 36 ἀστραπή is = φέγγος, the *shining, gleaming flash*).

§ 9. REBUKE TO THE PHARISEES AND LAWYERS.

(Luke xi. 37—54.)

As respects the following discourse against the φαρισαῖοι and νομικοί, the thoughts, which, according to Luke's account, it contained, are given by Matthew, but as his custom is, he conjoins them with others wanting in Luke, so as to form a complete whole. In this form the separate ideas will be found more fully explained on Matt. xxiii. We merely consider here the discourse in Luke viewed as a whole. Its form leaves no room for doubt that here again we have in Luke the account of an eyewitness, while the discourse in Matthew (ch. xxiii.) shows itself manifestly to be a composition consisting of kindred portions of discourses which might have been spoken by Jesus on very different occasions. For *in the first place*, the account of Luke starts from a definite historic occasion. During the Saviour's discourse which followed the cure of the dumb man, (xi. 14) a Pharisee came up and invited him to dine (in the exposition of ἀριστᾷν, ver. 37, there is no ground for deviating from the common meaning *prandere*.) As he observed that Jesus ate without having washed his hands, and loudly expressed his astonishment at this, after the meal was finished Christ at once commenced a conversation as to the connection of inward and outward purity. Owing to this observation of the Pharisee, the discourse was directed first against them,—the reason, however, which led Christ to extend it also to the νομικοί is stated by Luke at ch. xi. 15. One of the lawyers, namely, applied the words to himself, and therefore the Lord turned to that party and rebuked their errors. *In the second place*, the discourse concludes (ver. 53, 54) with a general remark by the writer, that such a public declaration had brought the opponents of Jesus to the firm determination to overthrow him as the destroyer of their whole power over the people. In Matthew all those points are wanting which show that the account of Luke had been drawn on the spot and from the life. Matthew on the contrary, gives an address in which he has put together all the antipharisaic elements to be found in the discourses of Jesus; these he has arranged with skill and discernment, into a new and entire whole. (In the closing verses of this section at Luke xi. 54, there occur some unusual expressions. As respects first the ἐνέχειν δεινῶς, it means as at Mark vi. 19, *insidiari*. In the LXX. it occurs at Gen. xlix. 23. Only at this passage in the New Testament does ἀποστοματίζειν occur. According to Timaeus in the Platonic Lexicon, when intransitive it is = ἀπό μνήμης λέγειν, *to recount from memory*. Transitively, however, it means *to cause one to tell* something, digging it as it were out of his mouth. Suidas says, ἀποστοματίζειν φασὶ τὸν διδάσκαλον ὅταν κελεύει τὸν παῖδα λέγειν ἄττα ἀπὸ στόματος. With this meaning the subsequent ἐνεδρεύειν well agrees, [which word does not again occur save at Acts xxiii. 21] as also does the expression θηρεῦσαι, which is intended to describe the ensnaring nature of the questions put by Christ's enemies, examples of which are brought forward at Matt. xxii. 15. sq. The word ἐνεδρεύειν, from ἔνεδρα, corresponds even in point of etymology with the Latin *insidiari*.)

§ 10. VARIOUS DISCOURSES OF JESUS.

(Luke xii. 1—59.)

To the contents of the following paragraphs the same remarks may be applied which were made on the foregoing. The same thoughts, for the most part, again occur also in Matthew, where they are arranged in various connections, according to the method adopted by that evangelist in combining portions of different discourses. Even if separate, gnome-like (axiomatic) declarations of Christ might have been spoken by the Saviour at different times, yet is it difficult to conceive that more lengthened portions of discourse, agreeing word for word, could have been uttered more than once. In examining the originality of the section, however, every thing in this instance again speaks in favour of Luke. For at the very beginning of the chapter, he again connects the discourse that follows with a definite historic occurrence. As soon as Jesus left the house of the Pharisee, and stepped out amidst the numerous masses of the assembled people, he continued addressing to his disciples the discourse respecting the Pharisees, pointing out the danger which threatened them from these self-seeking men, and referring them to that higher aid which stood ready for them. This discourse, which the Lord carried on with his disciples amidst a wide circle of surrounding people, was suddenly interrupted by an individual from amidst the crowd, with a request so strangely out of place, that the very contrast between this incident and the discourse of Jesus goes to prove the originality of the account used by Luke in this section. For this man, full of his little domestic affairs, asks that the Saviour would settle a quarrel about an inheritance in his family. The mild Son of man holds it not beneath his dignity to lead even this erring one back into another path. By narrating a parable, Jesus takes the trouble to make obvious to him the nothingness of earthly possessions (ver. 16—21). And then he resumes the address to his disciples, which had been interrupted, taking up in such a way the thread which had been let fall, that the intervening words are woven into the connection. The Father's care for those who seek after the spiritual, forms once more the subject of his discourse, with an intimation that all spiritual blessings are infinitely exalted above every thing earthly. After the possession of the former, therefore, the Lord exhorts his people to strive and not to slacken in their zeal, but to persevere like the expectant servants of their Lord. Here Peter again breaks in on the discourse of Jesus, (ver. 40) and asks to whom he meant to apply these words, to them alone or to all. This question leads Jesus to go still farther into the parable he had chosen, of servants who await their lord's return, and so to develop it as to convey the answer sought of him, and bring the apostles to the conclusion that he spake of his own departure and return. This then brings the Lord finally (ver. 54—59) to address a reproof to the crowd, in which he even charges them with that very hypocrisy against which he had at the commencement warned them. He reminds them of the visible signs of his presence, and earnestly exhorts them not to mistake these signs. Thus the whole is so connected, and shows itself by the intermediate questioning to be so plainly the original account of an eye-witness, that it cannot be dissevered. Its connection with what goes before makes us see in it plainly a portion of that great journal of travel which Luke used in writing his work. The separate thoughts, here given in their original connection, Matthew according to his custom re-arranged under certain general points of view.

Ver. 1. The account of Luke begins with a well-marked his-̀
torical connexion in point of time with the foregoing narrative,
(ἐν οἷς scil. χρόνοις in the sense of *meanwhile, during which period*,
synonymous with ἐν ᾧ Mark ii. 19; Luke v. 34.) While he was
at meat (Luke xi. 37,) the people assembled before the house of
the pharisee, in order to obtain a sight of the prophet. (The
μυριάδες denote, like the רְבָבוֹת great, but indefinite numbers.)
Here then the Lord begins an address of warning against the
Pharisees, directed in the first instance certainly to his disciples,
but plainly uttered in the presence of the people, (ver. 13, 54,)
whose ears many of his words may have reached. The exposition of the words was already given at Matt. xvi. 6. As the explanation of ζύμη, there is here expressly added the clause ἥτις ἐστὶν
ὑπόκρισις. The bringing forward of this in particular is very naturally accounted for from the fact that all the remarks of our Lord's
preceding rebuke, as also the whole blameworthy peculiarities
of the sect, centred in their ὑπόκρισις. To the spirit of the Gospel
indeed nothing is more opposed than hypocrisy, for, whether in
its grosser or more refined form, whether consciously or unconsciously cherished, it ever implies a contradiction between the
inner man and the outer form. This contradiction is removed
by Christianity, which establishes the ἁπλότης of the soul, and
attaches value to every outward appearance only so far as it is
the genuine expression of the inner life. (The term πρῶτον,
therefore, is to be taken as meaning, *first of all, above all*, as at
Matt. vi. 33.)

Ver. 2—12. The words which follow have been already explained, namely, ver. 2—9, at Matt. x. 26, sq., (compare Luke
viii. 17,) ver. 10, at Matt. xii. 31; Mark iii 28, ver. 11, 12; at
Matt. x. 19, 20. The connexion of the words with the admonition to beware of the Pharisees is also so simple as to be self-
evident. Only, there is something obscure in ver. 2, and ver. 3,
in regard to their connexion with what goes before and follows.
As to conjoining the discovery of what is concealed with the
warning against hypocrisy, in the sense of " the secrets of the
hypocrite shall one day be laid open," it is not to be thought of,
because at verse 3 the revealing agency is ascribed to the Apostles
themselves. We must rather supply, therefore, at this passage,
the words μὴ φοβηθῆτε, as is expressly done at Matt. x. 26.

On the one hand this open revelation of the inner man forms
the contrast to hypocrisy, and on the other the display, in its

full glory, of that Divine truth which the Apostles were called to advocate, necessarily consummates its triumph. Hence, even if opponents arise against it, the powerful protection of God will shield the champions of the truth. What is said at ver. 10, of the sin against the Holy Ghost, was fully considered on a quite different occasion. (Compare on Matt. xii. 31.) Yet is it at the same time not improbable that the Saviour in this connexion referred back to the main idea formerly expressed. For the warning against apostacy led him very naturally to speak of the lowest stage of declension. In contrast, however, to the sin *against* the Holy Ghost there is brought forward at the conclusion (ver. 12,) the help to be received *from* the Holy Ghost, the aid imparted to those who are steadfast to their faith in the Redeemer.

Ver. 13—16 The narrative which follows is peculiar to Luke, according to whom some one from among the crowd requested Jesus to support him in a lawsuit. This little episode is instructive in so far as it shows the way and manner in which Jesus conducted himself regarding those affairs which enter into *the external relations* of political and civil life. He wholly refrained from such interference, and confined his labours entirely to the internal and moral world, out of this no doubt there arose an entire reformation of all political and civil relations, brought about by the labours of Jesus, but at first he left these externals unassailed, seeking only to establish the new life within. An important hint this for all who are called to the work of the ministry! Interference with exterior relations characterises sectarian effort, which has to do not with men's hearts but with dominion over them, and their money. (Δικαστής occurs again at Acts vii. 27, 35, in the sense of *arbiter*, freely chosen umpire. Μεριστής, met with only here in the New Testament, means, according to Grotius, on the passage, qui familiae herciscundae, communi dividundo, aut finibus regundis arbiter sumitur.) To make the man who had so awkwardly interrupted his discourse, aware of his spiritual state, Jesus gives him in the following verses a warning against πλεονεξία. One may conceive of a wish being entertained for the division of an inheritance without πλεονεξία, but in the case of this man, the very moment he chose for making his application to Christ shows that worldliness had repressed all sympathy with things spiritual, and this entanglement is the root of πλεονεξία, the subjugation of life to things earthly. As respects the construction of the latter half of verse 15, it must be observed, first, that undoubtedly αὐτοῦ is the right reading, and that in this entirely Hebraizing passage the pronouns must be explained after the usage of the Hebrew language. The thought contained in the passage would be easy if the words ἐκ τῶν ὑπαρχόντων αὐτοῦ were wanting. By this additional clause some expositors (for example Paulus,) have been induced erroneously to supply a τι before the ἐκ τῶν κ. τ. λ. so as to bring out this meaning,—even if any one has many possessions, yet is the life of the body not part of his property, i. e. he has no control over his life. This explanation seems to agree with the following parable, according to which even the rich man speedily loses his bodily life. But ver. 21 at once opens to our view another sense in which the life may be understood by the words πλουτεῖν εἰς Θεόν. Only relatively is death a loss, for the πλουτῶν εἰς Θεόν it is a gain. It is most correct then to view ζωή as denoting true life, in so far as it implies σωτηρία. The construction then is simply this, that the thought has been in substance completely expressed by the words ὅτι οὐκ ἐν τῷ περισσεύειν τινὶ ἡ ζωὴ αὐτοῦ ἐστιν, the words ἐκ τῶν ὑπαρχόντων αὐτοῦ, however, which follow, bring forward from the preceding περισσεύειν this additional idea, that no spiritual power can be ascribed to the possession of earthly goods. There are then two opinions here combined in one—" Life consists not in superabundance," and " out of earthly portions nothing spiritual can flow." The parable which follows therefore teaches as well that earthly blessings may be lost, as the necessity of laying up imperishable treasures along with the possession of which ζωή is at the same time bestowed, and which θάνατος is so little able to take away that it rather introduces us to the full enjoyment of them.

Ver. 16—21. Here follows a parable, whose object by no means is to warn against the *abuse* of riches, but against riches themselves, that is, against the soul's placing its dependence on any transitory possession. This dependence may exist as well on the part of him who has *much* as of him who has *little*, although in the case of the former the temptation is greater. In the same way, however, can the true πτωχεία πνεύματος (Matt. v. 3,) exist amidst great possessions. According to the views of the world and the decisions of the law, the man whom Jesus brings forward in the parable does nothing unrighteous; rather does he act wisely; just as the man who from amidst the crowd wished to force on his brother to a division of the inheritance does nothing against the law. But in both cases predominance was given to that natural life which cleaves to the creature, devoting to it its whole affections, and in that condition man is a νεκρός, and consequently is transitory as the passing objects which he loves. With this state of soul the Saviour contrasts another and an opposite, in which man sets his affections on things eternal, and holds and uses all his transitory possessions not for their own sake, but to promote the everlasting welfare of himself and others. This being his state he is a πτωχός, even though he may have great possessions, while one in the condition of a beggar may be a πλουτῶν εἰς Θεόν. This expression is most characteristic in opposition to the θησαυρίζειν ἑαυτῷ. For in human effort every thing depends on the final object towards which it is directed. In man's usual efforts after the things of sense the I (self) is the object of all exertion; and that poor I, with its transient joy and peace, falls during this very effort a prey to φθορά; in genuine effort, however, it is God the eternal, unchangeable, immortal, (1 Tim. vi. 16,) who becomes the object followed after, and while man therefore is laying up treasure *for* God (εἰς is not to be confounded with ἐν or πρός,) he is at the same time laying up for himself, for where his treasure is, there also is his real I. (Matt. vi. 21.) Compare the beautiful treatise of Clemens Alex. τίς ὁ σωζόμενος πλούσιος, which contains a Commentary on the history at Mark x. 17, sq., full of rich and deep thoughts. In the Pauline epistles compare 1 Cor. vii. 29, sq., where we are taught to possess as though we possessed not. (Ver. 16, εὐφορέω, means to bear abundantly, fruitfully. In the New Testament it is found only here,—ver. 19, ἐρῶ τῇ ψυχῇ μου stands certainly for αὐτός; it is, however, to be carefully noted that the words σῶμα, ψυχή, and πνεῦμα are not used *promiscue* for the person who is the subject of discourse, but are severally applied in certain relations as these become more particularly prominent. In this case, for example, neither σῶμα nor πνεῦμα could have been employed. According to the Divine ordinance nourishment is required by the body, but the πνεῦμα has relation to nobler than sensuous blessings and food. The ψυχή, as being capable of education and development, can refer as well to the lower region of the σάρξ as to the higher one of the πνεῦμα. In this very thing consequently does the point of the thought before us lie, that he gave up to the σαρκικοῖς that ψυχή which he should have consecrated to the πνευματικοῖς.)

Ver. 22—31. In what follows of his discourse our Lord comes back to his disciples, taking again ver. 12 as his starting point from which to carry on his remarks, and keeping in view the contents of the parable. Warning them against anxious care for the world, he points his disciples to our heavenly Father as their true helper in every strait, and remarks that, while trusting in his aid, there was no necessity for such an anxious gathering together of the means of bodily support as is exhibited in the case of the rich man. The whole discourse, it may be added, is founded on the supposition, that circumstances might well give occasion and temptation enough for cherishing such anxieties. The particulars have already been more fully explained at Matt. vi. 25—32.

Ver. 32. With the words μὴ φοβοῦ the discourse obviously returns to the standing-point of ver. 4, where the Redeemer, styling the disciples his friends, exhorts them μὴ φοβηθῆτε. The confidential mode of his address however, μικρὸν ποίμνιον with which the foregoing φίλοι μου (ver. 4,) may be set down as parallel, does not seem to agree with the idea of a conversation before the multitude (ver. 1.) At least, in the passage, John xv. 14, 15, where the Lord also calls his disciples *his friends*, it is done in the innermost circle of those belonging to him. But in what follows, there immediately (ver. 33,) occurs the plainest reference to ver. 21, which words again were addressed to one amidst the crowd, (ver. 13,) so that it is not possible to divide this discourse into separate elements, as spoken (before the people and before the disciples,) at different times. It is impossible, especially because of ver. 41. The only supposition we can form therefore is, that the disciples were nearest to Jesus, standing close round him, and part of his words did not reach the multitude; but on the other hand the Saviour perhaps intended that to *some* his words should be completely audible, while *all* should receive at least the general impression of them. Thus the conclusion of his address, (ver. 54, sq.,) which contains a distinct appeal to the multitude, charges them with ὑπόκρισις, with a warning against which the discourse opened. (Compare ver. 1. with ver. 56) Even the marked, and at first sight strange separation of the μικρὸν ποίμνιον from the great multitude, (retained under the entanglements of Pharisaic influence,) was perhaps designed on this account by the Saviour, and even if many of the particular allusions were unintelligible to the crowd, (as, for instance, the account which follows of watching for his own return, must certainly have been unintelligible,) yet far less stress is laid on these than on the impress of rebuke and reproof which the whole discourse bears. This must have driven men to a decision for or against him; the better disposed would attach themselves to the little flock, the rest went over entirely to his enemies. And this circumstance itself shows that the discourse is in its right place in the account of the last journey to Jerusalem, for, only towards the close of the ministry of Jesus would it have been appropriate to make such a demand for a decisive choice.

In the idea of the ποίμνιον, however, there is implied a reference not merely to their connexion with Jesus as the shepherd, (John x. 12), but also, as the μικρόν indicates, to the relation in which the disciples stood to the world. The expression reminds us of the relation of sheep to wolves, (Matt x. 16). To comfort them, as it were, under the sufferings and persecutions of the world, the Saviour promises that the kingdom should be bestowed on them by the Father, under which term in this passage, as being the opposite of κόσμος (ver. 30) in its widest application, inwardly as well as outwardly, we must understand a state of things, in which God's will is supreme, and beneath that supremacy it must be well with the good. Most appropriately, however, does the δοῦναι here correspond with the ζητεῖν (ver. 31). For it was only with this,[1] that the promise of outward aid and support was primarily associated, and now the Saviour adds that the exalted object after which they strove was already their own. The preterite here is to be retained in its literal sense, for this reason, that the Saviour views the disciples as the first bearers of that new life which he was called to bring into the world, and looks on them in the election of grace. If Jesus speaks here quite generally, without mentioning the υἱὸς τῆς ἀπωλείας (as in the similar passage, John xvii. 12), this was certainly done, partly because he spoke in presence of the multitude, partly because the time of Judas was not yet past, and so there still remained the hope of winning him, and finally it might yet be said that even Judas was chosen, but made not his election sure (2 Peter i. 10) and so fell through his unfaithfulness.

---

[1] The ζητεῖν—the seeking.—T.

Ver. 33. In the following verses (down to ver. 36) the Redeemer subjoins admonitions to the effect that they should walk as children of the kingdom, and members of the little flock. The picture is carried out in contrast to the preceding representation of the worldling anxious for the interests of the body and of self. The latter amasses for himself possessions and goods, the former sells them, the latter seeks ease and pleasure (ver. 19) the former stands amidst struggles and contests (ver. 35). It may be a question, however, in what sense the exhortation expressed in general terms, πωλήσατε τὰ ὑπάρχοντα ὑμῶν, is to be understood. In the first place it is not to be conceived that we have here any general admonition to Christians, otherwise the passage, 1 Cor. vii. 29, sq. would contradict it. Freedom in a spiritual sense from all earthly possessions, is assuredly to be considered as the highest aim of every member of the kingdom; by it alone can the outward act acquire real significance. A second question, however, certainly arises, whether the Lord means here to give his disciples a special precept; and according to Matt. xix. 27, it appears by no means improbable that he does.[1] According to Matt. xix. 21 also, Jesus, in certain cases where a too strong attachment to worldly possessions was manifested, appears to have required the entire giving up of these goods, and to have meant his injunction to be understood in good earnest, and in a literal sense. Yet, in any case, we must say that the necessity for such external renunciation must be regarded as something of subordinate importance, for all outward blessings being as Clemens Alex. (in the treatise above referred to) says, κτήματα, and therefore to be held possession of, so may they lawfully be thus held, if only they do not acquire the mastery. In the case of the disciples, however, it might be of importance that in this respect as in others they should be seen resembling their Lord. The remaining words of ver. 33 (as also ver. 34) agree entirely with the verses, Matt. vi. 20, 21, already explained. Instead of the transitory, the eternal is enjoined on us as the sole object of our endeavours, inasmuch as the καρδία (along with the ψυχή

---

[1] Luke xxii. 36, however, shows that even on the part of the disciples themselves the expression πάντα ἀφήκαμεν is to be taken with limitations Compare also on John xxi 3. In the parallel passage at Matt. vi 19, only the negative side is brought forward to view, μὴ θησαυρίζετε ὑμῖν θησαυροὺς ἐπὶ τῆς γῆς.

whose centre lies in the καρδία) identifies itself, as it were, with the object sought after. The only thing peculiar to Luke is the additional clause ποιήσατε ἑαυτοῖς βαλάντια μὴ παλαιούμενα, in which the βαλάντιον (see Luke x. 4) stands for what is contained in the *crumena*. The treasures which grow not old, therefore, are equivalent to the Eternal. (The word ἀνέκλειπτος, *inexhaustible*, is in the New Testament found only here).

Ver. 35, 36. In regard to what follows in the account of Luke, there occur kindred elements at Matt. xxiv. 42, sq. The two passages are so closely akin, that we cannot well suppose Christ to have twice spoken the same words at different periods, and in different circumstances. It thus becomes a question, in which of the two evangelists the original connection of the words may have been preserved. To me it once more seems in this case probable, that (as was remarked generally on Luke xii. 1) Luke has the more closely recorded the circumstances. For the whole account of Luke is so peculiar, that it evidently reports to us a conversation which really took place, with its various turns and interruptions, while it is equally obvious that Matthew (ch. xxiv) combines portions of discourses which all refer to the same topic, namely the Lord's return to the earth. In favour of the view that Luke or the author of the account he made use of, has possibly introduced here something foreign to the occasion, there is merely the obscurity of the connexion, and the circumstance, that the following context seems to point to the Parousia, which is not referred to in what goes before. But though the connecting thread which pervades all is fine, it is not wanting. For, all that is said from ver. 4 and onwards of the persecutions awaiting the disciples, and from ver. 22 of their entire separation from worldly possessions, and striving after eternal blessings, was based upon the idea that the Lord's protecting presence was to cease, so that the μικρὸν ποίμνιον (ver. 32) must be so explained that the flock is viewed as bereft of their shepherd, and exposed in consequence to all the assaults of the enemy. With this leading idea what follows is closely connected, inasmuch as the disciples are commanded to continue true, throughout the period of abandonment which stood before them, and that faithfulness would meet its reward from the Lord on his return. Granting then, that in the preceding context, no express reference is made to his return, yet the abandonment of the disciples presupposes the departure of their Lord, and this departure presupposes necessarily that one day he shall return, and these two ideas form the supports on which the whole connexion of the passage rests. The multitude, who equally heard this address, must certainly have failed to understand the idea of his return, which was a difficulty even to the disciples, but it was not for them that the discourse was primarily intended, and then, figurative though it was, it bore a meaning intelligible to all, as admonishing them faithfully to adhere to the true Lord. This exhortation formed at the same time a warning against hypocrisy, (ver. 56), which was greatly needed by the multitude, who listened indeed eagerly to Jesus, but from fear of the Pharisees shrank from a decision in his favour. (Compare on Matt. xxiv. 51, where instead of the ἄπιστοι in Luke there stands the more accurate ὑποκριταί.) The principal thoughts in the following verses, in so far as they relate to the Parousia, will be found explained more fully at Matt. xxiv., to which passage we now refer. Verses 35, and 36, like verse 33, retain primarily the preceptive form. The ideas of these verses Luke has modified in a peculiar way. The general comparison of servants who wait for their Lord, is more nearly defined by the circumstance, that he is represented as returning *from* the feast (ἀναλύσει ἐκ τῶν γάμων). We cannot therefore view this passage as a parallel one to Matt. xxv. 1, sq., for, in that chapter, the bridegroom is represented as coming *to* the marriage feast, and the virgins as waiting for him. The similitude of the marriage feast points in every case to the relation of Christ to his church, (compare Matt. ix. 15). To the church, however, in its wider acceptation, all the members of Christ's body assuredly belong, and among them consequently the apostles are included. But, the separate members may be viewed as standing in different relations to each other, according as this or that disposition acquires a certain ascendancy over their character. Sometimes they are pre-eminent for active effort (δοῦλοι), sometimes their natures are more receptive, or contemplative, (παρθένοι), and the figurative modes of expression are modified accordingly. (Compare more detailed remarks on Matt. xxv. 1, sq.; 14, sq.) Here the apostles are represented as men of activity, and for this reason they appear as the stewards of God's house, in the absence of the Lord at the heavenly banquet, that is, at his union with the church above, to which there is an analogy in his union with the church of the saints on earth at his return—his coming *to* the marriage-feast. (Ὀσφύες περιεζωσμέναι and λύχνοι καιόμενοι are the usual figurative expressions denoting *to be prepared and ready*, ἕτοιμος γίνεσθαι ver. 40. Compare Jer. i. 17; 1 Pet. i. 13; Matt. xxv. 1.)

Ver. 37, 38. After this exhortation to a faithful decision in favour of the Lord, (the opposite of ὑπόκρισις ver. 46, compared with Matt. xxiv. 51,) there is subjoined the thanks and the blessing, bestowed on such faithfulness. First of all, the return of the Lord is represented as wholly uncertain, in regard to the watch of the night in which it may be expected, and the reward of faithfulness as *equally great*, whatever the period of time over which it was extended. (This recalls to mind the parable, Matt. xx. 1, sq., according to which, the labourers, though called at different periods, yet receive *equal* recompence. Our more detailed remarks may be consulted on the passage itself.) Naturally there seems greater difficulty entailed by the later coming of the Lord, and the longer waiting which this implies. (It is intentionally that no mention is made of the first night-watch, for the banquet itself falls within it. As, however, allusion is made only to the second and third, Jesus seems here to have made use of the old division of the night amongst the Jews into three night-watches. Compare on Matt. xiv. 25.)—The description of the reward given to the true servants, is altogether peculiar; these ideas are found only in Luke. For, the Lord reverses their relative positions; he becomes the servant, they are the masters. In a passage, which also is peculiar to himself, (chap. xvii. 7—10) Luke has described the usual practice, that when a servant returns from labour, his master first requires him to attend to his personal comfort, and then permits him to take his own food, without thanking him for these exertions, inasmuch as he has only done what he was bound to do. The contrast of these two passages may be explained in this way, that the aim of Luke xvii. 7, sq. is to bring forward the humble, unassuming state of mind of those truly faithful servants of the Lord who say ὅτι δοῦλοι ἀχρεῖοί ἐσμεν. The passage before us, on the other hand, brings to view the self-humbling nature of the Son of man, so rich in grace, who not only places his servants on a level with himself, but sets himself beneath them. Thus, while the former passage gives expression to righteousness, that before us expresses grace, in regard to the relation of the servants to their Lord The form, however, under which our Lord's self-sacrificing love for his servants is here set forth, is borrowed from that promise which runs through all Scripture, of a great feast which at the setting up of God's kingdom, our Lord shall hold with his own. (Compare on Matt. viii. 11.) This δεῖπνον τοῦ γάμου τοῦ ἀρνίου (Rev. xix. 9,) has its type in that last meal of Jesus when he instituted the sacrament of the supper, and according to John xiii. 1, sq. the Saviour acted on that occasion altogether in harmony with what is here promised; he conducted himself like the servant, and considered his disciples as the masters. What then took place, was an outward type of what once in the end of the day, the Lord shall do to his own people, who until death remain true to his commandments. (For further details see on Matt. xxvi. 29.) With this the Saturnalia of the ancients may not inappropriately be compared, which also in symbolic form, gave expression to the idea that one day mankind should form a family of brethren. Thus even the Lord of heaven is not ashamed to present himself as the first-born among many brethren, (Rom. viii. 29; Heb. ii. 11.)

Ver. 39, 40. The Saviour, however, adds (modifying the previously used comparison of the servant waiting for his Lord) as a warning, that the time of the master's return is altogether uncertain; it must therefore be expected that he may come at any moment, (ver. 35, 40, as parallel to ver. 38,) and even at that instant he may appear when least of all men anticipate his return. (As to this thought, so important to our understanding the doctrine of the Parousia, compare the more detailed remarks at Matt. xxiv. 43, 44.) Here, however, the comparison of a master at a distance, whose return is waited for by his servants, whom he had left behind to manage the household affairs, (compare ver. 42, sq.) is conjoined with another, which serves more fully to bring out the unexpected nature of his coming—the figure, namely, of the goodman of the house, who defending himself from the assault of a thief, and not knowing the hour of the thief's approach, must be continually on the watch. That this comparison has absolutely no meaning, beyond expressing the idea of suddenness, is certainly not probable. It is in the first place, used in the New Testament so commonly with reference to the return of Christ, (Matt. xxiv. 43; 2 Peter iii. 10; Rev. iii. 3; xvi. 15,) that we cannot fail to suppose some special reference to be implied in the expression. Further, we must not overlook the reason why some nobler comparison—of which so many must have presented themselves—was not selected in order to show forth the suddenness. And, finally, the accurate filling up of the figure in some of the passages, (for example here and at Matt. xxiv. 43,) according to which, the master of the house is set in opposition to the thief, and the breaking in of the latter depicted, is not calculated to support the opinion which refuses to lay any stress on the various features of the comparison itself. Rather does the remark made on Matt. ix. 16 apply here, that our Lord frequently uses figurative expressions taken from the standing-point of his enemies. In this case, the comparison of the κλέπτης is taken from the feelings of those, who amidst the life and movement of earth, view themselves as in their own proper home. These take fright at the coming of the Son of man, as at the inbreaking of a thief; through him they believe it is all over with their (supposed) property and possessions. Here, then, is seen the feeling of all worldly-minded men, concentrated as it were in the οἰκοδεσπότης, under whom we can (according to Matt. xii. 29; Luke xi. 21,) understand no other than the ἄρχων τοῦ κόσμου τούτου. Thus understood, the comparison acquires, on the one hand, its own definite meaning, and on the other, there is also assigned a ground for the uncertainty of our Lord's return, which will be more closely examined and remarked upon at Matt. xxiv. 43. It seems, however, an obscure point, how this comparison of the κλέπτης can be interwoven with that of the δοῦλοι, as is done in this passage, and at Matt. xxiv. 43. The ground of it is probably this. The Apostles themselves, although on the one side they are the representatives of the βασιλεία τ. Θ. (ver. 32), yet appear on the other, as by no means removed from the region of the κόσμος,—they still bear the worldly element within them (1 John ii. 16), and require for this reason very earnest admonitions to fidelity, and warnings against unfaithfulness (ver. 9, 10, 47, 48). In so far, however, as the disciples themselves still belong to the region of the κόσμος, in so far do they also share its character; they cherish fear, namely, for the manifestation of the Divine, and for this reason could the Lord here conjoin two things apparently foreign to each other.[1] Like the disciples,

---

[1] Schleiermacher (on Luke p 189) seems to me altogether groundlessly to doubt the authenticity of the connexion here. It is wholly improbable that this verse alone should be an interpolation in a discourse which hangs so closely together.

every believer bears a double character; as a member of the kingdom of God, he is a δοῦλος τοῦ Θεοῦ, in so far, however, as the old man and consequently the world lives within him, he carries in himself that which is enmity against God, and according to this position, he must partly long for, and partly dread the coming of the Lord, as that act which shall reveal the κρυπτὰ τῶν ἀνθρώπων. According to that standing-point of exalted contemplation, therefore, from which the Saviour spoke, he viewed all the separate individuals in the connexion which their lives bore to the whole, and found the key of heaven and hell, of bliss and anguish, in the hearts of each.

Ver. 41. It is easy to explain how Peter should here have put the question, whether this was spoken to them alone, or to all, (even to the ὄχλος ver. 1.) For, the discourse had in fact acquired a general character, inasmuch as *that* part of the disciples' nature had been brought into view, through which they were still connected with the world. Peter's question, therefore, in this connexion, is a plain testimony to the direct originality of the whole narrative.

Ver. 42—46. The Saviour's reply to the question of Peter is not given definitely, as the circumstances themselves required that it should not. The Saviour spake in presence of a great multitude of people, and his intention was that a different impression should be produced by his words on his disciples, and on the crowd; he could not therefore answer with absolute precision to the somewhat indiscreet question of Peter. To this it must be added, that in fact an absolutely definite decision would not have been founded on truth. For, however certain it is, that in the church of Christ every member should not be a master, (James iii. 1), yet, on the other hand, it is no less established that in a certain respect every believer is a δοῦλος τ. Θ, and must watch for the coming of the Lord. Accordingly, Jesus so answers the question, that in a full and literal sense he applies what was said to the disciples as the representatives of those called to be instructors in the Church. In the next place, however, he transfers it to all, (ver. 48), in so far as they can be considered as δοῦλοι, admitting even that their insight and intelligence is developed in a lower measure. In the following verses, the idea of ver. 36 is carried further out, and in such a way as to delineate those δοῦλοι who, holding sway over the other servants, regulate the whole household economy. In this, the reference to the Apostles cannot be mistaken. First, the fidelity, and then the unfaithfulness of such servants is depicted with their consequences, but as to these we reserve the particulars till we come to the exposition of Matt. xxiv. 45–51, which verses closely agree with those before us. Although, as was remarked above, we in this instance again give the preference to the position of these words in the account of Luke, as being that which they originally held; yet, in ver. 46, the reading μετὰ τῶν ἀπίστων, must yield to that of Matthew, who has μετὰ τῶν ὑποκριτῶν. In this reading the original expression seems to be preserved, and in the text of Luke the more general idea seems falsely to have crept in. The few critical authorities in favour of inserting ὑποκριτῶν in the text of Luke can claim meanwhile no regard. The reference to the ὑποκριταί accords strikingly with ver. 1, as compared with ver. 56. In this expression, moreover, preserved by Matt., we may find an indication that the words in Matt. are borrowed from the very connexion, as given here, a connexion which points so naturally to ὑπόκρισις.

SUPPLEMENTARY NOTE BY THE AUTHOR.

Respecting the note at p. 210 it should be kept in view that the terms there selected as descriptive of myths should be applied only to the so-called myths of the New Testament. An unintentionally fictitious construction of myths (a very different thing from deception or falsehood) must undoubtedly be assumed in the histories of other nations. In the New Testament, however, according to the principles laid down at Vol. I. p. 29, sq. it cannot exist, and, therefore, the assuming of myths here, is equivalent to the assumption of fraud and falsehood.

ERRATA.

In page 146, line 19, *for* ἀνούετε *read* ἀκούετε.
... 172, 3, *for* ἀδιλφοί *read* ἀδιλφαί.
... 174, 14, *for* πάντως *read* πάντως.
194, 5, *for* συνῆκα *read* συνῆκαν.
. 197, .. 39, *for* contrast *read* contest.
.. 198, .. 41, *for* πωτηρ *read* πατηρ
202, 9, *for* by *read* as by.
. ' 211, . 10, *for* first *read* second.
. 227, 28, *for* ἡγίρα *read* ἡμίρα
. 231, .. 43, *for* Himalayes of the *read* Himalayas, the.
267, .. 38, *for* this I would *read* this would.

*** The note at p. 190, and note 1 at p. 249, should have been marked T.

www.ingramcontent.com/pod-product-compliance
Lightning Source LLC
Chambersburg PA
CBHW050836230426
43667CB00012B/2028